CW01594299

ACARS

A Users Guide for the Aviation Enthusiast

by Lionel K Anderson MSc

ACARS
A Users Guide for the Aviation Enthusiast

First Edition 2010 by Las Atalayas Publishing

Author and Editor Lionel K Anderson MSc
Copyright © Lionel K Anderson 2010

The moral rights of the author have been asserted. All rights reserved. No part of this publication may be reproduced, stored in a retrieval system or transmitted in any form or by any means, electronic, mechanical or otherwise without the written permission of the Publisher.

ISBN 978-1-4457-8847-0

Design and Typesetting by kenandglen.com

Contents

Acknowledgements

I'd first like to thank Grzegorz Rafalski for his sunset photograph of Kraków John Paul II Balice International Airport that was used for the basis of the books cover.

I'd allso like to thank Hamish McTorsk and Bev Ewen-Smith for their help when I was researching infromation for this book.

Disclaimer

The use of radio receivers and scanners to monitor radio frequencies is not permitted in every country of the world. Similarly some countries and authorities prohibit the use of ACARS data. Thus readers are advised to check with their licensing authorities prior to doing so as the author cannot be held responsible for any legal consequences.

Glossary

ACARS	Aircraft Communications Addressing and Reporting System
ACMS	Aircraft Condition Monitoring System
AMS	ACARS Message Security, as specified in ARINC 823
AOA	ACARS Over AVLC. With the introduction of VDL Mode 2, the ACARS protocols were modified to take advantage of the higher data rate made possible by Mode 2. AOA is an interim step in replacing the ACARS protocols with ATN protocols.
ATN	Aeronautical Telecommunications Network. As air traffic increases, ACARS will no longer have the capacity or flexibility to handle the large amount of datalink communications. ATN is planned to replace ACARS in the future and will provide services such as authentication, security, and a true internetworking architecture. Europe is leading the US in the implementation of ATN.
AVLC	Aviation VHF Link Control. A particular protocol used for aeronautical datalink communications.
CDU	Control Display Unit
CMF	Communications Management Function. The software that runs in a CMU, and sometimes as a software partition in an integrated avionics computer.
CMU	Communications Management Unit. Successor to the MU, the CMU performs similar datalink routing functions, but has additional capacity to support more functions. CMU standards are defined in ARINC Characteristic 758.
FDAMS	Flight Data Acquisition and Management System
FMS	Flight Management System. FMS standards are defined in ARINC Characteristic 702 and 702A.
HFDL	High Frequency Data Link is an ACARS communications media used to exchange data such as Airline Operational Control (AOC) messages, Controller Pilot Data Link Communication (CPDLC) messages and Automatic Dependent Surveillance (ADS) messages between aircraft end-systems and corresponding ground-based HFDL ground stations.
HF	High Frequency. A portion of the RF spectrum.
LRU	Line Replaceable Unit. An avionics "black box" that can be replaced on the flight line, without downing the aircraft for maintenance.
MCDU	Multifunction Control Display Unit. A text-only device that displays messages to the aircrew and accepts crew input on an integrated keyboard. MCDU standards are defined in ARINC Characteristic 739. MCDUs have seven input ports and can be used with seven different systems, such as CMU or FMS. Each system connected to an MCDU generates its own display pages and accepts keyboard input, when it is selected as the system controlling the MCDU.
MIDU	Multi-Input Interactive Display Unit (often used as a third cockpit CDU).
MU	Management Unit. Often referred to as the ACARS MU, this is an avionics LRU that routes datalink messages to and from the ground.
OOOI	Shorthand for the basic flight phases—Out of the gate, Off the ground, On the ground, In the gate.
POA	Plain Old ACARS. Refers to the set of ACARS communications protocols in effect before the introduction of VDL Mode 2. The term is derived from POTS (Plain old telephone service) that refers to the wired analog telephone network.
SATCOM	Satellite Communications. Airborne SATCOM equipment includes a satellite data unit, high power amplifier, and an antenna with a steerable beam. A typical SATCOM installation can support a datalink channel as well as several voice channels.
VDL	VHF Data Link
VHF	Very High Frequency. A portion of the RF spectrum.

About the Author

Lionel K Anderson developed an early interest in aviation and aircraft during his schooldays living on the Isle of Wight. This encouraged him to build model aeroplanes and experiment with radio control designing and building simple system using thermionic valves and electro-mechanical escapements.

Those were the days when great things were happening in aviation and he recalls seeing the Fairey Delta 2, flown by Peter Twiss, overhead in 1956 when a new World Air Speed Record 1132mph was made, a significant achievement considering the old record had only been set the previous year by an American F100 Super Sabre, and was so much slower.

Leaving school he joined the British Army as an Apprentice Radar Mechanic and pursued a career in the maintenance of aircraft tracking and surveillance radars.

Later as a professional electronics engineer he was involved in the design and development of radar and microwave engineering systems.

Now retired he continues his many interests and activities in electronics and computing publishing a number of books on various allied subjects.

Chapter 1
Introduction

Aviation enthusiasts have for many years listened to air traffic voice messages by monitoring VHF air band transmissions using radio scanners or dedicated air band radio receivers. By monitoring the broadcast messages the enthusiast could ascertain only a limited amount of information in respect of an aircrafts positions and its route.

In the mid to late 1990s most communications between aircraft and the ground used voice communications. The expansion in air traffic generated the need for a faster and more efficient system for handling communications.

Aeronautical Radio Incorporated (ARINC) then developed the Aircraft Communications Addressing and Reporting System (ACARS), a digital data-link system for transmission of short and relatively simple messages between aircraft and ground stations and designed to utilise existing ground station and aircraft radio equipment, and enhance air-ground-air communications.

SITA, a multinational information technology company, later augmented their worldwide data network by adding ground radio stations to provide ACARS service.

ACARS carry a lot of traffic between aircraft and ground stations with the type of information in the ACARS transmissions varying widely. The ACARS messages can range from simple arrival/departure reports to lengthy aircraft computer downlinks of navigation, engine, and performance data as well as weather observations, flight plans, navigation positions, aircraft and engine performance data, arrival/departure/delay reports, equipment malfunction reports, crew reports and connecting gate lists.

As ACARS messages are transmitted in the VHF air band, it is now possible for the aviation enthusiast to receive the messages on their existing radio equipment and by connecting the receiver to a PC or laptop computer to decode the messages for display in a plain text format.

ACARS messages are either transmitted from an aircraft to a company ground station, called a downlink message, or transmitted from ground stations up to aircraft, called uplink messages.

Before a message is transmitted, the ACARS computer first listens to see if the frequency is clear before transmitting its message. This technique is sometimes called Self Organizing Time Division Multiplexing (SOTDM) or 'Listen before Transmit.' SOTDM applies equally to both aircraft and ground stations.

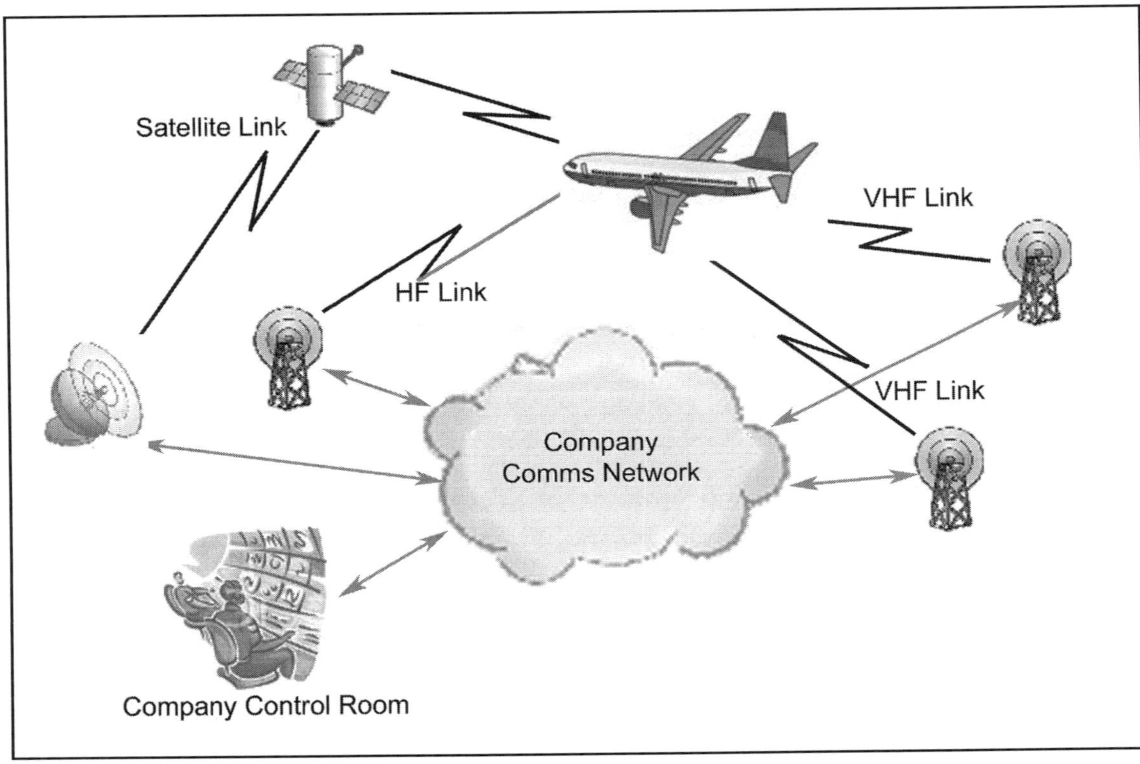

Figure 1 - An Airlines ACARS System

This book provides information about the format of ACARS messages and how they may be decoded.

Although this book concentrates on the VHF aspects of ACARS as it is written with the aviation enthusiast in mind, it should be mentioned that ACARS is an integrated system where communications between an aircraft and the airline company may satellite communications, as well as using a number of both VHF and HF transmitter receivers—all of which are linked together by the company's communications network.

Chapter 2
Receiving ACARS Radio Signals

The ACARS radio transmission is an amplitude-modulated (AM) signal to make it consistent with the historical use of AM voice mode on the aircraft bands in the early days of radio. The transmission is in the VHF band around 130 MHz and uses a 2400 bps NRZI-coded coherent audio frequency MSK (Minimum Shift Keying—a particular form of FSK) on AM to make use of standard aircraft AM communications equipment. A list of the frequencies commonly used for ACARS can be found in Appendix A.

The demodulated audio signal fits perfectly in the audio spectrum of an AM receiver (300-3000 Hz); thus, almost any make and model of air band receiver or scanner covering the VHF 130Mhz band is suitable for receiving ACARS transmissions.

In most cases the earphone output of your receiver can be used to connect the receiver to a standalone ACARS Decoder, to a PC, or to a Laptop Computer running one of the many suites of ACARS Decoder software.

It is essential that the air-band receiver or scanner should have a Squelch control such that the Squelch is turned off. It will also be necessary to adjust the volume control of the receiver so that the decoder is not overloaded. As a brief sync tone is sent before each transmission, many scanners' squelch will not open up fast enough, thus another reason to keep the squelch turned off. Suit some receivers and scanner are listed below.

N.B Squelch is normally used to remove the background noise and static when receiving voice transmissions. But as the ACARS signal is in effect a short burst of noise typically under one second in length, it necessary to be able to hear it.

Make	Model
Signal	R532/R53
Uniden	USC230, UBC-30XLT, USC230, UBC3500XLT
Yaesu	FT-817
Yupiteru	VT-125/150 , VT-225, MVT-3100, MVT-7100, MVT-7200

Table 1 - Typical Scanners used for ACARS

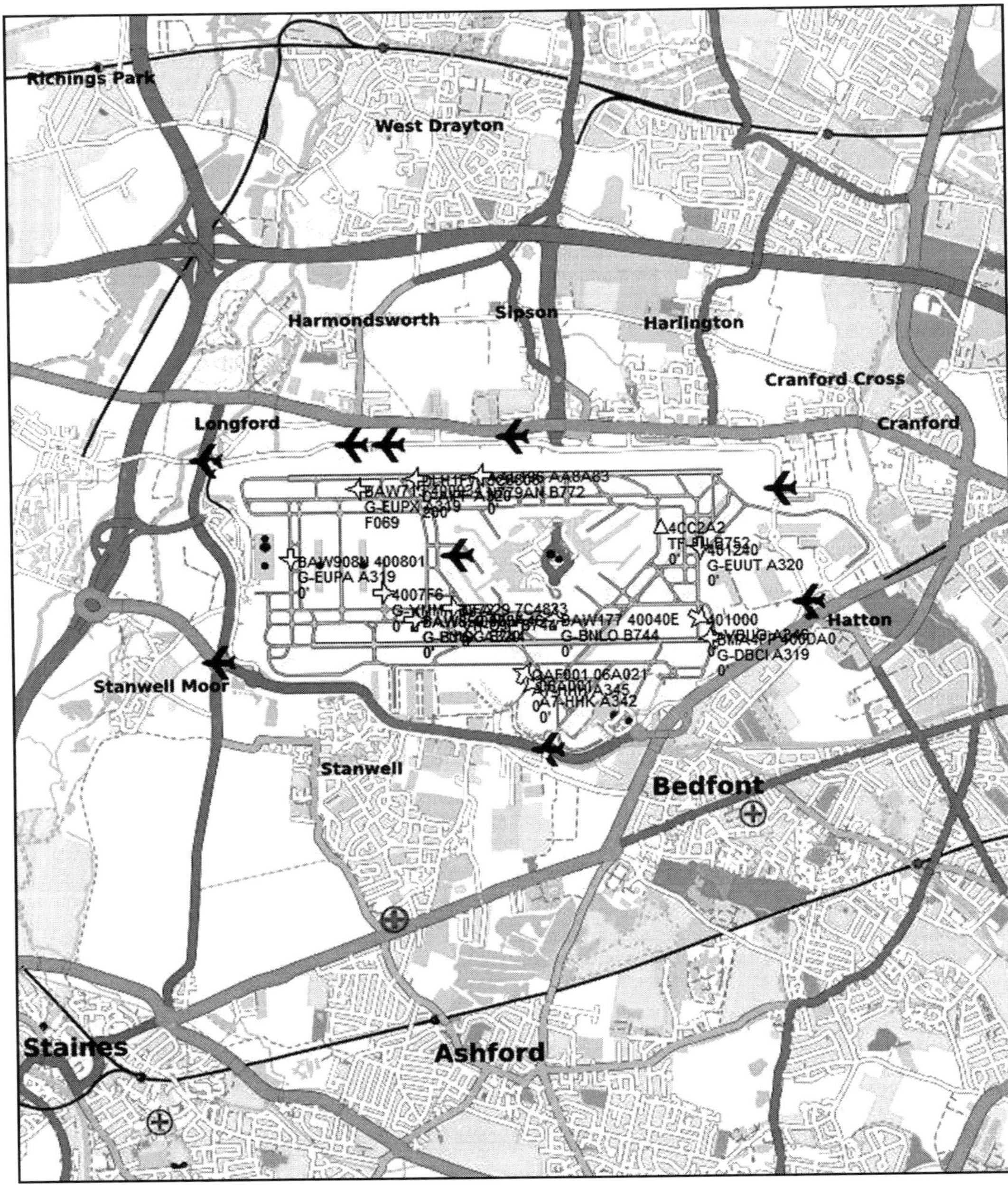

Figure 2 - London Heathrow Environs

Chapter 3

ACARS Message Frame Format

Each message frame consists of at least 50, and up to a maximum of 272 characters or bytes. Each character uses a 7-bit ACSII code with an additional eighth parity bit. This results in a total message transmission duration of between 0.17 and 0.91 seconds.

The message frame format is rigidly defined to include synchronization, address, acknowledgment, mode and error checking characters, in addition to the actual message text. Imbedded message-label characters indicate the type of message. The message format is shown in Table 2 below.

Parameter	Value	No of Characters
Pre-key	Tx warm-up/Rx AGC adjustment	16 characters
Bit Sync	Establish bit synchronisation	2 characters „+„ , „*„
Character Sync	Establish character synchronisation	2 characters SYN, SYN (16h)
Start of Heading	Start of Heading	1 character SOH (01h)
Mode	Ground system interface configuration	1 character
Address	Aircraft registration number	7 characters
Ack/Nak	Acknowledge/Non-Acknowledge flag	1 character
Label	Type of message	2 characters
Block Identifier	Message block number	1 character
STX	STX (02h) - if no text ETX (03h)	1 character
Flight No	Airline flight number	6 characters
Text	printable characters only	maximum 220 characters
Suffix	ETX or ETB (17h)	1 character
BCS	Block Check Sequence	16 bits
BCS Suffix	DLE (7fh)	1 character

Table 2 - ACARS Message Frame Format

The sixteen pre-key characters are all binary 1 values, thus resulting in the 0.05 second 2400 Hz beep that can be heard at the start of every message.

The Block Check Sequence field contains the value of an error-detection polynomial that can be used to determine if the entire message was received free of errors. Standard 7-bit ASCII is used, bit 8 is an odd parity bit used for the text field of the ACARS message, and the content may be free text or a mixture of formatted and free text.

ACARS communications are divided into Category A and Category B. An aircraft uses a Category A transmission to broadcast its messages to all listening ground stations. This is denoted by an ASCII ***2*** (Hex32) in the Mode field of the downlink message. When using Category B, an aircraft transmits its message to a single ground station. This is denoted by an ASCII character in the range **@** to **]** (Hex40 - Hex5D) in the Mode field of the downlink message.

All ground stations support Category A, but may uplink **'** to **}** (Hex27 - Hex7D) in the Mode field. The ground station may use either ***2*** or the range **'** to **}** (Hex27 - Hex7D) in the Mode field.

At the receiving end, a Block Check calculation is made and compared to the calculation appended to the packet by the transmitting station. If the downlink messages contain errors, no response will be given and the transmitting station will retransmit the packet a number of times until a positive acknowledgement is received and the message can be deleted from storage, or the aircrew be alerted to its nontransmission.

If an uplink message is found in error, the airborne equipment will generate a negative acknowledgement (NAK) which triggers an uplink retransmission. Retransmission is also triggered by timeout.

Positive acknowledgement from the aircraft consists of the transmission of the Uplink Block Identifier of the correctly received block. Positive acknowledgement from the ground station consists of a similar transmission of the Downlink Block Identifier. Acknowledgements are placed in the Technical Acknowledgement field. The general-response-message label is ***_DLE*** (Hex5F Hex7F). Messages with this label contain no information except acknowledgements and are used for link maintenance.

A typical raw undecoded message might look like this:

```
□□□□□□□□□□□□□□□□□<SYN><SYN><SOH>2..KC693<NAK>Q05<STX>S68!2\42H;C<
FS<ACK><BEL>##########+*#<NAK>*T#^U*#*<DC2>*#*T#U+L#MjU#UM#)5R#+E
#T*J#5U#+jU#<SYN>*U#U########################################vw<S
OH>2.<SO>II0?(0_□C<ETX>@<DLE>
```

Chapter 4

Decoding ACARS Messages

The raw message shown at the end of the last chapter could be decoded and translated into plane English as follows, "KC693 operating as MC4208 was first contacted at 19-18 on 21/06/2010 using Ground Station 2 with broadcast message number S68A was conducting Q0 type link test."

Fortunately, users don't have to work through the process of translating such raw messages as there are a readily available number of decoders that will do the job for them.

First, though, it is necessary to look at the structure of decoded messages and discuss some of the standard-message formats.

ACARS Downlink Messages

Consider this decoded message:

```
(#5)15-05-2010 15:33:36 M=06 ADDR= F-ZKXF TA=Q ML=Q0 B=9
MSN=D09D FID=AF9876
```

which can be displayed more simply in a table like that below.

Decoded	Interpretation
(#5)	Decoder generated message number
15-05-2010 18:43:32	Decoder generated timestamp (optional)
M=06	Mode Category A = A,
ADDR=F-KZXF	Aircraft address
TA=Q	Technical acknowledgement
ML=Q0	Message Label (message type)
B=9	Uplink/Downlink Block Identifier
MSN=D09D	Message Sequence Number
FID=AF9876	Flight Identifier

Table 3 - Typical ACARS Decoded Message Format

In this case, record #5 decoded at 15:33:36 contains a message from a French aircraft with registration F-ZKXF using logical channel 06 to transmit and acknowledge uplink block Q and a link test (Q0) with block identifier 9 and message sequence number 0635 (here the time in minutes and seconds after the hour is used—other formats are also in use). The flight is Air France AF9876.

A method commonly used by many software decoders for displaying the decoded details shown below.

ACARS mode: 06 Aircraft reg: F-ZKXF
Message label: Q0 Block id: 9 Msg. no: D09D
Flight id: AF9876

Some more examples of the more important or frequently seen ACARS messages:

```
M=06 ADDR= F-KZXF TA=NAK ML=_? B=3 MSN=2810 FID=AF9876
```

Decoded	Interpretation
(#7)	Decoder generated message number
16-05-2010 09:33:12	Decoder generated timestamp (optional)
M=06	Mode Category A = A,
ADDR=F-KZXF	Aircraft address
TA=NAK	Technical acknowledgement
ML=_?	Message Label (message type)
B=3	Uplink/Downlink Block Identifier
MSN=2810	Message Sequence Number
FID=AF9876	Flight Identifier

Using logical channel 06 an unsolicited (TA=NAK) general response _? without information is transmitted as block 3 from aircraft F-KZXF on flight AF9876 with sequence number 2810. General responses are mainly used for block acknowledgement purposes.

```
M=06 ADDR= ??????? TA=NAK ML=SQ B= 00XSSRH
```

Decoded	Interpretation
(#8)	Decoder generated message number
16-05-2010 15:13:52	Decoder generated timestamp (optional)
M=06	Mode Category A = A,
ADDR=??????	Aircraft address
TA=NAK	Technical acknowledgement
ML=SQ	Message Label (message type)

The message on the previous page is called a "squitter." That is an ID and Uplink test message that is transmitted at regular intervals from ground stations. This particular one is a squitter (SQ) version 0 (00) from a SITA (XS) ground station in Singapore (SRH). The ? denotes the ASCII NUL character (00h) used for broadcast. A block identifier is not used.

```
M=06 ADDR= F-KZXF TA=5 ML=:; B=131525
```

Decoded	Interpretation
(#8)	Decoder generated message number
16-05-2010 12:06:22	Decoder generated timestamp (optional)
M=06	Mode Category A = A,
ADDR=F-KZXF	Aircraft address
TA=5	Technical acknowledgement
ML=:;	Message Label (message type)
B=131525	Uplink/Downlink Block Identifier

This is a data transceiver auto tune message (:;) from ground station 06 commanding the ACARS transceiver of aircraft F-KZXF to change its frequency to 131.525 MHz. At the same time acknowledgement is given for the aircraft's downlink block 5.

Although users can enjoy the fun and challenge of decoding ACARS messages it is more normal to use one of the many software decoders readily available some of which are shown in Table 4 below.

Type	Name	Comments
Software	Airnav	Available from www.airnavsystems.com
Software	ACARSD	Probably the best ACARS decoding suite of programs. Available at www.acarsd.org/
Software	KG-ACARS	Available from http://sky.geocities.jp/kgacars/indexworld.html
Software	MultiMode	For MACs available from www.blackcatsystems.com
Software	PlanePlotter	An excellent software program that interfaces to a number of radar boxes as well as ACARS scanners. Available from www.coaa.co.uk
Software	RadioRaft	Available from http://radioraft.free.fr
Software	SkySpy	Available from www.dxzone.com/
Integrated	Winradio Digital Suite	The WiNRADiO Digital Suite is an optional software package fully integrated with WiNRADiO 1000, 1500 and 3000 receivers.

Table 4 - Popular ACARS Decoders

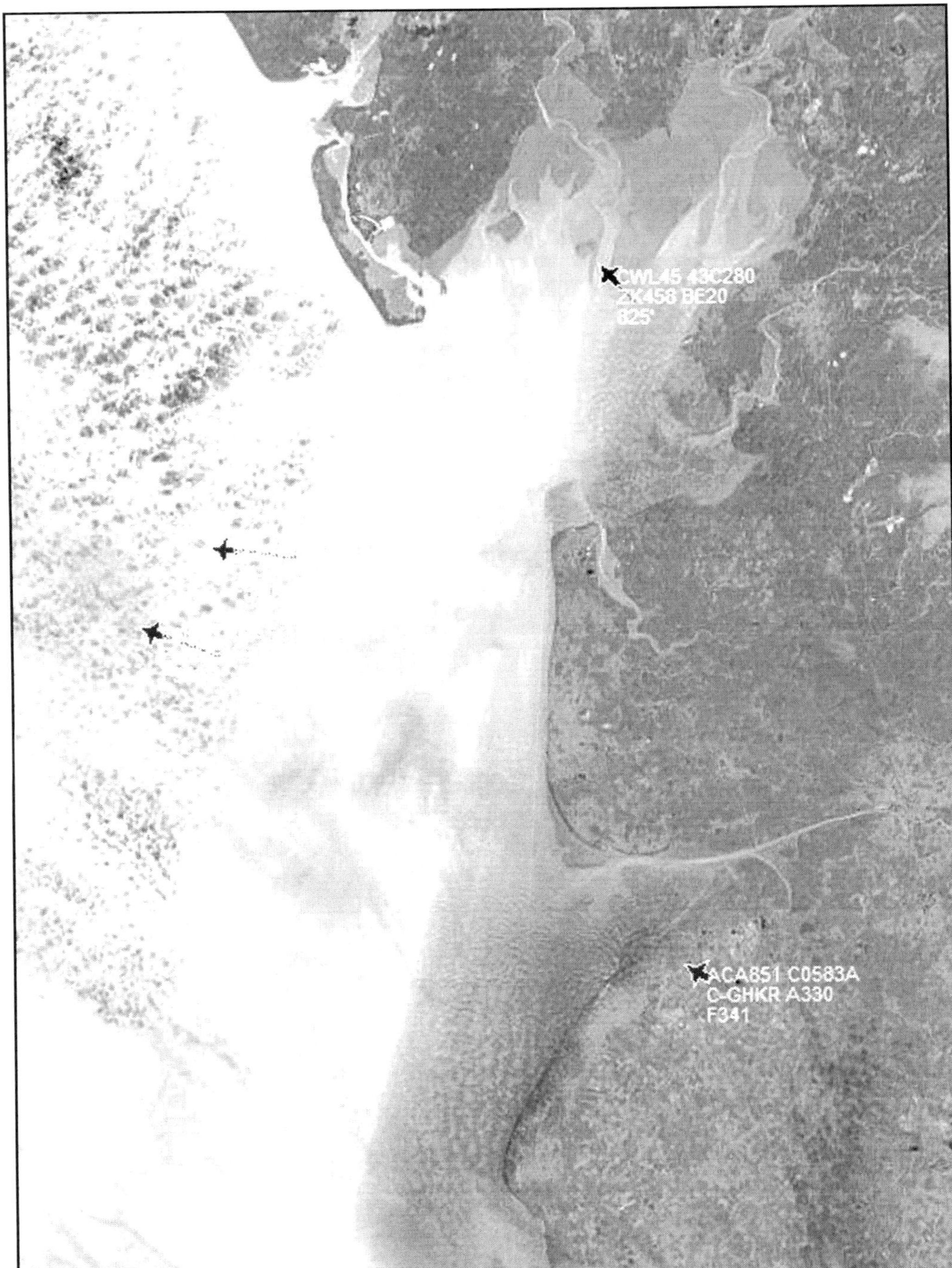

Figure 3 - North West England Satellite Type Overlay

Chapter 5

More on Decoding

Consider the ACARS message shown below. There are a number of significant components and these can be seen annotated.

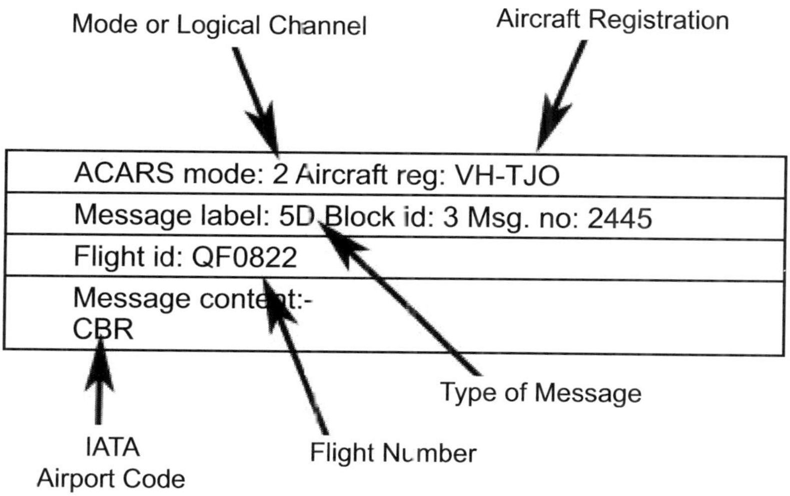

This particular message is from a Qantas Boeing 737-476 on Flight QF 882 from Melbourne. The 5D message label shows that the aircraft is requesting an Airport Terminal Information Service (ATIS) for its destination Canberra. (ATIS is the continuous broadcast of recorded non-control information in high activity terminal areas).

The ACARS Mode designator is the logical channel used to identify where an ACARS message is being transmitted to or from. They are associated with the aircrafts company and its location in the World. A list of many known codes is shown in Appendix B.

The Message Label is a shorthand code for the type of message being transmitted. Many of these codes are specific to a particular airline company. In some cases the same code will be used by different companies with different meanings. The most commonly used and known codes are shown in Appendix C.

The actual ACARS Message itself may contain a number of abbreviations and IATA codes. In the example shown above the code MBR is the IATA code for Melbourne International Airport. Cross reference listings of IATA/ICAO and ICAO/IATA airport codes are shown in Appendices E & F.

As will be seen in the following examples the ACARS Message may contain a number of 2, 3 or even 4 character abbreviations. Many of the common abbreviations used can be found in Appendix D.

Message Type 80

ACARS mode: 2 Aircraft reg: N630VA
Message label: 80 Block id: 9 Msg. no: M92A
Flight id: VX0418
Message content:- 418 ETA ON GND AT 0900Z SAY THE GATE

This was a Virgin American A320 from Los Angeles JFK New York telling the company they expected to land at 0900hrsZ and requesting what Gate they would be using to disembark.

Message Type B6

ACARS mode: M Aircraft reg: HS-TKD
Message label: 80 Block id: 7 Msg. no: F39A
Flight id: TG0461
Message content:- /MELCAYA.ADS.HS-TKD13E5EF6B3090C6A417401 F267A

Is aircraft HS-TKD, a Thai Airways International Boeing 777-300 on Flight TG 461 from Bangkok to Melbourne transmitting an Air Data systems (ADS) message to the Melbourne company office.

Message Type Q0

ACARS mode: M Aircraft reg: VH-EBM
Message label: Q0 Block id: 5 Msg. no: S88A
Flight id: QF0481
Message content:-

This is an example of a Q0 message which is just a simple Link Test.

Message Type 16

ACARS mode: 2 Aircraft reg: N654FE
Message label: 16 Block id: 4 Msg. no: M96A
Flight id: FX1747
Message content:- 241747/AUTPOS/LLD N415913 W0754453 /ALT 27896/SAT -026 /WND 265061/TAT ****/TAS 485/CRZ 079 /FOB 018240 /DAT 100624/TIM 092318

This is an automatic position report from a FedEx A300FR on Flight FX1747 from Indianapolis to Springfield.

Message Type A1

ACARS mode: 2 Aircraft reg: N361AA
Message label: SA Block id: 1 Msg. no: M93A
Flight id: AA0081
Message content:- /PIKCLYA.OC1/CLX 1229 100614 EGGX CLRNCE 016 AAL81 CLRD TO KDFW VIA GOMUP NAT A GOMUP 59N020W 61N030W 63N040W 63N050W 62N060W GRIBS JELCO FM GOMUP/1317 MNTN F320 M080 END OF MESSAGEA403

This is the oceanic clearance and routing over Greenland for an American Airlines Boeing 767-300 departing London Gatwick on Flight AA 81 to Dallas Fort Worth.

Message Type 5Z

ACARS mode: H Aircraft reg: SU-GBS
Message label: 5U Block id: 5 Msg. no: M09A
Flight id: MS0986
Message content:- SU HECA

This is a message from aircraft SU-GBS, a EgyptAir 777 on Flight MS 986 from New York to Cairo asking for the latest weather and also what an alternative aerodrome to the scheduled Cairo destination would be.

Message Type 5U

ACARS mode: 2 Aircraft reg: N936UW
Message label: 5Z Block id: 6 Msg. no: 5408
Flight id: US0750
Message content:- /TXT MTC 2 WRITEUPS AFT GA LLEY COFFEEMAKER WILL NOT BREW//F/OS ADI FLICKERS

This is a US Airways Boeing 757 on Flight US 750 from Philadelphia to Brussels sending an airline designated fault report.

Message Type QX

ACARS mode: 2 Aircraft reg: C-FGMF
Message label: QX Block id: 6 Msg. no: M71A
Flight id: AC0551
Message content:-

An Air Canada Embraer 190-100IGW Flight AC 551 from Vancouver to Montreal reporting that it is unable to process the ACARS message.

Message Type 25

ACARS mode: H Aircraft reg: TC-JGX
Message label: 25 Block id: 6 Msg. no: M43A
Flight id: TK1846
Message content:- /FOB 66/UTC 0739

An Turkish Airlines oeing 737-800 Flight TK 1846 from Athens to Istanbul reporting that it is carrying a specila load that will need handling upon arrival.

Message Type 1L

ACARS mode: H Aircraft reg: D-ABOF
Message label: 1L Block id: 8 Msg no: M03A
Flight id: DE0546
Message content:- 000872342030UXX+QBDFDNE)ODRGM

This was a Condor Boeing 737-330 reporting departure from Cologne on Flight DE 546 to Las Palmas.

Message Type HX

ACARS mode: H Aircraft reg: D-ABCG
Message label: HX Block id: 5 Msg no: S17A
Flight id: AB2740
Message content:- /SINGMXS.C1 ??? .SINGMXS 250742 AGM AN .D-ABCG/GL KGS1 - / SA 25/07:20 LGIR 250720Z 32011KT 9999 FEW018CB SCT

This was an Airbus A321 from Dusseldorf to Heraklion on flight AB 2740 notifying a problem with an uplink report.

Message Type 1M

ACARS mode: H Aircraft reg: OH-LBR
Message label: 1M Block id: 1 Msg no: M47A
Flight id: AY1731
Message content:- /FIN1731/ETA01/250610/EFHK/LGIR/LGIR/2JK0 0802//

This was an FinnAir Boeing 757-200 on Flight AY 1731 from Helsinki to Heraklion reporting an Estimated Time of Arrival (ETA) of 0802Z.

Message Type 1M

ACARS mode: N Aircraft reg: N757AN
Message label: 5Z Block id: 3 Msg no: M64A
Flight id: AA0168
Message content:- OS JFK /FPR

This is a an American Airlines designated downlink from a Boeing registration N757AN on Flight AA 168 from Tokyo to JFK New York requesting a flight plan for the journey.

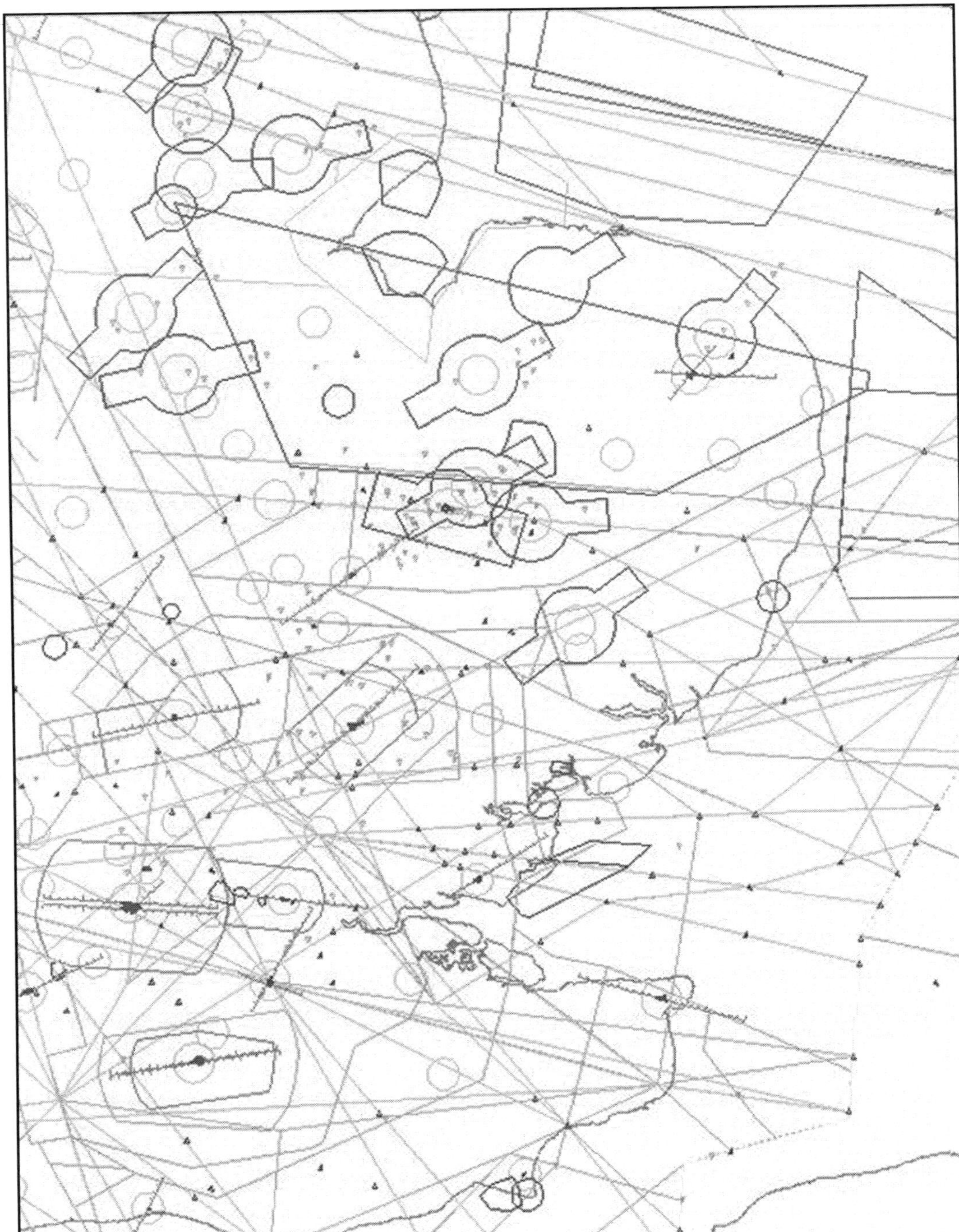

Figure 4 - Southern UK Airspace Overlay

Chapter 5

Further Information

It is hoped that the reader will have gained from reading the previous chapters an understanding of what ACARS is, the general format of messages and the decoded information contained in what is transmitted between an aircraft and the airline company.

The examples show just a few of the many message types but by using the tables in the appendices to the book a reader should be able to translate many received ACARS messages for themselves.

This book has concentrated on the reception of ACARS messages in the VHF air band as that part of the radio spectrum is that most used by the aviation enthusiast.

However mention should be made of the fact that aircraft and ground stations also use HF for ACARS communications over the oceans. This is because VHF is only suitable for line of sight communications and once an aircraft leaves the land mass it cannot communicate with any VHF stations.

For those wanting to explore HF ACARS then a HF receiver with SSB and stability is required. A good example of such a receiver is the Kenwood R-2000.

For decoding the HF ACARS message a suitable program is Charles Brains' "PC-HFDL ARINC 635-6" available for download from the Internet at http://www.chbrain.dircon.co.uk/download/PC-HFDL%202.042%20Setup.zip.

Finally for the more academically minded there is a list of related avionic specifications shown in Appendix I.

Free ACARS

Even if one doesn't have an airband receiver, scanner or decoding software one can still receive some live ACARS feeds and read ACARS messages from receiving stations around the world.

ACARSD is the first system which can be used as online ACARS Server and to use the ACARS Online Network all that is needed is to download a copy of of the ACARSD Client Software from “http://www.acarsd.org/download/clientNG-0.01.001.zip”.

After downloading the Zip file it should be extracted into a standalone folder typically C:ACARS_client.

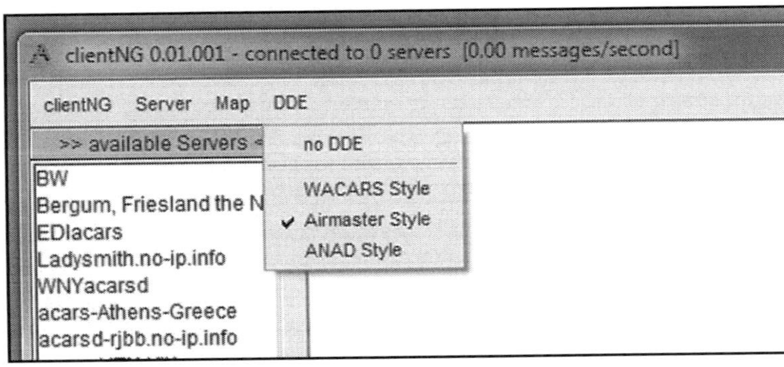

Figure 5 - clientNG DDE setting

The program is launched by running clientNG.exe. Once running the DDE menu should be set to “Airmaster Style” as shown in Figure 5 ensuring that the “no DDE” option is not checked. Then the main settings should be set as shown below in Fig 6.

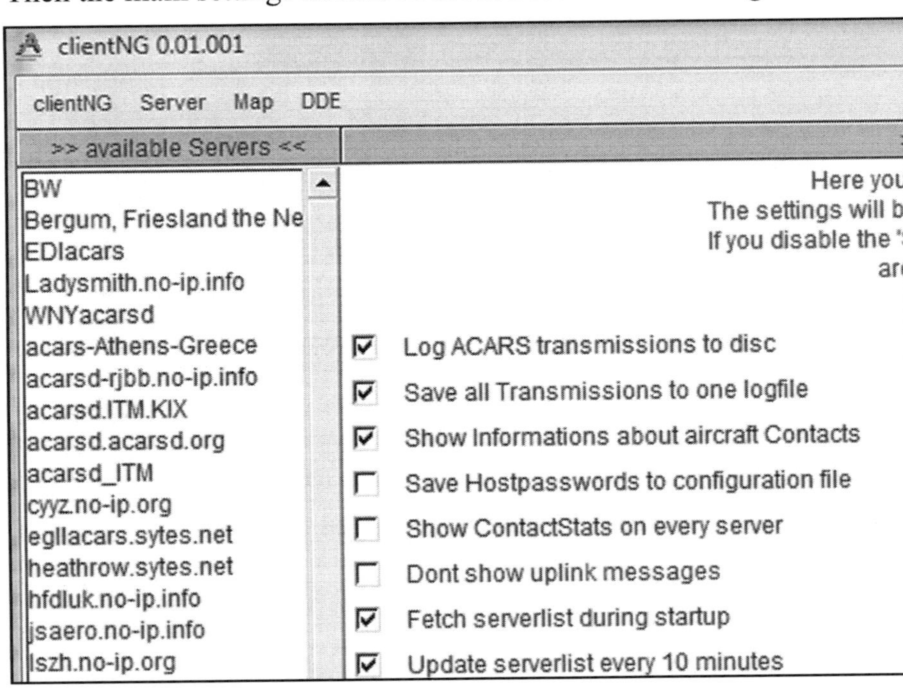

Figure 6 - clientNG main settings

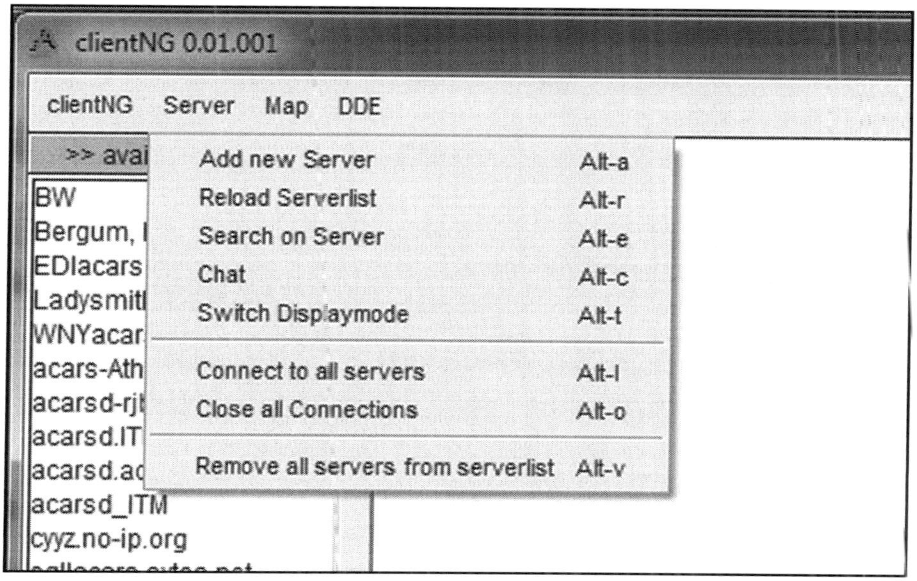

Figure 7 - clientNG Servers

To begin receiving ACARS messages the "Connect to all servers" option can be checked (or use the ALT-l keyboard shortcut) ob by double clicking on a named served.

Useful Web Sites

Today there is a tremendous amount of information available on the Internet on the subject and there are also a number of web sites providing help and support to the aviation enthusiast with an interest in ACARS some of which are listed below

Radarspotters

http://radarspotters.eu

A really useful site offering help and advice about buying, setting up and using virtual radar and software helping enthusiasts to get the most from the fascinating hobby. Radarspotters also has a well supported Web Forum that is free to use and totally independent of any product supplier.

FlightRadar24

http://www.flightradar24.com

Flightradar24.com shows live aircraft traffic in the airspace above Europe. It also has a friendly and useful forum.

Kinetic-Avionics

http://www.kinetic-avionics.co.uk/forums

Although primarily to support the SBS-1eR Virtual Radar this is a useful forum for the aviation enthusiast.

PlanePlotter User Group

http://groups.yahoo.com/group/planeplotter

A lively user group where one can find useful files, charts, utilities and answers to a wide range of questions specific to PlanePlotter.

ACARSSD

http://groups.yahoo.com/group/acarsd

A user group for the open discussion group of ACARSSD the free ACARS Decoder.

ACARSonline

http://uk.groups.yahoo.com/group/acarsonline

A user group for sharing ACARS messages.

Virtual Radar Server

http://www.virtualradarserver.co.uk/

VirtualRadar is a free .NET application that connects to a BaseStation instance that is transmitting messages from a Kinetics Avionics SBS-1 or SBS-1er ADS-B receiver.

Global Tuners

http://www.globaltuners.com/

GlobalTuners provides access to remotely controlled radio receivers all over the world allowing one can listen to and tune the various receivers.

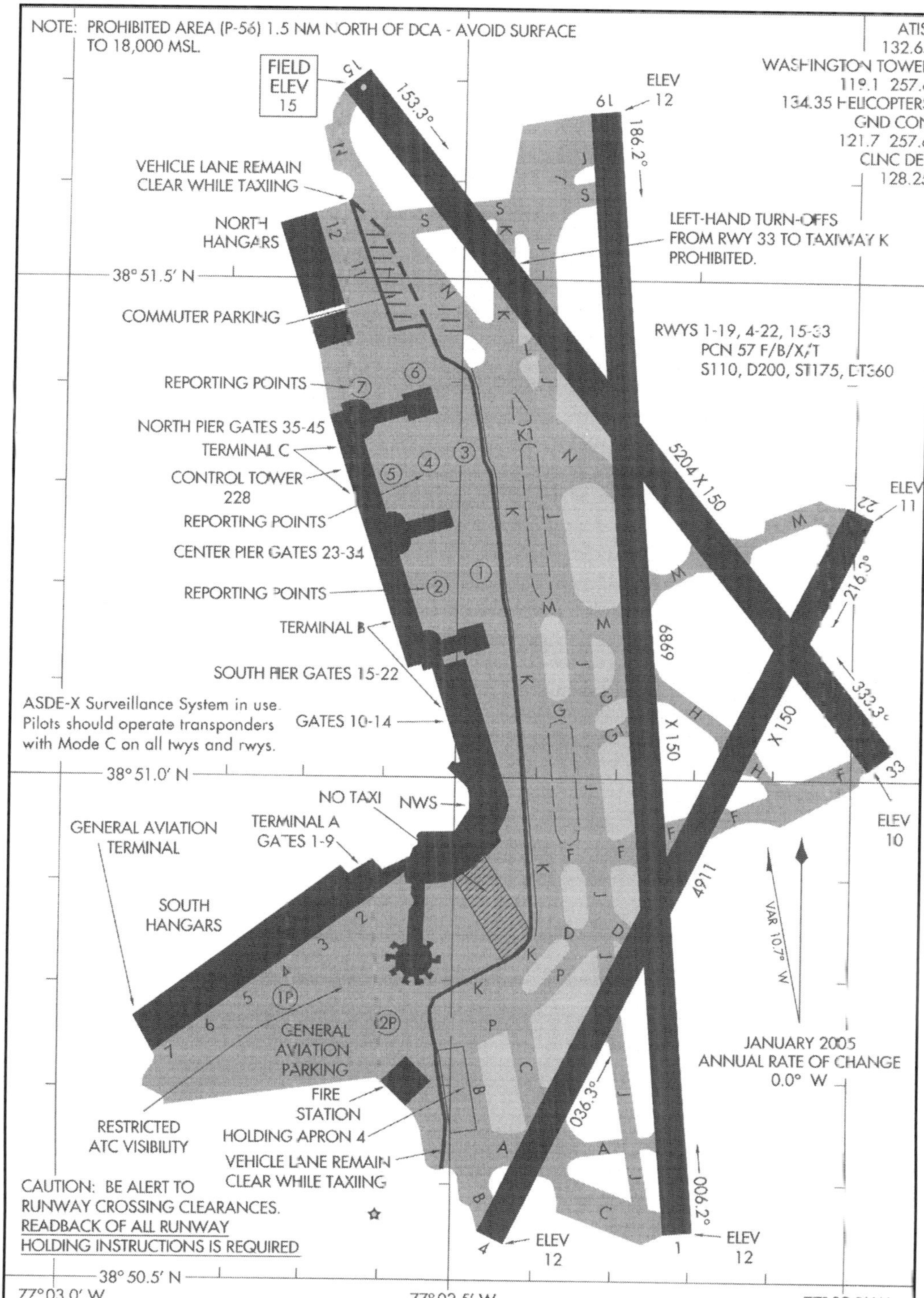

Figure 8 - Washington Dulles International Airport

ACARS VHF Frequencies (Mhz)

These frequencies are those typically used for the transmission and reception of ACARS mesages as known at the time of publication of this guide.

Frequency MHz	Area
129.125	North America
130.025	Secondary Channel in USA and Canada
130.425	USA
130.450	North America
131.125	USA
131.450	Japan
131.475	Air Canada Company Channel
131.525	European Secondary Channel
131.550	Worldwide Primary Channel
131.725	Europe Primary Channel
131.825	Lufthansa Company Channel
131.825	Air France Company Channel
131.850	Europe
136.700	USA
136.750	Europe & USA
136.800	USA
136.850	SITA in North America
136.900	Europe & USA Secondary Channel

ACARS Mode Codes

A character showing the ACARS Mode may be seen at the start of a message as shown in the example below.

ACARS mode: H Aircraft reg: F-ZKXF
Message label: H1 Block id: 9 Msg. no: D09D
Flight id: AF9876

Codes may vary from country to country so some typical codes are shown below.

Country	Code	Ground Station
Wordlwide	2	to free groundstations
UK	[	EastMidlands
UK	A	Aberdeen
UK	E	Edinburgh
UK	G	Glasgow
UK	H	London Heathrow
UK	L	Belfast
UK	M	Manchester
UK	N	Newcastle
UK	P	Prestwick
UK	R	Manchester
UK	T	LondonStansted
UK	U	Luton
UK	W	LondonGatwick
UK	X	Birmingham
Australia	A	Adelaide
Australia	B	Brisbane
Australia	C	Canberra
Australia	D	Darwin
Australia	M	Melbourne
Australia	P	Perth
Australia	S	Sydney
Austria	M	Vienna
Belgium	R	Brussel
Canada	B	Toronto
Canada	G	Ottawa
Canada	J	Windsor
Canada	L	Sudbury
Canada	M	Montreal
Canada	N	NorthBay
Canada	O	Toronto
Canada	R	Ottawa
Canada	S	Montreal
Finland	V	Helsinki
France	O	Paris
Germany	F	Frankfurt
Germany	G	Colonge
Germany	H	Hamburg
Germany	h	Hamburg
Germany	R	Stuttgart
Germany	T	Stuttgart
Germany	U	Düsseldorf
Hungary	A	Zagreb
Hungary	O	Budapest
Ireland	D	Dublin
Ireland	O	Cork
Ireland	S	Shannon
Italy	B	Milano
Italy	G	Genoa
Italy	g	Genoa
Japan	A	TokyoNarita
Japan	B	Nagoya
Japan	C	NemuroRokko
Japan	D	Komatsu
Japan	E	ChitoseOkayama
Japan	G	Hakodate
Japan	H	Akita
Japan	M	Haneda
Japan	N	Hachijyo
Nederlands	A	Amsterdam
Nederlands	C	Amsterdam
Nederlands	E	Amsterdam
Spain	B	Barcelona

ACARS Message Types

A character showing the ACARS Message type is normally found after the message label as shown in the example below.

ACARS mode: H Aircraft reg: F-ZKXF
Message label: H1 Block id: 9 Msg. no: D09D
Flight id: AF9876

Code	Message Type
00	Emergency Situation Report
51	Ground GMT Report Uplink
52	Ground UTC Report Uplink
54	Voice Go-ahead
57	Alternate Aircrew Initiated Position
5D	ATIS Request
5P	Temporary Suspension
5R	Aircrew Initiated Position Report
5U	Weather Request
5Y	Aircrew Revision to Previous
5Z	Airline Designated
7A	Aircrew Initiated Engine Data/Takeoff
7B	Aircrew Entered Miscellaneous Message
80-89	Airline Defined Message
A0	ATS Facility Notification
A1	Oceanic Clearance
A2	Unassigned
A3	Departure Clearance
A4	Flight Systems Message
A5	Unassigned
A6	Request ADS Reports
A7	Free Text from ATC
A8	Deliver Departure Slot
A9	ATIS Report
AA	ATC Communications
AB	Terminal Weather Information for Pilots
AC	Pushback Clearance Uplink
AD	Expected Taxi Clearance
AE	Unassigned

Code	Message Type
AF	CPC Command Response
B0	ATS Facility Notification
B1	Request Oceanic Clearance
B2	Oceanic Clearance Readback
B3	Request Departure Clearance
B4	Departure Clearance Readback
B5	Waypoint Position Report
B6	Provide ADS Report
B7	?Free Text? to ATC
B8	Request Departure Slot
B9	Request ATIS Report
BA	ATC Communication
BB	Terminal Weather Information for Pilots
BC	Pushback Clearance Request
BD	Expected Taxi Clearance Request
BE	CPC Log-on/Log-off Request
BF	CPC WILCO
BG	Unassigned
C0-C9	Cockpit Printer Messages
CA	Cockpit Printer Messages
CB	Printer Busy
CC	Printer in Local or Test Mode
CD	Printer Out of Paper
CE	Printer Buffer Overrun
CF	Printer Initialisation Before Completion
EI	Internet Email Message
F3	Dedicated Transceiver Advisory
H1	General Message
H2	Meteorological Report

Appendix C

Code	Message Type
H3	Icing Report
HF	HFDL Messages
HX	Undelivered Uplink Report
M2	User Defined Message
Q0	Link Test
Q1	Departure Report
Q2	Estimated Time of Arrival Report
Q3	Clock Update Advisory
Q4	Voice Circuit Busy (Not Supported)
Q5	Unable to Deliver Uplink Messages
Q6	Voice to Data Changeover Advisory
Q7	Delay Message
QA	OUT Fuel Report
QB	OFF Report
QC	ON Report
QD	IN / Fuel Report
QE	OUT / Fuel/Destination Report
QF	OFF/ Destination Report
QG	OUT / Return IN Report
QH	OUT Report
QK	Landing Report

Code	Message Type
QL	Arrival Report
QM	Arrival Information Report
QN	Diversion Report
QP	OUT Report
QQ	OFF Report
QR	ON Report
QS	IN Report
QT	OUT / Return IN Report
QX	Intercept / Unable to Process
RA	Command/Response
RB	Command/Response
REG	Registration
S1	VHF Network Statistics Report
S2	VHF Performance Report
S3	LRU Configuration Report
SA	Media Advisory
SQ	Squitter Message
UP	Message Acknowledgement
:;	Aircraft Transceiver Auto-Tune
_j	Reserved
_DEL	General Response (Demand Mode)

Abbreviations used in ACARS Messages

A character showing the ACARS Message type is normally found after the message label as shown in the example below.

ACARS mode: H Aircraft reg: F-ZKXF
Message label: H1 Block id: 9 Msg. no: D09D
Flight id: AF9876
Message content:- POS210711,N 34.539,E133.620,----,273,24376,83

Two Letter Abbreviations

AO	Passenger count in zone A (first class)
AL	Flight level
OA	Passenger count in zone A (first class)
OB	Passenger count in zone B (business class)
OA	Passenger in zone A (first class)
OB	Passenger count in zone B (business Class)
OC	Passenger count in zone C (coach class)
AL	Flight level
CG	Centre of gravity
CI	Cost index
CL	Cruising level
CR	Company route
CW	Cruise wind
CZ	Cruising speed
DA	Departure aerodrome
DG	Drag factor
DP	Dew point
DS	Destination station
DX	Long Distance
E1-9	Engine parameters
EO	Estimated time over
ET	Estimated time
FB	Amount of fuel boarded
FC	Estimated further clearance
FD	Fuel over destination
FF	Fuel flow factor in pounds per hour
FI	Flight Identification
FL	Flight level
FO	First officer
FR	Fault report prefix
FX	En Route fix
GL	Geographical location
HD	Aircraft heading
IC	Aircraft icing
IN	Time in
IR	In VHF radio range and Instrument Rated
LA	Identification of officer landing aircraft
LT	Light
MA	Message assurance
MN	Maintenance
MT	Maximum takeoff power computation
MU	Management Unit
N1	Speed of turbine 1
N2	Speed of turbine 2
NA	Navigation aid
NL	Number of landings
NP	Next report point
OB	Passenger count in zone B (business class)
OC	Passenger count in zone C (coach class)
OF	Time off
ON	Time on
OP	Oil pressure
OS	Other supplementary information
OT	Time out or oil temperature
OV	Present location
PB	Number of persons on board
PD	Point of departure
PW	Position weather
QN	Altimeter settings
RD	Departure runway
RF	Request flight level
RI	Return in time
RL	Requesting cruising level
RM	Remarks
RO	Return on time
RQ	Request
RT	Route information
RL	Request cruising level
SA	Alternative aerodrome
SI	Special communication addressing instruction
SK	Sky conditions
SL	SELCAL code
SP	Significant point
ST	Standard takeoff power
TA	Static air temperature
TB	Turbulence
TD	Takeoff temperature
TE	Time En Route
TM	Surface air temperature
TO	Time over
TP	Transmission path
V1	Velocity 1.
VR	Rotate
VR	Runway visual range
V2	Velocity 2
WL	Weather
WP	Way point

WR	Warning prefix
WV	Wind information
WR	Warning prefix
WX	Weather
ZW	Zero fuel weight

Three Letter Abbreviations

ADF	Automatic direction finding
ADS	Automatic dependent surveillance
AEP	Fixed ICAO format position report with weather
AGM	Start of standard message
ALT	Altitude
ALT	Altimeter
AML	Aircraft Maintenance Log
APP	Approach
APU	Auxiliary power unit
ATA	Actual time of arrival
AUW	All up weight
AWD	Automated weather data
BBG	in reference to HAZMAT cargo
BKN	Broken
CHP	Chop
CLR	Clear
CPT	Captain
CRZ	used in conjunction with engine cruise data
CTL	Control
CVG	Covering
DAL	Radio Ham
DAI	Display aircraft itinerary
DBI	Data base initialisation-update
DDG	in reference to HAZMAT cargo
DDX	Display dispatch message
DEV	Display aircraft deviations
DFR	Display flight routing
DLD	in reference to cargo
DTX	Display text
EAC	Expect approach clearance
EDA	Engine data Fo.Ctvs
EDF	Engine data Follows
EFC	Expect final clearance
EGT	Exhaust Gas Thrust
ENG	Engine data
EOK	Everything "OK"
EON	Expected touchdown time
EPR	Exhaust pressure ratio
ERR	Error message
ERT	Estimated ramp time
ELT	Estimated Landing Time
FAA	Federal Aviation Administration
FDD	Flight data recorder information
FDR	Flight data recorder
FLR	Fault report
FLR	Failure
FLT	Flight
FMC	Flight Management Computer
FMS	Flight Management System
FOB	Fuel on board
FPR	Flight Plan request
FQY	Frequency
FRM	Maintenance codes
FCS	Flight control systems
FTM	Used before waypoint name
GEN	Generator
GPU	Ground power unit
GMT	Greenwich Mean Time
HDG	Heading
IAS	Indicated air speed
IDG	Integrated Drive Generator
IFR	Instrument flight rules
LEG	Flight sequence from engine start to next engine stop
LIF	Request for Load information (weight and balance)
LND	Landing
LOM	Locator outer marker
LWT	Landing weight
MAC	Deviation of centre of gravity due to Loading in pct
MCH	Mach number
MEL	Minimum essential list of maintenance codes
MSA	Minimum safe altitude
MSL	Mean sea level
NDP	Non-directional beacon
NRP	No report
NVD	No visual defects
OAT	Outside air temperature
OCA	Ocean control area
OCC	Occasional (weather)
OFF	Off time
OUT	Out time
OVR	Over
PAX	Passenger
PCU	Power control unit
POD	Point of descent
POS	Position
PWD	Predicted Weather Data
PWI	Predicted Wind Info
QFE	Airport elevation altimeter pressure setting
QNF	Mean sea level altimeter pressure setting
RCA	Reached cruise speed altitude
REV	in reference to cargo
RGS	Remote Ground Station
REQ	Request
ROC	Rate of climb
ROD	Rate of descent
RVR	Runway visual range
RWY	Runway
SAT	Static air temperature
SMI	Standard message identifiers
SMT	Standard message text
STA	Station :
TAS	True airspeed
TAT	True air temperature
T/O	Take off
TDX	with regards to fuel

TEI	Text element identifiers
TIS	ATIS information
TKO	Takeoff
TOG	Take Off gross Weight
TPS	Runway information
TRB	Turbulence
TYP	Type
TYP	Type 1 weather request
TYP	Type 2 weather request
UHF	Ultra High Frequency
UTC	Universal Coordinate Time
VEC	Vector
VHF	Very High Frequency
VOR	VHF omni-directional radio range
WND	Wind (direction/velocity)
WOB	Weather observation
WRN	Warning
WXA	Weather at
WXR	Weather

Other Codes

ADNS	ARINC Data Network Service
APRCH	Approach
ARINC	Aeronautical Radio Inc.
ATIS	Automatic Terminal Information Service
ATISRQ	ATIS request
AWDAF	Automated Weather Data-Area Forecast
AWDFT	Automated Weather Data-Terminal Area Forecast
AWDSA	Automated Weather Data-Air route Forecast
CFDIU	Combined Flight Data Indicator Unit
CLIMB	Climbing
CRUISE	Cruise level
DESCEN	Descending
DFDAU	Digital Flight Data Acquisition Unit
DPTR	Departure
FAA	Federal Aviation Administration
FDR	Flight data recorder
FMC	Flight Management Computer
IATA	International Air Transportation Association
ICAP	International Civil Aviation Organization
INCLIMB	In climb
INRANG	In range of VHF
INRP	In report
IR	Instrument rated
INOP	Inoperative
LEVEL	Level flight
LIVE	Live cargo (animals)
MAAS	Meet and assist
NON-FDE	Faults Non Critical Faults, Aircraft is air worthy usual cabin and lighting faults
NOSIG	No Significant change
OFFRP	Off report
ONRP	On report
OUTRP	Out report
PLTOKL	Internal addressing within Computer System
PIREP	Pilot's report
POSWX	Position weather
RGS	Remote Ground Station
SMI	Standard Message Identifiers
SMT	Standard Message Text
TEI	Text Element Identifiers
TRIM	Required Compensation of MAC
UDCS	Undercast sky
UDCST	Undercast sky
WCHR	Wheelchair
WXRQ	Weather request
XPDR	Transponder

IATA / ICAO Airport Codes

IATA	ICAO	Airport & Country	IATA	ICAO	Airport & Country
AAC	HEAR	El Arish Intl, Egypt	AFA	SAMR	Suboficial Aytes Germano, Argentina
AAE	DABB	Annaba, Algeria	AFD	FAPA	Port Alfred, South Africa
AAL	EKYT	Aalborg Airport, Denmark	AGB	EDMA	Augsburg, Germany
AAM	FAMD	Malamala, South Africa	AGE	EDWG	Wangerooge, Germany
AAN	OMAL	Al Ain Intl, United Arab Emirates	AGF	LFBA	Agen, France
AAO	SVAN	Anaco, Venezuela	AGH	ESTA	Angelholm, Sweden
AAQ	URKA	Vityazevo Airport, Russia	AGJ	RORA	Aguni Airport, Japan
AAR	EKAH	Aarhus Airport, Denmark	AGM	BGAM	Angmagssalik Airport, Greenland
AAT	ZWAT	Altay Airport, China	AGP	LEMG	Malaga Airport, Spain
AAV	RPMA	Allah Valley Airport, Philippines	AGR	VIAG	Agra Airport, India
AAY	OYGD	Al, Yemen	AGS	KAGS	Augusta Regional, USA
AAZ	MGQZ	Quezaltenango Airport, Guatemala	AGU	MMAS	Lic. Jesus Teran Peredo Intl, Mexico
ABC	LEAB	Albacete Airport, Spain	AGV	SVAC	Oswaldo Guevara Mujica, Venezuela
ABD	CIAA	Abadan Airport, Iran	AGX	VOAT	Agatti Aerodrome, India
ABE	KABE	Lehigh Valley Intl, USA	AHB	OEAB	Abha Regional Airport, Saudi Arabia
ABH	YAPH	Alpha Airport, Australia	AHL	SYAH	Aishalton, Guyana
ABI	KABI	Abilene Regional Airport, USA	AHN	KAHN	Athens, USA
ABJ	DIAP	Felix Houphouet, Ivory Coast	AHO	LIEA	Alghero Airport, Italy
ABK	HAKD	Kebri Dehar, Ethiopia	AHU	GMTA	Cherif Al Idrissi, Morocco
ABO	TJAB	Antonio Juarbe Pol, Puerto Rico	AIG	FEFY	Yalinga, Central Africa
ABQ	KABQ	Albuquerque Intl Sunport, USA	AIT	NCAI	Avarua, Cook Islands
ABR	KABR	Aberdeen Regional Airport, USA	AJA	LFKJ	Campo Dell Oro Airport, France
ABS	HEBL	Abu Simbel Airport, Egypt	AJI	LTCO	Agri Airport, Turkey
ABV	DNAA	Nnamdi Azikiwe, Nigeria	AJJ	GQNJ	Akjoujt, Mauritania
ABX	YMAY	Albury Airport, Australia	AJN	FMCV	Ouani, Comoros
ABY	KABY	Southwest Georgia Regional, USA	AJR	ESNX	Arvidsjaur, Sweden
ABZ	EGPD	Aberdeen Airport, United Kingdom	AJU	SBAR	Santa Maria Airport, Brazil
ACA	MMAA	General Juan N. Alvarez Intl, Mexico	AJY	DRZA	Manu Dayak, Niger
ACC	DGAA	Kotoka Intl, Ghana	AKD	VAAK	Akola Airport, India
ACE	GCRR	Lanzarote Airport, Spain	AKF	HLKF	Kufra, Libya
ACH	LSZR	St Gallen, Switzerland	AKJ	RJEC	Asahikawa Airport, Japan
ACI	EGJA	Alderney Airport, United Kingdom	AKL	NZAA	Auckland Intl, New Zealand
ACK	KACK	Nantucket Memorial Airport, USA	AKN	PAKN	King Salmon Airport, USA
ACR	SKAC	Araracuara, Colombia	AKR	DNAK	Akure, Nigeria
ACT	KACT	Waco Regional Airport, USA	AKU	ZWAK	Aksu Airport, China
ACV	KACV	Arcata Airport, USA	AKV	CYKO	Akulivik, Canada
ACY	KACY	Atlantic City Intl, USA	AKX	UATT	Aktyubinsk, Kazakhstan
ACZ	OIZB	Zabol Airport, Iran	AKY	VYSW	Sittwe, Myanmar
ADA	LTAF	Adana Airport, Turkey	ALA	UAAA	Almaty, Kazakhstan
ADB	LTBJ	Izmir Adnan Menderes Airport, Turkey	ALB	KALB	Albany Intl, USA
ADD	HAAB	Addis Abeba Bole Intl, Ethiopia	ALC	LEAL	Alicante Airport, Spain
ADE	OYAA	Aden Intl, Yemen	ALD	SPAR	Alerta, Peru
ADF	LTCP	Adiyaman Airport, Turkey	ALF	ENAT	Alta Airport, Norway
ADH	UEAA	Aldan Airport, Russia	ALG	DAAG	Algiers, Algeria
ADI	FYAR	Arandis, Namibia	ALH	YABA	Albany Airport, Australia
ADJ	OJAM	Marka Intl, Jordan	ALJ	FAAB	Alexander Bay, South Africa
ADL	YPAD	Adelaide Intl, Australia	ALL	LIMG	Villanova d'Albenga Intl, Italy
ADP	VCCA	Anuradhapura, Sri Lanka	ALO	KALO	Waterloo Regional Airport, USA
ADQ	PADQ	Kodiak Airport, USA	ALP	OSAP	Aleppo Intl, Syria
ADU	OITL	Ardabil Airport, Iran	ALR	NZLX	Alexandra, New Zealand
AEH	FTTC	Abeche, Chad	ALU	HCMA	Alula, Somalia
AEO	GQNA	Aioun, Mauritania	ALW	KALW	Walla Walla Regional Airport, USA
AEP	SABE	Aeroparque Jorge Newbery, Argentina	ALY	HEAX	Alexandria Intl, Egypt
AES	ENAL	Alesund Airport, Norway	AMA	KAMA	Rick Husband Amarillo Intl, USA
AEX	KAEX	Alexandria Intl, USA	AMB	FMNE	Ambilobe, Madagascar
AEY	BIAR	Akureyri Airport, Iceland	AMC	FTTN	Am, Chad

IATA	ICAO	Airport & Country
AMD	VAAH	Sardar Vallabhbhai Patel Intl, India
AMH	HAAM	Arba Minch, Ethiopia
AMI	WRRA	Selaparang Airport, Indonesia
AMM	OJAI	Queen Alia Intl Jordan
AMO	FTTU	Mao, Chad
AMP	FMSY	Ampanihy, Madagascar
AMQ	WAPP	Pattimura Airport, Indonesia
AMS	EHAM	Amsterdam Schiphol, Netherlands
AMV	ULDD	Amderma Airport, Russia
ANC	PANC	Ted Stevens Anchorage Intl, USA
ANE	LFJR	Angers Loire Aeroport Airport, France
ANF	SCFA	Cerro Moreno Intl, Chile
ANG	LFBU	Angouleme, France
ANI	PANI	Aniak Airport, USA
ANJ	FCBZ	Zanaga, Congo
ANM	FMNH	Antsirabato, Madagascar
ANO	FQAG	Angoche, Mozambique
ANR	EBAW	Deurne Airport, Belgium
ANS	SPHY	Andahuaylas, Peru
ANU	TAPA	VC Bird Intl, Antigua and Barbuda
ANX	ENAN	Andoya Airport, Norway
AOC	EDAC	Altenburg, Germany
AOG	ZYAS	Anshan Airport, China
AOI	LIPY	Ancona Falconara Airport, Italy
AOJ	RJSA	Aomori Airport, Japan
AOK	LGKP	Karpathos Island National, Greece
AOO	KAOO	Altoona, USA
AOR	WMKA	Sultan Abdul Halim, Malaysia
AOT	LIMW	Aosta Airport, Italy
AOU	VLAP	Attopeu, Laos
APB	SLAP	Apolo, Bolivia
APF	KAPF	Naples Municipal Airport, USA
APL	FQNP	Nampula, Mozambique
APN	KAPN	Alpena County Regional Airport, USA
AQB	MGQC	Quiche Airport, Guatemala
AQG	ZSAQ	Anqing Airport, China
AQJ	OJAQ	Aqaba Intl, Jordan
AQP	SPQU	Rodriguez Ballon, Peru
ARH	ULAA	Talagi Airport, Russia
ARI	SCAR	Chacalluta Intl, Chile
ARK	HTAR	Arusha, Tanzania
ARM	YARM	Armidale Airport, Australia
ARN	ESSA	Arlanda, Sweden
ARR	SAVR	Alto Rio Senguer Airport, Argentina
ARW	LRAR	Arad Intl, Romania
ARY	YARA	Ararat Airport, Australia
ARZ	FNZE	N'zeto, Angola
ASB	UTAA	Ashgabat, Turkmenistan
ASD	MYAF	Andros Town Intl, Bahamas
ASE	KASE	Aspen, USA
ASF	URWA	Astrakhan Airport, Russia
ASG	NZAS	Ashburton, New Zealand
ASJ	RJKA	Amami Airport, Japan
ASK	DIYO	Yamoussoukro, Ivory Coast
ASO	HASO	Asosa, Ethiopia
ASP	YBAS	Alice Springs Airport, Australia
ASR	LTAU	Kayseri Erkilet Intl, Turkey
ASU	SGAS	Asuncion Silvio Pettirossi, Paraguay
ASV	HKAM	Amboseli, Kenya
ASW	HESN	Aswan Intl, Egypt
ATB	HSAT	Atbara, Sudan
ATC	MYCA	Arthurs Town Airport, Bahamas
ATF	SEAM	Chachoan, Ecuador
ATH	LGAV	Athens Intl, Greece
ATI	SUAG	Artigas Intl, Uruguay
ATJ	FMME	Antsirabe, Madagascar
ATL	KATL	Hartsfield, USA
ATQ	VIAR	Raja Sansi Intl, India
ATR	GQPA	Atar, Mauritania
ATV	FTTI	Ati, Chad
ATW	KATW	Outagamie County Regional, USA
ATZ	HEAT	Asyut Intl, Egypt
AUA	TNCA	Queen Beatrix Intl, Aruba
AUC	LFDH	Auch, France
AUC	SKUC	Santiago Perez, Colombia
AUF	LFLA	Auxerre, France
AUH	OMAA	Abu Dhabi Intl, United Arab Emirates
AUR	LFLW	Aurillac Airport, France
AUS	KAUS	Austin, USA
AVI	MUCA	Maximo Gomez Intl, Cuba
AVK	ZMAH	Arvaikheer, Mongolia
AVL	KAVL	Asheville Regional Airport, USA
AVN	LFMV	Avignon Airport, France
AVP	KAVP	Wilkes, USA
AVV	YAVV	Avalon Airport, Australia
AWA	HALA	Awasa, Ethiopia
AWZ	OIAW	Ahwaz Airport, Iran
AXA	TQPF	Anguilla Wallblake, Anguilla
AXD	LGAL	Alexandroupolis Intl, Greece
AXK	OYAT	Ataq, Yemen
AXM	SKAR	El Eden, Colombia
AXP	MYAP	Spring Point Airport, Bahamas
AXT	RJSK	Akita Airport, Japan
AXU	HAAX	Axum, Ethiopia
AYN	ZHAY	Anyang Airport, China
AYP	SPHO	Col Alfredo Mendivil Duarte, Peru
AYQ	YAYE	Ayers Rock Airport, Australia
AYT	LTAI	Antalya Airport, Turkey
AZD	OIYY	Shahid Sadooghi Airport Iran
AZI	OMAD	Bateen, United Arab Emirates
AZO	KAZO	Kalamazoo/Battle Creek Intl, USA
AZR	DAUA	Adrar, Algeria
AZZ	FNAM	Ambriz, Angola
BAG	RPUB	Loakan Airport, Philippines
BAH	OBBI	Bahrain Intl, Bahrain
BAI	MRBA	Buenos Aires Airport, Costa Rica
BAK	UBBB	Bina, Azerbaijan
BAL	LTCJ	Batman Airport, Turkey
BAN	FZVR	Basongo, Congo
BAQ	SKBQ	Ernesto Cortissoz, Colombia
BAV	ZBOW	Baotou Airport, China
BAX	UNBB	Barnaul Airport, Russia
BAY	LRBM	Baia Mare Airport, Romania
BBA	SCBA	Balmaceda, Chile
BBG	NGTU	Butaritari, Kiribati
BBH	EDBH	Ostseeflughafen Stralsund, Germany
BBI	VEBS	Biju Patnaik Airport, India
BBK	FBKE	Kasane, Botsuana
BBM	VDBG	Battambang, Cambodia
BBN	WBGZ	Bario, Malaysia

IATA	ICAO	Airport & Country
BBO	HCMI	Berbera, Somalia
BBP	EGHJ	Bembridge Airport, United Kingdom
BBQ	TAPH	Codrington Airport, Antigua & Barbuda
BBR	TFFB	Baillif Airport, Guadeloupe
BBS	EGLK	Blackbushe Airport, United Kingdom
BBT	FEFT	Berberati, Central Africa
BBU	LRBS	Bucharest Intl, Romania
BBV	DIGN	Nero, Ivory Coast
BBY	FEFM	Bambari, Central Africa
BBZ	FLZB	Zambezi, Zambia
BCA	MUBA	Gustavo Rizo Airport, Cuba
BCD	RPVB	Bacolod City Domestic, Philippines
BCL	MRBC	Barra del Colorado Airport, Costa Rica
BCM	LRBC	Bacau Intl, Romania
BCN	LEBL	Barcelona Intl, Spain
BCO	HABC	Baco, Ethiopia
BDA	TXKF	Hamilton Bermuda Intl, Bermuda
BDB	YBUD	Bundaberg Airport, Australia
BDH	OIBL	Bandar Lengeh Airport, Iran
BDI	FSSB	Bird Island, Seychelles
BDJ	WRBB	Syamsudin Noor Airport, Indonesia
BDK	DIBU	Soko, Ivory Coast
BDL	KBDL	Bradley Intl, USA
BDO	WIIB	Husein Sastranegara, Indonesia
BDQ	VABO	Vadodara Airport, India
BDS	LIBR	Casale Airport, Italy
BDT	FZFD	Gbadolite, Congo
BDU	ENDU	Bardufoss Airport, Norway
BDV	FZRB	Moba, Congo
BEB	EGPL	Benbecula Airport, United Kingdom
BED	KBED	Laurence G. Hanscom Field, USA
BEF	MNBL	Bluefields, Nicaragua
BEG	LYBE	Belgrade Nikola Tesla Airport, Serbia
BEI	HABE	Beica, Ethiopia
BEK	VOPN	Sri Sathya Sai Airport, India
BEL	SBBE	Val de C, Brazil
BEP	VOBI	Bellary Airport, India
BES	LFRB	Brest Bretagne Airport, France
BET	PABE	Bethel Airport, USA
BEU	YBIE	Bedourie Airport, Australia
BEV	LLBS	Teyman Airport, Israel
BEW	FQBR	Beira, Mozambique
BEY	OLBA	Beirut Intl, Lebanon
BFE	EDLI	Bielefeld, Germany
BFI	KBFI	King County Intl, USA
BFL	KBFL	Meadows Field Airport, USA
BFN	FABL	Bloemfontein, South Africa
BFO	FVCZ	Buffalo Range, Zimbabwe
BFS	EGAA	Belfast Intl, United Kingdom
BFU	ZSBB	Bengbu Airport, China
BFX	FKKU	Bafoussam, Cameroon
BGA	SKBG	Palonegro, Colombia
BGB	FOGB	Booue, Gabon
BGC	LPBG	Braganca Airport, Portugal
BGF	FEFF	M'poko, Central Africa
BGH	GQNE	Bogue, Mauritania
BGI	TBPB	Grantley Adams Intl, Barbados
BGL	VNBL	Baglung, Nepal
BGM	KBGM	Greater Binghamton Airport, USA
BGN	RPUZ	Bagabag Airport, Philippines

IATA	ICAO	Airport & Country
BGO	ENBR	Bergen Airport, Flesland, Norway
BGR	KBGR	Bangor Intl, USA
BGU	FEFG	Bangassou, Central Africa
BGY	LIME	Orio al Serio Intl, Italy
BGZ	LPBR	Braga Airport, Portugal
BHA	SESV	Los Perales, Ecuador
BHB	KBHB	Hancock County, USA
BHD	EGAC	Belfast City Airport, United Kingdom
BHE	NZWB	Woodbourne , New Zealand
BHH	OEBH	Bisha Domestic Airport, Saudi Arabia
BHI	SAZB	Comandante Espora, Argentina
BHJ	VABJ	Bhuj Rudra Mata Airport, India
BHK	UTSB	Bukhara, Uzbekistan
BHM	KBHM	Birmingham Intl, USA
BHN	OYBN	Beihan, Yemen
BHO	VABP	Bhopal Airport, India
BHP	VNBJ	Bhojpur, Nepal
BHQ	YBHI	Broken Hill Airport, Australia
BHR	VNBP	Bharatpur, Nepal
BHS	YBTH	Bathurst Airport, Australia
BHU	VABV	Bhavnagar Airport, India
BHV	OPBW	Bahawalpur Airport, Pakistan
BHX	EGBB	Birmingham Intl, United Kingdom
BHY	ZGBH	Beihai Airport, China
BIA	LFKB	Bastia, France
BIK	WABB	Frans Kaisiepo Airport, Indonesia
BIL	KBIL	Billings Logan Intl, USA
BIM	OABN	Bamyan, Afghanistan
BIM	MYBS	South Bimini Airport, Bahamas
BIO	LEBB	Bilbao Airport, Spain
BIQ	LFBZ	Biarritz, France
BIR	VNVT	Biratnagar, Nepal
BIS	KBIS	Bismarck Municipal Airport, USA
BIT	VNBT	Baitadi, Nepal
BIV	FEFR	Bria, Central Africa
BIY	FABE	Bisho, South Africa
BJA	DAAE	Bejaia, Algeria
BJB	OIMN	Bojnord Airport, Iran
BJF	ENBS	Batsfjord Airport, Norway
BJH	VNBG	Bajhang, Nepal
BJI	KBJI	Bemidji Regional Airport, USA
BJL	GBYD	Banjul Intl, Gambia
BJM	HBBA	Bujumbura Intl, Burundi
BJO	SLBJ	Bermejo, Bolivia
BJR	HABD	Bahir Dar, Ethiopia
BJU	VNBR	Bajura, Nepal
BJV	LTFE	Milas, Turkey
BJX	MMLO	Del Bajio Intl, Mexico
BJZ	LEBZ	Badajoz Airport, Spain
BKI	WBKK	Kota Kinabalu, Malaysia
BKJ	GUOK	Baralande, Guinea
BKK	VTBD	Bangkok Intl, Thailand
BKO	GABS	Senou, Mali
BKQ	YBCK	Blackall Airport, Australia
BKR	FTTK	Bokoro, Chad
BKY	FZMA	Kavumu, Congo
BKZ	HTBU	Bukoba, Tanzania
BLA	SVBC	Jose Antonio Anzoategui, Venezuela
BLE	ESSD	Borlange, Sweden
BLI	KBLI	Bellingham Intl, USA

IATA	ICAO	Airport & Country
BLK	EGNH	Blackpool Intl, United Kingdom
BLL	EKBI	Billund Airport, Denmark
BLN	YBLA	Benalla Airport, Australia
BLO	BIBL	Blonduos Airport, Iceland
BLP	SPBL	Huallaga, Peru
BLQ	LIPE	Aeroporto G. Marconi di Bologna, Italy
BLR	VOBG	Bangalore Intl, India
BLT	YBTR	Blackwater Airport, Australia
BLX	LIDB	Belluno Airport, Italy
BLZ	FWCL	Chileka, Malawi
BMA	ESSB	Bromma, Sweden
BMB	FZFU	Bumba, Congo
BMD	FMML	Tsiribihina, Madagascar
BME	YBRM	Broome Intl, Australia
BMI	KBMI	Central Illinois Regional Airport, USA
BMK	EDWR	Borkum, Germany
BMM	FOOB	Bitam, Gabon
BMV	VVBM	Buon Ma Thuot Airport, Vietnam
BMW	DATM	Bordj Mokhtar Airport, Algeria
BNA	KBNA	Nashville Intl, USA
BNB	FZGN	Boende, Congo
BNC	FZNP	Beni, Congo
BND	OIKB	Bandar Abbass Intl, Iran
BNE	YBBN	Brisbane Airport, Australia
BNI	DNBE	Benin, Nigeria
BNK	YBNA	Ballina, Australia
BNN	ENBN	Bronnoysund Airport, Norway
BNP	OPBN	Bannu Airport, Pakistan
BNR	DFOB	Banfora, Burkina Faso
BNS	SVBI	Barinas, Venezuela
BNX	LQBK	Banja Luka Intl, Bosnia
BOA	FZAJ	Boma, Congo
BOB	NTTB	Bora Bora Airport, French Polynesia
BOC	MPBO	Bocas Del Toro Intl, Panama
BOD	LFBD	Bordeaux Airport Airport, France
BOE	FCOB	Boundji, Congo
BOG	SKBO	Eldorado Intl, Colombia
BOH	EGHH	Bournemouth Airport, United Kingdom
BOI	KBOI	Boise Air Terminal, USA
BOJ	LBBG	Burgas Intl, Bulgaria
BOM	VABB	Chhatrapati Shivaji Intl, India
BON	TNCB	Flamingo Intl, Netherlands Antilles
BOO	ENBO	Bodo Airport, Norway
BOP	FEFO	Bouar, Central Africa
BOS	KBOS	Gen. Edward Lawrence Logan, USA
BOU	LFLD	Bourges Airport, France
BOY	DFOO	Bobo, Burkina Faso
BOZ	FEGZ	Bozoum, Central Africa
BPC	FKKV	Bamenda, Cameroon
BPH	RPMF	Bislig Airport, Philippines
BPN	WALL	Sepinggan Intl, Indonesia
BPS	SBPS	Porto Seguro Airport, Brazil
BPT	KBPT	Southeast Texas Regional, USA
BPY	FMNQ	Besalampy, Madagascar
BQA	RPUR	Baler Airport, Philippines
BQB	YBLN	Busselton Regional Airport, Australia
BQH	EGKB	Biggin Hill Airport, United Kingdom
BQK	KBQK	Brunswick Golden Isles Airport, USA
BQL	YBOU	Boulia Airport, Australia
BQN	TJBQ	Rafael Hernandez Airport, Puerto Rico
BQO	DIBN	Tehini, Ivory Coast
BQS	UHBB	Ignatyevo Airport, Russia
BQT	UMBB	Brest, Belarus
BRC	SAZS	San Carlos de Bariloche Intl, Argentina
BRD	KBRD	Brainerd Lakes Regional Airport, USA
BRE	EDDW	Airport Bremen, Germany
BRI	LIBD	Palese Macchie Airport, Italy
BRK	YBKE	Bourke Airport, Australia
BRM	SVBM	Barquisimeto, Venezuela
BRN	LSZB	Bern, Switzerland
BRO	KBRO	Brownsville/South Padre Island Intl, USA
BRQ	LKTB	Brno Turany Airport, Czech Republic
BRR	EGPR	Barra Airport, United Kingdom
BRS	EGGD	Bristol Intl, United Kingdom
BRT	YBTI	Bathurst Island Airport, Australia
BRU	EBBR	Brussels National Airport, Belgium
BRV	EDWB	Bremerhaven, Germany
BRW	PABR	Wiley Post, USA
BRX	MDBH	Maria Montez Intl, Dominican Repub
BSA	HCMF	Bosaso, Somalia
BSB	SBBR	Pres Juscelino Kubitschek, Brazil
BSC	SKBS	Jose Celestino Mutis, Colombia
BSD	ZPBS	Baoshan Airport, China
BSG	FGBT	Bata Airport, Equatorial Guinea
BSJ	YBNS	Bairnsdale Airport, Australia
BSN	FEFS	Bossangoa, Central Africa
BSO	RPUO	Basco Airport, Philippines
BST	OABT	Bost, Afghanistan
BSU	FZEN	Basankusu, Congo
BSX	VYPN	Pathein, Myanmar
BTA	FKKO	Bertoua, Cameroon
BTB	FCOT	Betou, Congo
BTC	VCCB	Batticaloa AB, Sri Lanka
BTE	GFBN	Bonthe, Sierra Leone
BTH	WIKB	Hang Nadim Airport, Indonesia
BTJ	WITT	Sultan Iskandarmuda, Indonesia
BTK	UIBB	Bratsk Airport, Russia
BTM	KBTM	Bert Mooney Airport, USA
BTQ	HRYI	Butare, Rwanda
BTR	KBTR	Baton Rouge Metropolitan, USA
BTS	LZIB	Bratislava, Slovakia
BTU	WBGB	Bintulu, Malaysia
BTV	KBTV	Burlington Intl, USA
BUD	LHBP	Budapest Ferihegy Intl, Hungary
BUF	KBUF	Buffalo Niagara Intl, USA
BUG	FNBG	Benguela, Angola
BUJ	DAAD	Bou Saada Airport, Algeria
BUK	OYBQ	Al, Yemen
BUN	SKBU	Buenaventura, Colombia
BUO	HCMV	Burao, Somalia
BUQ	FVBU	Bulawayo, Zimbabwe
BUR	KBUR	Bob Hope Airport, USA
BUX	FZKA	Bunia, Congo
BUZ	OIBB	Bushehr Airport, Iran
BVA	LFOB	Beauvais, France
BVB	SBBV	Boa Vista Intl, Brazil
BVC	GVBA	Rabil, Cape Verde
BVE	LFBV	Brive, France

IATA	ICAO	Airport & Country
BVG	ENBV	Berlevag Airport, Norway
BWA	VNBW	Bhairahawa, Nepal
BWE	EDVE	Flughafen Braunschweig, Germany
BWF	EGNL	Barrow/, United Kingdom
BWH	WMKB	Butterworth, Malaysia
BWI	KBWI	Baltimore, USA
BWK	LDSB	Airport Brac, Croatia
BWN	WBSB	Brunei Intl, Brunei Darussalam
BWQ	YBRW	Brewarrina Airport, Australia
BWT	YWYY	Burnie Airport, Australia
BWU	YSBK	Bankstown Airport, Australia
BXE	GOTB	Bakel, Senegal
BXH	UAAH	Balkhash, Kazakhstan
BXI	DIBI	Boundiali, Ivory Coast
BXR	OIKM	Bam Airport, Iran
BXU	RPME	Bancasi Airport, Philippines
BYC	SLYA	Yacuiba, Bolivia
BYK	DIBK	Bouake, Ivory Coast
BYM	MUBY	Carlos Manuel de Cespedes, Cuba
BYN	ZMBH	Bayankhongor, Mongolia
BYU	EDQD	Bayreuth, Germany
BZD	YBRN	Balranald Airport, Australia
BZE	MZBZ	Philip S W Goldson Intl, Belize
BZG	EPBY	Bydgoszcz Ignacy, Poland
BZL	VGBR	Barisal Airport, Bangladesh
BZN	KBZN	Gallatin Field Airport, USA
BZO	LIPB	Bolzano Dolomiti Airport, Italy
BZR	LFMU	Beziers, France
BZU	FZKJ	Buta, Congo
BZV	FCBB	Maya, Congo
CAA	MHCA	Catacamas, Honduras
CAB	FNCA	Cabinda, Angola
CAE	KCAE	Columbia Metropolitan Airport, USA
CAG	LIEE	Cagliari, Italy
CAH	VVCM	Ca Mau Airport, Vietnam
CAI	HECA	Cairo Intl, Egypt
CAJ	SVCN	Canaima, Venezuela
CAK	KCAK	Akron, USA
CAL	EGEC	Campbeltown Airport, United Kingdom
CAM	SLCA	Camiri, Bolivia
CAN	ZGGG	Guangzhou Baiyun Intl, China
CAP	MTCH	Cap Haitien Intl, Haiti
CAQ	SKCU	Caucasia, Colombia
CAS	GMMC	Anfa, Morocco
CAT	MYCB	New Bight Airport, Bahamas
CAX	EGNC	Carlisle Airport, United Kingdom
CAY	SOCA	Cayenne, French Guiana
CAZ	YCBA	Cobar Airport, Australia
CBB	SLCB	Jorge Wilsterman, Bolivia
CBG	EGSC	Cambridge City, United Kingdom
CBJ	MDCR	Cabo Rojo Airport, Dominican Repub
CBL	SVCB	Ciudad Bolivar, Venezuela
CBO	RPMC	Awang Airport, Philippines
CBP	LPCO	Coimbra Airport, Portugal
CBQ	DNCA	Calabar, Nigeria
CBR	YSCB	Canberra Intl, Australia
CBV	MGCB	Coban Airport, Guatemala
CCC	MUOC	Cayo Coco Airport, Cuba
CCF	LFMK	Carcassonne en Pays, France
CCH	SCCC	Chile Chico, Chile

IATA	ICAO	Airport & Country
CCJ	VOCL	Calicut Intl, India
CCK	YPCC	Cocos Island Intl, Australia
CCL	YCCA	Chinchilla Airport, Australia
CCN	OACC	Charkhcharan, Afghanistan
CCP	SCIE	Carriel Sur Intl, Chile
CCS	SVMI	Simon Bolivar Intl, Venezuela
CCU	VECC	Netaji Subhash Airport Intl, India
CCZ	MYBC	Chub Cay Intl, Bahamas
CDC	KCDC	Cedar City Regional Airport, USA
CDG	LFPG	Paris, France
CDO	FACD	Cradock, South Africa
CDP	VOCP	Cuddapah Airport, India
CDU	YSCN	Camden Airport, Australia
CDV	PACV	Merle K. Mudhole Smith Airport, USA
CDY	RPMU	Cagayan de Sulu Airport, Philippines
CEB	RPVM	Mactan, Philippines
CEC	KCEC	Jack McNamara Field Airport, USA
CED	YCDU	Ceduna Airport, Australia
CEG	EGNR	Hawarden Airport, United Kingdom
CEH	FWCD	Chelinda, Malawi
CEI	VTCT	Chiang Rai Intl, Thailand
CEK	USCC	Balandino Airport, Russia
CEN	MMCN	Ciudad Obregon Intl, Mexico
CEO	FNWK	Wako Kungo, Angola
CEP	SLCP	Concepcion, Bolivia
CEQ	LFMD	Cannes, France
CER	LFRC	Cherbourg, France
CET	LFOU	Cholet Lepontreau Airport, France
CFE	LFLC	Clermont, France
CFG	MUCF	Jaime Gonzalez Airport, Cuba
CFN	EIDL	Donegal Airport, Ireland
CFR	LFRK	Caen, France
CFS	YSCH	Coffs Harbour Airport, Australia
CFU	LGKR	Corfu Intl, Greece
CGB	SBCY	Marechal Rondon Airport, Brazil
CGH	SBSP	Congonhas Intl, Brazil
CGK	WIII	Soekarno, Indonesia
CGM	RPMH	Camiguin Airport, Philippines
CGN	EDDK	Koln – Bonn, Germany
CGO	ZHCC	Zhengzhou Xinzheng Intl, China
CGP	VGEG	Shah Amanat Intl, Bangladesh
CGQ	ZYCC	Changchun Longjia Intl, China
CGR	SBCG	Campo Grande Intl, Brazil
CGU	SVPR	Manuel Carlos Piar, Venezuela
CGY	RPML	Lumbia Airport, Philippines
CHA	KCHA	Chattanooga Metropolitan, USA
CHB	OPCL	Chilas Airport, Pakistan
CHC	NZCH	Christchurch Intl, New Zealand
CHF	RKPE	R, South Korea
CHH	SPPY	Chachapoyas, Peru
CHM	SPEO	Teniente Jaime A De Montreuil, Peru
CHO	KCHO	Charlottesville, USA
CHQ	LGSA	Chania Intl, Greece
CHR	LFLX	Chateauroux, France
CHS	KCHS	Charleston Intl, USA
CHT	NZCI	Chatham Is/Tuuta, New Zealand
CHV	LPCH	Chaves Airport, Portugal
CHW	ZLJQ	Jiuquan Airport, China
CHX	MPCH	Cap. Manuel Nino Intl, Panama
CIA	LIRA	Ciampino Airport, Italy

IATA	ICAO	Airport & Country
CIC	KCIC	Chico Municipal Airport, USA
CID	KCID	The Eastern Iowa Airport, USA
CIF	ZBCF	Chifeng Airport, China
CIH	ZBCZ	Changzhi Airport, China
CIJ	SLCO	Cobija, Bolivia
CIM	SKCM	Cimitarra, Colombia
CIP	FLCP	Chipata, Zambia
CIS	PCIS	Canton Afld, Kiribati
CIU	KCIU	Chippewa County Intl, USA
CIX	SPHI	Jose Abelardo, Peru
CJA	SPJR	Armando Revoredo Iglesias, Peru
CJB	VOCB	Coimbatore Airport, India
CJC	SCCF	El Loa, Chile
CJJ	RKTU	Chongju Intl, South Korea
CJL	OPCH	Chitral Airport, Pakistan
CJS	MMCS	Abraham Gonzalez Intl, Mexico
CJU	RKPC	Cheju Intl, South Korea
CKB	KCKB	Marion Regional Airport, USA
CKG	ZUCK	Chongqing Jiangbei Intl, China
CKH	UESO	Chokurdakh Airport, Russia
CKI	YCKI	Croker Island Airport, Australia
CKT	OIMC	Sarakhs Airport, Iran
CKY	GUCY	Gbessia, Guinea
CKZ	LTBH	Canakkale Airport, Turkey
CLA	VGCM	Comilla Airport, Bangladesh
CLE	KCLE	Cleveland, USA
CLJ	LRCL	Cluj, Romania
CLL	KCLL	Easterwood Airport, USA
CLM	KCLM	William R. Fairchild Intl, USA
CLO	SKCL	Alfonso Bonilla Aragon Intl, Colombia
CLQ	MMIA	Lic. Miguel de Madrid Airport, Mexico
CLT	KCLT	Charlotte/Douglas Intl, USA
CLY	LFKC	Calvi, France
CLZ	SVCL	Calabozo, Venezuela
CMB	VCBI	Bandaranaike Intl, Sri Lanka
CMD	YCTM	Cootamundra Airport, Australia
CME	MMCE	Ciudad del Carmen Intl, Mexico
CMF	LFLB	Chambery, France
CMG	SBCR	Corumb, Brazil
CMH	KCMH	Port Columbus Intl, USA
CMI	KCMI	University of Illinois, USA
CMK	FWCM	Club Makokola, Malawi
CMM	MGCR	Carmelita Airport, Guatemala
CMN	GMMN	Mohamed V, Morocco
CMO	HCMO	Obbia, Somalia
CMQ	YCMT	Clermont Airport, Australia
CMR	LFGA	Colmar, France
CMS	HCMS	Scusciuban, Somalia
CMW	MUCM	Ignacio Agramonte Intl, Cuba
CMX	KCMX	Houghton County Memorial, USA
CNB	YCNM	Coonamble Airport, Australia
CND	LRCK	Constanta Intl, Romania
CNF	SBCF	Tancredo Neves Intl, Brazil
CNG	LFBG	Cognac, France
CNJ	YCCY	Cloncurry Airport, Australia
CNN	UELL	Chulman Airport, Russia
CNP	BGCO	Constable Pynt Airport, Greenland
CNR	SCRA	Chanaral, Chile
CNS	YBCS	Cairns Intl, Australia
CNX	VTCC	Chiang Mai Intl, Thailand

IATA	ICAO	Airport & Country
COD	KCOD	Yellowstone Regional Airport, USA
COG	SKCD	Mandinga, Colombia
COH	VECO	Cooch Behar Airport, India
COJ	YCBB	Coonabarabran Airport, Australia
COO	DBBB	Cadjehoun, Benin
COQ	ZMCD	Choibalsan, Mongolia
COR	SACO	Ingeniero Ambrosio Intl, Argentina
COS	KCOS	Colorado Springs Municipal, USA
COU	KCOU	Columbia Regional Airport, USA
COV	LPCV	Covilha Airport, Portugal
COX	MYAK	Congo Town Airport, Bahamas
COZ	MDCZ	Constanza Airport, Dominican Repub
CPA	GLCP	Cape Palmas, Liberia
CPD	YCBP	Coober Pedy Airport, Australia
CPE	MMCP	Ing. Alberto Acuna Ongay Intl, Mexico
CPH	EKCH	Copenhagen Kastrup Intl, Denmark
CPL	SKHA	Gen Navas Pardo, Colombia
CPO	SCHA	Chamonate, Chile
CPP	RPUK	Calapan Airport, Philippines
CPR	KCPR	Natrona County Intl, USA
CPT	FACT	Cape Town Intl, South Africa
CPX	TJCP	Benjamin Rivera Noriega, Puerto Rico
CQF	LFAC	Calais, France
CRA	LRCV	Craiova Airport, Romania
CRB	YCBR	Collarenebri Airport, Australia
CRC	SKGO	Santa Ana, Colombia
CRD	SAVC	General Enrique Mosconi, Argentina
CRI	MYCI	Colonial Hill Airport, Bahamas
CRK	RPLC	Diosdado Macapagal Intl, Philippines
CRL	EBCI	Brussels South Charleroi, Belgium
CRM	RPVF	Catarman National Airport, Philippines
CRP	KCRP	Corpus Christi Intl, USA
CRQ	KCRQ	McClellan, USA
CRV	LIBC	Crotone Airport, Italy
CRW	KCRW	Yeager Airport, USA
CSB	LRCS	Caransebes Airport, Romania
CSF	LFPC	Creil Airport, France
CSG	KCSG	Columbus Metropolitan Airport, USA
CSK	GOGS	Cap Skiring, Senegal
CSX	ZGHA	Changsha Huanghua Intl, China
CSY	UWKS	Cheboksary Airport, Russia
CTA	LICC	Catania, Italy
CTC	SANC	Coronel Felipe Varela, Argentina
CTF	MGCT	Coatepeque Airport, Guatemala
CTG	SKCG	Rafael Nunez, Colombia
CTL	YBCV	Charleville Airport, Australia
CTM	MMCM	Chetumal Intl, Mexico
CTS	RJCC	New Chitose Airport, Japan
CTT	LFMQ	Le Castellet Airport, France
CTU	ZUUU	Chengdu Shuangliu Intl, China
CUC	SKCC	Camilo Daza Intl, Colombia
CUE	SECU	Mariscal Lamar, Ecuador
CUF	LIMZ	Cuneo Levaldigi Airport, Italy
CUL	MMCL	Federal de Bachigualato Intl, Mexico
CUM	SVCU	Antonio Jose De Sucre, Venezuela
CUN	MMUN	Cancun Intl, Mexico
CUO	SKCR	Caruru, Colombia
CUP	SVCP	Jose Francisco Bermudez, Venezuela
CUQ	YCOE	Coen Airport, Australia
CUR	TNCC	Hato Intl, Netherlands Antilles

IATA	ICAO	Airport & Country
CUU	MMCU	Gen Roberto Fierro Villalobos, Mexico
CUY	YCUE	Cue Airport, Australia
CUZ	SPZO	Velazco Astete, Peru
CVC	YCEE	Cleve Airport, Australia
CVE	SKCV	Covenas, Colombia
CVF	LFLJ	Courchevel Airport, France
CVG	KCVG	Northern Kentucky Intl, USA
CVJ	MMCB	General Mariano Matamoros, Mexico
CVM	MMCV	General Pedro J. Mendez, Mexico
CVQ	YCAR	Carnarvon Airport, Australia
CVT	EGBE	Coventry Airport, United Kingdom
CVU	LPCR	Corvo Airport, Portugal
CVX	KCVX	Charlevoix Municipal Airport, USA
CWA	KCWA	Central Wisconsin Airport, USA
CWB	SBCT	Afonso Pena Intl, Brazil
CWL	EGFF	Cardiff Intl, United Kingdom
CWT	YCWR	Cowra Airport, Australia
CWW	YCOR	Corowa Airport, Australia
CXB	VGCB	Cox's Bazar Airport, Bangladesh
CXI	PLCH	Cassidy Intl, Kiribati
CXN	HCMC	Candala, Somalia
CXR	VVCR	Cam Ranh Airport, Vietnam
CYB	MWCB	Gerrard, Cayman Islands
CYG	YCRG	Corryong Airport, Australia
CYO	MUCL	Vilo Acuna Airport, Cuba
CYP	RPVC	Calbayog Airport, Philippines
CYR	SUCA	Colonia International, Uruguay
CYS	KCYS	Cheyenne Regional Airport, USA
CYU	RPLO	Cuyo Airport, Philippines
CYZ	RPUY	Cauayan Airport, Philippines
CZE	SVCR	Jose L Chirinos Intl, Venezuela
CZL	DABC	Constantine, Algeria
CZM	MMCZ	Cozumel Intl, Mexico
CZS	SBCZ	Cruzeiro do Sul Intl, Brazil
CZU	SKCZ	Las Brujas, Colombia
CZX	ZSCG	Changzhou Airport, China
DAB	KDAB	Daytona Beach Intl, USA
DAC	VGZR	Zia Intl, Bangladesh
DAD	VVDN	Da Nang Intl, Vietnam
DAK	HEDK	Dakhla Airport, Egypt
DAL	KDAL	Dallas Love Field, USA
DAM	OSDI	Damascus Intl, Syria
DAP	VNDL	Darchula, Nepal
DAR	HTDA	Dar, Tanzania
DAT	ZBDT	Datong Airport, China
DAV	MPDA	Enrique Malek Intl, Panama
DAY	KDAY	James M. Cox Dayton Intl, USA
DBA	OPDB	Dalbandin Airport, Pakistan
DBM	HADM	Debre Marcos, Ethiopia
DBO	YSDU	Dubbo Airport, Australia
DBQ	KDBQ	Dubuque Regional Airport, USA
DBT	HADT	Debre Tabor, Ethiopia
DBV	LDDU	Dubrovnik Airport, Croatia
DCA	KDCA	Washington National Airport, USA
DCF	TDCF	Canefield Airport, Dominica
DCM	LFCK	Castres, France
DDG	ZYDD	Dandong Airport, China
DEA	OPDG	Dera Ghazi Khan Airport, Pakistan
DEB	LHDC	Debrecen Intl, Hungary
DEC	KDEC	Decatur Airport, USA

IATA	ICAO	Airport & Country
DED	VIDN	Jolly Grant Airport, India
DEI	FSSD	Denis Island, Seychelles
DEL	VIDP	Indira Gandhi Intl, India
DEM	HADD	Dembi Dollo, Ethiopia
DEN	KDEN	Denver Intl, USA
DES	FSDR	Desroches, Seychelles
DEZ	OSDZ	Deir Zzor, Syria
DFW	KDFW	Dallas, USA
DGE	YMDG	Mudgee Airport, Australia
DGO	MMDO	General Guadalupe Victoria, Mexico
DGT	RPVD	Sibulan Airport, Philippines
DGU	DFOD	Dedougou, Burkina Faso
DHI	VNDH	Dhangadhi, Nepal
DHM	VIGG	Gaggal Airport, India
DHN	KDHN	Dothan Regional Airport, USA
DIB	VEC1	Chabua Airport, India
DIE	FMNA	Arrachart, Madagascar
DIJ	LFSD	Dijon, France
DIL	WPDL	Comoro Airport, East Timor
DIM	DIDK	Dimbokro Ville, Ivory Coast
DIN	VVDB	Dien Bien Phu Airport, Vietnam
DIR	HADR	A.T.D. Yilma Intl, Ethiopia
DIS	FCPL	Dolisie, Congo
DIU	VA1P	Diu Airport, India
DIY	LTCC	Diyarbakir Airport, Turkey
DJE	DTTJ	Zarzis, Tunesia
DJG	DAAJ	Djanet, Algeria
DJJ	WAJJ	Sentani Airport, Indonesia
DJM	FCBD	Djambala, Congo
DJO	DIDL	Daloa, Ivory Coast
DKR	GOOY	Leopold Sedar Senghor, Senegal
DLA	FKKD	Douala, Cameroon
DLC	ZYTL	Dalian Zhoushuizi Intl, China
DLD	ENDI	Geilo Airport, Norway
DLE	LFGJ	Dole, France
DLG	PADL	Dillingham Airport, USA
DLH	KDLH	Duluth Intl, USA
DLI	VVDL	Lien Khuong Airport, Vietnam
DLM	LTBS	Dalaman Airport, Turkey
DME	UUDD	Domodedovo Intl, Russia
DMM	OEDF	King Fahd Intl, Saudi Arabia
DMU	VEMR	Dimapur Airport, India
DND	EGPN	Dundee Airport, United Kingdom
DNH	ZLDH	Dunhuang Airport, China
DNK	UKDD	Dnipropetrovsk Airport, Ukraine
DNO	YDLQ	Deniliquin Airport, Australia
DNP	VNDG	Dang, Nepal
DNR	LFRD	Dinard, France
DNX	HSGG	Galegu, Sudan
DNZ	LTAY	Denizli Cardak Airport, Turkey
DOD	HTDO	Dodoma, Tanzania
DOG	HSDN	Dongola, Sudan
DOH	OTBD	Doha Intl, Qatar
DOK	UKCC	Donetsk Airport, Ukraine
DOL	LFRG	Deauville, France
DOM	TDPD	Melville Hall Airport, Dominica
DOP	VNDP	Dolpa, Nepal
DOR	DFEE	Dori Ville, Burkina Faso
DPE	LFAB	Dieppe, France
DPL	RPMG	Dipolog Airport, Philippines

IATA	ICAO	Airport & Country
DPO	YDPO	Devonport Airport, Australia
DPS	WADD	Bali Intl, Indonesia
DRB	YDBY	Derby Airport, Australia
DRK	MRDK	Drake Bay Airport, Costa Rica
DRN	YDBI	Dirranbandi Airport, Australia
DRO	KDRO	Durango, USA
DRS	EDDC	Flughafen Dresden, Germany
DRW	YPDN	Darwin Intl, Australia
DSA	EGCN	Doncaster Sheffield, United Kingdom
DSC	FKKS	Dschang, Cameroon
DSD	TFFA	Grande Anse Airport, Guadeloupe
DSE	HADC	Combolcha, Ethiopia
DSK	OPDI	Dera Ismail Khan Airport, Pakistan
DSM	KDSM	Des Moines Intl, USA
DTE	RPUD	Daet Airport, Philippines
DTM	EDLW	Dortmund Airport 21, Germany
DTW	KDTW	Detroit Metropolitan, USA
DUB	EIDW	Dublin Intl, Ireland
DUD	NZDN	Dunedin, New Zealand
DUJ	KDUJ	DuBois, USA
DUN	BGDU	Dundas Airport, Greenland
DUQ	CAM3	Duncan, Canada
DUR	FADN	Durban Intl, South Africa
DUS	EDDL	Dusseldorf International, Germany
DUT	PADU	Unalaska Airport, USA
DVO	RPMD	Francisco Bangoy Intl, Philippines
DWA	FWDW	Dwangwa, Malawi
DWB	FMNO	Soalala, Madagascar
DWD	OEDW	Dawadmi Domestic, Saudi Arabia
DXB	OMDB	Dubai Intl, United Arab Emirates
DYA	YDYS	Dysart Airport, Australia
DYR	UHMA	Ugolny Airport, Russia
DYU	UTDD	Dushanbe, Tajikistan
DZN	UAKD	Zhezkazgan, Kazakhstan
DZO	SUDU	Santa Bernardina Intl, Uruguay
EAB	OYAB	Abbs, Yemen
EAM	OENG	Najran Domestic Airport, Saudi Arabia
EAS	LESO	San Sebastian Airport, Spain
EAT	KEAT	Pangborn Memorial Airport, USA
EAU	KEAU	Chippewa Valley Regional, USA
EBA	LIRJ	Aeroporto Marina di Campo, Italy
EBB	HUEN	Entebbe Intl, Uganda
EBD	HSOB	El Obeid, Sudan
EBG	SKEB	El Bagre, Colombia
EBJ	EKEB	Esbjerg Airport, Denmark
EBM	DTTR	El Borma, Tunesia
EBU	LFMH	Saint, France
EBW	FKKW	Ebolowa, Cameroon
ECH	YECH	Echuca Airport, Australia
ECN	LCEN	Ercan Intl, Cyprus
EDI	EGPH	Edinburgh Airport, United Kingdom
EDL	HKED	Eldoret, Kenya
EDM	LFRI	La Roche sur Yon, France
EDO	LTFD	Edremit Korfez Airport, Turkey
EFD	KEFD	Ellington Field, USA
EFL	LGKF	Kefalonia Island Intl, Greece
EGC	LFBE	Bergerac, France
EGE	KEGE	Eagle County Regional Airport, USA
EGN	HSGN	Geneina, Sudan
EGO	UUOB	Belgorod Airport, Russia
EGS	BIEG	Egilsstaoir Airport, Iceland
EIS	TUPJ	Beef I Intl, British Virgin Islands
EIY	LLEY	Ein Yahav Airfield, Israel
EJA	SKEJ	Yariguies, Colombia
EJH	OEWJ	Wedjh Domestic Airport, Saudi Arabia
EKO	KEKO	Elko Regional Airport, USA
EKT	ESSU	Eskilstuna, Sweden
ELB	SKBC	El Banco Apt., Colombia
ELC	YELD	Elcho Island Airport, Australia
ELF	HSFS	El Fasher, Sudan
ELG	DAUE	El Golea Airport, Algeria
ELH	MYEH	North Eleuthera Airport, Bahamas
ELM	KELM	Elmira/Corning Regional Airport, USA
ELP	KELP	El Paso Intl, USA
ELQ	OEGS	Gassim Regional Airport, Saudi Arabia
ELS	FAEL	East London, South Africa
ELT	HETR	El Tor Airport, Egypt
ELU	DAUO	El Oued, Algeria
EMA	EGNX	East Midlands Airport, United Kingdom
EMD	YEML	Emerald Airport, Australia
EME	EDWE	Emden, Germany
EMG	FAEM	Empangeni, South Africa
EMN	GQNI	Nema, Mauritania
ENA	PAEN	Kenai Municipal Airport, USA
ENC	LFSN	Nancy, France
ENF	EFET	Enontekio Airport, Finland
ENK	EGAB	Enniskillen, United Kingdom
ENO	SGEN	Quiteria, Paraguay
ENS	EHTW	Enschede Airport Twente, Netherlands
ENT	PKMA	Enewetak Aux Af, Marshall Islands
ENU	DNEN	Enugu, Nigeria
ENY	ZLYA	Yan'an Airport, China
EOH	SKMD	Olaya Herrera, Colombia
EOR	SVED	El Dorado, Venezuela
EOZ	SVEZ	Elorza, Venezuela
EPA	OEPA	Qaisumah Domestic, Saudi Arabia
EPL	LFSG	Epinal, France
EPR	YESP	Esperance Airport, Australia
EPS	MDPO	El Portillo Airport, Dominican Republic
EPU	EEPU	Parnu Airport, Estonia
EQS	SAVE	Esquel Airport, Argentina
ERA	HCMU	Erigavo, Somalia
ERC	LTCD	Erzincan Airport, Turkey
ERF	EDDE	Erfurt, Germany
ERH	GMFK	Moulay Ali Cherif, Morocco
ERI	KERI	Erie Intl, USA
ERS	FYWE	Eros, Namibia
ERZ	LTCE	Erzurum Airport, Turkey
ESB	LTAC	Ankara Esenboga Intl, Turkey
ESH	OESH	Sharorah Domestic, Saudi Arabia
ESH	EGKA	Shoreham Airport, United Kingdom
ESM	SETN	General Rivadeneira, Ecuador
ESR	SCES	El Salvador Bajo, Chile
ESS	EDLE	Essen – Mulheim, Germany
ETE	HAMM	Metema, Ethiopia
ETH	LLET	Eilat Airport, Israel
ETZ	LFJL	Metz, France
EUG	KEUG	Eugene Airport, USA
EUQ	RPVS	Evelio Javier Airport, Philippines
EUX	TNCE	F.D. Roosevelt, Netherlands Antilles

IATA	ICAO	Airport & Country
EVE	ENEV	Harstad, Norway
EVG	ESND	Sveg, Sweden
EVN	UGEE	Zvartnots, Armenia
EVV	KEVV	Evansville Regional Airport, USA
EVX	LFOE	Evreux, France
EWB	KEWB	New Bedford Regional Airport, USA
EWD	OEWD	Wadi al, Saudi Arabia
EWN	KEWN	Craven County Regional Airport, USA
EWO	FCCE	Ewo, Congo
EWR	KEWR	Newark Liberty Intl, USA
EXT	EGTE	Exeter Intl, United Kingdom
EYL	GAYE	Yelimane, Mali
EYP	SKYP	El Yopal, Colombia
EYS	HKES	Eliye Springs, Kenya
EYW	KEYW	Key West Intl, USA
EZE	SAEZ	Ezeiza Intl, Argentina
EZS	LTCA	Elazig Airport, Turkey
FAA	GUFH	Badala, Guinea
FAB	EGLF	Farnborough Airfield, United Kingdom
FAE	EKVG	Vagar Airprot, Faroe Islands
FAH	OAFR	Farah, Afghanistan
FAI	PAFA	Fairbanks Intl, USA
FAJ	TJFA	Diego Jimenez Torres, Puerto Rico
FAN	ENLI	Farsund Airport, Norway
FAO	LPFR	Faro Airport, Portugal
FAR	KFAR	Hector Intl, USA
FAT	KFAT	Fresno Yosemite Intl, USA
FAY	KFAY	Fayetteville Regional Airport, USA
FBD	OAFZ	Faizabad, Afghanistan
FBM	FZQA	Lubumbashi Intl, Congo
FCB	FAFB	Sentra Oes, South Africa
FCN	ETMN	Cuxhaven – Nordholz, Germany
FCO	LIRF	Fiumicino, Italy
FDE	ENBL	F, Norway
FDF	TFFF	Le Lamentin, Martinique
FDH	EDNY	Friedrichshafen, Germany
FDO	SADF	San Fernando Airport, Argentina
FDU	FZBO	Bandundu, Congo
FEB	VNSR	Sanfebagar, Nepal
FEK	DIFK	Ferkessedougou, Ivory Coast
FER	HKFG	Ferguson's Gulf, Kenya
FEZ	GMFF	Saiss, Morocco
FFU	SCFT	Futaleufu, Chile
FGD	GQPF	F'derik, Mauritania
FHR	KFHR	Friday Harbor Airport, USA
FIG	GUFA	Katourou, Guinea
FIH	FZAA	N'djili Intl, Congo
FIZ	YFTZ	Fitzroy Crossing Airport, Australia
FIZ	YFTZ	Fitzroy Crossing Airport, Australia
FJR	OMFJ	Fujairah Intl, United Arab Emirates
FKB	EDSB	Karlsruhe/Baden, Germany
FKI	FZIC	Bangoka Intl, Congo
FKJ	RJNF	Fukui Airport, Japan
FKS	RJSF	Fukushima Airport, Japan
FLA	SKFL	Gustavo Artunduaga P, Colombia
FLG	KFLG	Flagstaff Pulliam Airport, USA
FLL	KFLL	Fort Lauderdale, USA
FLN	SBFL	Herc, Brazil
FLO	KFLO	Florence Regional Airport, USA
FLR	LIRQ	A. Vespucci Florence Airport, Italy

IATA	ICAO	Airport & Country
FLS	YFLI	Flinders Island Airport, Australia
FLW	LPFL	Flores Airport, Portugal
FMA	SARF	Formosa Intl, Argentina
FMI	FZRF	Kalemie, Congo
FMM	EDJA	Allgau Airport / Memmingen, Germany
FMN	KFMN	Four Corners Regional Airport, USA
FMO	EDDG	Munster, Germany
FNA	GFLL	Lungi, Sierra Leone
FNB	ETNU	Neubrandenburg, Germany
FNC	LPMA	Madeira Airport, Portugal
FNG	DFEF	Fada N'Gourma, Burkina Faso
FNH	HAFN	Fincha, Ethiopia
FNJ	ZKPY	Sunan, North Korea
FNJ	ZKPY	Sunan, South Korea
FNT	KFNT	Bishop Intl, USA
FOC	ZSFZ	Fuzhou Chengle Intl, China
FOE	KFOE	Forbes Field, USA
FOG	LIBF	Gino Lisa Airport, Italy
FOM	FKKM	Nkounja, Cameroon
FON	MRAN	La Fortuna Airport, Costa Rica
FOR	SBFZ	Pinto Martins Intl, Brazil
FOS	YFRT	Forrest Airport, Australia
FOU	FOGF	Fougamou, Gabon
FPO	MYGF	Grand Bahama Intl , Bahamas
FRA	EDDF	Frankfurt am Main, Germany
FRB	YFBS	Forbes Airport, Australia
FRK	FSSF	Fregate, Seychelles
FRL	LIPK	Forli Airport, Italy
FRO	ENFL	Floro Airport, Norway
FRS	MGTK	Mundo Maya Intl, Guatemala
FRU	UAFM	Manas, Kyrgyzstan
FRW	FBFT	Francistown, Botsuana
FSC	LFKF	Figari, France
FSD	KFSD	Sioux Falls Regional Airport, USA
FSM	KFSM	Fort Smith Regional Airport, USA
FSP	LFVP	St. Pierre Airport, Saint
FTU	FMSD	Tolagnaro, Madagascar
FTX	FCOO	Owando, Congo
FUE	GCFV	Fuerteventura Airport, Spain
FUG	ZSFY	Fuyang Airport, China
FUJ	RJFE	Goto, Japan
FUK	RJFF	Fukuoka Airport, Japan
FUN	NGFU	Funafuti Intl, Tuvalu
FWA	KFWA	Fort Wayne Intl, USA
FXO	FQCB	Cuamba, Mozambique
FYN	ZWFY	Fuyun Airport, China
FYT	FTTY	Faya Largeau, Chad
FZO	EGTG	Filton Aerodrome, United Kingdom
GAF	DTTF	Ksar, Tunesia
GAJ	RJSC	Yamagata Airport, Japan
GAL	PAGA	Edward G. Pitka Sr. Airport, USA
GAN	VRMG	Gan, Maldives
GAO	MUGT	Mariana Grajales Airport, Cuba
GAQ	GAGO	Korogoussou, Mali
GAS	HKGA	Garissa, Kenya
GAT	LFNA	Tallard Airport, France
GAU	VEGT	Guwahati Intl, India
GAW	VYGG	Gantgaw, Myanmar
GAY	VEGY	Gaya Airport, India
GBE	FBSK	Sir Seretse Khama Intl, Botsuana

IATA	ICAO	Airport & Country
GBJ	TFFM	Marie Galante Airport, Guadeloupe
GBK	GFGK	Gbangbatoke, Sierra Leone
GBZ	NZGB	Great Barrier, New Zealand
GCC	KGCC	Gillette, USA
GCI	EGJB	Guernsey Airport, United Kingdom
GCJ	FAGC	Grand Central, South Africa
GCM	MWCR	Roberts Intl, Cayman Islands
GCN	KGCN	Grand Canyon National Park, USA
GDG	UHBI	Magdagachi Airport, Russia
GDJ	FZWC	Gandajika, Congo
GDL	MMGL	Don Miguel Hidalgo y Costilla, Mexico
GDN	EPGD	Gdansk Lech Walesa Airport, Poland
GDO	SVGD	Guasdualito, Venezuela
GDQ	HAGN	Azezo, Ethiopia
GDT	MBGT	Grand Turk Intl, Turks & Caicos
GDX	UHMM	Sokol Airport, Russia
GEA	NWWM	Magenta, New Caledonia
GEG	KGEG	Spokane Intl, USA
GEO	SYCJ	Cheddi Jagan Intl, Guyana
GER	MUNG	Rafael Cabrera Airport, Cuba
GES	RPMR	General Santos Intl, Philippines
GET	YGEL	Geraldton Airport, Australia
GEV	ESNG	Gallivare, Sweden
GFF	YGTH	Griffith Airport, Australia
GFK	KGFK	Grand Forks Intl, USA
GFN	YGFN	Grafton Airport, Australia
GFR	LFRF	Granville, France
GFY	FYGF	Grootfontein, Namibia
GGG	KGGG	East Texas Regional Airport, USA
GGO	DIGL	Guiglo, Ivory Coast
GGT	MYEF	Exuma Intl, Bahamas
GHA	DAUG	Ghardaia, Algeria
GHB	MYEM	Governor's Harbour Airport, Bahamas
GHC	MYBG	Great Harbour Cay Airport, Bahamas
GIB	LXGB	Gibraltar, Gibraltar
GID	HBBE	Gitega, Burundi
GIG	SBGL	Galeao, Brazil
GII	GUSI	Siguiri, Guinea
GIL	OPGT	Gilgit Airport, Pakistan
GIR	SKGI	Santiago Vila, Colombia
GIS	NZGS	Gisborne, New Zealand
GIY	FAGI	Giyani, South Africa
GIZ	OEGN	Gizan Regional Airport, Saudi Arabia
GJL	DAAV	Jijel, Algeria
GJT	KGJT	Walker Field Airport, USA
GKA	AYGA	Goroka, Papua New Guinea
GKH	VNGK	Gorkha, Nepal
GLA	EGPF	Glasgow Intl, United Kingdom
GLF	MRGF	Golfito Airport, Costa Rica
GLI	YGLI	Glen Innes Airport, Australia
GLK	HCMR	Galcaio, Somalia
GLL	ENKL	Gol Airport, Norway
GLO	EGBJ	Gloucester Airport, United Kingdom
GLT	YGLA	Gladstone Airport, Australia
GMA	FZFK	Gemena, Congo
GMB	HAGM	Gambella, Ethiopia
GME	UMGG	Gomel, Belarus
GMN	NZGM	Greymouth, New Zealand
GMZ	GCGM	La Gomera Airport, Spain
GNA	UMMG	Grodno, Belarus

IATA	ICAO	Airport & Country
GNB	LFLS	Grenoble, France
GND	TGPY	Point Salines Intl, Grenada
GNN	HAGH	Ghinnir, Ethiopia
GNV	KGNV	Gainesville Regional Airport, USA
GNZ	FBGZ	Ghanzi, Botsuana
GOA	LIMJ	Genoa Cristoforo Colombo, Italy
GOB	HAGB	Robe, Ethiopia
GOH	BGGH	Nuuk Airport, Greenland
GOI	VAGO	Dabolim Airport , India
GOJ	UWGG	Strigino Airport, Russia
GOM	FZNA	Goma Intl, Congo
GOQ	ZLGM	Golmud Airport, China
GOR	HAGR	Gore, Ethiopia
GOT	ESGG	Landvetter, Sweden
GOU	FKKR	Garoua, Cameroon
GOV	YPGV	Gove Airport, Australia
GOY	VCCG	Amparai, Sri Lanka
GOZ	LBGO	Gorna Oryahovitsa Airport, Bulgaria
GPA	LGRX	Araxos National Airport, Greece
GPI	KGPI	Glacier Park Intl, USA
GPI	SKGP	Guapi, Colombia
GPL	MRGP	Guapiles Airport, Costa Rica
GPN	YGPT	Garden Point Airport, Australia
GPO	SAZG	General Pico Airport, Argentina
GPS	SEGS	Seymour, Ecuador
GPS	SEGS	Seymour Airport, Ecuador
GPT	KGPT	Gulfport, USA
GRB	KGRB	Austin Straubel Intl, USA
GRG	OAGZ	Gardez, Afghanistan
GRJ	FAGG	George, South Africa
GRK	KGRK	Killeen, USA
GRO	LEGE	Girona, Spain
GRQ	EHGG	Groningen Airport Eelde, Netherlands
GRR	KGRR	Gerald R. Ford Intl, USA
GRS	LIRS	Grosseto Airport, Italy
GRU	SBGR	Guarulhos Intl, Brazil
GRW	LPGR	Graciosa Airport, Portugal
GRX	LEGR	Granada, Spain
GRZ	LOWG	Graz, Austria
GSE	ESGP	Goteborg City Airport, Sweden
GSO	KGSO	Piedmont Triad Intl, USA
GSP	KGSP	Greenville, USA
GSQ	HEOW	Shark El Oweinat Intl, Egypt
GSR	HCMG	Gardo, Somalia
GSU	HSGF	Gedaref, Sudan
GTE	YGTE	Groote Eylandt Airport, Australia
GTF	KGTF	Great Falls Intl, USA
GTN	NZGT	Glentanner, New Zealand
GTR	KGTR	Golden Triangle Regional Airport, USA
GUA	MGGT	Guatemala La Aurora Intl, Guatemala
GUB	MMGR	Guerrero Negro Airport, Mexico
GUC	KGUC	Gunnison, USA
GUD	GAGM	Goundam, Mali
GUH	YGDH	Gunnedah Airport, Australia
GUI	SVGI	Guiria, Venezuela
GUL	YGLB	Goulburn Airport, Australia
GUM	PGUM	Guam Intl, Guam
GUQ	SVGU	Guanare, Venezuela
GUW	UATG	Atyrau, Kazakhstan
GVA	LSGG	Geneva, Switzerland

IATA	ICAO	Airport & Country
GVX	ESSK	Gavle, Sweden
GWA	VYGW	Gwa, Myanmar
GWD	OPGD	Gwadar Intl, Pakistan
GWE	FVTL	Thornhill, Zimbabwe
GWL	VIGR	Gwalior Airport, India
GWT	EDXW	Sylt, Germany
GWY	EICM	Galway Airport, Ireland
GXF	OYSY	Sayun, Yemen
GXG	FNNG	Negage, Angola
GXQ	SCCY	Teniente Vidal, Chile
GYA	SLGY	Cap Av Emilio Beltran, Bolivia
GYE	SEGU	Simon Bolivar Intl, Ecuador
GYI	HRYG	Gisenyi, Rwanda
GYM	MMGM	Gen Jose Maria Yanez Intl, Mexico
GYN	SBGO	Santa Genoveva Airport, Brazil
GZT	LTAJ	Oguzeli Airport, Turkey
HAA	ENHK	Hasvik Airport, Norway
HAC	RJTH	Hachijojima Airport, Japan
HAD	ESMT	Halmstad, Sweden
HAH	FMCH	Prince Said Ibrahim, Comoros
HAJ	EDDV	Hannover, Germany
HAK	ZJHK	Haikou Meilan Intl, China
HAM	EDDH	Hamburg, Germany
HAN	VVNB	Noi Bai Intl, Vietnam
HAQ	VRMH	Hanimaadhoo, Maldives
HAS	OEHL	Hail Regional Airport, Saudi Arabia
HAU	ENHD	Haugesund Airport, Norway
HAV	MUHA	Jose Marti Intl, Cuba
HAW	EGFE	Haverfordwest, United Kingdom
HBA	YMHB	Hobart Intl, Australia
HBE	HEBA	Borg El Arab Intl, Egypt
HBT	OEKK	Hafr al, Saudi Arabia
HBX	VA1A	Hubli Airport, India
HCM	HCME	Eil, Somalia
HCQ	YHLC	Halls Creek Airport, Australia
HDD	OPKD	Hyderabad Airport, Pakistan
HDF	EDAH	Heringsdorf, Germany
HDF	EDAH	Heringsdorf, Germany
HDM	OIHH	Hamadan Airport, Iran
HDN	KHDN	Yampa Valley Airport, USA
HDS	FAHT	Hoedspruit, South Africa
HDY	VTSS	Hat Yai Intl, Thailand
HEA	OAHR	Herat, Afghanistan
HEH	VYHH	Heho, Myanmar
HEI	EDXB	Heide, Germany
HEK	ZYHE	Heihe Airport, China
HEL	EFHK	Helsinki, Finland
HEM	EFHF	Helsinki, Finland
HER	LGIR	Heraklion Intl, Greece
HET	ZBHH	Hohhot Baita Intl, China
HEX	MDHE	Herrera Intl, Dominican Republic
HFA	LLHA	Haifa Airport, Israel
HFE	ZSOF	Hefei Luogang Intl, China
HFN	BIHN	Hornafjorour Airport, Iceland
HFS	ESOH	Hagfors, Sweden
HFT	ENHF	Hammerfest Airport, Norway
HGH	ZSHC	Hangzhou Xiaoshan Intl, China
HGL	EDXH	Helgoland, Germany
HGN	VTCH	Mae Hong Son Airport, Thailand
HGO	DIKO	Korhogo, Ivory Coast

IATA	ICAO	Airport & Country
HGR	KHGR	Hagerstown Regional Airport, USA
HGS	GFHA	Hastings, Sierra Leone
HGU	AYMH	Mount Hagen, Papua New Guinea
HHN	EDFH	Frankfurt, Germany
HHQ	VTPH	Hua Hin Airport, Thailand
HID	YHID	Horn Island Airport, Australia
HIJ	RJOA	Hiroshima Airport, Japan
HIL	RPVH	Hilongos Airport, Philippines
HIR	AGGH	Honiara Intl, Solomon Islands
HJR	VAKJ	Khajuraho Airport, India
HKD	RJCH	Hakodate Airport, Japan
HKK	NZHK	Hokitika, New Zealand
HKT	VTSP	Phuket Intl, Thailand
HLA	FALA	Lanseria, South Africa
HLD	ZBLA	Hailar Dongshan Airport, China
HLF	ESSF	Hultsfred, Sweden
HLH	ZBUL	Ulanhot Airport, China
HLN	KHLN	Helena Regional Airport, USA
HLP	WIIH	Halim Perdanakusuma Intl, Indonesia
HLS	YSTH	St Helens Airport, Australia
HLT	YHML	Hamilton Airport, Australia
HLU	NWWH	Nesson, New Caledonia
HLW	FAHL	Hluhluwe, South Africa
HLZ	NZHN	Hamilton Intl, New Zealand
HME	DAUH	Hassi Messaoud, Algeria
HMI	ZWHM	Hami Airport, China
HMO	MMHO	Ignacio Pesqueira Garcia, Mexico
HMR	ENHA	Hamar Airport, Norway
HMV	ESUT	Hemavan, Sweden
HNA	RJSI	Hanamaki Airport, Japan
HND	RJTT	Tokyo Intl , Japan
HNL	PHNL	Honolulu Intl, USA
HNM	PHHN	Hana Airport, USA
HNY	ZGHY	Hengyang Airport, China
HOA	HKHO	Hola, Kenya
HOD	OYHD	Hodeidah Intl, Yemen
HOG	MUHG	Frank Pais Airport, Cuba
HOM	PAHO	Homer Airport, USA
HOQ	EDQM	Hof, Germany
HOR	LPHR	Horta Airport, Portugal
HOU	KHOU	William P. Hobby Airport, USA
HOV	ENOV	Orsta, Norway
HOX	VYHL	Hommalin, Myanmar
HPA	NFTL	Ha'apai, Tonga
HPH	VVCI	Cat Bi Airport, Vietnam
HPN	KHPN	Westchester County Airport, USA
HRB	ZYHB	Harbin Taiping Intl, China
HRE	FVHA	Harare Intl, Zimbabwe
HRG	HEGN	Hurghada Intl, Egypt
HRK	UKHH	Osnova Airport, Ukraine
HRL	KHRL	Valley Intl, USA
HRS	FAHR	Harrismith, South Africa
HSG	RJFS	Saga Airport, Japan
HSM	YHSM	Horsham Airport, Australia
HSN	ZSZS	Zhoushan Airport, China
HSV	KHSV	Huntsville Intl, USA
HTA	UIAA	Kadala Airport, Russia
HTI	YBHM	Hamilton Island Airport, Australia
HTN	ZWTN	Hotan Airport, China
HTR	RORH	Hateruma Airport, Japan

IATA	ICAO	Airport & Country
HTS	KHTS	Tri, USA
HTU	YHPN	Hopetoun Airport, Australia
HTZ	SKHC	Hato Corozal, Colombia
HUE	HAHU	Humera, Ethiopia
HUG	MGHT	Huehuetenango Airport, Guatemala
HUI	VVPB	Phu Bai Airport, Vietnam
HUQ	HLON	Hon, Libya
HUU	SPNC	Alferez David Figueroa Fernan, Peru
HUV	ESNH	Hudiksvall, Sweden
HUX	MMBT	Bah, Mexico
HUY	EGNJ	Humberside Airport, United Kingdom
HVA	FMNL	Analalava, Madagascar
HVB	YHBA	Hervey Bay Airport, Australia
HVG	ENHV	Honningsvag Airport, Norway
HVN	KHVN	Tweed, USA
HWN	FVWN	Hwange National Park, Zimbabwe
HXD	KHXD	Hilton Head Airport, USA
HXX	YHAY	Hay Airport, Australia
HYA	KHYA	Barnstable Municipal Airport, USA
HYD	VOHY	Hyderabad Airport, India
HYN	ZSLQ	Huangyan Luqiao Airport, China
HYV	EFHV	Hyvinkaa Airport, Finland
HZB	LFQT	Merville, France
HZG	ZLHZ	Hanzhong Airport, China
IAD	KIAD	Washington Dulles Intl, USA
IAH	KIAH	George Bush Intercontinental, USA
IAM	DAUZ	Zarzaitine, Algeria
IAS	LRIA	Iasi Intl, Romania
IBA	DNIB	New Ibadan, Nigeria
IBE	SKIB	Perales, Colombia
IBP	SPBR	Iberia, Peru
IBZ	LEIB	Ibiza Airport, Spain
ICA	SVIC	Icabaru, Venezuela
ICR	MUNC	Nicaro Airport, Cuba
ICT	KICT	Wichita Mid, USA
IDA	KIDA	Idaho Falls Regional Airport, USA
IDB	ESUE	Idre, Sweden
IDF	FZCB	Idiofa, Congo
IDR	VAID	Devi Ahilyabai Holkar Intl, India
IDY	LFEY	d'Yeu, France
IEG	EPZG	Zielona Gora Intl, Poland
IEJ	RORE	Iejima Airport, Japan
IEV	UKKK	Zhuliany Intl, Ukraine
IFJ	BIIS	Isafjorour Airport, Iceland
IFN	OIFM	Isfahan Intl, Iran
IFO	UKLI	Ivano, Ukraine
IFP	KIFP	Laughlin/Bullhead Intl, USA
IGA	MYIG	Inagua Airport , Bahamas
IGN	RPMI	Maria Cristina Airport, Philippines
IGO	SKIG	Chigorodo, Colombia
IGR	SARI	Cataratas del Iguazu Intl, Argentina
IGS	ETSI	Ingolstadt, Germany
IGU	SBFI	Foz do Iguacu Intl, Brazil
IHN	OYQN	Qishn, Yemen
IHO	FMSI	Ihosy, Madagascar
IKA	OIIE	Imam Khomeini Intl, Iran
IKI	RJDB	Iki Airport, Japan
IKL	FZGV	Ikela, Congo
IKT	UUII	Irkutsk Intl, Russia
ILF	CZBD	Ilford, Canada

IATA	ICAO	Airport & Country
ILK	FMMQ	Atsinanana, Madagascar
ILM	KILM	Wilmington Intl, USA
ILO	RPVI	Mandurriao Airport, Philippines
ILP	NWWE	Moue, New Caledonia
ILR	DNIL	Ilorin, Nigeria
ILU	HKKL	Kilaguni, Kenya
ILY	EGPI	Islay Airport, United Kingdom
ILZ	LZZI	Zilina Airport, Slovakia
IMB	SYIB	Imbaimadai, Guyana
IMF	VEIM	Imphal Airport, India
IMK	VNST	Simikot, Nepal
IMO	FEFZ	Zemio, Central Africa
IMP	SBIZ	Prefeito Renato Moreira Airport, Brazil
INC	ZLIC	Yinchuan Helanshan Airport, China
IND	KIND	Indianapolis Intl, USA
INF	DATG	In Guezzam Airport Algeria
INH	FQIN	Inhambane, Mozambique
INI	LYNI	Nis Constantine the Great Intl, Serbia
INL	KINL	Falls Intl, USA
INN	LOWI	Innsbruck, Austria
INO	FZBA	Inongo, Congo
INU	ANAU	Nauru Intl, Nauru
INV	EGPE	Inverness Airport, United Kingdom
INZ	DAUI	In Salah Airport, Algeria
IOA	LGIO	Ioannina National Airport, Greece
IOM	EGNS	Isle of Man Airport, United Kingdom
ION	FCOI	Impfondo, Congo
IOS	SBIL	Jorge Amado Airport, Brazil
IPE	RPMV	Ipil Airport, Philippines
IPH	WMKI	Sultan Azlan Shah, Malaysia
IPI	SKIP	San Luis, Colombia
IPL	KIPL	Imperial County Airport, USA
IPT	KIPT	Williamsport Regional Airport, USA
IQN	ZLQY	Qingyang Airport, China
IQQ	SCDA	Diego Aracena Intl, Chile
IQT	SPQT	Col Francisco Secada Vignetta, Peru
IRG	YLHR	Lockhart River Airport, Australia
IRI	HTIR	Iringa, Tanzania
IRJ	SANL	Capit, Argentina
IRO	FEFI	Birao, Central Africa
IRP	FZJH	Isiro, Congo
ISA	YBMA	Mount Isa Airport, Australia
ISB	OPRN	Islamabad Intl, Pakistan
ISC	EGHE	St. Mary's Airport, United Kingdom
ISE	LTFC	Suleyman Demirel Airport, Turkey
ISG	ROIG	Ishigaki Airport, Japan
ISP	KISP	Long Island MacArthur Airport, USA
IST	LTBA	Istanbul Ataturk Intl, Turkey
ITH	KITH	Ithaca Tompkins Regional, USA
ITM	RJOO	Osaka Intl , Japan
ITO	PHTO	Hilo Intl, USA
IVA	FMNJ	Ampapamena, Madagascar
IVC	NZNV	Invercargill, New Zealand
IVL	EFIV	Ivalo Airport, Finland
IVR	YIVL	Inverell Airport, Australia
IWJ	RJOW	Iwami Airport, Japan
IXA	VEAT	Agartala Airport, India
IXB	VEBD	Bagdogra Airport, India
IXC	VICG	Chandigarh Airport, India
IXE	VOML	Mangalore Airport, India

IATA	ICAO	Airport & Country
IXG	VABM	Belgaum Airport, India
IXH	VEKR	Kailashahar Airport, India
IXI	VELR	Lilabari Airport, India
IXJ	VIJU	Jammu Airport, India
IXK	VAKS	Junagadh Airport, India
IXM	VOMD	Madurai Airport, India
IXN	VEKW	Khowai Airport, India
IXQ	VEKM	Kamalpur Airport, India
IXR	VERC	Birsa Munda Airport, India
IXS	VEKU	Silchar Airport, India
IXT	VEPG	Pasighat Airport, India
IXU	VAAU	Aurangabad Airport, India
IXV	VEAN	Along Airport, India
IXW	VEJS	Jamshedpur Airport, India
IXY	VAKE	Kandla Airport, India
IXZ	VOPB	Port Blair Airport, India
IYK	KIYK	Inyokern Airport, USA
IZO	RJOC	Izumo Airport, Japan
JAA	OAJL	Jalalabad, Afghanistan
JAC	KJAC	Jackson Hole Airport, USA
JAD	YPJT	Jandakot Airport, Australia
JAF	VCCJ	Kankesanturai AB, Sri Lanka
JAI	VIJP	Jaipur Airport, India
JAK	MTJA	Jacmel, Haiti
JAL	MMJA	El Lencero Airport, Mexico
JAN	KJAN	Jackson, USA
JAU	SPJJ	Jauja, Peru
JAV	BGJN	Jakobshavn Airport, Greenland
JAX	KJAX	Jacksonville Intl, USA
JCH	BGCH	Christianshab Airport, Greenland
JCU	GECT	Ceuta Heliport, Spain
JDH	VIJO	Jodhpur Airport, India
JDZ	ZSJD	Jingdezhen Airport, China
JED	OEJN	King Abdulaziz Intl, Saudi Arabia
JEE	MTJE	Jeremie, Haiti
JEG	BGEM	Auisiait Airport, Greenland
JER	EGJJ	Jersey Airport, United Kingdom
JFK	KJFK	John F. Kennedy Intl, USA
JFR	BGFH	Frederikshab Airport, Greenland
JGA	VAJM	Jamnagar Airport, India
JGB	VE46	Jagdalpur Airport, India
JGO	BGGN	Godhavn Airport, Greenland
JHB	WMKJ	Sultan Ismail, Malaysia
JHG	ZPJH	Jinghong Gasa Airport, China
JHS	BGHB	Holsteinsborg Airport, Greenland
JHW	KJHW	Chautauqua County Airport, USA
JIB	HFFF	Djibouti Ambouli, Djibouti
JIK	LGIK	Ikaria Island National Airport, Greece
JIL	ZYJL	Jilin Airport, China
JIM	HAJM	Aba Segud, Ethiopia
JIN	HUJI	Jinja, Uganda
JIU	ZSJJ	Jiujiang Lushan Airport, China
JIW	OPJI	Jiwani Airport, Pakistan
JJI	SPJI	Juanjui, Peru
JJN	ZSQZ	Quanzhou Jinjiang Airport, China
JKG	ESGJ	Jonkoping, Sweden
JKH	LGHI	Chios Island National Airport, Greece
JKR	VNJP	Janakpur, Nepal
JLN	KJLN	Joplin Regional Airport, USA
JLR	VAJB	Jabalpur Airport, India
JMK	LGMK	Mykonos Island National, Greece
JMO	VNJS	Jomsom, Nepal
JMU	ZYJM	Jiamusi Airport, China
JNB	FAJS	Johannesburg Intl, South Africa
JNG	ZLJN	Jining Airport, China
JNN	BGNN	Nanortalik Airport, Greenland
JNS	BGNS	Narssaq Airport, Greenland
JNU	PAJN	Juneau Intl, USA
JNX	LGNX	Naxos Island National Airport, Greece
JNZ	ZYJZ	Jinzhou Airport, China
JOE	EFJO	Joensuu Airport, Finland
JOG	WIIJ	Adisucipto Intl, Indonesia
JOI	SBJV	Joinville, Brazil
JOL	RPMJ	Jolo Airport, Philippines
JOM	HTNJ	Njombe, Tanzania
JOS	DNJO	Jos, Nigeria
JPA	SBJP	Presidente Castro Pinto Intl, Brazil
JQE	MPJE	Jaque, Panama
JRH	VEJT	Jorhat Airport, India
JRO	HTKJ	Kilimanjaro Intl, Tanzania
JSA	VIJR	Jaisalmer Airport, India
JSH	LGST	Sitia Public Airport, Greece
JSI	LGSK	Skiathos Island National, Greece
JSR	VGJR	Jessore Airport, Bangladesh
JST	KJST	John Murtha Johnstown, USA
JSY	LGSO	Syros Island National Airport, Greece
JTR	LGSR	Santorini National Airport, Greece
JTY	LGPL	Astypalaia Island National, Greece
JUB	HSSJ	Juba, Sudan
JUI	EDWJ	Juist, Germany
JUL	SPJL	Inca Manco Capac, Peru
JUM	VNJL	Jumla, Nepal
JUV	BGUP	Upernavik Airport, Greenland
JVA	FMMK	Ankavandra, Madagascar
JWA	FBJW	Jwaneng, Botsuana
JYV	EFJY	Jyvaskyla Airport, Finland
KAA	FLKS	Kasama, Zambia
KAB	FVKB	Kariba, Zimbabwe
KAC	OSKL	Kamishly, Syria
KAD	DNKA	New Kaduna, Nigeria
KAG	RKNN	Kangnung Aero, South Korea
KAJ	EFKI	Kajaani Airport, Finland
KAN	DNKN	Mallam Aminu Kano, Nigeria
KAO	EFKS	Kuusamo Airport, Finland
KAP	FZSK	Kapanga, Congo
KAR	SYKM	Kamarang, Guyana
KAT	NZKT	Kaitaia, New Zealand
KAU	EFKA	Kauhava Airport, Finland
KAV	SVKA	Bolivar, Venezuela
KAW	VYKT	Kawthoung, Myanmar
KBA	GFKB	Kabala, Sierra Leone
KBI	FKKB	Kribi, Cameroon
KBL	OAKB	Kabul Intl, Afghanistan
KBN	FZWT	Tunta, Congo
KBO	FZRM	Kabalo, Congo
KBP	UKBB	Boryspil Intl, Ukraine
KBQ	FWKG	Kasungu, Malawi
KBR	WMKC	Sultan Ismail Petra, Malaysia
KBS	GFBO	Bo, Sierra Leone
KBV	VTSG	Krabi Airport, Thailand

IATA	ICAO	Airport & Country
KBZ	NZKI	Kaikoura, New Zealand
KCA	ZWKC	Kuqa Airport, China
KCH	WBGG	Kuching Intl, Malaysia
KCM	LTCN	Kahramanmaras Airport, Turkey
KCU	HUMI	Masindi, Uganda
KCZ	RJOK	Kochi Airport, Japan
KDA	GOGK	Kolda, Senegal
KDC	DBBK	Kandi, Benin
KDD	OPKH	Khuzdar Airport, Pakistan
KDH	OAKN	Kandahar, Afghanistan
KDI	WAAU	Wolter Monginsidi Airport, Indonesia
KDL	EEKA	Kardla Airport, Estonia
KDN	FOGE	Ndende, Gabon
KDO	VRMT	Kaadedhdhoo, Maldives
KDU	OPSD	Skardu Airport, Pakistan
KEC	FZQG	Kasenga, Congo
KED	GQNK	Kaedi, Mauritania
KEE	FCOK	Kelle, Congo
KEF	BIKF	Keflavik Intl, Iceland
KEJ	UNEE	Kemorovo Airport Russia
KEL	EDHK	Kiel, Germany
KEM	EFKE	Kemi, Finland
KEN	GFKE	Kenema, Sierra Leone
KEO	DIOD	Odienne, Ivory Coast
KEP	VNNG	Nepalgunj, Nepal
KER	OIKK	Kerman Airport, Iran
KES	CZEE	Kelsey, Canada
KET	VYKG	Kengtung, Myanmar
KEW	CPV8	Keewaywin, Canada
KEY	HKKR	Kericho, Kenya
KFA	GQNF	Kiffa, Mauritania
KGA	FZUA	Kananga, Congo
KGC	YKSC	Kingscote Airport, Australia
KGD	UMKK	Khrabrovo Airport, Russia
KGF	UAKK	Karaganda, Kazakhstan
KGG	GOTK	Kedougou, Senegal
KGI	YPKG	Kalgoorlie, Australia
KGJ	FWKA	Karonga, Malawi
KGL	HRYR	Gregoire Kayibanda, Rwanda
KGN	FZOK	Kasongo, Congo
KGS	LGKO	Kos Island Intl, Greece
KGY	YKRY	Kingaroy Airport, Australia
KHD	OICK	Khoram Abad Airport, Iran
KHG	ZWSH	Kashgar Airport, China
KHH	RCKH	Kaohsiung Intl, Taiwan
KHI	OPKC	Jinnah Intl, Pakistan
KHJ	EFKJ	Kauhajoki Airport, Finland
KHK	OIBQ	Khark Airport, Iran
KHM	VYKI	Kanti, Myanmar
KHN	ZSCN	Nanchang Intl, China
KHS	OOKB	Khasab AB, Oman
KHT	OAKS	Khost, Afghanistan
KHV	UHHH	Novy Airport, Russia
KHW	FBKR	Khwai River, Botsuana
KID	ESMK	Kristianstad, Sweden
KIF	CNM5	Kingfisher Lake, Canada
KIH	OIBK	Kish Airport, Iran
KIJ	RJSN	Niigata Airport, Japan
KIM	FAKM	Kimberley, South Africa
KIN	MKJP	Norman Manley Intl, Jamaica
KIR	EIKY	Kerry Airport, Ireland
KIS	HKKI	Kisumu, Kenya
KIT	LGKC	Kithira Island National Airport, Greece
KIV	LUKK	Chisinau, Moldova
KIW	FLSO	Southdowns, Zambia
KIX	RJBB	Kansai Intl, Japan
KIY	HTKI	Kilwa Masoko, Tanzania
KJA	UNKL	Krasnoyarsk Yemelyanovo, Russia
KJK	EBKT	Kortrijk, Belgium
KJP	ROKR	Kerama Airport, Japan
KKC	VTUK	Khon Kaen Airport, Thailand
KKE	NZKK	Kerikeri, New Zealand
KKJ	RJFR	New Kitakyushu Airport, Japan
KKN	ENKR	Kirkenes Airport, Norway
KKO	NZKO	Kaikohe, New Zealand
KKW	FZCA	Kikwit, Congo
KKX	RJKI	Kikai Airport, Japan
KLB	FLKL	Kalabo, Zambia
KLC	GOOK	Kaolack, Senegal
KLH	VAKP	Kolhapur Airport, India
KLI	FZFP	Kotakoli, Congo
KLO	RPVK	Kalibo Airport, Philippines
KLR	ESMQ	Kalmar, Sweden
KLU	LOWK	Klagenfurt, Austria
KLV	LKKV	Karlovy Vary Intl, Czech Republic
KLX	LGKL	Kalamata Intl, Greece
KLY	FZOD	Kalima, Congo
KLZ	FAKZ	Kleinsee, South Africa
KME	HRZA	Kamembe, Rwanda
KMG	ZPPP	Kunming Wujiaba Intl, China
KMH	FAKU	Johan Pienaar, South Africa
KMI	RJFM	Miyazaki Airport, Japan
KMJ	RJFT	Kumamoto Airport, Japan
KMK	FCPA	Makabana, Congo
KMN	FZSA	Kamina Base, Congo
KMP	FYKT	Keetmanshoop, Namibia
KMS	DGSI	Kumasi, Ghana
KMU	HCMK	Kisimayu, Somalia
KMZ	FLKO	Kaoma, Zambia
KNA	SCVM	Vina Del Mar, Chile
KND	FZOA	Kindu, Congo
KNJ	FCBK	Kindamba, Congo
KNM	FZTK	Kaniama, Congo
KNN	GUXD	Kankan, Guinea
KNQ	NWWD	Kone, New Caledonia
KNS	YKII	King Island Airport, Australia
KNU	VIKA	Kanpur Airport, India
KNX	YPKU	Kununurra Airport, Australia
KNZ	GAKA	Kenieba, Mali
KOA	PHKO	Kona Intl at Keahole, USA
KOC	NWWK	Koumac, New Caledonia
KOE	WRKK	El Tari Airport, Indonesia
KOF	FAKP	Komatipoort, South Africa
KOI	EGPA	Kirkwall Airport, United Kingdom
KOJ	RJFK	Kagoshima Airport, Japan
KOK	EFKK	Kruunupyy Airport, Finland
KOO	FZRQ	Kongolo, Congo
KOP	VTUW	Nakhon Phanom Airport, Thailand
KOW	ZSGZ	Ganzhou Airport, China
KPO	RKTH	Pohang Aero, South Korea

IATA	ICAO	Airport & Country
KPS	YKMP	Kempsey Airport, Australia
KRA	YKER	Kerang Airport, Australia
KRB	YKMB	Karumba Airport, Australia
KRE	HBBO	Kirundo, Burundi
KRF	ESNK	Kramfors, Sweden
KRH	EGKR	Redhill Airport, United Kingdom
KRK	EPKK	John Paul II Intl Krakow, Poland
KRL	ZWKL	Korla Airport, China
KRM	SYKR	Karanambo, Guyana
KRN	ESNQ	Kiruna, Sweden
KRP	EKKA	Karup Airport, Denmark
KRR	URKK	Pashkovsky Airport, Russia
KRS	ENCN	Kristiansand Airport, Norway
KRT	HSSS	Khartoum, Sudan
KRY	ZWKM	Karamay Airport, China
KSA	PTSA	Kosrae, Micronesia
KSC	LZKZ	Kosice Airport, Slovakia
KSD	ESOK	Karlstad, Sweden
KSE	HUKS	Kasese, Uganda
KSF	EDVK	Kassel, Germany
KSH	OICC	Shahid Ashrafi Esfahani Airport, Iran
KSI	GUKU	Kissi, Guinea
KSJ	LGKS	Kassos Island Public Airport, Greece
KSK	ESKK	Karlskoga, Sweden
KSL	HSKA	Kassala, Sudan
KSN	UAUU	Narimanovka, Kazakhstan
KSO	LGKA	Kastoria National Airport, Greece
KSS	GASK	Sikasso, Mali
KST	HSKI	Kosti, Sudan
KSU	ENKB	Kristiansund Airport, Norway
KSW	LLKS	Qiryat Shemona Airport, Israel
KSY	LTCF	Kars Airport, Turkey
KSZ	ULKK	Kotlas Airport, Russia
KTA	YPKA	Karratha Airport, Australia
KTD	RORK	Kita, Japan
KTE	WMKE	Kerteh, Malaysia
KTL	HKKT	Kitale, Kenya
KTM	VNKT	Tribhuvan Intl, Nepal
KTN	PAKT	Ketchikan Intl, USA
KTO	SYKT	Kato, Guyana
KTQ	EFIT	Kitee Airport, Finland
KTT	EFKT	Kittila Airport, Finland
KTU	VIKO	Kota Airport, India
KTW	EPKT	Katowice Intl, Poland
KTX	GAKO	Koutiala, Mali
KUA	WMKD	Kuantan, Malaysia
KUF	UWWW	Kurumoch Airport, Russia
KUH	RJCK	Kushiro Airport, Japan
KUL	WMKK	Kuala Lumpur Intl, Malaysia
KUM	RJFC	Yakushima Airport, Japan
KUO	EFKU	Kuopio Airport, Finland
KUS	BGKK	Kulusuk Airport, Greenland
KUU	VIBR	Bhuntar Airport, India
KUV	RKJK	Kunsan Ab, South Korea
KVA	LGKV	Kavala Intl, Greece
KVB	ESGR	Skovde, Sweden
KVD	UBBG	Gyandzha, Azerbaijan
KVX	USKK	Kirov Airport, Russia
KWA	PKWA	Bucholz Aaf, Marshall Islands
KWE	ZUGY	Guiyang Longdongbao Airport, China
KWG	UKDR	Lozuvatka Intl, Ukraine
KWH	OAHN	Khwahan, Afghanistan
KWI	OKBK	Kuwait Intl, Kuwait
KWJ	RKJJ	Kwangju Aero, South Korea
KWL	ZGKL	Guilin Liangjiang Intl, China
KWM	YKOW	Kowanyama Airport, Australia
KWZ	FZQM	Kolwezi, Congo
KXE	FAKD	Klerksdorp, South Africa
KYA	LTAN	Konya Airport, Turkey
KYE	OLKA	Rene Mouawad AB, Lebanon
KYP	VYKP	Kyaukpyu, Myanmar
KYS	GAKY	Kayes, Mali
KYZ	UNKY	Kyzyl Airport, Russia
KZI	LGKZ	Kozani National Airport, Greece
KZN	UWKD	Kazan Airport, Russia
KZS	LGKJ	Kastelorizo Island Public, Greece
LAD	FNLU	Luanda, Angola
LAE	AYLA	Nadzab, Papua New Guinea
LAF	KLAF	Purdue University Airport, USA
LAI	LFRO	Lannion, France
LAK	CYKD	Aklavik, Canada
LAN	KLAN	Capital City Airport, USA
LAO	RPLI	Laoag Intl, Philippines
LAP	MMLP	Manuel Marquez de Leon Intl, Mexico
LAS	KLAS	McCarran Intl, USA
LAU	HKLU	Lamu/Manda, Kenya
LAW	KLAW	Lawton, USA
LAX	KLAX	Los Angeles Intl, USA
LAY	FALY	Ladysmith, South Africa
LBA	EGNM	Leeds Bradford Intl, United Kingdom
LBB	KLBB	Lubbock Preston Smith Intl, USA
LBC	EDHL	Lubeck, Germany
LBD	UTDL	Khudzhand, Tajikistan
LBE	KLBE	Arnold Palmer Regional Airport, USA
LBG	LFPB	Paris, France
LBI	LFCI	Albi, France
LBO	FZVI	Lusambo, Congo
LBQ	FOGR	Lambarene, Gabon
LBS	NFNL	Labasa, Fiji
LBU	WBKL	Labuan I, Malaysia
LBV	FOOL	Leon M'ba, Gabon
LBX	RPLU	Lubang Airport, Philippines
LBY	LFRE	Labaule, France
LCA	LCLK	Larnaca Intl, Cyprus
LCC	LIBN	Lecce Airport, Italy
LCD	FALO	Louis Trichardt, South Africa
LCE	MHLC	Goloson Intl, Honduras
LCG	LECO	A Coruna Airport, Spain
LCH	KLCH	Lake Charles Regional Airport, USA
LCJ	EPLL	Lodz Wladyslaw Reymont, Poland
LCL	MULM	La Coloma Airport, Cuba
LCO	FCBL	Lague, Congo
LCV	LIQL	Tassignano Airport, Italy
LCY	EGLC	London City Airport, United Kingdom
LDA	VEMH	Malda Airport, India
LDB	SBLO	Londrina Airport, Brazil
LDE	LFBT	Tarbes, France
LDH	YLHI	Lord Howe Island Airport, Australia
LDI	HTLI	Lindi, Tanzania
LDK	ESGL	Lidkoping, Sweden

IATA	ICAO	Airport & Country
LDN	VNLD	Lamidada, Nepal
LDU	WBKD	Lahad Datu, Malaysia
LDY	EGAE	City of Derry Airport, United Kingdom
LEA	YPLM	Learmonth Airport, Australia
LED	ULLI	Pulkovo Airport, Russia
LEH	LFOH	Le Havre, France
LEI	LEAM	Almeria Intl, Spain
LEJ	EDDP	Leipzig, Germany
LEK	GULB	Tata, Guinea
LEN	LELN	Leon Airport, Spain
LEQ	EGHC	Land's End Airport, United Kingdom
LER	YLST	Leinster Airport, Australia
LET	SKLT	Alfredo Vasquez Cobo, Colombia
LEX	KLEX	Blue Grass Airport, USA
LEY	EHLE	Lelystad Airport, Netherlands
LEZ	MHLE	La Esperanza, Honduras
LFR	SVLF	La Fria, Venezuela
LFT	KLFT	Lafayette Regional Airport, USA
LFW	DXXX	Tokoin, Togo
LGA	KLGA	LaGuardia Airport, USA
LGB	KLGB	Long Beach Municipal Airport, USA
LGG	EBLG	Liege Airport, Belgium
LGH	YLEC	Leigh Creek Airport, Australia
LGI	MYLD	Deadman's Cay Airport, Bahamas
LGK	WMKL	Langkawi Intl, Malaysia
LGP	RPLP	Legazpi Airport, Philippines
LGQ	SELA	Lago Agrio, Ecuador
LGR	SCHR	Cochrane, Chile
LGS	SAMM	Comodoro Ricardo, Argentina
LGW	EGKK	London Gatwick, United Kingdom
LHA	EDTL	Lahr, Germany
LHD	PALH	Lake Hood Seaplane Base, USA
LHE	OPLA	Allama Iqbal Intl, Pakistan
LHG	YLRD	Lightning Ridge Airport, Australia
LHR	EGLL	London Heathrow, United Kingdom
LHW	ZLAN	Lanzhou Airport, China
LIE	FZFA	Libenge, Congo
LIF	NWWL	Ouanaham, New Caledonia
LIG	LFBL	Limoges Airport, France
LIH	PHLI	Lihue Airport, USA
LIL	LFQQ	Lille, France
LIM	SPIM	Jorge Chavez Intl, Peru
LIN	LIML	Linate Airport, Italy
LIO	MRLM	Limon Intl, Costa Rica
LIQ	FZGA	Lisala, Congo
LIR	MRLB	Daniel Oduber Intl, Costa Rica
LIS	LPPT	Portela Airport, Portugal
LIT	KLIT	Little Rock National Airport, USA
LIW	VYLK	Loikaw, Myanmar
LIX	FWLK	Likoma, Malawi
LJA	FZVA	Lodja, Congo
LJG	ZPLJ	Lijiang Airport, China
LJU	LJLJ	Aerodrom Ljubljana, Slovenia
LKL	ENNA	Lakselv Airport, Norway
LKN	ENLK	Leknes Airport, Norway
LKO	VILK	Amausi Airport, India
LKY	HTLM	Lake Manyara, Tanzania
LLA	ESPA	Kallax, Sweden
LLE	FAMN	Malelane, South Africa
LLI	HALL	Lalibella, Ethiopia
LLW	FWLI	Lilongwe Intl, Malawi
LLY	RPMX	Liloy Airport, Philippines
LMB	FWSM	Salima, Malawi
LME	LFRM	Le Mans, France
LMM	MMLM	Federal del Valle del Fuerte, Mexico
LMP	LICD	Lampedusa Airport, Italy
LMQ	HLMB	Marsa Brega, Libya
LMR	FALC	Finsch Mine, South Africa
LMT	KLMT	Klamath Falls Airport, USA
LNK	KLNK	Lincoln Airport, USA
LNO	YLEO	Leonora Airport, Australia
LNS	KLNS	Lancaster Airport, USA
LNY	PHNY	Lanai Airport, USA
LNZ	LOWL	Linz, Austria
LOB	SCAN	San Rafael, Chile
LOE	VTUL	Loei Airport, Thailand
LOK	HKLO	Lodwar, Kenya
LOS	DNMM	Murtala Muhammed, Nigeria
LOV	MMMV	Venustiano Carranza Intl, Mexico
LOY	HKLY	Loyangalani, Kenya
LPA	GCLP	Gran Canaria Intl, Spain
LPB	SLLP	El Alto Intl, Bolivia
LPD	SKLP	La Pedrera, Colombia
LPI	ESSL	Saab, Sweden
LPL	EGGP	Liverpool, United Kingdom
LPP	EFLP	Lappeenranta Airport, Finland
LPQ	VLLB	Luang Prabang, Laos
LPT	VTCL	Lampang Airport, Thailand
LPX	EVLA	Liepaja Intl, Latvia
LPY	LFHP	Le Puy, France
LQM	SKLG	Caucaya, Colombia
LRB	FXLR	Leribe, Lesotho
LRD	KLRD	Laredo Intl, USA
LRE	YLRE	Longreach Airport, Australia
LRH	LFBH	La Rochelle, France
LRL	DXNG	Niamtougou, Togo
LRM	MDLR	La Romana Intl, Dominican Republic
LRT	LFRH	Lorient, France
LSC	SCSE	La Florida, Chile
LSE	KLSE	La Crosse Municipal Airport, USA
LSH	VYLS	Lashio, Myanmar
LSI	EGPB	Sumburgh Airport, United Kingdom
LSL	MRLC	Los Chiles Airport, Costa Rica
LSQ	SCGE	Maria Dolores, Chile
LSS	TFFS	Les Saintes Airport, Guadeloupe
LST	YMLT	Launceston Airport, Australia
LSY	YLIS	Lismore Airport, Australia
LTA	FATZ	Tzaneen, South Africa
LTB	YLTV	Latrobe Valley Airport, Australia
LTC	FTTH	Lai, Chad
LTI	ZMAT	Altai, Mongolia
LTK	OSLK	Bassel Al, Syria
LTL	FOOR	Lastourville, Gabon
LTM	SYLT	Lethem, Guyana
LTN	EGGW	London Luton Airport, United Kingdom
LTO	MMLT	Loreto Intl, Mexico
LTQ	LFAT	Le Touquet, France
LUA	VNLK	Lukla, Nepal
LUB	SYLP	Lumid Pau, Guyana
LUD	FYLZ	Luderitz, Namibia

IATA	ICAO	Airport & Country
LUG	LSZA	Lugano Airport, Switzerland
LUH	VILD	Sahnewal Airport, India
LUN	FLLS	Lusaka Intl, Zambia
LUO	FNUE	Luena, Angola
LUQ	SAOU	San Luis Airport, Argentina
LUS	FZCE	Lusanga, Congo
LUX	ELLX	Luxembourg Intl, Luxembourg
LVA	LFOV	Laval, France
LVI	FLLI	Livingstone, Zambia
LVP	OIBV	Lavan Airport, Iran
LWK	EGET	Tingwall Airport, United Kingdom
LWO	UKLL	Lviv Airport, Ukraine
LWS	KLWS	Lewiston, USA
LWY	WBGW	Lawas, Malaysia
LXA	ZULS	Lhasa Gonggar Airport, China
LXG	VLLN	Luang Namtha, Laos
LXR	HELX	Luxor Intl, Egypt
LXS	LGLM	Lemnos Intl, Greece
LXU	FLLK	Lukulu, Zambia
LYA	ZHLY	Luoyang Airport, China
LYC	ESNL	Lycksele, Sweden
LYG	ZSLG	Lianyungang Airport, China
LYH	KLYH	Lynchburg Regional Airport, USA
LYN	LFLY	Lyon, France
LYP	OPFA	Faisalabad Intl, Pakistan
LYR	ENSB	Svalbard Airport, Norway
LYS	LFLL	Lyon Saint Exupery Airport, France
LYX	EGMD	Ashford Airport, United Kingdom
LZA	FZUG	Luiza, Congo
LZC	MMLC	Lazaro Cardenas Airport, Mexico
LZH	ZGZH	Liuzhou Airport, China
LZI	FZAL	Luozi, Congo
MAA	VOMM	Chennai Intl, India
MAB	SBMA	Maraba Airport, Brazil
MAD	LEMD	Madrid Barajas Intl, Spain
MAF	KMAF	Midland Intl, USA
MAG	AYMD	Madang, Papua New Guinea
MAH	LEMH	Menorca Airport, Spain
MAI	FWMG	Mangochi, Malawi
MAJ	PKMJ	Marshall Is Intl, Marshall Islands
MAK	HSSM	Malakal, Sudan
MAM	MMMA	General Servando Canales, Mexico
MAN	EGCC	Manchester Intl, United Kingdom
MAO	SBEG	Eduardo Gomes Intl, Brazil
MAQ	VTPM	Mae Sot Airport, Thailand
MAR	SVMC	La Chinita Intl, Venezuela
MAT	FZAM	Matadi, Congo
MAX	GOSM	Ouro Sogui, Senegal
MAY	MYAB	Clarence Bain Airport, Bahamas
MAZ	TJMZ	Eugenio Mar, Puerto Rico
MBA	HKMO	Moi, Kenya
MBC	FOGG	Mbigou, Gabon
MBD	FAMM	Mafikeng Intl, South Africa
MBE	RJEB	Monbetsu Airport , Japan
MBI	HTMB	Mbeya, Tanzania
MBJ	MKJS	Sangster Intl, Jamaica
MBO	RPUM	Mamburao Airport, Philippines
MBP	SPBB	Moyobamba, Peru
MBQ	HUMA	Mbarara, Uganda
MBS	KMBS	MBS Intl, USA

IATA	ICAO	Airport & Country
MBT	RPVJ	Masbate Airport, Philippines
MBW	YMMB	Moorabbin Airport, Australia
MBX	LJMB	Maribor Airport, Slovenia
MCA	GUMA	Macenta, Guinea
MCH	SEMH	General Serrano, Ecuador
MCI	KMCI	Kansas City Intl, USA
MCJ	SKAO	San Jose De Maicao, Colombia
MCM	LNMC	Monaco Heliport, Monaco
MCN	KMCN	Middle Georgia Regional Airport, USA
MCO	KMCO	Orlando Intl, USA
MCP	SBMQ	Macapa Intl, Brazil
MCQ	LHMC	Miskolc Airport, Hungary
MCR	MGMM	Melchor de Mencos, Guatemala
MCT	OOMS	Seeb Intl, Oman
MCU	LFBK	Montlucon, France
MCW	KMCW	Mason City Municipal Airport, USA
MCY	YBMC	Sunshine Coast Airport, Australia
MCZ	SBMO	Zumbi dos Palmares Airport, Brazil
MDC	WAMM	Sam Ratulangi Airport, Indonesia
MDE	SKRG	Jose Maria Cordova, Colombia
MDG	ZYMD	Mudanjiang Airport, China
MDK	FZEA	Mbandaka, Congo
MDL	VYCZ	Chanmyathazi, Myanmar
MDQ	SAZM	Mar Del Plata Intl, Argentina
MDT	KMDT	Harrisburg Intl, USA
MDW	KMDW	Chicago Midway Intl, USA
MDZ	SAME	El Plumerillo Intl, Argentina
MEB	YMEN	Essendon Airport, Australia
MEC	SEMT	Eloy Alfaro Intl, Ecuador
MED	OEMA	Moh Bin Abdulaziz, Saudi Arabia
MEE	NWWR	La Roche Aero, New Caledonia
MEG	FNMA	Malange, Angola
MEH	ENMH	Mehamn Airport, Norway
MEI	KMEI	Meridian Regional Airport, USA
MEL	YMML	Melbourne Intl, Australia
MEM	KMEM	Memphis Intl, USA
MEN	LFNB	Mende, France
MES	WIMM	Polonia Intl, Indonesia
MEW	FZVM	Mweka, Congo
MEX	MMMX	Mexico City Intl, Mexico
MEY	VNMG	Meghauli, Nepal
MFA	HTMA	Mafia, Tanzania
MFC	FXMF	Mafeteng, Lesotho
MFE	KMFE	McAllen, USA
MFF	FOOD	Moanda, Gabon
MFG	OPMF	Muzaffarabad Airport, Pakistan
MFN	NZMF	Milford Sound, New Zealand
MFQ	DRRM	Maradi, Niger
MFR	KMFR	Rogue Valley Intl, USA
MFS	SKMF	Miraflores, Colombia
MFU	FLMF	Mfuwe, Zambia
MFX	LFKX	Meribel Airport, France
MGA	MNMG	Augusto Cesar Sandino, Nicaragua
MGB	YMTG	Mount Gambier Airport, Australia
MGD	SLMG	Magdalena, Bolivia
MGF	SBMG	Maringa Domestic Airport, Brazil
MGH	FAMG	Margate, South Africa
MGK	VYMT	Mong Tong, Myanmar
MGL	EDLN	Monchengladbach, Germany
MGM	KMGM	Montgomery Regional Airport, USA

IATA	ICAO	Airport & Country
MGN	SKMG	Baracoa, Colombia
MGQ	HCMM	Mogadishu, Somalia
MGU	VYMN	Manaung, Myanmar
MGW	KMGW	Morgantown Municipal Airport, USA
MGX	FOGI	Moabi, Gabon
MGZ	VYME	Myeik, Myanmar
MHA	SYMD	Mahdia, Guyana
MHD	OIMM	Mashhad Intl, Iran
MHG	EDFM	Mannheim, Germany
MHH	MYAM	Marsh Harbour Airport, Bahamas
MHK	KMHK	Manhattan Regional Airport, USA
MHP	UMMM	Minsk, Belarus
MHQ	EFMA	Mariehamn Airport, Finland
MHT	KMHT	Manchester, USA
MHU	YHOT	Mount Hotham Airport, Australia
MHW	SLAG	Monteagudo, Bolivia
MIA	KMIA	Miami Intl, USA
MID	MMMD	Manuel Crescencio Rej, Mexico
MIK	EFMI	Mikkeli Airport, Finland
MIM	YMER	Merimbula Airport, Australia
MIP	LLMR	Mitzpe Ramon Airfield, Israel
MIR	DTMB	Habib Bourguiba, Tunesia
MIU	DNMA	Maiduguri, Nigeria
MJA	FMSJ	Manja, Madagascar
MJC	DIMN	Man, Ivory Coast
MJD	OPMJ	Moenjodaro Airport, Pakistan
MJF	ENMS	Mosjoen Airport, Norway
MJL	FOGM	Mouila Ville, Gabon
MJM	FZWA	Mbuji, Congo
MJN	FMNM	Amborovy, Madagascar
MJT	LGMT	Mytilene Intl, Greece
MJV	LELC	Murcia, Spain
MJZ	UERR	Mirny Airport, Russia
MKB	FOOE	Mekambo, Gabon
MKE	KMKE	General Mitchell Intl, USA
MKG	KMKG	Muskegon County Airport, USA
MKH	FXMK	Mokhotlong, Lesotho
MKI	FEFB	M'boki, Central Africa
MKJ	FCOM	Makoua, Congo
MKK	PHMK	Molokai Airport, USA
MKM	WBGK	Mukah, Malaysia
MKR	YMEK	Meekatharra Airport, Australia
MKS	HAMA	Mekane Salam, Ethiopia
MKT	KMKT	Mankato Regional Airport, USA
MKU	FOOK	Makokou, Gabon
MKY	YBMK	Mackay Airport, Australia
MKZ	WMKM	Malacca, Malaysia
MLA	LMML	Luqa, Malta
MLB	KMLB	Melbourne Intl, USA
MLE	VRMM	Male Intl, Maldives
MLH	LFSB	EuroAirport Basel, France
MLI	KMLI	Quad City Intl, USA
MLM	MMMM	General Francisco J. Mujica, Mexico
MLN	GEML	Melilla Airport, Spain
MLO	LGML	Milos Island National Airport, Greece
MLP	RPMM	Malabang Airport, Philippines
MLU	KMLU	Monroe Regional Airport, USA
MLW	GLMR	Spriggs Payne, Liberia
MLX	LTAT	Malatya Erhac Airport, Turkey
MLZ	SUMO	Cerro Largo Intl, Uruguay
MMB	RJCM	Memanbetsu Airport, Japan
MMD	ROMD	Minami, Japan
MME	EGNV	Durham Tees Valley, United Kingdom
MMF	FKKF	Mamfe, Cameroon
MMG	YMOG	Mount Magnet Airport, Australia
MMJ	RJAF	Matsumoto Airport, Japan
MMK	ULMM	Murmansk Airport, Russia
MMO	GVMA	Maio, Cape Verde
MMP	SKMP	San Bernardo, Colombia
MMX	ESMS	Sturup, Sweden
MMY	ROMY	Miyako Airport, Japan
MMZ	OAMN	Maimama, Afghanistan
MNC	FQNC	Nacala, Mozambique
MNG	YMGD	Maningrida Airport, Australia
MNJ	FMSM	Mananjary, Madagascar
MNL	RPLL	Ninoy Aquino Intl, Philippines
MNO	FZRA	Manono, Congo
MNR	FLMG	Mongu, Zambia
MNS	FLMA	Mansa, Zambia
MNU	VYMM	Mawlamyine, Myanmar
MOA	MUMO	Orestes Acosta Airport, Cuba
MOB	KMOB	Mobile Regional Airport, USA
MOD	KMOD	Modesto City, USA
MOE	VYMO	Momeik, Myanmar
MOG	VYMS	Mong, Myanmar
MOL	ENML	Molde Airport, Norway
MOM	GQNL	Letfotar, Mauritania
MON	NZMC	Mount Cook, New Zealand
MOQ	FMMV	Morondava, Madagascar
MOT	KMOT	Minot Intl, USA
MOV	YMRB	Moranbah Airport, Australia
MPA	FYKM	Katima Mulilo, Namibia
MPD	OPMP	Sindhri Airport, Pakistan
MPH	RPVE	Godofredo P. Ramos, Philippines
MPK	RKJM	Mokpo, South Korea
MPL	LFMT	Montpellier, France
MPM	FQMA	Maputo, Mozambique
MPN	EGYP	Mount Pleasant, Falkland Islands
MPT	WPMN	Maliana Airport, East Timor
MQF	USCM	Magnitogorsk Airport, Russia
MQL	YMIA	Mildura Airport, Australia
MQM	LTCR	Mardin Airport, Turkey
MQN	ENRA	Mo i Rana Airport, Norway
MQQ	FTTD	Moundou, Chad
MQU	SKQU	Mariquita, Colombia
MQX	HAMK	Alula Aba Nega, Ethiopia
MRD	SVMD	Alberto Carnevalli, Venezuela
MRG	YMBA	Mareeba Airport, Australia
MRI	PAMR	Merrill Field, USA
MRO	NZMS	Masterton, New Zealand
MRQ	RPUW	Marinduque Airport, Philippines
MRR	SEMA	J M Velasco Ibarra, Ecuador
MRS	LFML	Marseille, France
MRU	FIMP	Mauritius Intl, Mauritius
MRV	URMM	Mineralnye Vody Airport, Russia
MRX	OIAM	Mahshahr Airport, Iran
MRY	KMRY	Monterey Peninsula Airport, USA
MRZ	YMOR	Moree Airport, Australia
MSA	CZMD	Muskrat Dam, Canada
MSE	EGMH	Kent Intl, United Kingdom

IATA	ICAO	Airport & Country
MSH	OOMA	Masirah AB, Oman
MSM	FZCV	Masi, Congo
MSN	KMSN	Dane County Regional Airport, USA
MSO	KMSO	Missoula Intl, USA
MSP	KMSP	Minneapolis, USA
MSQ	UMMS	Minsk, Belarus
MSR	LTCK	Mus Airport, Turkey
MST	EHBK	Maastricht Aachen, Netherlands
MSU	FXMM	Moshoeshoe I Intl, Lesotho
MSX	FCMM	Mossendjo, Congo
MSY	KMSY	Louis Armstrong New Orleans, USA
MTA	NZMA	Matamata, New Zealand
MTF	HAMT	Mizan Teferi, Ethiopia
MTJ	KMTJ	Montrose Regional Airport, USA
MTR	SKMR	Los Garzones, Colombia
MTS	FDMS	Matsapha Airport, Swaziland
MTT	MMMT	Coatzacoalcos National, Mexico
MTY	MMMY	General Mariano Escobedo, Mexico
MTZ	LLMZ	Masada Airfield, Israel
MUA	AGGM	Munda, Solomon Islands
MUB	FBMN	Maun, Botsuana
MUC	EDDM	Munchen, Germany
MUH	HEMM	Mersa Matruh Airport, Egypt
MUK	NCMK	Akatoka Manava, Cook Islands
MUN	SVMT	Maturin Intl, Venezuela
MUR	WBGM	Marudi, Malaysia
MUX	OPMT	Multan Intl, Pakistan
MUY	FCBM	Mouyondzi, Congo
MUZ	HTMU	Musoma, Tanzania
MVB	FOON	M'vengue, Gabon
MVD	SUMU	Carrasco Intl, Uruguay
MVO	FTTM	Mongo, Chad
MVP	SKMU	Fabio A Leon Bentley, Colombia
MVR	FKKL	Salak, Cameroon
MVV	LFHM	Megeve Airport, France
MVX	FOGV	Minvoul, Gabon
MVY	KMVY	Martha's Vineyard Airport, USA
MVZ	FVMV	Masvingo, Zimbabwe
MWA	KMWA	Williamson County Regional, USA
MWE	HSMR	Merowe, Sudan
MWN	HTMD	Mwadui, Tanzania
MWQ	VYMW	Magway, Myanmar
MWZ	HTMW	Mwanza, Tanzania
MXI	RPMQ	Imelda R. Marcos Airport, Philippines
MXJ	DNMN	Minna, Nigeria
MXL	MMML	General Rodolfo S, Mexico
MXM	FMSR	Morombe, Madagascar
MXN	LFRU	Morlaix, France
MXP	LIMC	Malpensa Intl, Italy
MXT	FMMO	Maintirano, Madagascar
MXX	ESKM	Siljan, Sweden
MYA	YMRY	Moruya Airport, Australia
MYB	FOOY	Mayumba, Gabon
MYD	HKML	Malindi, Kenya
MYE	RJTQ	Miyakejima Airport, Japan
MYG	MYMM	Mayaguana Airport, Bahamas
MYJ	RJOM	Matsuyama Airport, Japan
MYN	OYMB	Marib, Yemen
MYQ	VOMY	Mysore Airport, India
MYR	KMYR	Myrtle Beach Intl, USA

IATA	ICAO	Airport & Country
MYT	VYMK	Pamti, Myanmar
MYW	HTMT	Mtwara, Tanzania
MYY	WBGR	Miri, Malaysia
MYZ	FWMY	Monkey Bay, Malawi
MZB	FQMP	Mocimboa Da Praia, Mozambique
MZC	FOOM	Mitzic, Gabon
MZI	GAMB	Barbe, Mali
MZM	LFSF	Metz, France
MZO	MUMZ	Sierra Maestra Airport, Cuba
MZR	OAMS	Mazar, Afghanistan
MZT	MMMZ	General Rafael Buelna Intl, Mexico
MZU	VEMZ	Muzzafarpur Airport, India
MZX	HAML	Masslo, Ethiopia
N/A	VTCR	Chiang Rai Airport, Thailand
NAA	YNBR	Narrabri Airport, Australia
NAE	DBBN	Natitingou, Benin
NAG	VANP	Dr. Babasaheb Ambedkar Intl, India
NAI	SYAN	Annai, Guyana
NAK	VTUQ	Nakhon Ratchasima Airport, Thailand
NAL	URMN	Nalchik Airport, Russia
NAN	NFFN	Nadi Intl, Fiji
NAO	ZUNC	Nanchong Airport, China
NAP	LIRN	Naples Intl, Italy
NAQ	BGQA	Qaanaaq Airport, Greenland
NAS	MYNN	Nassau Intl, Bahamas
NAT	SBNT	Augusto Severo Intl, Brazil
NAV	LTAZ	Nevsehir Kapadokya Airport, Turkey
NAW	VTSC	Narathiwat Airport, Thailand
NAY	ZBBB	Beijing Nanyuan Airport, China
NBO	HKJK	Jomo Kenyatta, Kenya
NCE	LFMN	Nice, France
NCH	HTNA	Nachingwea, Tanzania
NCL	EGNT	Newcastle Airport, United Kingdom
NCS	FANC	Newcastle, South Africa
NCY	LFLP	Annecy, France
NDB	GQPP	Nouadhibou, Mauritania
NDE	HKMA	Mandera, Kenya
NDG	ZYQQ	Qiqihar Airport, China
NDJ	FTTJ	N'Djamena, Chad
NDL	FEFN	N'dele, Central Africa
NDM	HAMN	Mendi, Ethiopia
NDU	FYRU	Rundu, Namibia
NEJ	HANJ	Nejjo, Ethiopia
NEK	HANK	Nekemte, Ethiopia
NEU	VLSN	Sam Neua, Laos
NGA	YYNG	Young Airport, Australia
NGB	ZSNB	Ningbo Lishe Intl, China
NGE	FKKN	N'gaoundere, Cameroon
NGO	RJGG	Chubu Intl , Japan
NGS	RJFU	Nagasaki Airport, Japan
NGV	FNGI	N'giva, Angola
NGX	VNMA	Manang, Nepal
NHF	HSNW	New Halfa, Sudan
NIA	GLNA	Nimba, Liberia
NIM	DRRN	Diori Hamani, Niger
NIO	FZBI	Nioki, Congo
NIT	LFBN	Souche Airport, France
NIX	GANR	Nioro, Mali
NJC	USNN	Nizhnevartovsk Airport, Russia
NKC	GQNN	Nouakchott, Mauritania

IATA	ICAO	Airport & Country
NKG	ZSNJ	Nanjing Lukou Intl, China
NKM	RJNA	Nagoya Airport , Japan
NKY	FCBY	Yokangassi, Congo
NLA	FLND	Ndola, Zambia
NLD	MMNL	Quetzalcoatl Intl, Mexico
NLK	YSNF	Norfolk Island Airport, Australia
NLO	FZAB	N'dolo, Congo
NLP	FANS	Nelspruit, South Africa
NLV	UKON	Mykolaiv Airport, Ukraine
NMB	VADN	Daman Airport, India
NMC	MYEN	Norman's Cay Airport, Bahamas
NMS	VYNS	Namsang, Myanmar
NNG	ZGNN	Nanning Wuxu Intl, China
NNI	FYNA	Namutoni, Namibia
NNM	ULAM	Naryan, Russia
NNR	EICA	Connemara Regional Airport, Ireland
NNT	VTCN	Nan Airport, Thailand
NNY	ZHNY	Nanyang Airport, China
NOC	EIKN	Knock Intl, Ireland
NOM	MRNS	Nosara Airport, Costa Rica
NOR	BINF	Norofjorour Airport, Iceland
NOS	FMNN	Fascene, Madagascar
NOU	NWWW	Tontouta, New Caledonia
NOV	FNHU	Albano Machado, Angola
NOZ	UNWW	Novokuznetsk Spichenkovo, Russia
NPE	NZNR	Napier, New Zealand
NPL	NZNP	New Plymouth, New Zealand
NQT	EGBN	Nottingham Airport United Kingdom
NQY	EGDQ	Newquay Cornwall United Kingdom
NRA	YNAR	Narrandera Airport, Australia
NRD	EDWY	Norderney, Germany
NRK	ESSP	Kungsangen, Sweden
NRL	EGEN	North Ronaldsay, Isle of Man
NRM	GANK	Keibane, Mali
NRN	EDLV	Airport Weeze, Germany
NRT	RJAA	Narita Intl, Japan
NSI	FKYS	Nsimalen, Cameroon
NSK	UOOO	Norilsk Airport, Russia
NSN	NZNS	Nelson, New Zealand
NST	VTSN	Cha Ian Airport, Thailand
NTB	ENNO	Notodden Airport, Norway
NTE	LFRS	Nantes Atlantique Airport, France
NTL	YWLM	Newcastle, Australia
NTN	YNTN	Normanton Airport, Australia
NTQ	RJNW	Noto Airport, Japan
NTT	NFTP	Niuatoputapu, Tonga
NTY	FAPN	Pilanesberg, South Africa
NUD	HSNH	El Nahud, Sudan
NUE	EDDN	Nurnberg, Germany
NUU	HKNK	Nakuru, Kenya
NVA	SKNV	Benito Salas, Colombia
NVK	ENNK	Narvik Airport, Norway
NVS	LFQG	Nevers, France
NVT	SBNF	Ministro Victor Konder Intl, Brazil
NWA	FMCI	Moheli, Comoros
NWI	EGSH	Norwich Intl, United Kingdom
NYE	HKNI	Nyeri, Kenya
NYI	DGSN	Sunyani, Ghana
NYK	HKNY	Nanyuki, Kenya
NYO	ESKN	Skavsta, Sweden

IATA	ICAO	Airport & Country
NYU	VYBG	Bagan, Myanmar
NZE	GUNZ	Konia, Guinea
OAG	YORG	Orange Airport, Australia
OAJ	KOAJ	Albert J. Ellis Airport, USA
OAK	KOAK	Metropolitan Oakland Intl, USA
OAM	NZOU	Oamaru, New Zealand
OAX	MMOX	Xoxocotlan Intl, Mexico
OBI	EDMO	Oberpfaffenhofen, Germany
OBO	RJCB	Obihiro Airport , Japan
OBS	LFHO	Aubenas Ardeche Airport, France
OBY	BGSC	Scoresbysund Airport, Greenland
OCC	SECO	Francisco De Orellana, Ecuador
OCV	SKOC	Aguas Claras, Colombia
ODB	LEBA	Cordoba Airport, Spain
ODE	EKOD	Odense Airport, Denmark
ODS	UKOO	Odessa Airport, Ukraine
ODY	VLOS	Oudomsay, Laos
OEM	SMPA	Vincent Faiks, Suriname
OER	ESNO	Ornskoldsvik, Sweden
OFI	DIOF	Ouango Fitini, Ivory Coast
OGG	PHOG	Kahului Airport, USA
OGN	ROYN	Yonaguni Airport, Japan
OGO	DIAU	Abengourou, Ivory Coast
OGR	FTTB	Bongor, Chad
OGX	DAUU	Ouargla Airport, Algeria
OGZ	URMO	Beslan Airport, Russia
OHA	NZOH	Ohakea, New Zealand
OHD	LWOH	Ohrid, Macedonia
OHD	LWOH	Ohrid Airport, Macedonia
OHR	EDXY	Wyk, Germany
OIM	RJTO	Oshima Airport, Japan
OIR	RJEO	Okushiri Airport, Japan
OIT	RJFO	Oita Airport, Japan
OKA	ROAH	Naha Airport, Japan
OKC	KOKC	Will Rogers World Airport, USA
OKE	RJKB	Okinoerabu Airport, Japan
OKF	FYOO	Okaukuejo, Namibia
OKI	RJNO	Oki Airport, Japan
OKJ	RJOB	Okayama Airport, Japan
OKN	FOGQ	Okondja, Gabon
OLA	ENOL	Orland Main Air Station, Norway
OLB	LIEO	Olbia, Italy
OMA	KOMA	Eppley Airfield, USA
OMB	FOOH	Omboue Hospital, Gabon
OMC	RPVO	Ormoc Airport, Philippines
OMD	FYOG	Oranjemund, Namibia
OME	PAOM	Nome Airport, USA
OMM	OONR	Marmul, Oman
OMO	LQMO	Mostar Intl, Bosnia
OMR	LROD	Oradea Intl, Romania
OMS	UNOO	Tsentralny Airport, Russia
OND	FYOA	Ondangwa, Namibia
ONJ	RJSR	Odate, Japan
ONT	KONT	Ontario Intl, USA
ONX	MPEJ	Enrique Adolfo Jimenez, Panama
OOL	YBCG	Gold Coast Airport, Australia
OOM	YCOM	Cooma, Australia
OPO	LPPR	Francisco Sa Carneiro, Portugal
ORB	ESOE	Orebro, Sweden
ORD	KORD	Chicago O'Hare Intl, USA

IATA	ICAO	Airport & Country
ORE	LFOJ	Orleans, France
ORF	KORF	Norfolk Intl, USA
ORG	SMZO	Zorg En Hoop, Suriname
ORH	KORH	Worcester Regional Airport, USA
ORJ	SYOR	Orinduik, Guyana
ORK	EICK	Cork Intl, Ireland
ORM	EGBK	Sywell Aerodrome, United Kingdom
ORN	DAOO	Ouran, Algeria
ORP	FBOR	Orapa, Botsuana
ORU	SLOR	Juan Mendoza, Bolivia
ORW	OPOR	Ormara Airport, Pakistan
ORY	LFPO	Paris, France
OSD	ESPC	Froson, Sweden
OSI	LDOS	Osijek Airport, Croatia
OSK	ESMO	Oskarshamn, Sweden
OSL	ENGM	Oslo Gardermoen Airport, Norway
OSN	RKSO	Osan Ab, South Korea
OSR	LKMT	Ostrava, Czech Republic
OSS	UAFO	Osh, Kyrgyzstan
OST	EBOS	Ostend, Belgium
OSW	UWOR	Orsk Airport, Russia
OSY	ENNM	Namsos Airport, Norway
OTC	FTTL	Berim, Chad
OTH	KOTH	Southwest Oregon Regional, USA
OTL	GQNB	Boutilimit, Mauritania
OTP	LROP	Bucharest Intl, Romania
OTR	MRCC	Coto 47 Airport, Costa Rica
OTU	SKOT	Otu, Colombia
OTZ	PAOT	Ralph Wien Memorial Airport, USA
OUA	DFFD	Ouagadougou, Burkina Faso
OUD	GMFO	Angads, Morocco
OUE	FCOU	Ouesso, Congo
OUG	DFCC	Ouahigouya, Burkina Faso
OUH	FAOH	Oudtshoorn, South Africa
OUI	VLHS	Ban Houeisay, Laos
OUL	EFOU	Oulu Airport, Finland
OUR	FKKI	Batouri, Cameroon
OUT	FTTS	Bousso, Chad
OUZ	GQPZ	Tazadit, Mauritania
OVA	FMSL	Bekily, Madagascar
OVB	UNNT	Novosibirsk Tolmachevo, Russia
OVD	LEAS	Asturias Airport, Spain
OXB	GGOV	Osvaldo Vieira, Guinea Bissau
OXF	EGTK	Oxford Airport, United Kingdom
OXR	KOXR	Oxnard Airport, USA
OYE	FOGO	Oyem, Gabon
OYL	HKMY	Oda, Kenya
OZC	RPMO	Labo Airport, Philippines
OZH	UKDE	Zaporizhzhia Intl, Ukraine
OZZ	GMMZ	Ouarzazate, Morocco
PAA	VYPA	Hpa, Myanmar
PAB	VABI	Bilaspur Airport, India
PAD	EDLP	Paderborn, Germany
PAF	HUPA	Pakuba, Uganda
PAG	RPMP	Pagadian Airport, Philippines
PAH	KPAH	Barkley Regional Airport, USA
PAJ	OPPC	Parachinar Airport, Pakistan
PAL	SKPQ	German Olano Ab, Colombia
PAN	VTSK	Pattani Airport, Thailand
PAP	MTPP	Port, Haiti

IATA	ICAO	Airport & Country
PAS	LGPA	Paros National Airport, Greece
PAT	VEPT	Patna Airport, India
PAU	VYPK	Pauk, Myanmar
PAX	MTPX	Port De Paix, Haiti
PAZ	MMPA	El Tajin National Airport, Mexico
PBC	MMPB	Hermanos Serdan Intl, Mexico
PBD	VAPR	Porbandar Airport, India
PBE	SKPR	Puerto Berrio, Colombia
PBH	VQPR	Paro Airport, Bhutan
PBI	KPBI	Palm Beach Intl, USA
PBL	SVPC	Gen. Bartolome Salom, Venezuela
PBM	SMJP	J.A. Pengel Intl, Suriname
PBN	FNPA	Porto Amboim, Angola
PBO	YPBO	Paraburdoo Airport, Australia
PBP	MRIA	Punta Islita Airport, Costa Rica
PBR	MGPB	Puerto Barrios Airport, Guatemala
PBU	VYPT	Putao, Myanmar
PBZ	FAPG	Plettenberg Bay, South Africa
PCL	SPCL	David Abenzur Rengifo, Peru
PCP	FPPR	Principe, Sao Tome and Principe
PCR	SKPC	Puerto Carreno, Colombia
PCW	KPCW	Erie, USA
PDA	SKPD	Obando, Colombia
PDG	WIPT	Minangkabau Intl, Indonesia
PDL	LPPD	Joao Paulo II Airport, Portugal
PDP	SULS	Capitan Curbelo Intl, Uruguay
PDS	MMPG	Piedras Negras Intl, Mexico
PDT	KPDT	Eastern Oregon Regional Airport, USA
PDU	SUPU	Tydeo Larre Borges Intl, Uruguay
PDV	LBPD	Plovdiv Intl, Bulgaria
PDX	KPDX	Portland Intl, USA
PED	LKPD	Pardubice Airport, Czech Republic
PEE	USPP	Bolshoye Savino Airport, Russia
PEG	LIRZ	San Egidio Airport, Italy
PEI	SKPE	Matecana, Colombia
PEK	ZBAA	Beijing Capital Intl, China
PEM	SPTU	Padre Aldamiz, Peru
PEN	WMKP	Penang Intl, Malaysia
PER	YPPH	Perth Intl, Australia
PES	ULPB	Besovets Airport, Russia
PEU	MHPL	Puerto Lempira, Honduras
PEW	OPPS	Peshawar Intl, Pakistan
PEZ	UWPP	Penza Airport, Russia
PFJ	BIPA	Patreksfjorour Airport, Iceland
PFN	KPFN	Panama City, USA
PFO	LCPH	Paphos Intl, Cyprus
PFR	FZVS	Ilebo, Congo
PGA	KPGA	Page Municipal Airport, USA
PGF	LFMP	Perpignan, France
PGH	VIPT	Pantnagar Airport, India
PGV	KPGV	Pitt, USA
PGX	LFBX	Perigueux, France
PHC	DNPO	Port Harcourt, Nigeria
PHE	YPPD	Port Hedland Intl, Australia
PHF	KPHF	Williamsburg Intl, USA
PHL	KPHL	Philadelphia Intl, USA
PHS	VTPP	Phitsanulok Airport, Thailand
PHW	FAPH	Hendrik Van Eck, South Africa
PHX	KPHX	Phoenix Sky Harbor Intl, USA
PIA	KPIA	Greater Peoria Regional Airport, USA

IATA	ICAO	Airport & Country
PIB	KPIB	Hattiesburg, USA
PID	MYPI	New Providence Airport, Bahamas
PIE	KPIE	St. Petersburg, USA
PIH	KPIH	Pocatello Regional Airport, USA
PIK	EGPK	Glasgow Prestwick, United Kingdom
PIO	SPSO	Pisco, Peru
PIR	KPIR	Pierre Regional Airport, USA
PIS	LFBI	Poitiers, France
PIT	KPIT	Pittsburgh Intl, USA
PIU	SPUR	Capt Guillermo Concha Iberico, Peru
PIW	CZMN	Pikwitonei, Canada
PIX	LPPI	Pico Airport, Portugal
PJA	ESUP	Pajala, Sweden
PJG	OPPG	Panjgur Airport, Pakistan
PJM	MRPJ	Puerto Jimenez Airport, Costa Rica
PKB	KPKB	Mid, USA
PKC	UHPP	Yelizovo Airport, Russia
PKE	YPKS	Parkes Airport, Australia
PKK	VYPU	Pakhokku, Myanmar
PKO	DBBP	Parakou, Benin
PKR	VNPK	Pokhara, Nepal
PKT	YPKT	Port Keats Airport, Australia
PKU	WIBB	Sultan Syarif Kasim II, Indonesia
PKV	ULOO	Pskov Airport, Russia
PKW	FBSP	Selebi, Botsuana
PKY	WRBP	Tjilik Riwut Airport, Indonesia
PKZ	VLPS	Pakse, Laos
PLF	FTTP	Pala, Chad
PLH	EGHD	Plymouth City Airport, United Kingdom
PLM	WIPP	Sultan Mahmud Badaruddin Indonesia
PLN	KPLN	Pellston Regional Airport , USA
PLO	YPLC	Port Lincoln Airport Australia
PLU	SBBH	Pampulha Domestic Airport, Brazil
PLW	WAML	Mutiara Airport, Indonesia
PLZ	FAPE	Port Elizabeth, South Africa
PMA	HTPE	Pemba, Tanzania
PMC	SCTE	El Tepual Intl, Chile
PMF	LIMP	Parma Airport, Italy
PMG	SBPP	Ponta Pora Intl, Brazil
PMI	LEPA	Palma de Mallorca Airport, Spain
PMO	LICJ	Palermo Intl, Italy
PMR	NZPM	Palmerston North, New Zealand
PMS	OSPR	Palmyra, Syria
PMV	SVMG	Del Caribe Intl, Venezuela
PMW	SBPJ	Palmas Airport, Brazil
PMY	SAVY	El Tehuelche Airport, Argentina
PMZ	MRPM	Palmar Sur Airport, Costa Rica
PNA	LEPP	Pamplona Airport, Spain
PNH	VDPP	Pochentong Intl, Cambodia
PNI	PTPN	Pohnpei Intl, Micronesia
PNK	WIOO	Supadio Airport, Indonesia
PNL	LICG	Pantelleria Airport, Italy
PNQ	VAPO	Pune Airport, India
PNR	FCPP	A. Neto, Congo
PNS	KPNS	Pensacola Regional Airport, USA
PNT	SCNT	Teniente Julio Gallardo, Chile
PNY	VOPC	Pondicherry Airport, India
POA	SBPA	Salgado Filho Intl, Brazil
POD	GOSP	Podor, Senegal
POG	FOOG	Port Gentil, Gabon

IATA	ICAO	Airport & Country
POL	FQPB	Pemba, Mozambique
POM	AYPY	Port Moresby, Papua New Guinea
PON	MGPP	Poptun Airport, Guatemala
POP	MDPP	Gregorio Luperon, Dominican Repub
POR	EFPO	Pori Airport, Finland
POS	TTPP	Piarco Intl, Trinidad & Tobago
POW	LJPZ	Portoroz Airport, Slovenia
POX	LFPT	Pontoise, France
POZ	EPPO	Poznan, Poland
PPI	YPIR	Port Pirie Airport, Australia
PPN	SKPP	Guillermo Leon Valencia, Colombia
PPP	YBPN	Proserpine, Australia
PPQ	NZPP	Paraparaumu, New Zealand
PPS	RPVP	Puerto Princesa Airport, Philippines
PPU	VYPP	Hpapun, Myanmar
PPW	EGEP	Papa Westray Airport, Orkney isles
PQC	VVPQ	Duong Dong Airport, Vietnam
PQI	KPQI	Northern Maine Regional Airport, USA
PQQ	YPMQ	Port Macquarie Airport, Australia
PRA	SAAP	General Urquiza Airport, Argentina
PRG	LKPR	Prague Ruzyne Intl, Czech Republic
PRH	VTCP	Phrae Airport, Thailand
PRI	FSPP	Praslin, Seychelles
PRK	FAPK	Prieska, South Africa
PRM	LPPM	Portimao Airport, Portugal
PRN	LYPR	Pristina Intl, Serbia
PRP	LFKO	Tavaria Airport, France
PRU	VYPY	Pyay, Myanmar
PRY	FAWB	Wonderboom, South Africa
PSA	LIRP	Galileo Galilei Airport, Italy
PSC	KPSC	Tri, USA
PSD	HEPS	Port Said Airport, Egypt
PSE	TJPS	Mercedita Airport, Puerto Rico
PSG	PAPG	Petersburg James A. Johnson, USA
PSI	OPPI	Pasni Airport, Pakistan
PSL	EGPT	Perth Airport , United Kingdom
PSM	KPSM	Pease Intl Tradeport Airport, USA
PSO	SKPS	Antonio Narino, Colombia
PSP	KPSP	Palm Springs Intl, USA
PSR	LIBP	Abruzzo Intl, Italy
PSS	SARP	Gen Jose de San Martin, Argentina
PSZ	SLPS	Salvador Ogaya, Bolivia
PTG	FAPI	Pietersburg, South Africa
PTJ	YPOD	Portland Airport, Australia
PTM	SVPT	Palmarito, Venezuela
PTP	TFFR	Pointe, Guadeloupe
PTX	SKPI	Pitalito, Colombia
PTY	MPTO	Tocumen Intl, Panama
PTZ	SESM	Rio Amazonas, Ecuador
PUF	LFBP	Pau, France
PUG	YPAG	Port Augusta Airport, Australia
PUI	VEPU	Purnea Airport, India
PUJ	MDPC	Punta Cana Intl, Dominican Republic
PUN	FZOP	Punia, Congo
PUQ	SCCI	Carlos Ibanez Del Campo Intl, Chile
PUS	RKPK	Kimhae Intl, South Korea
PUU	SKAS	Tres De Mayo, Colombia
PUW	KPUW	Pullman, USA
PUY	LDPL	Pula Airport, Croatia
PUZ	MNPC	Puerto Cabezas, Nicaragua

IATA	ICAO	Airport & Country
PVA	SKPV	Providencia, Colombia
PVC	KPVC	Provincetown Municipal Airport, USA
PVD	KPVD	Theodore Francis Green Statet, USA
PVG	ZSPD	Shanghai Pudong Intl, China
PVK	LGPZ	Aktion National Airport, Greece
PVO	SEPV	Reales Tamarindos, Ecuador
PVR	MMPR	Lic. Gustavo Diaz Ordaz Intl, Mexico
PVS	UHMD	Provideniya Bay Airport, Russia
PWE	UHMP	Pevek Airport, Russia
PWM	KPWM	Portland Intl Jetport, USA
PWO	FZQC	Pweto, Congo
PXM	MMPS	Puerto Escondido Intl, Mexico
PXO	LPPS	Porto Santo Airport, Portugal
PXU	VVPK	Pleiku Airport, Vietnam
PYE	NCPY	Tongareva, Cook Islands
PYH	SVPA	Puerto Ayacucho, Venezuela
PYJ	UERP	Polyarny Airport, Russia
PZA	SKPZ	Paz De Ariporo, Colombia
PZB	FAPM	Pietermaritzburg, South Africa
PZH	OPZB	Zhob Airport, Pakistan
PZU	HSPN	Port Sudan, Sudan
PZY	LZPP	Piestany Airport, Slovakia
QBC	CYBD	Bella Coola, Canada
QBG	LYPA	Pancevo Airport, Serbia
QBQ	LFQM	Besancon, France
QGY	LHPR	Gyor, Hungary
QHI	VTBS	Sattahip Airport, Thailand
QKX	ENKA	Kautokeino Airport, Norway
QLA	EGHL	Lasham Airfield, United Kingdom
QLT	LIRL	Latina Airport, Italy
QND	LYNS	Novi Sad Airport, Serbia
QPD	MUPR	Pinar del R, Cuba
QPW	BGKA	Kangaatsiaq Airport, Greenland
QRA	FAGM	Rand, South Africa
QRC	SCRG	De La Independencia, Chile
QRM	YNRM	Narromine Airport, Australia
QRR	YWRN	Warren Airport, Australia
QRV	LFQD	Arras, France
QSA	LELL	Sabadell Airport, Spain
QSN	MUNB	San Nicolas de Bari Airport, Cuba
QWV	LYVA	Valjevo Airport, Serbia
RAB	AYRB	Rabaul, Papua New Guinea
RAE	OERR	Arar Domestic Airport, Saudi Arabia
RAG	NZRA	Raglan, New Zealand
RAH	OERF	Rafha Domestic Airport, Saudi Arabia
RAI	GVFM	Francisco Mendes, Cape Verde
RAJ	VARK	Rajkot Airport, India
RAK	GMMX	Menara, Morocco
RAN	LIDR	Ravenna Airport, Italy
RAO	SBRP	Leite Lopes Airport, Brazil
RAP	KRAP	Rapid City Regional Airport, USA
RAR	NCRG	Rarotonga Intl, Cook Islands
RAS	OIGG	Rasht Airport, Iran
RAV	SKCN	Cravo Norte, Colombia
RAZ	OPRT	Rawalakot Airport, Pakistan
RBA	GMME	Sale, Morocco
RBC	YROI	Robinvale Airport, Australia
RBJ	RJCR	Rebun Airport, Japan
RBO	SLRB	Robore, Bolivia
RBQ	SLRQ	Rurrenabaque, Bolivia

IATA	ICAO	Airport & Country
RBR	SBRB	Presidente Medici Airport, Brazil
RBS	YORB	Orbost Airport, Australia
RBT	HKMB	Marsabit, Kenya
RCB	FARB	Richards Bay, South Africa
RCH	SKRH	Almirante Padilla, Colombia
RCL	YRED	Redcliffe Airport, Australia
RCO	LFDN	Rochefort, France
RCQ	SATR	Daniel Jurkic Airport, Argentina
RCS	EGTO	Rochester Airport, United Kingdom
RCU	SAOC	Las Higueras Airport, Argentina
RDD	KRDD	Redding Municipal Airport, USA
RDG	KRDG	Reading Regional Airport, USA
RDM	KRDM	Redmond Municipal Airport, USA
RDT	GOSR	Richard Toll, Senegal
RDU	KRDU	Raleigh, USA
RDZ	LFCR	Rodez, France
REC	SBRF	Guararapes Intl, Brazil
REG	LICR	Reggio Calabria Airport, Italy
REN	UWOO	Tsentralny Airport, Russia
REP	VDSR	Siem Reap, Cambodia
RER	MGRT	Retalhuleu Airport, Guatemala
RES	SARE	Resistencia Intl, Argentina
RET	ENRS	Rost Airport, Norway
REU	LERS	Reus Airport, Spain
REX	MMRX	General Lucio Blanco Intl, Mexico
REY	SLRY	Reyes, Bolivia
RFN	BIRG	Raufarhofn Airport, Iceland
RFP	NTTR	Raiatea Airport, French Polynesia
RGA	SAWE	Hermes Quijada Airport, Argentina
RGH	VEBG	Balurghat Airport, India
RGI	NTTG	Rangiroa Airport, French Polynesia
RGL	SAWG	Piloto Civil N. Fernandez, Argentina
RGN	VYYY	Yangon Intl, Myanmar
RHE	LFSR	Reims, France
RHG	HRYU	Ruhengeri, Rwanda
RHI	KRHI	Rhinelander, USA
RHO	LGRP	Rhodes Intl, Greece
RHP	VNRC	Ramechhap, Nepal
RIB	SLRI	Cap De Av Selin Zeitun Lopez, Bolivia
RIC	KRIC	Richmond Intl, USA
RIJ	SPJA	Rioja, Peru
RIK	MRCR	Carrillo Airport, Costa Rica
RIM	SPLN	San Nicolas, Peru
RIS	RJER	Rishiri Airport, Japan
RIW	KRIW	Riverton Regional Airport, USA
RIX	EVRA	Riga Intl, Latvia
RIY	OYRN	Riyan, Yemen
RJA	VORY	Rajahmundry Airport, India
RJB	VNRB	Rajbiraj, Nepal
RJH	VGRJ	Rajshahi Airport, Bangladesh
RJK	LDRI	Rijeka Airport, Croatia
RJL	LELO	Logrono, Spain
RJN	OIKR	Rafsanjan Airport, Iran
RKD	KRKD	Knox County Regional Airport, USA
RKE	EKRK	Copenhagen Roskilde, Denmark
RKT	OMRK	Khaimah Intl, United Arab Emirates
RKV	BIRK	Reykjavik Airport, Iceland
RLG	ETNL	Rostock, Germany
RMA	YROM	Roma Airport, Australia
RMF	HEMA	Marsa Alam Intl, Egypt

IATA	ICAO	Airport & Country
RMI	LIPR	Federico Fellini Intl, Italy
RMK	YREN	Renmark Airport, Australia
RML	VCCC	Ratmalana, Sri Lanka
RNB	ESDF	Ronneby, Sweden
RNE	LFLO	Roanne, France
RNJ	RORY	Yoron Airport, Japan
RNN	EKRN	Ronne Bornholm Airport, Denmark
RNO	KRNO	Tahoe Intl, USA
RNS	LFRN	Rennes, France
ROA	KROA	Roanoke Regional Airport, USA
ROB	GLRB	Roberts Intl, Liberia
ROC	KROC	Greater Rochester Intl, USA
ROD	FARS	Robertson, South Africa
ROK	YBRK	Rockhampton Airport, Australia
ROP	PGRO	Rota Island, Northern Mariana Islands
ROR	PTRO	Babelthuap/Koror, Micronesia
ROR	PTRO	Koror, Palau
ROS	SAAR	Rosario Intl, Argentina
ROT	NZRO	Rotorua, New Zealand
ROV	URRR	Rostov, Russia
RPM	YNGU	Ngukurr Airport, Australia
RPN	LLIB	Rosh Pina Airport, Israel
RPR	VARP	Raipur Airport, India
RRG	FIMR	Plaine Corail, Mauritius
RRK	VERK	Rourkela Airport, India
RRS	ENRO	Roros Airport, Norway
RSA	SAZR	Santa Rosa Airport Argentina
RSD	MYER	Rock Sound Intl, Bahamas
RST	KRST	Rochester Intl, USA
RSU	RKJY	Yeosu, South Korea
RSW	KRSW	Southwest Florida Intl, USA
RTA	NFNR	Rotuma, Fiji
RTB	MHRO	Roatan Intl, Honduras
RTC	VARG	Ratnagiri Airport, India
RTM	EHRD	Rotterdam Airport, Netherlands
RTS	YRTI	Rottnest Island Airport, Australia
RTW	UWSS	Tsentralny Airport, Russia
RUA	HUAR	Arua, Uganda
RUH	OERK	King Khalid Intl, Saudi Arabia
RUK	VNRK	Rukumkot, Nepal
RUM	VNRT	Rumjatar, Nepal
RUN	FMEE	St Denis Gillot, Reunion
RUP	VERU	Rupsi Airport, India
RUV	MGRB	Rubelsanto Airport, Guatemala
RVA	FMSG	Farafangana, Madagascar
RVE	SKSA	Los Colonizadores, Colombia
RVK	ENRM	Rorvik Airport, Norway
RVN	EFRO	Rovaniemi Airport, Finland
RVO	FARI	Reivilo, South Africa
RVY	SURV	Rivera Intl, Uruguay
RWN	UKLR	Rivne Airport, Ukraine
RXS	RPVR	Roxas Airport, Philippines
RYG	ENRY	Moss Airport, Rygge, Norway
RYK	OPRK	Shaikh Zayed Intl, Pakistan
RYN	LFCY	Royan, France
RZE	EPRZ	Rzeszow, Poland
RZR	OINR	Ramsar Airport, Iran
SAA	RPVG	Guiuan Airport, Philippines
SAB	TNCS	Juancho, Netherlands Antilles
SAF	KSAF	Santa Fe Municipal Airport, USA

IATA	ICAO	Airport & Country
SAH	OYSN	Sanaa Intl, Yemen
SAK	BIKR	Alexander Airport, Iceland
SAN	KSAN	San Diego Intl, USA
SAP	MHLM	La Mesa Intl, Honduras
SAQ	MYAN	San Andros Airport, Bahamas
SAT	KSAT	San Antonio Intl, USA
SAV	KSAV	Savannah Intl, USA
SAW	LTFJ	Istanbul Sabiha Gokcen Intl, Turkey
SAW	KSAW	Sawyer Intl, USA
SAY	LIQS	Siena Airport, Italy
SBA	KSBA	Santa Barbara Municipal Airport, USA
SBH	TFFJ	Saint, Guadeloupe
SBI	GUSB	Sambailo, Guinea
SBK	LFRT	Saint, France
SBN	KSBN	South Bend Regional Airport, USA
SBP	KSBP	San Luis Obispo County, USA
SBQ	OPSB	Sibi Airport, Pakistan
SBU	FASB	Springbok, South Africa
SBY	KSBY	Salisbury, USA
SBZ	LRSB	Sibiu Intl, Romania
SCC	PASC	Deadhorse Airport, USA
SCI	SVPM	Paramillo, Venezuela
SCK	KSCK	Stockton Metropolitan Airport, USA
SCL	SCEL	Arturo Merino Benitez Intl, Chile
SCN	EDDR	Saarbrucken, Germany
SCQ	LEST	Santiago Airport, Spain
SCS	EGPM	Scatsta Airport, United Kingdom
SCT	OYSQ	Moori, Yemen
SCU	MUCU	Antonio Maceo Intl, Cuba
SCV	LRSV	Suceava Airport, Romania
SCW	UUYY	Syktyvkar Airport, Russia
SCY	SEST	San Cristobal, Ecuador
SDB	FALW	Langebaanweg Ab, South Africa
SDD	FNUB	Lubango, Angola
SDE	SANE	Vicecomodoro Aragonez, Argentina
SDF	KSDF	Louisville Intl, USA
SDG	OICS	Sanandaj Airport, Iran
SDJ	RJSS	Sendai Airport, Japan
SDK	WBKS	Sandakan, Malaysia
SDL	ESNN	Sundsvall, Sweden
SDN	ENSD	Sandane Airport, Norway
SDQ	MDSD	Las Americas, Dominican Republic
SDR	LEXJ	Santander Airport, Spain
SDS	RJSD	Sado Airport, Japan
SDT	OPSS	Saidu Sharif Airport, Pakistan
SDU	SBRJ	Santos Dumont Regional, Brazil
SDV	LLSD	Sde Dov Airport, Israel
SDY	KSDY	Sidney, USA
SEA	KSEA	Seattle, USA
SEB	HLLS	Sebha, Libya
SEL	RKSS	Kimpo Intl, South Korea
SEN	EGMC	Southend Airport, United Kingdom
SEU	HTSN	Seronera, Tanzania
SEY	GQNS	Selibabi, Mauritania
SEZ	FSIA	Seychelles Intl, Seychelles
SFA	DTTX	Thyna, Tunesia
SFB	KSFB	Orlando Sanford Intl, USA
SFC	TFFC	Saint, Guadeloupe
SFD	SVSR	San Fernando De Apure, Venezuela
SFE	RPUS	San Fernando Airport, Philippines

IATA	ICAO	Airport & Country
SFG	TFFG	Grand Case Airport, Guadeloupe
SFI	GMMS	Safi, Morocco
SFJ	BGSF	Kangerlussuaq Airport, Greenland
SFO	KSFO	San Francisco Intl, USA
SFQ	LTCH	Sanliurfa Airport, Turkey
SFS	RPLB	Subic Bay Intl, Philippines
SFT	ESNS	Skelleftea, Sweden
SGA	OASN	Sheghnan, Afghanistan
SGC	USRR	Surgut Airport, Russia
SGD	EKSB	Soenderborg Airport, Denmark
SGE	EDGS	Siegerlandflughafen, Germany
SGF	KSGF	Springfield, USA
SGN	VVTS	Tan Son Nhat Intl, Vietnam
SGO	YSGE	Saint George Airport, Australia
SGS	RPMN	Sanga, Philippines
SGU	KSGU	St. George Municipal Airport, USA
SGX	HTSO	Songea, Tanzania
SGZ	VTSH	Songkhla Airport, Thailand
SHA	ZSSS	Shanghai Hongqiao Airport, China
SHB	RJCN	Nakashibetsu Airport, Japan
SHE	ZYTX	Shenyang Taoxian Intl, China
SHI	RORS	Shimojishima Airport, Japan
SHJ	OMSJ	Sharjah Intl, United Arab Emirates
SHK	FXSH	Sehonghong, Lesotho
SHL	VEBI	Shillong Airport, India
SHM	RJBD	Nanki, Japan
SHO	RKND	Sokcho Aero, South Korea
SHP	ZBSH	Qinhuangdao Shanhaiguan, China
SHQ	YSPT	Southport Airport, Australia
SHR	KSHR	Sheridan County Airport, USA
SHS	ZHSS	Shashi Airport, China
SHT	YSHT	Shepparton Airport, Australia
SHV	KSHV	Shreveport Regional Airport, USA
SHY	HTSY	Shinyanga, Tanzania
SIA	RPNS	Siargao Airport, Philippines
SIB	FCBS	Sibiti, Congo
SID	GVAC	Amilcar Cabral, Cape Verde
SIE	LPSI	Sines Airport, Portugal
SIF	VNSI	Simara, Nepal
SIG	TJIG	Isla Grande Airport, Puerto Rico
SII	GMMF	Sidi Ifni, Morocco
SIJ	BISI	Siglufjordur Airport, Iceland
SIN	WSSS	Singapore Changi Intl, Singapore
SIO	YSMI	Smithton Airport, Australia
SIP	UKFF	Simferopol Airport, Ukraine
SIR	LSGS	Sion Airport, Switzerland
SIS	FASS	Sishen, South Africa
SIT	PASI	Sitka Rocky Gutierrez Airport, USA
SJA	SPJN	San Juan De Marcona, Peru
SJB	SLJO	San Joaquin, Bolivia
SJC	KSJC	Norman Y. Mineta San Jos, USA
SJD	MMSD	Los Cabos Intl, Mexico
SJE	SKSJ	Jorge E Gonzalez, Colombia
SJI	RPUH	McGuire Field, Philippines
SJJ	LQSA	Sarajevo Intl, Bosnia
SJM	MDSJ	San Juan de la Maguana, Dom Repub
SJO	MROC	Juan Santamaria Intl, Costa Rica
SJP	SBSR	Sao Jose do Rio Preto Airport, Brazil
SJT	KSJT	San Angelo Regional Airport, USA
SJU	TJSJ	Luis Munoz Marin Intl, Puerto Rico
SJV	SLJV	San Javier, Bolivia
SJW	ZBSJ	Shijiazhuang Daguocun Intl, China
SJY	EFIL	Seinajoki Airport, Finland
SJZ	LPSJ	Sao Jorge Airport, Portugal
SKD	UTSS	Samarkand, Uzbekistan
SKE	ENSN	Skien Airport, Norway
SKG	LGTS	Thessaloniki Intl, Greece
SKH	VNSK	Surkhet, Nepal
SKN	ENSK	Stokmarknes Airport, Norway
SKO	DNSO	Siddiq Abubakar Iii Intl, Nigeria
SKP	LWSK	Skopje, Macedonia
SKP	LWSK	Skopje Airport, Macedonia
SKR	HASK	Shakiso, Ethiopia
SKU	LGSY	Skyros Island National Airport, Greece
SKV	HESC	St Catherine Intl, Egypt
SKZ	OPSK	Sukkur Airport, Pakistan
SLA	SASA	El Aybal Airport, Argentina
SLC	KSLC	Salt Lake City Intl, USA
SLD	LZSL	Sliac Airport, Slovakia
SLI	MDLI	La Isabela Intl, Dominican Republic
SLI	FLSW	Solwezi, Zambia
SLL	OOSA	Salalah, Oman
SLM	LESA	Salamanca Airport, Spain
SLP	MMSP	Ponciano Arriaga Intl, Mexico
SLU	TLPC	George F.L. Charles, Saint Lucia
SLV	VISM	Shimla Airport, India
SLW	MMIO	Plan de Guadalupe Intl, Mexico
SLZ	SBSL	Marechal Cunha Machado Intl, Brazil
SMA	LPAZ	Santa Maria Airport, Portugal
SMB	SCSB	Franco Bianco, Chile
SMF	KSMF	Sacramento Intl, USA
SMG	SPRN	Santa Maria De Fatima, Peru
SMI	LGSM	Samos Intl, Greece
SML	MYLS	Stella Maris Airport, Bahamas
SMR	SKSM	Simon Bolivar, Colombia
SMS	FMMS	Sainte, Madagascar
SMV	LSZS	Samedan Airport, Switzerland
SMX	KSMX	Santa Maria Public Airport, USA
SMY	GOTS	Simenti, Senegal
SNA	KSNA	John Wayne Airport, USA
SNB	YSNB	Snake Bay Airport, Australia
SNC	SESA	Gen Ulpiano Paez, Ecuador
SNE	GVSN	Preguica, Cape Verde
SNF	SVSP	Sub Teniente Nestor Arias, Venezuela
SNI	GLGE	Sinoe, Liberia
SNM	SLSM	San Ignacio De Moxos, Bolivia
SNN	EINN	Shannon Airport, Ireland
SNO	VTUI	Sakon Nakhon Airport, Thailand
SNR	LFRZ	Saint, France
SNU	MUSC	Abel Santa Maria Airport, Cuba
SNV	SVSE	Santa Elena De Uairen, Venezuela
SNW	VYTD	Mazin, Myanmar
SNX	MDSB	Sabana de la Mar, Dominican Repub
SOB	LHSM	S, Hungary
SOC	WRSQ	Adisumarmo Intl, Indonesia
SOE	FCOS	Souanke, Congo
SOF	LBSF	Sofia Airport, Bulgaria
SOG	ENSG	Sogndal Airport, Norway
SOJ	ENSR	Sorkjosen Airport, Norway
SOK	FXSM	Semonkong, Lesotho

IATA	ICAO	Airport & Country
SOM	SVST	San Tome, Venezuela
SON	NVSS	Santo, Vanuatu
SOO	ESNY	Soderhamn, Sweden
SOT	EFSO	Sodankyla Airport, Finland
SOU	EGHI	Southampton Airport, United Kingdom
SOX	SKSO	Alberto Lieras Camargo, Colombia
SOZ	LFKS	Solenzara, France
SPC	GCLA	La Palma Airport, Spain
SPD	VGSD	Saidpur Airport, Bangladesh
SPI	KSPI	Abraham Lincoln Capital Airport, USA
SPN	PGSN	Obyan Intl, Northern Mariana Islands
SPP	FNME	Menongue, Angola
SPS	KSPS	Sheppard Air Force Base, USA
SPU	LDSP	Airport Split, Croatia
SPY	DISP	San Pedro, Ivory Coast
SQH	VVNS	Na San Airport, Vietnam
SQO	ESUD	Storuman, Sweden
SRD	SLRA	San Ramon, Bolivia
SRE	SLSU	Juana Azurduy De Padilla, Bolivia
SRG	WIIS	Achmad Yani Airport, Indonesia
SRH	FTTA	Sarh, Chad
SRI	WRLS	Temindung Airport Indonesia
SRJ	SLSB	Capitan German Quiroga, Bolivia
SRN	YSRN	Strahan Airport, Australia
SRP	ENSO	Stord Airport, Sorstokken, Norway
SRQ	KSRQ	Sarasota, USA
SRT	HUSO	Soroti, Uganda
SRY	OINZ	Dasht, Iran
SRZ	SLET	El Trompillo, Bolivia
SSA	SBSV	Dep Luis Eduardo Magalhaes, Brazil
SSD	SCSF	Victor Lafon, Chile
SSE	VASL	Sholapur Airport, India
SSG	FGSL	Malabo Airport, Equatorial Guinea
SSH	HESH	Sharm El Sheikh Int, Egypt
SSJ	ENST	Sandnessjoen Airport, Norway
SSN	RKSM	Seoul Ab, South Korea
SSQ	CSR8	La Sarre, Canada
SSY	FNBC	M'banza Congo, Angola
STA	EKVJ	Stauning Airport, Denmark
STC	KSTC	St. Cloud Regional Airport, USA
STD	SVSO	Mayor Buenaventura Vivas,Venezuela
STI	MDST	Cibao Intl, Dominican Republic
STL	KSTL	Lambert, USA
STM	SBSN	Santarem Airport, Brazil
STN	EGSS	London Stansted, United Kingdom
STR	EDDS	Stuttgart, Germany
STT	TIST	King, US Virgin Islands
STV	VASU	Surat Airport, India
STW	URMT	Shpakovskoye Airport, Russia
STX	TISX	Henry E Rohlsen, US Virgin Islands
STY	SUSO	Salto Nueva Hesperides Intl, Uruguay
SUB	WRSJ	Juanda Airport, Indonesia
SUF	LICA	Lamezia Terme Intl, Italy
SUG	RPMS	Surigao Airport, Philippines
SUI	UGSS	Babushara Airport, Georgia
SUJ	LRSM	Satu Mare Intl, Romania
SUL	OPSU	Sui Airport, Pakistan
SUN	KSUN	Friedman Memorial Airport, USA
SUQ	SESC	Sucua, Ecuador
SUR	CJV7	Summer Beaver, Canada
SUT	HTSU	Sumbawanga, Tanzania
SUV	NFNA	Nausori Intl, Fiji
SUX	KSUX	Sioux Gateway Airport, USA
SVB	FMNS	Sambava South, Madagascar
SVD	TVSV	E T Joshua, St. Vincent & Grenadines
SVG	ENZV	Stavanger Airport, Sola, Norway
SVI	SKSV	San Vicente Del Caguan, Colombia
SVJ	ENSH	Svolvae Airport, Norway
SVL	EFSA	Savonlinna Airport, Finland
SVO	UUEE	Sheremetyevo Intl, Russia
SVP	FNKU	Bie, Angola
SVQ	LEZL	Seville Airport, Spain
SVX	USSS	Koltsovo Intl, Russia
SWA	ZGOW	Shantou Airport, China
SWC	YSWL	Stawell Airport, Australia
SWF	KSWF	Stewart Intl, USA
SWH	YSWH	Swan Hill Airport, Australia
SWP	FYSM	Swakopmund, Namibia
SWS	EGFH	Swansea Airport, United Kingdom
SWU	RKSW	Suwon, South Korea
SWX	FBSW	Shakawe, Botsuana
SXB	LFST	Strasbourg Airport, France
SXE	YWSL	West Sale Airport, Australia
SXF	EDDB	Berlin Schonefeld, Germany
SXG	FLSN	Senanga, Zambia
SXI	OIBS	Sirri Island Airport, Iran
SXL	EISG	Sligo Airport, Ireland
SXM	TNCM	Princess Juliana, Netherlands Antilles
SXR	VISR	Srinagar Airport, India
SXU	HASD	Soddo, Ethiopia
SXV	VOSM	Salem Airport, India
SXZ	LTCL	Siirt Airport, Turkey
SYC	SPOV	Shiringayoc O Hda Mejia, Peru
SYD	YSSY	Sydney Intl, Australia
SYE	OYSH	Saadah, Yemen
SYJ	OIKY	Sirjan Airport, Iran
SYK	BIST	Stykkisholmur Airport, Iceland
SYM	ZPSM	Simao Airport, China
SYO	RJSY	Shonai Airport, Japan
SYQ	MRPV	Tobias Bolanos Intl, Costa Rica
SYR	KSYR	Syracuse Hancock Intl, USA
SYW	OPSN	Sehwan Sharif Airport, Pakistan
SYX	ZGSY	Sanya Fenghuang Intl, China
SYY	EGPO	Stornoway Airport, United Kingdom
SYZ	OISS	Shiraz Intl, Iran
SZA	FNSO	Soyo, Angola
SZB	WMSA	Sultan Abdul Aziz Shah, Malaysia
SZE	EGSY	Sheffield City Airport, United Kingdom
SZF	LTFH	Samsun Carsamba Airport, Turkey
SZG	LOWS	Salzburg, Austria
SZJ	MUSN	Siguanea Airport, Cuba
SZK	FASZ	Skukuza, South Africa
SZV	ZSSZ	Suzhou Guangfu Airport, China
SZW	EDOP	Schwerin – Parchim, Germany
SZX	ZGSZ	Shenzhen Bao'an Intl, China
SZY	EPSY	Szczytno, Poland
SZZ	EPSC	Szczecin, Poland
TAC	RPVA	Daniel Z. Romualdez, Philippines
TAE	RKTN	Taegu Aero, South Korea
TAG	RPVT	Tagbilaran Airport, Philippines

IATA	ICAO	Airport & Country
TAI	OYTZ	Ganed, Yemen
TAK	RJOT	Takamatsu Airport, Japan
TAM	MMTM	Gen Francisco Javier Mina, Mexico
TAO	ZSQD	Qingdao Liuting Intl, China
TAP	MMTP	Tapachula Intl, Mexico
TAR	LIBG	Grottaglie Airport, Italy
TAS	UTTT	Tashkent Yuzhny, Uzbekistan
TAT	LZTT	Tatry Airport, Slovakia
TAW	SUTB	Tacuarembo, Uruguay
TAY	EETU	Tartu Airport, Estonia
TBB	VVTH	Dong Tac Airport, Vietnam
TBH	RPVU	Tugdan Airport, Philippines
TBJ	DTKA	Tabarka 7 Novembre, Tunesia
TBO	HTTB	Tabora, Tanzania
TBP	SPME	Pedro Canga, Peru
TBS	UGGG	Lochini, Georgia
TBS	UGGG	Tbilisi Intl, Georgia
TBU	NFTF	Fua'amotu Intl, Tonga
TBY	FBTS	Tshabong, Botsuana
TBZ	OITT	Tabriz Intl, Iran
TCA	YTNK	Tennant Creek Airport, Australia
TCB	MYAT	Treasure Cay Airport, Bahamas
TCE	LRTC	Tulcea Airport, Romania
TCH	FOOT	Tchibanga, Gabon
TCO	SKCO	La Florida, Colombia
TCP	HETB	Taba Intl, Egypt
TCQ	SPTN	Col Carlos Ciriani Santa Rosa, Peru
TCX	OIMT	Tabas Airport, Iran
TDA	SKTD	Trinidad, Colombia
TDD	SLTR	Jorge Henrich Arauz, Bolivia
TDG	RPMW	Tandag Airport, Philippines
TDV	FMSN	Samangoky, Madagascar
TEA	MHTE	Tela, Honduras
TED	EKTS	Thisted Airport, Denmark
TEE	DABS	Tebessa, Algeria
TEG	DFET	Tenkodogo, Burkina Faso
TEI	VETJ	Tezu Airport, India
TEM	YTEM	Temora Airport, Australia
TEQ	LTBU	Corlu Airport, Turkey
TET	FQTT	Chingozi, Mozambique
TEX	KTEX	Telluride Regional Airport, USA
TEY	BITE	Pingeyri Airport, Iceland
TEZ	VETZ	Tezpur Airport, India
TFN	GCXO	Tenerife Los Rodeos Airport, Spain
TFS	GCTS	Tenerife Reina Sofia Airport, Spain
TGD	LYPG	Podgorica, Montenegro
TGG	WMKN	Sultan Mahmud, Malaysia
TGI	SPGM	Tingo Maria, Peru
TGM	LRTM	Targu Mures Intl, Romania
TGO	ZBTL	Tongliao Airport, China
TGR	DAUK	Touggourt, Algeria
TGT	HTTG	Tanga, Tanzania
TGU	MHTG	Toncontin Intl, Honduras
TGZ	MMTG	Llano San Juan Airport, Mexico
THC	GLTN	Tchien, Liberia
THE	SBTE	Senador Petronio Portella, Brazil
THF	EDDI	Berlin Tempelhof, Germany
THG	YTNG	Thangool Airport, Australia
THI	GQNC	Tichit, Mauritania
THK	VLTK	Thakhek, Laos

IATA	ICAO	Airport & Country
THL	VYTL	Tachilek, Myanmar
THN	ESGT	Trollhattan, Sweden
THO	BITH	Sauoanes Airport, Iceland
THR	OIII	Mehrabad Intl, Iran
THS	VTPO	Sukhothai Airport, Thailand
THT	GQNT	Tamchakett, Mauritania
THU	BGTL	Thule Air Base, Greenland
THZ	DRRT	Tahoua, Niger
TIA	LATI	Rinas Mother Teresa Airport, Albania
TIB	SKTB	Tibu, Colombia
TID	DAOB	Tiaret, Algeria
TIE	HATP	Tippi, Ethiopia
TIF	OETF	Taif Regional Airport, Saudi Arabia
TIJ	MMTJ	General Abelardo, Mexico
TIR	VOTP	Tirupati Airport, India
TIU	NZTU	Timaru, New Zealand
TIV	LYTV	Tivat Airport, Montenegro
TIY	GQND	Tidjikja, Mauritania
TJA	SLTJ	Capt Oriel Lea Plaza, Bolivia
TKC	FKKC	Tiko, Cameroon
TKD	DGTK	Takoradi, Ghana
TKG	WIIT	Radin Inten II Airport, Indonesia
TKK	PTKK	Chuuk Intl, Micronesia
TKN	RJKN	Tokunoshima Airport, Japan
TKQ	HTKA	Kigoma, Tanzania
TKR	VGSG	Thakuragaon Airport, Bangladesh
TKT	VTPT	Tak Airport, Thailand
TKU	EFTU	Turku Airport, Finland
TLB	OPTA	Tarbela Dam Airport, Pakistan
TLC	MMTO	Lic. Adolfo Lopez Mateos, Mexico
TLD	FBTL	Tuli Block, Botsuana
TLE	FMST	Toliara, Madagascar
TLH	KTLH	Tallahassee Regional Airport, USA
TLL	EETN	Tallinn Airport, Estonia
TLM	DAON	Messali El Hadj Airport, Algeria
TLS	LFBO	Toulouse, France
TLV	LLBG	Ben Gurion Intl, Israel
TLX	SCTL	Panguilemo, Chile
TMD	GQNH	Timbedra, Mauritania
TME	SKTM	Tame, Colombia
TMI	VNTR	Tumlingtar, Nepal
TMJ	UTST	Termez, Uzbekistan
TML	DGLE	Tamale, Ghana
TMM	FMMT	Toamasina, Madagascar
TMO	SVTM	Tumeremo, Venezuela
TMP	EFTP	Tampere, Finland
TMR	DAAT	Tamanrasset, Algeria
TMS	FPST	Sao Tom, Sao Tome and Principe
TMU	MRTR	Tambor Airport, Costa Rica
TMW	YSTW	Tamworth Airport, Australia
TMX	DAUT	Timimoun Airport, Algeria
TMZ	NZTH	Thames, New Zealand
TNA	ZSJN	Jinan Yaoqiang Airport, China
TND	MUTD	Alberto Delgado Airport, Cuba
TNE	RJFG	Tanegashima Airport, Japan
TNF	LFPN	Toussus – le Noble Airport, France
TNG	GMTT	Ibn Batouta, Morocco
TNH	ZYTN	Tonghua Liuhe Airport, China
TNI	VIST	Satna Airport, India
TNJ	WIKN	Kijang Airport, Indonesia

IATA	ICAO	Airport & Country
TNO	MRTM	Tamarindo Airport, Costa Rica
TNR	FMMI	Ivato, Madagascar
TNS	CBX5	Cantung, Canada
TOE	DTTZ	Nefta, Tunesia
TOJ	LETO	Madrid Torrejon Airport, Spain
TOL	KTOL	Toledo Express Airport, USA
TOM	GATB	Tombouctou, Mali
TOQ	SCBE	Barriles, Chile
TOS	ENTC	Tromso Airport, Norway
TOU	NWWU	Touho, New Caledonia
TOY	RJNT	Toyama Airport, Japan
TOZ	DITM	Mahana, Ivory Coast
TPA	KTPA	Tampa Intl, USA
TPC	SETR	Tarapoa, Ecuador
TPE	RCTP	Chiang Kai, Taiwan
TPG	WMBI	Taiping, Malaysia
TPN	SETI	Tiputini, Ecuador
TPP	SPST	Cdte.Guillermo D Castillo Par, Peru
TPQ	MMEP	Amado Nervo National Airport, Mexico
TPS	LICT	Vincenzo Florio Airport, Italy
TQS	SKTQ	Tres Esquinas, Colombia
TRA	RORT	Tarama Airport, Japan
TRB	SKTU	Gonzalo Mejia, Colombia
TRC	MMTC	Torreon Intl, Mexico
TRD	ENVA	Trondheim Airport, Norway
TRE	EGPU	Tiree Airport, United Kingdom
TRF	ENTO	Sandefjord Airport, Norway
TRG	NZTG	Tauranga, New Zealand
TRI	KTRI	Tri, USA
TRK	WRLR	Juwata Airport, Indonesia
TRN	LIMF	Torino Caselle Airport, Italy
TRO	YTRE	Taree Airport, Australia
TRR	VCCT	China Bay AB, Sri Lanka
TRS	LIPQ	Friuli Venezia Giulia Airport, Italy
TRU	SPRU	Cap Carlos Martinez De Pinill, Peru
TRV	VOTV	Thiruvananthapuram Intl, India
TRW	NGTA	Bonriki Intl, Kiribati
TRY	HUTO	Tororo, Uganda
TRZ	VOTR	Tiruchirapalli Airport, India
TSA	RCSS	Taipei Songshan Airport, Taiwan
TSB	FYTM	Tsumeb, Namibia
TSC	SETH	Taisha, Ecuador
TSE	UACC	Astana, Kazakhstan
TSF	LIPH	Treviso Airport, Italy
TSH	FZUK	Tshikapa, Congo
TSJ	RJDT	Tsushima Airport, Japan
TSN	ZBTJ	Tianjin Binhai Intl, China
TSR	LRTR	Timisoara Intl, Romania
TST	VTST	Trang Airport, Thailand
TSV	YBTL	Townsville Intl, Australia
TTA	GMAT	Plage Blanche, Morocco
TTB	LIET	Tortoli, Italy
TTC	SCTT	Las Breas, Chile
TTH	OOTH	Thumrait AB, Oman
TTJ	RJOR	Tottori Airport, Japan
TTN	KTTN	Trenton, USA
TTQ	MRAO	Tortuguero Airport, Costa Rica
TTS	FMNT	Tsaratanana, Madagascar
TTU	GMTN	Sania Ramel, Morocco
TUA	SETU	El Rosal, Ecuador

IATA	ICAO	Airport & Country
TUC	SANT	Benjamin Matienzo Intl Argentina
TUD	GOTT	Tambacounda, Senegal
TUF	LFOT	Tours, France
TUG	RPUT	Tuguegarao Airport, Philippines
TUI	OETR	Turaif Domestic Airport, Saudi Arabia
TUK	OPTU	Turbat Airport, Pakistan
TUL	KTUL	Tulsa Intl, USA
TUM	YTMU	Tumut Airport, Australia
TUN	DTTA	Carthage, Tunesia
TUO	NZAP	Taupo, New Zealand
TUP	KTUP	Tupelo Regional Airport, USA
TUS	KTUS	Tucson Intl, USA
TUU	OETB	Tabuk Regional Airport, Saudi Arabia
TUV	SVTC	Tucupita, Venezuela
TUX	CBX7	Tumbler Ridge, Canada
TVA	FMMR	Morafenobe, Madagascar
TVC	KTVC	Cherry Capital Airport, USA
TVY	VYDW	Dawei, Myanmar
TWB	YTWB	Toowoomba Airport, Australia
TWF	KTWF	Magic Valley Regional Airport, USA
TWU	WBKW	Tawau, Malaysia
TXK	KTXK	Texarkana Regional Airport, USA
TXL	EDDT	Berlin Tegel, Germany
TXN	ZSTX	Huangshan Tunxi Intl, China
TXU	DITB	Tabou, Ivory Coast
TYB	YTIB	Tibooburra Airport, Australia
TYF	ESST	Fryklanda, Sweden
TYL	SPYL	Capitan Montes, Peru
TYM	MYES	Staniel Cay Airport, Bahamas
TYN	ZBYN	Taiyuan Wusu Airport, China
TYR	KTYR	Tyler Pounds Regional Airport, USA
TYS	KTYS	McGhee Tyson Airport, USA
TYT	SUTR	Treinta Y Tres, Uruguay
TZL	LQTZ	Tuzla Intl, Bosnia
TZX	LTCG	Trabzon Airport, Turkey
UAK	BGBW	Narssarssuaq Airport, Greenland
UAQ	SANU	San Juan Airport, Argentina
UAS	HKSB	Buffalo Spring, Kenya
UBJ	RJDC	Yamaguchi Ube Airport Japan
UBP	VTUU	Ubon Ratchathani Airport, Thailand
UCN	GLBU	Buckanan, Liberia
UCT	UUYH	Ukhta Airport, Russia
UDI	SBUL	Uberlandia Airport, Brazil
UDJ	UKLU	Uzhhorod Airport, Ukraine
UDN	LIPD	Campoformido Airport, Italy
UDR	VAUD	Udaipur Airport, India
UEL	FQQL	Quelimane, Mozambique
UEO	ROKJ	Kumejima Airport, Japan
UET	OPQT	Quetta Intl, Pakistan
UFA	UWUU	Ufa Airport, Russia
UGA	ZMBN	Bulgan, Mongolia
UGC	UTNU	Urgench, Uzbekistan
UGO	FNUG	Uige, Angola
UHE	LKKU	Kunovice Airport, Czech Republic
UIB	SKUI	El Carano, Colombia
UIH	VVPC	Phu Cat Airport, Vietnam
UIN	KUIN	Quincy Regional Airport, USA
UIO	SEQU	Mariscal Sucre Intl, Ecuador
UIP	LFRQ	Quimper, France
UIT	N55	Jaluit, Marshall Islands

IATA	ICAO	Airport & Country
UKB	RJBE	Kobe Airport, Japan
UKR	OYMK	Mukeiras, Yemen
ULC	SCTI	Los Cerrillos, Chile
ULD	FAUL	Prince M.Buthelezi, South Africa
ULI	TT02	Ulithi, Micronesia
ULN	ZMUB	Buyant, Mongolia
ULP	YQLP	Quilpie Airport, Australia
ULQ	SKUL	Farfan, Colombia
ULU	HUGU	Gulu, Uganda
UMD	BGUM	Uummannaq Airport, Greenland
UME	ESNU	Umea, Sweden
UMI	SPIL	Quincemil, Peru
UND	OAUZ	Kunduz, Afghanistan
UNE	FXQN	Qacha's Nek, Lesotho
UNI	TVSU	Union I. Intl, St. Vincent & Grenadines
UNN	VTSR	Ranong Airport, Thailand
UNV	KUNV	University Park Airport, USA
UPG	WAAA	Hasanuddin Airport, Indonesia
UPL	MRUP	Upala Airport, Costa Rica
UPN	MMPN	Gen. Ignacio Lopez Rayon, Mexico
UPV	EGDJ	Upavon Airfield, United Kingdom
URA	UARR	Uralsk, Kazakhstan
URC	ZWWW	Diwopu Airport, China
URE	EEKE	Kuressaare Airport, Estonia
URM	SVUM	Uriman, Venezuela
URO	LFOP	Rouen, France
URT	VTSB	Surat Thani Airport, Thailand
URY	OEGT	Gurayat Domestic, Saudi Arabia
USH	SAWH	Ushuaia Intl, Argentina
USM	VTSM	Samui Airport, Thailand
USN	RKPU	Ulsan, South Korea
USU	RPVV	Busuanga Airport, Philippines
UTA	FVMU	Mutare, Zimbabwe
UTH	VTUD	Udon Thani Airport, Thailand
UTN	FAUP	Upington, South Africa
UTP	VTBU	U, Thailand
UTP	VTUD	Udon Thani Intl, Thailand
UTR	VTPU	Uttaradit Airport, Thailand
UTT	FAUT	K.D. Matanzima, South Africa
UTW	FAQT	Queenstown, South Africa
UUD	UIUU	Mukhino Airport, Russia
UUN	ZMBU	Baruun, Mongolia
UUS	UHSS	Yuzhno, Russia
UVE	NWWV	Ouloup, New Caledonia
UVF	TLPL	Hewanorra Intl, Saint Lucia
UVL	HEKG	El Kharga Airport, Egypt
UYL	HSNL	Nyala, Sudan
UYN	ZLYL	Yulin Airport, China
VAA	EFVA	Vaasa Airport, Finland
VAF	LFLU	Valence, France
VAH	SLVG	Vallegrande, Bolivia
VAN	LTCI	Van Ferit Melen Airport, Turkey
VAR	LBWN	Varna Intl, Bulgaria
VAS	LTAR	Sivas Airport, Turkey
VAT	FMMY	Vatomandry, Madagascar
VAV	NFTV	Vava'u, Tonga
VAW	ENSS	Vardo Airport, Norway
VBS	LIPO	Montichiari Airport, Italy
VBY	ESSV	Visby, Sweden
VCA	VVCT	Tra Noc Airport, Vietnam

IATA	ICAO	Airport & Country
VCE	LIPZ	Marco Polo Venice Airport, Italy
VCH	SUVO	Vichadero, Uruguay
VCP	SBKP	Viracopos Intl, Brazil
VCR	SVCO	Carora, Venezuela
VCS	VVCS	Co Ong Airport, Vietnam
VCT	KVCT	Victoria Regional Airport, USA
VCV	KVCV	Southern California Logistics, USA
VDA	LLOV	Ovda Intl, Israel
VDB	ENFG	Fagernes Airport, Norway
VDE	GCHI	El Hierro Airport, Spain
VDM	SAVV	Gobernador Castello, Argentina
VDP	SVVP	Valle De La Pascua, Venezuela
VDS	ENVD	Vadso Airport, Norway
VDZ	PAVD	Valdez Airport, USA
VER	MMVR	General Heriberto Jara Intl, Mexico
VEY	BIVM	Vestmannaeyjar Airport, Iceland
VFA	FVFA	Victoria Falls, Zimbabwe
VGA	VOBZ	Vijayawada Airport, India
VGN	RPUQ	Mindoro Airport, Philippines
VGO	LEVX	Vigo Airport, Spain
VGT	KVGT	North Las Vegas Airport, USA
VGZ	SKVG	Villagarzon, Colombia
VHC	FNSA	Saurimo, Angola
VHM	ESNV	Vilhelmina, Sweden
VHY	LFLV	Vichy, France
VIC	LIPT	Vicenza Trissino Airport, Italy
VIE	LOWW	Wien, Austria
VIG	SVVG	Juan Pablo Perez Alfonzo, Venezuela
VII	VVVH	Vinh Airport, Vietnam
VIJ	TUPW	Virgin Gorda, British Virgin Islands
VIN	UKWW	Vinnytsia Airport, Ukraine
VIR	FAVG	Virginia, South Africa
VIT	LEVT	Vitoria Airport, Spain
VIX	SBVT	Goiabeiras Airport, Brazil
VKG	VVRG	Rach Gia Airport, Vietnam
VKO	UUWW	Vnukovo Airport, Russia
VLC	LEVC	Valencia Airport, Spain
VLD	KVLD	Valdosta Regional Airport, USA
VLI	NVVV	Bauerfield, Vanuatu
VLL	LEVD	Valladolid Airport, Spain
VLM	SLVM	Rafael Pabon, Bolivia
VLN	SVVA	Arturo Michelena Intl, Venezuela
VLR	SCLL	Vallenar, Chile
VLV	SVVL	Dr. Antonio Nicolas Briceno, Venezuela
VME	SAOR	Villa Reynolds Airport, Argentina
VNA	VLSV	Saravane, Laos
VNE	LFRV	Vannes, France
VNS	VIBN	Varanasi Airport, India
VNX	FQVL	Vilankulu, Mozambique
VOG	URWW	Gumrak Airport, Russia
VOH	FMNV	Vohimarina, Madagascar
VOL	LGBL	Aghialos National Airport, Greece
VOZ	UUOO	Chertovitskoye Airport, Russia
VPS	KVPS	Okaloosa Regional Airport, USA
VPY	FQCH	Chimoio, Mozambique
VQS	TJVQ	Vieques Airport, Puerto Rico
VRA	MUVR	Juan Gualberto Gomez, Cuba
VRC	RPUV	Virac Airport, Philippines
VRE	FAVR	Vredendal, South Africa
VRK	EFVR	Varkaus Airport, Finland

IATA	ICAO	Airport & Country
VRL	LPVR	Vila Real Airport, Portugal
VRN	LIPX	Verona Airport, Italy
VRO	MUKW	Kawama Airport, Cuba
VRU	FAVB	Vryburg, South Africa
VSA	MMVA	Carlos Rovirosa Perez, Mexico
VSE	LPVZ	Viseu Airport, Portugal
VST	ESOW	Hasslo, Sweden
VTB	UMII	Vitebsk, Belarus
VTE	VLVT	Wattay Intl, Laos
VTL	LFXC	Vittel, France
VTL	LFSZ	Vittel, France
VTS	EVVA	Ventspils Intl, Latvia
VTU	MUVT	Hermanos Ameijeiras Airport, Cuba
VTZ	VEVZ	Visakhapatnam Airport, India
VUP	SKVP	Alfonso Lopez, Colombia
VVB	FMMH	Mahanoro, Madagascar
VVC	SKVV	Vanguardia, Colombia
VVI	SLVR	Viru Viru Intl, Bolivia
VVK	ESSW	Vastervik, Sweden
VVO	UHWW	Vladivostok Intl, Russia
VXC	FQLC	Lichinga, Mozambique
VXE	GVSV	S. Pedro, Cape Verde
VXO	ESMX	Kronoberg, Sweden
VYD	FAVY	Vryheid, South Africa
WAC	HAWC	Wacca, Ethiopia
WAG	NZWU	Wanganui, New Zealand
WAI	FMNW	Ambalabe, Madagascar
WAK	FMSZ	Ankazoabo, Madagascar
WAM	FMMZ	Ambatondrazaka, Madagascar
WAQ	FMMG	Antsalova, Madagascar
WAT	EIWF	Waterford Airport, Ireland
WAW	EPWA	Warsaw Frederic Chopin, Poland
WBD	FMNF	Avaratra, Madagascar
WBO	FMSB	Antsoa, Madagascar
WCH	SCTN	Chaiten, Chile
WDH	FYWH	Hosea Kutako Intl, Namibia
WEF	ZSWF	Weifang Airport, China
WEI	YBWP	Weipa Airport, Australia
WEL	FAWM	Welkom, South Africa
WFI	FMSF	Fianarantsoa, Madagascar
WGA	YSWG	Wagga Wagga Airport, Australia
WGC	VOWA	Warangal Airport, India
WGE	YWLG	Walgett Airport, Australia
WGT	YWGT	Wangaratta Airport, Australia
WHF	HSSW	Wadi Halfa, Sudan
WHK	NZWK	Whakatane, New Zealand
WHS	EGEH	Whalsay Airport, United Kingdom
WIC	EGPC	Wick Airport, United Kingdom
WIL	HKNW	Wilson, Kenya
WIN	YWTN	Winton Airport, Australia
WIR	NZWO	Wairoa, New Zealand
WJR	HKWJ	Waghala, Kenya
WJU	RKNW	Wonju, South Korea
WKA	NZWF	Wanaka, New Zealand
WKB	YWKB	Warracknabeal Airport, Australia
WKI	FVWT	Hwange Town, Zimbabwe
WKJ	RJCW	Wakkanai Airport, Japan
WLG	NZWN	Wellington Intl, New Zealand
WMA	FMNX	Mandritsara, Madagascar
WMD	FMSC	Mandabe, Madagascar
WME	YMNE	Mount Keith Airport, Australia
WML	FMMC	Malaimbandy, Madagascar
WMN	FMNR	Maroantsetra, Madagascar
WMR	FMNC	Avaratra, Madagascar
WNN	CKL3	Wunnumin Lake, Canada
WNP	RPUN	Naga Airport, Philippines
WNR	YWDH	Windorah Airport, Australia
WNS	OPNH	Nawabshah Airport, Pakistan
WNZ	ZSWZ	Wenzhou Intl, China
WOL	YWOL	Wollongong Airport, Australia
WPA	SCAS	Cabo Juan Roman, Chile
WPB	FMNG	Port Berge, Madagascar
WPC	CZPC	Pincher Creek, Canada
WPR	SCFM	Capitan Fuentes Martinez, Chile
WPU	SCGZ	Guardiamarina Zanartu, Chile
WRE	NZWR	Whangarei, New Zealand
WRO	EPWR	Copernicus Airport Wroclaw, Poland
WRY	EGEW	Westray Airport, United Kingdom
WSZ	NZWS	Westport, New Zealand
WTA	FMMU	Tambohorano, Madagascar
WTS	FMMX	Tsiroanomandidy, Madagascar
WUH	ZHHH	Wuhan Tianhe Airport, China
WUN	YWLU	Wiluna Airport, Australia
WUS	ZSWY	Nanping Wuyishan Airport, China
WUU	HSWW	Wau, Sudan
WUX	ZSWX	Wuxi Airport, China
WUZ	ZGWZ	Wuzhou Changzhoudao Airport, China
WVB	FYWB	Walvis Bay, Namibia
WVK	FMSK	Manakara, Madagascar
WVN	EDWI	Wilhelmshaven, Germany
WWA	YWWL	West Wyalong Airport, Australia
WWK	AYWK	Wewak Intl, Papua New Guinea
WYA	YWHA	Whyalla Airport, Australia
WYE	GFYE	Yengema, Sierra Leone
XAB	LFOI	Abbeville, France
XBE	CNE3	Bearskin Lake, Canada
XBJ	OIMB	Birjand Airport, Iran
XBQ	LFOQ	Blois, France
XBR	CNL3	Brockville, Canada
XCH	YPXM	Christmas Island Airport, Australia
XCL	CJS3	Cluff Lake, Canada
XCM	CNZ3	Chatham, Canada
XFN	ZHXF	Xiangfan Airport, China
XFW	EDHI	Finkenwerder, Germany
XGA	DFOG	Amilcar Cabral, Burkina Faso
XGG	DFEG	Gorom, Burkina Faso
XGN	FNXA	Xangongo, Angola
XGR	CYLU	Kangiqsualujjuaq, Canada
XIC	ZUXC	Xichang Qingshan Airport, China
XIY	ZLXY	Xi'an Xianyang Intl, China
XJM	OPMA	Mangla Airport, Pakistan
XKA	DFEL	Kantchari, Burkina Faso
XKH	VLXK	Xieng Khouang, Laos
XKS	CYAQ	Kasabonika, Canada
XLB	CZWH	Lac Brochet, Canada
XLS	GOSS	St Louis, Senegal
XMC	YMCO	Mallacoota Airport, Australia
XMI	HTMI	Masasi, Tanzania
XMN	ZSAM	Xiamen Gaoqi Intl, China
XMP	CFC4	Macmillan Pass, Canada

IATA	ICAO	Airport & Country
XMS	SEMC	Macas, Ecuador
XNA	KXNA	Northwest Arkansas Regional, USA
XNN	ZLXN	Xining Airport, China
XNT	ZBXT	Xingtai Airport, China
XNU	DFCN	Nouna, Burkina Faso
XPK	CZFG	Pukatawagan, Canada
XPP	CZNG	Poplar River, Canada
XQP	MRQP	La Managua Airport, Costa Rica
XRR	CYDM	Ross River, Canada
XRY	LEJR	Jerez Airport, Spain
XSI	CZSN	South Indian Lake, Canada
XTG	YTGM	Thargomindah Airport, Australia
XTL	CYBQ	Tadoule Lake, Canada
XTO	YTAM	Taroom Airport, Australia
XUZ	ZSXZ	Xuzhou Airport, China
XXG	LFQF	Autun, France
XYE	VYYE	Ye, Myanmar
YAA	CAJ4	Anahim Lake, Canada
YAC	CYAC	Cat Lake, Canada
YAG	CYAG	Ft Frances Mun, Canada
YAI	SCCH	Gen. Bernardo O'higgins, Chile
YAK	PAYA	Yakutat Airport, USA
YAL	CYAL	Alert Bay, Canada
YAM	CYAM	Sault Ste Marie, Canada
YAO	FKKY	Yaounde/Ville, Cameroon
YAP	PTYA	Yap Intl, Micronesia
YAT	CYAT	Attawapiskat, Canada
YAW	CYAW	Halifax, Canada
YAX	CKB6	Wapakeka, Canada
YAY	CYAY	St Anthony, Canada
YAZ	CYAZ	Tofino, Canada
YBB	CYBB	Pelly Bay, Canada
YBC	CYBC	Baie, Canada
YBE	CYBE	Uranium City, Canada
YBG	CYBG	Bagotville, Canada
YBI	CCE4	Black Tickle, Canada
YBK	CYBK	Baker Lake, Canada
YBL	CYBL	Campbell River, Canada
YBM	CAB5	Bronson Creek, Canada
YBP	ZUYB	Yibin Airport, China
YBR	CYBR	Brandon Muni, Canada
YBT	CYBT	Brochet, Canada
YBV	CYBV	Berens River, Canada
YBY	CYBF	Bonnyville, Canada
YCA	CAH3	Courtenay, Canada
YCB	CYCB	Cambridge Bay, Canada
YCC	CYCC	Cornwall Regl, Canada
YCD	CYCD	Nanaimo, Canada
YCE	CYCE	Huron, Canada
YCG	CYCG	Castlegar, Canada
YCH	CYCH	Miramichi, Canada
YCK	CEB3	Colville Lake, Canada
YCL	CYCL	Charlo, Canada
YCM	CYSN	St Catharines, Canada
YCN	CYCN	Cochrane, Canada
YCO	CYCO	Kugluktuk, Canada
YCQ	CYCQ	Chetwynd, Canada
YCR	CYCR	Sinclair Meml, Canada
YCS	CYCS	Chesterfield Inlet, Canada
YCT	CYCT	Coronation, Canada

IATA	ICAO	Airport & Country
YCW	CYCW	Chilliwack, Canada
YCY	CYCY	Clyde River, Canada
YCZ	CYCZ	Fairmont Hot Springs, Canada
YDA	CYDA	Dawson, Canada
YDB	CYDB	Burwash, Canada
YDC	CER3	Industrial, Canada
YDF	CYDF	Deer Lake, Canada
YDG	CYID	Digby, Canada
YDI	CCB4	Davis Inlet, Canada
YDJ	CJL2	Hatchet Lake, Canada
YDL	CYDL	Dease Lake, Canada
YDN	CYDN	Barker, Canada
YDO	CYDO	Dolbeau, Canada
YDP	CYDP	Nain, Canada
YDQ	CYDQ	Dawson Creek, Canada
YDT	CZBB	Boundary Bay, Canada
YDU	CJL8	Kasba Lake, Canada
YDV	CZTA	Bloodvein River, Canada
YEC	RKTY	Yechon Aero, South Korea
YEG	CYEG	Edmonton Intl, Canada
YEH	OIBI	Asalouyeh Airport, Iran
YEI	LTBR	Bursa Yenisehir Airport, Turkey
YEK	CYEK	Arviat, Canada
YEL	CYEL	Elliot Lake Mun, Canada
YEM	CYEM	Manitoulin East Muni., Canada
YEN	CYEN	Estevan, Canada
YER	CYER	Ft Severn, Canada
YET	CYET	Edson, Canada
YEU	CYEU	Eureka, Canada
YEV	CYEV	Zubko, Canada
YEY	CYEY	Amos Mun, Canada
YFA	CYFA	Ft Albany, Canada
YFB	CYFB	Iqaluit, Canada
YFC	CYFC	Fredericton, Canada
YFH	CYFH	Ft Hope, Canada
YFJ	CFJ2	Wekweti, Canada
YFO	CYFO	Flin Flon, Canada
YFR	CYFR	Ft Resolution, Canada
YFS	CYFS	Ft Simpson, Canada
YFX	CCK4	Fox Harbour, Canada
YGB	CYGB	Gillies Bay, Canada
YGC	CEQ5	Grande Cache, Canada
YGH	CYGH	Ft Good Hope, Canada
YGK	CYGK	Kingston, Canada
YGL	CYGL	La Grande Riviere, Canada
YGM	CYGM	Gimli Industrial Park, Canada
YGO	CYGO	Gods Lake Narrows, Canada
YGP	CYGP	Gaspe, Canada
YGQ	CYGQ	Greenstone Regl, Canada
YGR	CYGR	Iles, Canada
YGT	CYGT	Igloolik, Canada
YGV	CYGV	Havre St, Canada
YGW	CYGW	Kuujjuarapik, Canada
YGX	CYGX	Gillam, Canada
YGZ	CYGZ	Grise Fiord, Canada
YHA	CCP4	Port Hope Simpson, Canada
YHB	CYHB	Hudson Bay, Canada
YHD	CYHD	Dryden Regl, Canada
YHE	CYHE	Hope, Canada
YHF	CYHF	Hearst Mun, Canada

IATA	ICAO	Airport & Country
YHG	CCH4	Charlottetown, Canada
YHI	CYHI	Holman, Canada
YHK	CYHK	Gjoa Haven, Canada
YHM	CYHM	Hamilton, Canada
YHN	CYHN	Hornepayne Mun, Canada
YHO	CYHO	Hopedale, Canada
YHR	CYHR	Chevery, Canada
YHS	CAP3	Sechelt, Canada
YHT	CYHT	Haines Junction, Canada
YHU	CYHU	Montreal, Canada
YHY	CYHY	Hay River, Canada
YHZ	CYHZ	Halifax Intl, Canada
YIB	CYIB	Atikokan Mun, Canada
YIF	CYIF	St, Canada
YIH	ZHYC	Yichang Airport, China
YIK	CYIK	Ivujivik, Canada
YIN	ZWYN	Yining Airport, China
YIO	CYIO	Pond Inlet, Canada
YIV	CYIV	Island Lake, Canada
YIW	ZSYW	Yiwu Airport, China
YJA	CEC4	Jasper, Canada
YJF	CYJF	Ft Liard, Canada
YJN	CYJN	St, Canada
YJT	CYJT	Stephenville, Canada
YKA	CYKA	Kamloops, Canada
YKC	CYKC	Collins Bay, Canada
YKD	CNS7	Kincardine, Canada
YKF	CYKF	Kitchener/Waterloo Regl, Canada
YKG	CYAS	Kangirsuk, Canada
YKJ	CYKJ	Key Lake, Canada
YKL	CYKL	Schefferville, Canada
YKM	KYKM	Yakima Air Terminal, USA
YKQ	CYKQ	Waskaganish, Canada
YKS	UEEE	Yakutsk Airport, Russia
YKX	CYKX	Kirkland Lake, Canada
YKY	CYKY	Kindersley, Canada
YKZ	CYKZ	Toronto, Canada
YLB	CYLB	Lac La Biche, Canada
YLD	CYLD	Chapleau, Canada
YLE	CEM3	Wha Ti, Canada
YLH	CYLH	Lansdowne House, Canada
YLI	EFYL	Ylivieska Airport, Finland
YLJ	CYLJ	Meadow Lake, Canada
YLL	CYLL	Lloydminster, Canada
YLQ	CYLQ	La Tuque, Canada
YLR	CYLR	Leaf Rapids, Canada
YLS	CSH4	Lebel, Canada
YLT	CYLT	Alert, Canada
YLW	CYLW	Kelowna, Canada
YMA	CYMA	Mayo, Canada
YMB	CAD5	Merritt, Canada
YME	CYME	Matane, Canada
YMG	CYMG	Manitouwadge, Canada
YMH	CYMH	Marys Harbour, Canada
YMJ	CYMJ	Moose Jaw, Canada
YML	CYML	Charlevoix, Canada
YMM	CYMM	Ft Mc Murray, Canada
YMN	CYFT	Makkovik, Canada
YMO	CYMO	Moosonee, Canada
YMP	CAT5	Port Mc Neill, Canada

IATA	ICAO	Airport & Country
YMS	SPMS	Moises Benzaquen Rengifo, Peru
YMT	CYMT	Chapais, Canada
YMW	CYMW	Maniwaki, Canada
YMX	CYMX	Montreal Intl, Canada
YNA	CYNA	Natashquan, Canada
YNB	OEYN	Yanbu Domestic Airport, Saudi Arabia
YNC	CYNC	Wemindji, Canada
YND	CYND	Ottawa/Gatineau, Canada
YNE	CYNE	Norway House, Canada
YNH	CYNH	Hudson's Hope, Canada
YNJ	ZYYJ	Yanji Airport, China
YNL	CYNL	Points North Landing, Canada
YNM	CYNM	Matagami, Canada
YNS	CYHH	Nemiscau, Canada
YNT	ZSYT	Yantai Laishan Airport, China
YOC	CYOC	Old Crow, Canada
YOD	CYOD	Cold Lake, Canada
YOG	CNT3	Ogoki Post, Canada
YOH	CYOH	Oxford House, Canada
YOJ	CYOJ	High Level, Canada
YOL	DNYO	Yola, Nigeria
YOO	CYOO	Oshawa, Canada
YOP	CYOP	Rainbow Lake, Canada
YOS	CYOS	Billy Bishop Reg'l, Canada
YOW	CYOW	Ottawa, Canada
YPA	CYPA	Prince Albert, Canada
YPC	CYPC	Paulatuk, Canada
YPD	CNK4	Georgian Bay, Canada
YPE	CYPE	Peace River, Canada
YPG	CYPG	Southport, Canada
YPH	CYPH	Inukjuak, Canada
YPJ	CYLA	Aupaluk, Canada
YPL	CYPL	Pickle Lake, Canada
YPM	CYPM	Pikangikum, Canada
YPN	CYPN	Port Menier, Canada
YPO	CYPO	Peawanuck, Canada
YPQ	CYPQ	Peterborough, Canada
YPR	CYPR	Prince Rupert, Canada
YPS	CYPD	Port Hawkesbury, Canada
YPW	CYPW	Powell River, Canada
YPX	CYPX	Puvirnituq, Canada
YPY	CYPY	Ft Chipewyan, Canada
YPZ	CYPZ	Burns Lake, Canada
YQA	CYQA	Muskoka, Canada
YQB	CYQB	Quebec, Canada
YQC	CYHA	Quaqtaq, Canada
YQD	CYQD	The Pas, Canada
YQF	CYQF	Red Deer Industrial, Canada
YQG	CYQG	Windsor, Canada
YQH	CYQH	Watson Lake, Canada
YQI	CYQI	Yarmouth, Canada
YQK	CYQK	Kenora, Canada
YQL	CYQL	Lethbridge, Canada
YQM	CYQM	Moncton, Canada
YQN	CYQN	Nakina, Canada
YQQ	CYQQ	Comox, Canada
YQR	CYQR	Regina, Canada
YQS	CYQS	St Thomas Mun, Canada
YQT	CYQT	Thunder Bay, Canada
YQU	CYQU	Grande Prairie, Canada

IATA	ICAO	Airport & Country
YQV	CYQV	Yorkton, Canada
YQW	CYQW	North Battleford, Canada
YQX	CYQX	Gander Intl, Canada
YQY	CYQY	Sydney, Canada
YQZ	CYQZ	Quesnel, Canada
YRA	CEV4	Rae Lakes, Canada
YRB	CYRB	Resolute Bay, Canada
YRF	CYCA	Cartwright Nws, Canada
YRG	CCZ2	Rigolet, Canada
YRI	CYRI	Riviere, Canada
YRJ	CYRJ	Roberval, Canada
YRL	CYRL	Red Lake, Canada
YRM	CYRM	Rocky Mountain House, Canada
YRO	CYRO	Rockcliffe, Canada
YRQ	CYRQ	Trois, Canada
YRS	CYRS	Red Sucker Lake, Canada
YRT	CYRT	Rankin Inlet, Canada
YRV	CYRV	Revelstoke, Canada
YSB	CYSB	Sudbury, Canada
YSC	CYSC	Sherbrooke, Canada
YSD	CYSD	Suffield, Canada
YSE	CYSE	Squamish, Canada
YSF	CYSF	Stony Rapids, Canada
YSH	CYSH	Montague, Canada
YSJ	CYSJ	Saint John, Canada
YSK	CYSK	Sanikiluaq, Canada
YSL	CYSL	St, Canada
YSM	CYSM	Ft Smith, Canada
YSN	CZAM	Salmon Arm, Canada
YSO	CCD4	Postville, Canada
YSP	CYSP	Marathon, Canada
YSR	CYSR	Nanisivik, Canada
YST	CYST	St Theresa Point, Canada
YSU	CYSU	Summerside, Canada
YSY	CYSY	Sachs Harbour, Canada
YTA	CYTA	Pembroke, Canada
YTD	CZLQ	Thicket Portage, Canada
YTE	CYTE	Cape Dorset, Canada
YTF	CYTF	Alma, Canada
YTH	CYTH	Thompson, Canada
YTJ	CYTJ	Terrace Bay, Canada
YTL	CYTL	Big Trout Lake, Canada
YTQ	CYTQ	Tasiujaq, Canada
YTR	CYTR	Trenton, Canada
YTS	CYTS	Timmins, Canada
YTT	CJY3	Tisdale, Canada
YTX	CBM5	Telegraph Creek, Canada
YTZ	CYTZ	Toronto, Canada
YUB	CYUB	Tuktoyaktuk, Canada
YUD	CYMU	Umiujaq, Canada
YUL	CYUL	Montreal Intl, Canada
YUM	ZPLX	Luxi Mangshi Airport, China
YUM	KYUM	Yuma Intl / MCAS Yuma, USA
YUT	CYUT	Repulse Bay, Canada
YUX	CYUX	Hall Beach, Canada
YUY	CYUY	Rouyn, Canada
YVA	FMCN	Iconi, Comoros
YVB	CYVB	Bonaventure, Canada
YVC	CYVC	La Ronge, Canada
YVE	CYVK	Vernon, Canada
YVG	CYVG	Vermilion, Canada
YVM	CYVM	Qikiqtarjuaq, Canada
YVO	CYVO	Val, Canada
YVP	CYVP	Kuujjuaq, Canada
YVQ	CYVQ	Norman Wells, Canada
YVR	CYVR	Vancouver Intl, Canada
YVT	CYVT	Buffalo Narrows, Canada
YVV	CYVV	Wiarton, Canada
YVZ	CYVZ	Deer Lake, Canada
YWA	CYWA	Petawawa, Canada
YWB	CYKG	Kangiqsujuaq Wakeham Bay, Canada
YWG	CYWG	Winnipeg Intl, Canada
YWJ	CYWJ	Deline, Canada
YWK	CYWK	Wabush, Canada
YWL	CYWL	Williams Lake, Canada
YWM	CCA6	Williams Harbour, Canada
YWP	CYWP	Webequie, Canada
YWY	CYWY	Wrigley, Canada
YXC	CYXC	Cranbrook, Canada
YXD	CYXD	Edmonton City Center, Canada
YXE	CYXE	Saskatoon/Diefenbaker, Canada
YXH	CYXH	Medicine Hat, Canada
YXJ	CYXJ	Ft St John, Canada
YXK	CYXK	Rimouski, Canada
YXL	CYXL	Sioux Lookout, Canada
YXN	CYXN	Whale Cove, Canada
YXP	CYXP	Pangnirtung, Canada
YXQ	CYXQ	Beaver Creek, Canada
YXR	CYXR	Earlton, Canada
YXS	CYXS	Prince George, Canada
YXT	CYXT	Terrace, Canada
YXU	CYXU	London, Canada
YXX	CYXX	Abbotsford, Canada
YXY	CYXY	Whitehorse Intl, Canada
YXZ	CYXZ	Wawa, Canada
YYB	CYYB	North Bay, Canada
YYC	CYYC	Calgary Intl, Canada
YYD	CYYD	Smithers, Canada
YYE	CYYE	Ft Nelson, Canada
YYF	CYYF	Penticton, Canada
YYG	CYYG	Charlottetown, Canada
YYH	CYYH	Taloyoak, Canada
YYJ	CYYJ	Victoria Intl, Canada
YYL	CYYL	Lynn Lake, Canada
YYM	CYYM	Cowley, Canada
YYN	CYYN	Swift Current, Canada
YYQ	CYYQ	Churchill, Canada
YYR	CYYR	Goose, Canada
YYT	CYYT	St John's Intl, Canada
YYU	CYYU	Kapuskasing, Canada
YYW	CYYW	Armstrong, Canada
YYY	CYYY	Mont, Canada
YYZ	CYYZ	Toronto, Canada
YZE	CYZE	Gore Bay, Canada
YZF	CYZF	Yellowknife, Canada
YZG	CYZG	Salluit, Canada
YZH	CYZH	Slave Lake, Canada
YZP	CYZP	Sandspit, Canada
YZR	CYZR	Sarnia, Canada
YZS	CYZS	Coral Harbour, Canada

IATA	ICAO	Airport & Country
YZT	CYZT	Port Hardy, Canada
YZU	CYZU	Whitecourt, Canada
YZV	CYZV	Sept, Canada
YZW	CYZW	Teslin, Canada
YZX	CYZX	Greenwood, Canada
ZAC	CZAC	York Landing, Canada
ZAD	LDZD	Zadar Airport, Croatia
ZAG	LDZA	Zagreb Airport, Croatia
ZAH	OIZH	Zahedan Intl, Iran
ZAJ	OAZJ	Zaranj, Afghanistan
ZAL	SCVD	Pichoy, Chile
ZAM	RPMZ	Zamboanga Intl, Philippines
ZAO	LFCC	Cahors, France
ZAR	DNZA	Zaria, Nigeria
ZAT	ZPZT	Zhaotong Airport, China
ZAZ	LEZG	Zaragoza Airport, Spain
ZBF	CZBF	Bathurst, Canada
ZBM	CZBM	Bromont, Canada
ZBR	OIZC	Konarak Airport, Iran
ZBY	VLSB	Sayaboury, Laos
ZCL	MMZC	La Calera Airport, Mexico
ZCO	SCTC	Maquehue, Chile
ZEC	FASC	Secunda, South Africa
ZEL	CYJQ	Bella Bella, Canada
ZEM	CZEM	Eastmain River, Canada
ZER	VEZO	Zero Airport, India
ZFA	CZFA	Faro, Canada
ZFD	CZFD	Fond, Canada
ZFM	CZFM	Ft Mc Pherson, Canada
ZFN	CZFN	Tulita, Canada
ZFW	CEB5	Fairview, Canada
ZGC	ZLLL	Lanzhou Zhongchuan Airport, China
ZGF	CZGF	Grand Forks, Canada
ZGI	CZGI	Gods River, Canada
ZGM	FLNA	Ngoma, Zambia
ZGR	CZGR	Little Grand Rapids, Canada
ZHA	ZGZJ	Zhanjiang Airport, China
ZHP	CZHP	High Prairie, Canada
ZIC	SCTO	Victoria, Chile
ZIG	GOGG	Ziguinchor, Senegal

IATA	ICAO	Airport & Country
ZIH	MMZH	Ixtapa, Mexico
ZJG	CZJG	Jenpeg, Canada
ZJN	CZJN	Swan River, Canada
ZKB	FLKY	Kasaba Bay, Zambia
ZKE	CZKE	Kashechewan, Canada
ZKM	FOOS	Sette, Gabon
ZKP	FLKE	Kasompe, Zambia
ZLO	MMZO	Playa de Oro Intl, Mexico
ZLR	SCLN	Linares, Chile
ZMG	EDBM	Magdeburg, Germany
ZMH	CZML	108 Mile, Canada
ZMT	CZMT	Masset, Canada
ZND	DRZR	Zinder, Niger
ZNE	YNWN	Newman Airport, Australia
ZNZ	HTZA	Kisauni, Tanzania
ZOS	SCJO	Canal Bajo/Carlos H Siebert, Chile
ZPB	CZPB	Sachigo Lake, Canada
ZPC	SCPC	Pucon, Chile
ZPO	CZPO	Pinehouse Lake, Canada
ZQN	NZQN	Queenstown, New Zealand
ZRH	LSZH	Zurich Airport, Switzerland
ZRJ	CZRJ	Weagamow Lake, Canada
ZSA	MYSM	San Salvador Airport , Bahamas
ZSJ	CZSJ	Sandy Lake, Canada
ZSS	DISS	Sassandra, Ivory Coast
ZST	CZST	Stewart, Canada
ZTH	LGZA	Zakynthos Intl, Greece
ZTM	CZTM	Shamattawa, Canada
ZUC	CZUC	Ignace Mun, Canada
ZUD	SCAC	Pupelde, Chile
ZUH	ZGSD	Zhuhai Intl, China
ZUM	CZUM	Churchill Falls, Canada
ZVA	FMMN	Miandrivazo, Madagascar
ZVK	VLSK	Savannakhet, Laos
ZWA	FMND	Andapa, Madagascar
ZWL	CZWL	Wollaston Lake, Canada
ZYI	ZUZY	Zunyi Airport, China
ZYL	VGSY	Osmani Intl, Bangladesh
ZZE	LYUZ	Uzice Airport, Serbia
ZZU	FWUU	Mzuzu, Malawi

ICAO / IATA Airport Codes

ICAO	IATA	Airport & Country
AGGH	HIR	Honiara Intl, Solomon Islands
AGGM	MUA	Munda, Solomon Islands
ANAU	INU	Nauru Intl, Nauru
AYGA	GKA	Goroka, Papua New Guinea
AYLA	LAE	Nadzab, Papua New Guinea
AYMD	MAG	Madang, Papua New Guinea
AYMH	HGU	Mount Hagen, Papua New Guinea
AYPY	POM	Port Moresby, Papua New Guinea
AYRB	RAB	Rabaul, Papua New Guinea
AYWK	WWK	Wewak Intl, Papua New Guinea
BGAM	AGM	Angmagssalik Airport, Greenland
BGBW	UAK	Narssarssuaq Airport, Greenland
BGCH	JCH	Christianshab Airport, Greenland
BGCO	CNP	Constable Pynt Airport, Greenland
BGDU	DUN	Dundas Airport, Greenland
BGEM	JEG	Auisiait Airport, Greenland
BGFH	JFR	Frederikshab Airport, Greenland
BGGH	GOH	Nuuk Airport, Greenland
BGGN	JGO	Godhavn Airport, Greenland
BGHB	JHS	Holsteinsborg Airport, Greenland
BGJN	JAV	Jakobshavn Airport, Greenland
BGKA	QPW	Kangaatsiaq Airport, Greenland
BGKK	KUS	Kulusuk Airport, Greenland
BGNN	JNN	Nanortalik Airport, Greenland
BGNS	JNS	Narssaq Airport, Greenland
BGQA	NAQ	Qaanaaq Airport, Greenland
BGSC	OBY	Scoresbysund Airport, Greenland
BGSF	SFJ	Kangerlussuaq Airport, Greenland
BGTL	THU	Thule Air Base, Greenland
BGUM	UMD	Uummannaq Airport, Greenland
BGUP	JUV	Upernavik Airport, Greenland
BIAR	AEY	Akureyri Airport, Iceland
BIBL	BLO	Blonduos Airport, Iceland
BIEG	EGS	Egilsstaoir Airport, Iceland
BIHN	HFN	Hornafjorour Airport, Iceland
BIIS	IFJ	Isafjorour Airport, Iceland
BIKF	KEF	Keflavik Intl, Iceland
BIKR	SAK	Alexander Airport, Iceland
BINF	NOR	Norofjorour Airport, Iceland
BIPA	PFJ	Patreksfjorour Airport, Iceland
BIRG	RFN	Raufarhofn Airport, Iceland
BIRK	RKV	Reykjavik Airport, Iceland
BISI	SIJ	Siglufjordur Airport, Iceland
BIST	SYK	Stykkisholmur Airport, Iceland
BITE	TEY	Pingeyri Airport, Iceland
BITH	THO	Sauoanes Airport, Iceland
BIVM	VEY	Vestmannaeyjar Airport, Iceland
CAB5	YBM	Bronson Creek, Canada
CAD5	YMB	Merritt, Canada
CAH3	YCA	Courtenay, Canada
CAJ4	YAA	Anahim Lake, Canada
CAM3	DUQ	Duncan, Canada
CAP3	YHS	Sechelt, Canada
CAT5	YMP	Port Mc Neill, Canada
CBM5	YTX	Telegraph Creek, Canada
CBX5	TNS	Cantung, Canada
CBX7	TUX	Tumbler Ridge, Canada

ICAO	IATA	Airport & Country
CCA6	YWM	Williams Harbour, Canada
CCB4	YDI	Davis Inlet, Canada
CCD4	YSO	Postville, Canada
CCE4	YBI	Black Tickle, Canada
CCH4	YHG	Charlottetown, Canada
CCK4	YFX	Fox Harbour, Canada
CCP4	YHA	Port Hope Simpson, Canada
CCZ2	YRG	Rigolet, Canada
CEB3	YCK	Colville Lake, Canada
CEB5	ZFW	Fairview, Canada
CEC4	YJA	Jasper, Canada
CEM3	YLE	Wha Ti, Canada
CEQ5	YGC	Grande Cache, Canada
CER3	YDC	Industrial, Canada
CEV4	YRA	Rae Lakes, Canada
CFC4	XMP	Macmillan Pass, Canada
CFJ2	YFJ	Wekweti, Canada
CJL2	YDJ	Hatchet Lake, Canada
CJL8	YDU	Kasba Lake, Canada
CJS3	XCL	Cluff Lake, Canada
CJV7	SUR	Summer Beaver, Canada
CJY3	YTT	Tisdale, Canada
CKB6	YAX	Wapakeka, Canada
CKL3	WNN	Wunnumin Lake, Canada
CNE3	XBE	Bearskin Lake, Canada
CNK4	YPD	Georgian Bay, Canada
CNL3	XBR	Brockville, Canada
CNM5	KIF	Kingfisher Lake, Canada
CNS7	YKD	Kincardine, Canada
CNT3	YOG	Ogoki Post, Canada
CNZ3	XCM	Chatham, Canada
CPV8	KEW	Keewaywin, Canada
CSH4	YLS	Lebel, Canada
CSR8	SSQ	La Sarre, Canada
CYAC	YAC	Cat Lake, Canada
CYAG	YAG	Ft Frances Mun, Canada
CYAL	YAL	Alert Bay, Canada
CYAM	YAM	Sault Ste Marie, Canada
CYAQ	XKS	Kasabonika, Canada
CYAS	YKG	Kangirsuk, Canada
CYAT	YAT	Attawapiskat, Canada
CYAW	YAW	Halifax, Canada
CYAY	YAY	St Anthony, Canada
CYAZ	YAZ	Tofino, Canada
CYBB	YBB	Pelly Bay, Canada
CYBC	YBC	Baie, Canada
CYBD	QBC	Bella Coola, Canada
CYBE	YBE	Uranium City, Canada
CYBF	YBY	Bonnyville, Canada
CYBG	YBG	Bagotville, Canada
CYBK	YBK	Baker Lake, Canada
CYBL	YBL	Campbell River, Canada
CYBQ	XTL	Tadoule Lake, Canada
CYBR	YBR	Brandon Muni, Canada
CYBT	YBT	Brochet, Canada
CYBV	YBV	Berens River, Canada
CYCA	YRF	Cartwright Nws, Canada

ICAO	IATA	Airport & Country
CYCB	YCB	Cambridge Bay, Canada
CYCC	YCC	Cornwall Regl, Canada
CYCD	YCD	Nanaimo, Canada
CYCE	YCE	Huron, Canada
CYCG	YCG	Castlegar, Canada
CYCH	YCH	Miramichi, Canada
CYCL	YCL	Charlo, Canada
CYCN	YCN	Cochrane, Canada
CYCO	YCO	Kugluktuk, Canada
CYCQ	YCQ	Chetwynd, Canada
CYCR	YCR	Sinclair Meml, Canada
CYCS	YCS	Chesterfield Inlet, Canada
CYCT	YCT	Coronation, Canada
CYCW	YCW	Chilliwack, Canada
CYCY	YCY	Clyde River, Canada
CYCZ	YCZ	Fairmont Hot Springs, Canada
CYDA	YDA	Dawson, Canada
CYDB	YDB	Burwash, Canada
CYDF	YDF	Deer Lake, Canada
CYDL	YDL	Dease Lake, Canada
CYDM	XRR	Ross River, Canada
CYDN	YDN	Barker, Canada
CYDO	YDO	Dolbeau, Canada
CYDP	YDP	Nain, Canada
CYDQ	YDQ	Dawson Creek, Canada
CYEG	YEG	Edmonton Intl, Canada
CYEK	YEK	Arviat, Canada
CYEL	YEL	Elliot Lake Mun, Canada
CYEM	YEM	Manitoulin East Muni., Canada
CYEN	YEN	Estevan, Canada
CYER	YER	Ft Severn, Canada
CYET	YET	Edson, Canada
CYEU	YEU	Eureka, Canada
CYEV	YEV	Zubko, Canada
CYEY	YEY	Amos Mun, Canada
CYFA	YFA	Ft Albany, Canada
CYFB	YFB	Iqaluit, Canada
CYFC	YFC	Fredericton, Canada
CYFH	YFH	Ft Hope, Canada
CYFO	YFO	Flin Flon, Canada
CYFR	YFR	Ft Resolution, Canada
CYFS	YFS	Ft Simpson, Canada
CYFT	YMN	Makkovik, Canada
CYGB	YGB	Gillies Bay, Canada
CYGH	YGH	Ft Good Hope, Canada
CYGK	YGK	Kingston, Canada
CYGL	YGL	La Grande Riviere, Canada
CYGM	YGM	Gimli Industrial Park, Canada
CYGO	YGO	Gods Lake Narrows, Canada
CYGP	YGP	Gaspe, Canada
CYGQ	YGQ	Greenstone Regl, Canada
CYGR	YGR	Iles, Canada
CYGT	YGT	Igloolik, Canada
CYGV	YGV	Havre St, Canada
CYGW	YGW	Kuujjuarapik, Canada
CYGX	YGX	Gillam, Canada
CYGZ	YGZ	Grise Fiord, Canada
CYHA	YQC	Quaqtaq, Canada
CYHB	YHB	Hudson Bay, Canada
CYHD	YHD	Dryden Regl, Canada

ICAO	IATA	Airport & Country
CYHE	YHE	Hope, Canada
CYHF	YHF	Hearst Mun, Canada
CYHH	YNS	Nemiscau, Canada
CYHI	YHI	Holman, Canada
CYHK	YHK	Gjoa Haven, Canada
CYHM	YHM	Hamilton, Canada
CYHN	YHN	Hornepayne Mun, Canada
CYHO	YHO	Hopedale, Canada
CYHR	YHR	Chevery, Canada
CYHT	YHT	Haines Junction, Canada
CYHU	YHU	Montreal, Canada
CYHY	YHY	Hay River, Canada
CYHZ	YHZ	Halifax Intl, Canada
CYIB	YIB	Atikokan Mun, Canada
CYID	YDG	Digby, Canada
CYIF	YIF	St, Canada
CYIK	YIK	Ivujivik, Canada
CYIO	YIO	Pond Inlet, Canada
CYIV	YIV	Island Lake, Canada
CYJF	YJF	Ft Liard, Canada
CYJN	YJN	St, Canada
CYJQ	ZEL	Bella Bella, Canada
CYJT	YJT	Stephenville, Canada
CYKA	YKA	Kamloops, Canada
CYKC	YKC	Collins Bay, Canada
CYKD	LAK	Aklavik, Canada
CYKF	YKF	Kitchener/Waterloo Regl, Canada
CYKG	YWB	Kangiqsujuaq Wakeham Bay Canada
CYKJ	YKJ	Key Lake, Canada
CYKL	YKL	Schefferville, Canada
CYKO	AKV	Akulivik, Canada
CYKQ	YKQ	Waskaganish, Canada
CYKX	YKX	Kirkland Lake, Canada
CYKY	YKY	Kindersley, Canada
CYKZ	YKZ	Toronto, Canada
CYLA	YPJ	Aupaluk, Canada
CYLB	YLB	Lac La Biche, Canada
CYLD	YLD	Chapleau, Canada
CYLH	YLH	Lansdowne House, Canada
CYLJ	YLJ	Meadow Lake, Canada
CYLL	YLL	Lloydminster, Canada
CYLQ	YLQ	La Tuque, Canada
CYLR	YLR	Leaf Rapids, Canada
CYLT	YLT	Alert, Canada
CYLU	XGR	Kangiqsualujjuaq, Canada
CYLW	YLW	Kelowna, Canada
CYMA	YMA	Mayo, Canada
CYME	YME	Matane, Canada
CYMG	YMG	Manitouwadge, Canada
CYMH	YMH	Marys Harbour, Canada
CYMJ	YMJ	Moose Jaw, Canada
CYML	YML	Charlevoix, Canada
CYMM	YMM	Ft Mc Murray, Canada
CYMO	YMO	Moosonee, Canada
CYMT	YMT	Chapais, Canada
CYMU	YUD	Umiujaq, Canada
CYMW	YMW	Maniwaki, Canada
CYMX	YMX	Montreal Intl, Canada
CYNA	YNA	Natashquan, Canada
CYNC	YNC	Wemindji, Canada

ICAO	IATA	Airport & Country
CYND	YND	Ottawa/Gatineau, Canada
CYNE	YNE	Norway House, Canada
CYNH	YNH	Hudson's Hope, Canada
CYNL	YNL	Points North Landing, Canada
CYNM	YNM	Matagami, Canada
CYOC	YOC	Old Crow, Canada
CYOD	YOD	Cold Lake, Canada
CYOH	YOH	Oxford House, Canada
CYOJ	YOJ	High Level, Canada
CYOO	YOO	Oshawa, Canada
CYOP	YOP	Rainbow Lake, Canada
CYOS	YOS	Billy Bishop Reg'l, Canada
CYOW	YOW	Ottawa, Canada
CYPA	YPA	Prince Albert, Canada
CYPC	YPC	Paulatuk, Canada
CYPD	YPS	Port Hawkesbury, Canada
CYPE	YPE	Peace River, Canada
CYPG	YPG	Southport, Canada
CYPH	YPH	Inukjuak, Canada
CYPL	YPL	Pickle Lake, Canada
CYPM	YPM	Pikangikum, Canada
CYPN	YPN	Port Menier, Canada
CYPO	YPO	Peawanuck, Canada
CYPQ	YPQ	Peterborough, Canada
CYPR	YPR	Prince Rupert, Canada
CYPW	YPW	Powell River, Canada
CYPX	YPX	Puvirnituq, Canada
CYPY	YPY	Ft Chipewyan, Canada
CYPZ	YPZ	Burns Lake, Canada
CYQA	YQA	Muskoka, Canada
CYQB	YQB	Quebec, Canada
CYQD	YQD	The Pas, Canada
CYQF	YQF	Red Deer Industrial, Canada
CYQG	YQG	Windsor, Canada
CYQH	YQH	Watson Lake, Canada
CYQI	YQI	Yarmouth, Canada
CYQK	YQK	Kenora, Canada
CYQL	YQL	Lethbridge, Canada
CYQM	YQM	Moncton, Canada
CYQN	YQN	Nakina, Canada
CYQQ	YQQ	Comox, Canada
CYQR	YQR	Regina, Canada
CYQS	YQS	St Thomas Mun, Canada
CYQT	YQT	Thunder Bay, Canada
CYQU	YQU	Grande Prairie, Canada
CYQV	YQV	Yorkton, Canada
CYQW	YQW	North Battleford, Canada
CYQX	YQX	Gander Intl, Canada
CYQY	YQY	Sydney, Canada
CYQZ	YQZ	Quesnel, Canada
CYRB	YRB	Resolute Bay, Canada
CYRI	YRI	Riviere, Canada
CYRJ	YRJ	Roberval, Canada
CYRL	YRL	Red Lake, Canada
CYRM	YRM	Rocky Mountain House, Canada
CYRO	YRO	Rockcliffe, Canada
CYRQ	YRQ	Trois, Canada
CYRS	YRS	Red Sucker Lake, Canada
CYRT	YRT	Rankin Inlet, Canada
CYRV	YRV	Revelstoke, Canada

ICAO	IATA	Airport & Country
CYSB	YSB	Sudbury, Canada
CYSC	YSC	Sherbrooke, Canada
CYSD	YSD	Suffield, Canada
CYSE	YSE	Squamish, Canada
CYSF	YSF	Stony Rapids, Canada
CYSH	YSH	Montague, Canada
CYSJ	YSJ	Saint John, Canada
CYSK	YSK	Sanikiluaq, Canada
CYSL	YSL	St, Canada
CYSM	YSM	Ft Smith, Canada
CYSN	YCM	St Catharines, Canada
CYSP	YSP	Marathon, Canada
CYSR	YSR	Nanisivik, Canada
CYST	YST	St Theresa Point, Canada
CYSU	YSU	Summerside, Canada
CYSY	YSY	Sachs Harbour, Canada
CYTA	YTA	Pembroke, Canada
CYTE	YTE	Cape Dorset, Canada
CYTF	YTF	Alma, Canada
CYTH	YTH	Thompson, Canada
CYTJ	YTJ	Terrace Bay, Canada
CYTL	YTL	Big Trout Lake, Canada
CYTQ	YTQ	Tasiujaq, Canada
CYTR	YTR	Trenton, Canada
CYTS	YTS	Timmins, Canada
CYTZ	YTZ	Toronto, Canada
CYUB	YUB	Tuktoyaktuk, Canada
CYUL	YUL	Montreal Intl, Canada
CYUT	YUT	Repulse Bay, Canada
CYUX	YUX	Hall Beach, Canada
CYUY	YUY	Rouyn, Canada
CYVB	YVB	Bonaventure, Canada
CYVC	YVC	La Ronge, Canada
CYVG	YVG	Vermilion, Canada
CYVK	YVE	Vernon, Canada
CYVM	YVM	Qikiqtarjuaq, Canada
CYVO	YVO	Val, Canada
CYVP	YVP	Kuujjuaq, Canada
CYVQ	YVQ	Norman Wells, Canada
CYVR	YVR	Vancouver Intl, Canada
CYVT	YVT	Buffalo Narrows, Canada
CYVV	YVV	Wiarton, Canada
CYVZ	YVZ	Deer Lake, Canada
CYWA	YWA	Petawawa, Canada
CYWG	YWG	Winnipeg Intl, Canada
CYWJ	YWJ	Deline, Canada
CYWK	YWK	Wabush, Canada
CYWL	YWL	Williams Lake, Canada
CYWP	YWP	Webequie, Canada
CYWY	YWY	Wrigley, Canada
CYXC	YXC	Cranbrook, Canada
CYXD	YXD	Edmonton City Center, Canada
CYXE	YXE	Saskatoon/Diefenbaker, Canada
CYXH	YXH	Medicine Hat, Canada
CYXJ	YXJ	Ft St John, Canada
CYXK	YXK	Rimouski, Canada
CYXL	YXL	Sioux Lookout, Canada
CYXN	YXN	Whale Cove, Canada
CYXP	YXP	Pangnirtung, Canada
CYXQ	YXQ	Beaver Creek, Canada

ICAO	IATA	Airport & Country
CYXR	YXR	Earlton, Canada
CYXS	YXS	Prince George, Canada
CYXT	YXT	Terrace, Canada
CYXU	YXU	London, Canada
CYXX	YXX	Abbotsford, Canada
CYXY	YXY	Whitehorse Intl, Canada
CYXZ	YXZ	Wawa, Canada
CYYB	YYB	North Bay, Canada
CYYC	YYC	Calgary Intl, Canada
CYYD	YYD	Smithers, Canada
CYYE	YYE	Ft Nelson, Canada
CYYF	YYF	Penticton, Canada
CYYG	YYG	Charlottetown, Canada
CYYH	YYH	Taloyoak, Canada
CYYJ	YYJ	Victoria Intl, Canada
CYYL	YYL	Lynn Lake, Canada
CYYM	YYM	Cowley, Canada
CYYN	YYN	Swift Current, Canada
CYYQ	YYQ	Churchill, Canada
CYYR	YYR	Goose, Canada
CYYT	YYT	St John's Intl, Canada
CYYU	YYU	Kapuskasing, Canada
CYYW	YYW	Armstrong, Canada
CYYY	YYY	Mont, Canada
CYYZ	YYZ	Toronto, Canada
CYZE	YZE	Gore Bay, Canada
CYZF	YZF	Yellowknife, Canada
CYZG	YZG	Salluit, Canada
CYZH	YZH	Slave Lake, Canada
CYZP	YZP	Sandspit, Canada
CYZR	YZR	Sarnia, Canada
CYZS	YZS	Coral Harbour, Canada
CYZT	YZT	Port Hardy, Canada
CYZU	YZU	Whitecourt, Canada
CYZV	YZV	Sept, Canada
CYZW	YZW	Teslin, Canada
CYZX	YZX	Greenwood, Canada
CZAC	ZAC	York Landing, Canada
CZAM	YSN	Salmon Arm, Canada
CZBB	YDT	Boundary Bay, Canada
CZBD	ILF	Ilford, Canada
CZBF	ZBF	Bathurst, Canada
CZBM	ZBM	Bromont, Canada
CZEE	KES	Kelsey, Canada
CZEM	ZEM	Eastmain River, Canada
CZFA	ZFA	Faro, Canada
CZFD	ZFD	Fond, Canada
CZFG	XPK	Pukatawagan, Canada
CZFM	ZFM	Ft Mc Pherson, Canada
CZFN	ZFN	Tulita, Canada
CZGF	ZGF	Grand Forks, Canada
CZGI	ZGI	Gods River, Canada
CZGR	ZGR	Little Grand Rapids, Canada
CZHP	ZHP	High Prairie, Canada
CZJG	ZJG	Jenpeg, Canada
CZJN	ZJN	Swan River, Canada
CZKE	ZKE	Kashechewan, Canada
CZLQ	YTD	Thicket Portage, Canada
CZMD	MSA	Muskrat Dam, Canada
CZML	ZMH	108 Mile, Canada

ICAO	IATA	Airport & Country
CZMN	PIW	Pikwitonei, Canada
CZMT	ZMT	Masset, Canada
CZNG	XPP	Poplar River, Canada
CZPB	ZPB	Sachigo Lake, Canada
CZPC	WPC	Pincher Creek, Canada
CZPO	ZPO	Pinehouse Lake, Canada
CZRJ	ZRJ	Weagamow Lake, Canada
CZSJ	ZSJ	Sandy Lake, Canada
CZSN	XSI	South Indian Lake, Canada
CZST	ZST	Stewart, Canada
CZTA	YDV	Bloodvein River, Canada
CZTM	ZTM	Shamattawa, Canada
CZUC	ZUC	Ignace Mun, Canada
CZUM	ZUM	Churchill Falls, Canada
CZWH	XLB	Lac Brochet, Canada
CZWL	ZWL	Wollaston Lake, Canada
DAAD	BUJ	Bou Saada Airport, Algeria
DAAE	BJA	Bejaia, Algeria
DAAG	ALG	Algiers, Algeria
DAAJ	DJG	Djanet, Algeria
DAAT	TMR	Tamanrasset, Algeria
DAAV	GJL	Jijel, Algeria
DABB	AAE	Annaba, Algeria
DABC	CZL	Constantine, Algeria
DABS	TEE	Tebessa, Algeria
DAOB	TID	Tiaret, Algeria
DAON	TLM	Messali El Hadj Airport, Algeria
DAOO	ORN	Ouran, Algeria
DATG	INF	In Guezzam Airport, Algeria
DATM	BMW	Bordj Mokhtar Airport, Algeria
DAUA	AZR	Adrar, Algeria
DAUE	ELG	El Golea Airport, Algeria
DAUG	GHA	Ghardaia, Algeria
DAUH	HME	Hassi Messaoud, Algeria
DAUI	INZ	In Salah Airport, Algeria
DAUK	TGR	Touggourt, Algeria
DAUO	ELU	El Oued, Algeria
DAUT	TMX	Timimoun Airport, Algeria
DAUU	OGX	Ouargla Airport, Algeria
DAUZ	IAM	Zarzaitine, Algeria
DBBB	COO	Cadjehoun, Benin
DBBK	KDC	Kandi, Benin
DBBN	NAE	Natitingou, Benin
DBBP	PKO	Parakou, Benin
DFCC	OUG	Ouahigouya, Burkina Faso
DFEE	DOR	Dori Ville, Burkina Faso
DFEF	FNG	Fada N'Gourma, Burkina Faso
DFEG	XGG	Gorom, Burkina Faso
DFEL	XKA	Kantchari, Burkina Faso
DFET	TEG	Tenkodogo, Burkina Faso
DFFD	OUA	Ouagadougou, Burkina Faso
DFOB	BNR	Banfora, Burkina Faso
DFOD	DGU	Dedougou, Burkina Faso
DFOG	XGA	Amilcar Cabral, Burkina Faso
DFON	XNU	Nouna, Burkina Faso
DFOO	BOY	Bobo, Burkina Faso
DGAA	ACC	Kotoka Intl, Ghana
DGLE	TML	Tamale, Ghana
DGSI	KMS	Kumasi, Ghana
DGSN	NYI	Sunyani, Ghana

ICAO	IATA	Airport & Country
DGTK	TKD	Takoradi, Ghana
DIAP	ABJ	Felix Houphouet, Ivory Coast
DIAU	OGO	Abengourou, Ivory Coast
DIBI	BXI	Boundiali, Ivory Coast
DIBK	BYK	Bouake, Ivory Coast
DIBN	BQO	Tehini, Ivory Coast
DIBU	BDK	Soko, Ivory Coast
DIDK	DIM	Dimbokro Ville, Ivory Coast
DIDL	DJO	Daloa, Ivory Coast
DIFK	FEK	Ferkessedougou, Ivory Coast
DIGL	GGO	Guiglo, Ivory Coast
DIGN	BBV	Nero, Ivory Coast
DIKO	HGO	Korhogo, Ivory Coast
DIMN	MJC	Man, Ivory Coast
DIOD	KEO	Odienne, Ivory Coast
DIOF	OFI	Ouango Fitini, Ivory Coast
DISP	SPY	San Pedro, Ivory Coast
DISS	ZSS	Sassandra, Ivory Coast
DITB	TXU	Tabou, Ivory Coast
DITM	TOZ	Mahana, Ivory Coast
DIYO	ASK	Yamoussoukro, Ivory Coast
DNAA	ABV	Nnamdi Azikiwe, Nigeria
DNAK	AKR	Akure, Nigeria
DNBE	BNI	Benin, Nigeria
DNCA	CBQ	Calabar, Nigeria
DNEN	ENU	Enugu, Nigeria
DNIB	IBA	New Ibadan, Nigeria
DNIL	ILR	Ilorin, Nigeria
DNJO	JOS	Jos, Nigeria
DNKA	KAD	New Kaduna, Nigeria
DNKN	KAN	Mallam Aminu Kano, Nigeria
DNMA	MIU	Maiduguri, Nigeria
DNMM	LOS	Murtala Muhammed, Nigeria
DNMN	MXJ	Minna, Nigeria
DNPO	PHC	Port Harcourt, Nigeria
DNSO	SKO	Siddiq Abubakar Iii Intl, Nigeria
DNYO	YOL	Yola, Nigeria
DNZA	ZAR	Zaria, Nigeria
DRRM	MFQ	Maradi, Niger
DRRN	NIM	Diori Hamani, Niger
DRRT	THZ	Tahoua, Niger
DRZA	AJY	Manu Dayak, Niger
DRZR	ZND	Zinder, Niger
DTKA	TBJ	Tabarka 7 Novembre, Tunesia
DTMB	MIR	Habib Bourguiba, Tunesia
DTTA	TUN	Carthage, Tunesia
DTTF	GAF	Ksar, Tunesia
DTTJ	DJE	Zarzis, Tunesia
DTTR	EBM	El Borma, Tunesia
DTTX	SFA	Thyna, Tunesia
DTTZ	TOE	Nefta, Tunesia
DXNG	LRL	Niamtougou, Togo
DXXX	LFW	Tokoin, Togo
EBAW	ANR	Deurne Airport, Belgium
EBBR	BRU	Brussels National Airport, Belgium
EBCI	CRL	Brussels South Charleroi, Belgium
EBKT	KJK	Kortrijk, Belgium
EBLG	LGG	Liege Airport, Belgium
EBOS	OST	Ostend, Belgium
EDAC	AOC	Altenburg, Germany

ICAO	IATA	Airport & Country
EDAH	HDF	Heringsdorf, Germany
EDAH	HDF	Heringsdorf, Germany
EDBH	BBH	Ostseeflughafen Stralsund, Germany
EDBM	ZMG	Magdeburg, Germany
EDDB	SXF	Berlin Schonefeld, Germany
EDDC	DRS	Flughafen Dresden, Germany
EDDE	ERF	Erfurt, Germany
EDDF	FRA	Frankfurt am Main, Germany
EDDG	FMO	Munster, Germany
EDDH	HAM	Hamburg, Germany
EDDI	THF	Berlin Tempelhof, Germany
EDDK	CGN	Koln – Bonn, Germany
EDDL	DUS	Dusseldorf International, Germany
EDDM	MUC	Munchen, Germany
EDDN	NUE	Nurnberg, Germany
EDDP	LEJ	Leipzig, Germany
EDDR	SCN	Saarbrucken, Germany
EDDS	STR	Stuttgart, Germany
EDDT	TXL	Berlin Tegel, Germany
EDDV	HAJ	Hannover, Germany
EDDW	BRE	Airport Bremen, Germany
EDFH	HHN	Frankfurt, Germany
EDFM	MHG	Mannheim, Germany
EDGS	SGE	Siegerlandflughafen, Germany
EDHI	XFW	Finkenwerder, Germany
EDHK	KEL	Kiel, Germany
EDHL	LBC	Lubeck, Germany
EDJA	FMM	Allgau Airport / Memmingen, Germany
EDLE	ESS	Essen – Mulheim, Germany
EDLI	BFE	Bielefeld, Germany
EDLN	MGL	Monchengladbach, Germany
EDLP	PAD	Paderborn, Germany
EDLV	NRN	Airport Weeze, Germany
EDLW	DTM	Dortmund Airport 21, Germany
EDMA	AGB	Augsburg, Germany
EDMO	OBI	Oberpfaffenhofen, Germany
EDNY	FDH	Friedrichshafen, Germany
EDOP	SZW	Schwerin – Parchim, Germany
EDQD	BYU	Bayreuth, Germany
EDQM	HOQ	Hof, Germany
EDSB	FKB	Karlsruhe/Baden, Germany
EDTL	LHA	Lahr, Germany
EDVE	BWE	Flughafen Braunschweig, Germany
EDVK	KSF	Kassel, Germany
EDWB	BRV	Bremerhaven, Germany
EDWE	EME	Emden, Germany
EDWG	AGE	Wangerooge, Germany
EDWI	WVN	Wilhelmshaven, Germany
EDWJ	JUI	Juist, Germany
EDWR	BMK	Borkum, Germany
EDWY	NRD	Norderney, Germany
EDXB	HEI	Heide, Germany
EDXH	HGL	Helgoland, Germany
EDXW	GWT	Sylt, Germany
EDXY	OHR	Wyk, Germany
EEKA	KDL	Kardla Airport, Estonia
EEKE	URE	Kuressaare Airport, Estonia
EEPU	EPU	Parnu Airport, Estonia
EETN	TLL	Tallinn Airport, Estonia
EETU	TAY	Tartu Airport, Estonia

ICAO	IATA	Airport & Country
EFET	ENF	Enontekio Airport, Finland
EFHF	HEM	Helsinki, Finland
EFHK	HEL	Helsinki, Finland
EFHV	HYV	Hyvinkaa Airport, Finland
EFIL	SJY	Seinajoki Airport, Finland
EFIT	KTQ	Kitee Airport, Finland
EFIV	IVL	Ivalo Airport, Finland
EFJO	JOE	Joensuu Airport, Finland
EFJY	JYV	Jyvaskyla Airport, Finland
EFKA	KAU	Kauhava Airport, Finland
EFKE	KEM	Kemi, Finland
EFKI	KAJ	Kajaani Airport, Finland
EFKJ	KHJ	Kauhajoki Airport, Finland
EFKK	KOK	Kruunupyy Airport, Finland
EFKS	KAO	Kuusamo Airport, Finland
EFKT	KTT	Kittila Airport, Finland
EFKU	KUO	Kuopio Airport, Finland
EFLP	LPP	Lappeenranta Airport, Finland
EFMA	MHQ	Mariehamn Airport, Finland
EFMI	MIK	Mikkeli Airport, Finland
EFOU	OUL	Oulu Airport, Finland
EFPO	POR	Pori Airport, Finland
EFRO	RVN	Rovaniemi Airport, Finland
EFSA	SVL	Savonlinna Airport, Finland
EFSO	SOT	Sodankyla Airport, Finland
EFTP	TMP	Tampere, Finland
EFTU	TKU	Turku Airport, Finland
EFVA	VAA	Vaasa Airport, Finland
EFVR	VRK	Varkaus Airport, Finland
EFYL	YLI	Ylivieska Airport, Finland
EGAA	BFS	Belfast Intl, United Kingdom
EGAB	ENK	Enniskillen, United Kingdom
EGAC	BHD	Belfast City Airport, United Kingdom
EGAE	LDY	City of Derry Airport, United Kingdom
EGBB	BHX	Birmingham Intl, United Kingdom
EGBE	CVT	Coventry Airport, United Kingdom
EGBJ	GLO	Gloucester Airport, United Kingdom
EGBK	ORM	Sywell Aerodrome, United Kingdom
EGBN	NQT	Nottingham Airport, United Kingdom
EGCC	MAN	Manchester Intl, United Kingdom
EGCN	DSA	Doncaster Sheffield, United Kingdom
EGDJ	UPV	Upavon Airfield, United Kingdom
EGDQ	NQY	Newquay Cornwall, United Kingdom
EGEC	CAL	Campbeltown Airport, United Kingdom
EGEH	WHS	Whalsay Airport, United Kingdom
EGEN	NRL	North Ronaldsay, Isle of Man
EGEP	PPW	Papa Westray Airport, Orkney isles
EGET	LWK	Tingwall Airport, United Kingdom
EGEW	WRY	Westray Airport, United Kingdom
EGFE	HAW	Haverfordwest, United Kingdom
EGFF	CWL	Cardiff Intl, United Kingdom
EGFH	SWS	Swansea Airport, United Kingdom
EGGD	BRS	Bristol Intl, United Kingdom
EGGP	LPL	Liverpool, United Kingdom
EGGW	LTN	London Luton Airport, United Kingdom
EGHC	LEQ	Land's End Airport, United Kingdom
EGHD	PLH	Plymouth City Airport, United Kingdom
EGHE	ISC	St. Mary's Airport, United Kingdom
EGHH	BOH	Bournemouth Airport, United Kingdom
EGHI	SOU	Southampton Airport, United Kingdom

ICAO	IATA	Airport & Country
EGHJ	BBP	Bembridge Airport, United Kingdom
EGHL	QLA	Lasham Airfield, United Kingdom
EGJA	ACI	Alderney Airport, United Kingdom
EGJB	GCI	Guernsey Airport, United Kingdom
EGJJ	JER	Jersey Airport, United Kingdom
EGKA	ESH	Shoreham Airport, United Kingdom
EGKB	BQH	Biggin Hill Airport, United Kingdom
EGKK	LGW	London Gatwick, United Kingdom
EGKR	KRH	Redhill Airport, United Kingdom
EGLC	LCY	London City Airport, United Kingdom
EGLF	FAB	Farnborough Airfield, United Kingdom
EGLK	BBS	Blackbushe Airport, United Kingdom
EGLL	LHR	London Heathrow, United Kingdom
EGMC	SEN	Southend Airport, United Kingdom
EGMD	LYX	Ashford Airport, United Kingdom
EGMH	MSE	Kent Intl, United Kingdom
EGNC	CAX	Carlisle Airport, United Kingdom
EGNH	BLK	Blackpool Intl, United Kingdom
EGNJ	HUY	Humberside Airport, United Kingdom
EGNL	BWF	Barrow/, United Kingdom
EGNM	LBA	Leeds Bradford Intl, United Kingdom
EGNR	CEG	Hawarden Airport, United Kingdom
EGNS	IOM	Isle of Man Airport, United Kingdom
EGNT	NCL	Newcastle Airport, United Kingdom
EGNV	MME	Durham Tees Valley, United Kingdom
EGNX	EMA	East Midlands Airport, United Kingdom
EGPA	KOI	Kirkwall Airport, United Kingdom
EGPB	LSI	Sumburgh Airport, United Kingdom
EGPC	WIC	Wick Airport, United Kingdom
EGPD	ABZ	Aberdeen Airport, United Kingdom
EGPE	INV	Inverness Airport, United Kingdom
EGPF	GLA	Glasgow Intl, United Kingdom
EGPH	EDI	Edinburgh Airport, United Kingdom
EGPI	ILY	Islay Airport, United Kingdom
EGPK	PIK	Glasgow Prestwick, United Kingdom
EGPL	BEB	Benbecula Airport, United Kingdom
EGPM	SCS	Scatsta Airport, United Kingdom
EGPN	DND	Dundee Airport, United Kingdom
EGPO	SYY	Stornoway Airport, United Kingdom
EGPR	BRR	Barra Airport, United Kingdom
EGPT	PSL	Perth Airport , United Kingdom
EGPU	TRE	Tiree Airport, United Kingdom
EGSC	CBG	Cambridge City, United Kingdom
EGSH	NWI	Norwich Intl, United Kingdom
EGSS	STN	London Stansted, United Kingdom
EGSY	SZE	Sheffield City Airport, United Kingdom
EGTE	EXT	Exeter Intl, United Kingdom
EGTG	FZO	Filton Aerodrome, United Kingdom
EGTK	OXF	Oxford Airport, United Kingdom
EGTO	RCS	Rochester Airport, United Kingdom
EGYP	MPN	Mount Pleasant, Falkland Islands
EHAM	AMS	Amsterdam Schiphol, Netherlands
EHBK	MST	Maastricht Aachen, Netherlands
EHGG	GRQ	Groningen Airport Eelde, Netherlands
EHLE	LEY	Lelystad Airport, Netherlands
EHRD	RTM	Rotterdam Airport, Netherlands
EHTW	ENS	Enschede Airport Twente, Netherlands
EICA	NNR	Connemara Regional Airport, Ireland
EICK	ORK	Cork Intl, Ireland

ICAO	IATA	Airport & Country
EICM	GWY	Galway Airport, Ireland
EIDL	CFN	Donegal Airport, Ireland
EIDW	DUB	Dublin Intl, Ireland
EIKN	NOC	Knock Intl, Ireland
EIKY	KIR	Kerry Airport, Ireland
EINN	SNN	Shannon Airport, Ireland
EISG	SXL	Sligo Airport, Ireland
EIWF	WAT	Waterford Airport, Ireland
EKAH	AAR	Aarhus Airport, Denmark
EKBI	BLL	Billund Airport, Denmark
EKCH	CPH	Copenhagen Kastrup Intl, Denmark
EKEB	EBJ	Esbjerg Airport, Denmark
EKKA	KRP	Karup Airport, Denmark
EKOD	ODE	Odense Airport, Denmark
EKRK	RKE	Copenhagen Roskilde, Denmark
EKRN	RNN	Ronne Bornholm Airport, Denmark
EKSB	SGD	Soenderborg Airport, Denmark
EKTS	TED	Thisted Airport, Denmark
EKVG	FAE	Vagar Airprot, Faroe Islands
EKVJ	STA	Stauning Airport, Denmark
EKYT	AAL	Aalborg Airport, Denmark
ELLX	LUX	Luxembourg Intl, Luxembourg
ENAL	AES	Alesund Airport, Norway
ENAN	ANX	Andoya Airport, Norway
ENAT	ALF	Alta Airport, Norway
ENBL	FDE	F, Norway
ENBN	BNN	Bronnoysund Airport, Norway
ENBO	BOO	Bodo Airport, Norway
ENBR	BGO	Bergen Airport, Flesland, Norway
ENBS	BJF	Batsfjord Airport, Norway
ENBV	BVG	Berlevag Airport, Norway
ENCN	KRS	Kristiansand Airport, Norway
ENDI	DLD	Geilo Airport, Norway
ENDU	BDU	Bardufoss Airport, Norway
ENEV	EVE	Harstad, Norway
ENFG	VDB	Fagernes Airport, Norway
ENFL	FRO	Floro Airport, Norway
ENGM	OSL	Oslo Gardermoen Airport, Norway
ENHA	HMR	Hamar Airport, Norway
ENHD	HAU	Haugesund Airport, Norway
ENHF	HFT	Hammerfest Airport, Norway
ENHK	HAA	Hasvik Airport, Norway
ENHV	HVG	Honningsvag Airport, Norway
ENKA	QKX	Kautokeino Airport, Norway
ENKB	KSU	Kristiansund Airport, Norway
ENKL	GLL	Gol Airport, Norway
ENKR	KKN	Kirkenes Airport, Norway
ENLI	FAN	Farsund Airport, Norway
ENLK	LKN	Leknes Airport, Norway
ENMH	MEH	Mehamn Airport, Norway
ENML	MOL	Molde Airport, Norway
ENMS	MJF	Mosjoen Airport, Norway
ENNA	LKL	Lakselv Airport, Norway
ENNK	NVK	Narvik Airport, Norway
ENNM	OSY	Namsos Airport, Norway
ENNO	NTB	Notodden Airport, Norway
ENOL	OLA	Orland Main Air Station, Norway
ENOV	HOV	Orsta, Norway
ENRA	MQN	Mo i Rana Airport, Norway
ENRM	RVK	Rorvik Airport, Norway
ENRO	RRS	Roros Airport, Norway
ENRS	RET	Rost Airport, Norway
ENRY	RYG	Moss Airport, Rygge, Norway
ENSB	LYR	Svalbard Airport, Norway
ENSD	SDN	Sandane Airport, Norway
ENSG	SOG	Sogndal Airport, Norway
ENSH	SVJ	Svolvae Airport, Norway
ENSK	SKN	Stokmarknes Airport, Norway
ENSN	SKE	Skien Airport, Norway
ENSO	SRP	Stord Airport, Sorstokken, Norway
ENSR	SOJ	Sorkjosen Airport, Norway
ENSS	VAW	Vardo Airport, Norway
ENST	SSJ	Sandnessjoen Airport, Norway
ENTC	TOS	Tromso Airport, Norway
ENTO	TRF	Sandefjord Airport, Norway
ENVA	TRD	Trondheim Airport, Norway
ENVD	VDS	Vadso Airport, Norway
ENZV	SVG	Stavanger Airport, Sola, Norway
EPBY	BZG	Bydgoszcz Ignacy, Poland
EPGD	GDN	Gdansk Lech Walesa Airport, Poland
EPKK	KRK	John Paul II Intl Krakow, Poland
EPKT	KTW	Katowice Intl, Poland
EPLL	LCJ	Lodz Wladyslaw Reymont, Poland
EPPO	POZ	Poznan, Poland
EPRZ	RZE	Rzeszow, Poland
EPSC	SZZ	Szczecin, Poland
EPSY	SZY	Szczytno, Poland
EPWA	WAW	Warsaw Frederic Chopin, Poland
EPWR	WRO	Copernicus Airport Wroclaw, Poland
EPZG	IEG	Zielona Gora Intl, Poland
ESDF	RNB	Ronneby, Sweden
ESGG	GOT	Landvetter, Sweden
ESGJ	JKG	Jonkoping, Sweden
ESGL	LDK	Lidkoping, Sweden
ESGP	GSE	Goteborg City Airport, Sweden
ESGR	KVB	Skovde, Sweden
ESGT	THN	Trollhattan, Sweden
ESKK	KSK	Karlskoga, Sweden
ESKM	MXX	Siljan, Sweden
ESKN	NYO	Skavsta, Sweden
ESMK	KID	Kristianstad, Sweden
ESMO	OSK	Oskarshamn, Sweden
ESMQ	KLR	Kalmar, Sweden
ESMS	MMX	Sturup, Sweden
ESMT	HAD	Halmstad, Sweden
ESMX	VXO	Kronoberg, Sweden
ESND	EVG	Sveg, Sweden
ESNG	GEV	Gallivare, Sweden
ESNH	HUV	Hudiksvall, Sweden
ESNK	KRF	Kramfors, Sweden
ESNL	LYC	Lycksele, Sweden
ESNN	SDL	Sundsvall, Sweden
ESNO	OER	Ornskoldsvik, Sweden
ESNQ	KRN	Kiruna, Sweden
ESNS	SFT	Skelleftea, Sweden
ESNU	UME	Umea, Sweden
ESNV	VHM	Vilhelmina, Sweden
ESNX	AJR	Arvidsjaur, Sweden
ESNY	SOO	Soderhamn, Sweden
ESOE	ORB	Orebro, Sweden

ICAO	IATA	Airport & Country
ESOH	HFS	Hagfors, Sweden
ESOK	KSD	Karlstad, Sweden
ESOW	VST	Hasslo, Sweden
ESPA	LLA	Kallax, Sweden
ESPC	OSD	Froson, Sweden
ESSA	ARN	Arlanda, Sweden
ESSB	BMA	Bromma, Sweden
ESSD	BLE	Borlange, Sweden
ESSF	HLF	Hultsfred, Sweden
ESSK	GVX	Gavle, Sweden
ESSL	LPI	Saab, Sweden
ESSP	NRK	Kungsangen, Sweden
ESST	TYF	Fryklanda, Sweden
ESSU	EKT	Eskilstuna, Sweden
ESSV	VBY	Visby, Sweden
ESSW	VVK	Vastervik, Sweden
ESTA	AGH	Angelholm, Sweden
ESUD	SQO	Storuman, Sweden
ESUE	IDB	Idre, Sweden
ESUP	PJA	Pajala, Sweden
ESUT	HMV	Hemavan, Sweden
ETMN	FCN	Cuxhaven – Nordholz, Germany
ETNL	RLG	Rostock, Germany
ETNU	FNB	Neubrandenburg, Germany
ETSI	IGS	Ingolstadt, Germany
EVLA	LPX	Liepaja Intl, Latvia
EVRA	RIX	Riga Intl, Latvia
EVVA	VTS	Ventspils Intl, Latvia
FAAB	ALJ	Alexander Bay, South Africa
FABE	BIY	Bisho, South Africa
FABL	BFN	Bloemfontein, South Africa
FACD	CDO	Cradock, South Africa
FACT	CPT	Cape Town Intl, South Africa
FADN	DUR	Durban Intl, South Africa
FAEL	ELS	East London, South Africa
FAEM	EMG	Empangeni, South Africa
FAFB	FCB	Sentra Oes, South Africa
FAGC	GCJ	Grand Central, South Africa
FAGG	GRJ	George, South Africa
FAGI	GIY	Giyani, South Africa
FAGM	QRA	Rand, South Africa
FAHL	HLW	Hluhluwe, South Africa
FAHR	HRS	Harrismith, South Africa
FAHT	HDS	Hoedspruit, South Africa
FAJS	JNB	Johannesburg Intl, South Africa
FAKD	KXE	Klerksdorp, South Africa
FAKM	KIM	Kimberley, South Africa
FAKP	KOF	Komatipoort, South Africa
FAKU	KMH	Johan Pienaar, South Africa
FAKZ	KLZ	Kleinsee, South Africa
FALA	HLA	Lanseria, South Africa
FALC	LMR	Finsch Mine, South Africa
FALO	LCD	Louis Trichardt, South Africa
FALW	SDB	Langebaanweg Ab, South Africa
FALY	LAY	Ladysmith, South Africa
FAMD	AAM	Malamala, South Africa
FAMG	MGH	Margate, South Africa
FAMM	MBD	Mafikeng Intl, South Africa
FAMN	LLE	Malelane, South Africa
FANC	NCS	Newcastle, South Africa

ICAO	IATA	Airport & Country
FANS	NLP	Nelspruit, South Africa
FAOH	OUH	Oudtshoorn, South Africa
FAPA	AFD	Port Alfred, South Africa
FAPE	PLZ	Port Elizabeth, South Africa
FAPG	PBZ	Plettenberg Bay, South Africa
FAPH	PHW	Hendrik Van Eck, South Africa
FAPI	PTG	Pietersburg, South Africa
FAPK	PRK	Prieska, South Africa
FAPM	PZB	Pietermaritzburg, South Africa
FAPN	NTY	Pilanesberg, South Africa
FAQT	UTW	Queenstown, South Africa
FARB	RCB	Richards Bay, South Africa
FARI	RVO	Reivilo, South Africa
FARS	ROD	Robertson, South Africa
FASB	SBU	Springbok, South Africa
FASC	ZEC	Secunda, South Africa
FASS	SIS	Sishen, South Africa
FASZ	SZK	Skukuza, South Africa
FATZ	LTA	Tzaneen, South Africa
FAUL	ULD	Prince M.Buthelezi, South Africa
FAUP	UTN	Upington, South Africa
FAUT	UTT	K.D. Matanzima, South Africa
FAVB	VRU	Vryburg, South Africa
FAVG	VIR	Virginia, South Africa
FAVR	VRE	Vredendal, South Africa
FAVY	VYD	Vryheid, South Africa
FAWB	PRY	Wonderboom, South Africa
FAWM	WEL	Welkom, South Africa
FBFT	FRW	Francistown, Botsuana
FBGZ	GNZ	Ghanzi, Botsuana
FBJW	JWA	Jwaneng, Botsuana
FBKE	BBK	Kasane, Botsuana
FBKR	KHW	Khwai River, Botsuana
FBMN	MUB	Maun, Botsuana
FBOR	ORP	Orapa, Botsuana
FBSK	GBE	Sir Seretse Khama Int., Botsuana
FBSP	PKW	Selebi, Botsuana
FBSW	SWX	Shakawe, Botsuana
FBTL	TLD	Tuli Block, Botsuana
FBTS	TBY	Tshabong, Botsuana
FCBB	BZV	Maya, Congo
FCBD	DJM	Djambala, Congo
FCBK	KNJ	Kindamba, Congo
FCBL	LCO	Lague, Congo
FCBM	MUY	Mouyondzi, Congo
FCBS	SIB	Sibiti, Congo
FCBY	NKY	Yokangassi, Congo
FCBZ	ANJ	Zanaga, Congo
FCMM	MSX	Mossendjo, Congo
FCOB	BOE	Boundji, Congo
FCOE	EWO	Ewo, Congo
FCOI	ION	Impfondo, Congo
FCOK	KEE	Kelle, Congo
FCOM	MKJ	Makoua, Congo
FCOO	FTX	Owando, Congo
FCOS	SOE	Souanke, Congo
FCOT	BTB	Betou, Congo
FCOU	OUE	Ouesso, Congo
FCPA	KMK	Makabana, Congo
FCPL	DIS	Dolisie, Congo

ICAO	IATA	Airport & Country
FCPP	PNR	A. Neto, Congo
FDMS	MTS	Matsapha Airport, Swaziland
FEFB	MKI	M'boki, Central Africa
FEFF	BGF	M'poko, Central Africa
FEFG	BGU	Bangassou, Central Africa
FEFI	IRO	Birao, Central Africa
FEFM	BBY	Bambari, Central Africa
FEFN	NDL	N'dele, Central Africa
FEFO	BOP	Bouar, Central Africa
FEFR	BIV	Bria, Central Africa
FEFS	BSN	Bossangoa, Central Africa
FEFT	BBT	Berberati, Central Africa
FEFY	AIG	Yalinga, Central Africa
FEFZ	IMO	Zemio, Central Africa
FEGZ	BOZ	Bozoum, Central Africa
FGBT	BSG	Bata Airport, Equatorial Guinea
FGSL	SSG	Malabo Airport, Equatorial Guinea
FIMP	MRU	Mauritius Intl, Mauritius
FIMR	RRG	Plaine Corail, Mauritius
FKKB	KBI	Kribi, Cameroon
FKKC	TKC	Tiko, Cameroon
FKKD	DLA	Douala, Cameroon
FKKF	MMF	Mamfe, Cameroon
FKKI	OJR	Batouri, Cameroon
FKKL	MVR	Salak, Cameroon
FKKM	FOM	Nkounja, Cameroon
FKKN	NGE	N'gaoundere, Cameroon
FKKO	BTA	Bertoua, Cameroon
FKKR	GOU	Garoua, Cameroon
FKKS	DSC	Dschang, Cameroon
FKKU	BFX	Bafoussam, Cameroon
FKKV	BPC	Bamenda, Cameroon
FKKW	EBW	Ebolowa, Cameroon
FKKY	YAO	Yaounde/Ville, Cameroon
FKYS	NSI	Nsimalen, Cameroon
FLCP	CIP	Chipata, Zambia
FLKE	ZKP	Kasompe, Zambia
FLKL	KLB	Kalabo, Zambia
FLKO	KMZ	Kaoma, Zambia
FLKS	KAA	Kasama, Zambia
FLKY	ZKB	Kasaba Bay, Zambia
FLLI	LVI	Livingstone, Zambia
FLLK	LXU	Lukulu, Zambia
FLLS	LUN	Lusaka Intl, Zambia
FLMA	MNS	Mansa, Zambia
FLMF	MFU	Mfuwe, Zambia
FLMG	MNR	Mongu, Zambia
FLNA	ZGM	Ngoma, Zambia
FLND	NLA	Ndola, Zambia
FLSN	SXG	Senanga, Zambia
FLSO	KIW	Southdowns, Zambia
FLSW	SLI	Solwezi, Zambia
FLZB	BBZ	Zambezi, Zambia
FMCH	HAH	Prince Said Ibrahim, Comoros
FMCI	NWA	Moheli, Comoros
FMCN	YVA	Iconi, Comoros
FMCV	AJN	Ouani, Comoros
FMEE	RUN	St Denis Gillot, Reunion
FMMC	WML	Malaimbandy, Madagascar
FMME	ATJ	Antsirabe, Madagascar

ICAO	IATA	Airport & Country
FMMG	WAQ	Antsalova, Madagascar
FMMH	VVB	Mahanoro, Madagascar
FMMI	TNR	Ivato, Madagascar
FMMK	JVA	Ankavandra, Madagascar
FMML	BMD	Tsiribihina, Madagascar
FMMN	ZVA	Miandrivazo, Madagascar
FMMO	MXT	Maintirano, Madagascar
FMMQ	ILK	Atsinanana, Madagascar
FMMR	TVA	Morafenobe, Madagascar
FMMS	SMS	Sainte, Madagascar
FMMT	TMM	Toamasina, Madagascar
FMMU	WTA	Tambohorano, Madagascar
FMMV	MOQ	Morondava, Madagascar
FMMX	WTS	Tsiroanomandidy, Madagascar
FMMY	VAT	Vatomandry, Madagascar
FMMZ	WAM	Ambatondrazaka, Madagascar
FMNA	DIE	Arrachart, Madagascar
FMNC	WMR	Avaratra, Madagascar
FMND	ZWA	Andapa, Madagascar
FMNE	AMB	Ambilobe, Madagascar
FMNF	WBD	Avaratra, Madagascar
FMNG	WPB	Port Berge, Madagascar
FMNH	ANM	Antsirabato, Madagascar
FMNJ	IVA	Ampapamena, Madagascar
FMNL	HVA	Analalava, Madagascar
FMNM	MJN	Amborovy, Madagascar
FMNN	NOS	Fascene, Madagascar
FMNO	DWB	Soalala, Madagascar
FMNQ	BPY	Besalampy, Madagascar
FMNR	WMN	Maroantsetra, Madagascar
FMNS	SVB	Sambava South, Madagascar
FMNT	TTS	Tsaratanana, Madagascar
FMNV	VOH	Vohimarina, Madagascar
FMNW	WAI	Ambalabe, Madagascar
FMNX	WMA	Mandritsara, Madagascar
FMSB	WBO	Antsoa, Madagascar
FMSC	WMD	Mandabe, Madagascar
FMSD	FTU	Tolagnaro, Madagascar
FMSF	WFI	Fianarantsoa, Madagascar
FMSG	RVA	Farafangana, Madagascar
FMSI	IHO	Ihosy, Madagascar
FMSJ	MJA	Manja, Madagascar
FMSK	WVK	Manakara, Madagascar
FMSL	OVA	Bekily, Madagascar
FMSM	MNJ	Mananjary, Madagascar
FMSN	TDV	Samangoky, Madagascar
FMSR	MXM	Morombe, Madagascar
FMST	TLE	Toliara, Madagascar
FMSY	AMP	Ampanihy, Madagascar
FMSZ	WAK	Ankazoabo, Madagascar
FNAM	AZZ	Ambriz, Angola
FNBC	SSY	M'banza Congo, Angola
FNBG	BUG	Benguela, Angola
FNCA	CAB	Cabinda, Angola
FNGI	NGV	N'giva, Angola
FNHU	NOV	Albano Machado, Angola
FNKU	SVP	Bie, Angola
FNLU	LAD	Luanda, Angola
FNMA	MEG	Malange, Angola
FNME	SPP	Menongue, Angola

ICAO	IATA	Airport & Country
FNNG	GXG	Negage, Angola
FNPA	PBN	Porto Amboim, Angola
FNSA	VHC	Saurimo, Angola
FNSO	SZA	Soyo, Angola
FNUB	SDD	Lubango, Angola
FNUE	LUO	Luena, Angola
FNUG	UGO	Uige, Angola
FNWK	CEO	Wako Kungo, Angola
FNXA	XGN	Xangongo, Angola
FNZE	ARZ	N'zeto, Angola
FOGB	BGB	Booue, Gabon
FOGE	KDN	Ndende, Gabon
FOGF	FOU	Fougamou, Gabon
FOGG	MBC	Mbigou, Gabon
FOGI	MGX	Moabi, Gabon
FOGM	MJL	Mouila Ville, Gabon
FOGO	OYE	Oyem, Gabon
FOGQ	OKN	Okondja, Gabon
FOGR	LBQ	Lambarene, Gabon
FOGV	MVX	Minvoul, Gabon
FOOB	BMM	Bitam, Gabon
FOOD	MFF	Moanda, Gabon
FOOE	MKB	Mekambo, Gabon
FOOG	POG	Port Gentil, Gabon
FOOH	OMB	Omboue Hospital, Gabon
FOOK	MKU	Makokou, Gabon
FOOL	LBV	Leon M'ba, Gabon
FOOM	MZC	Mitzic, Gabon
FOON	MVB	M'vengue, Gabon
FOOR	LTL	Lastourville, Gabon
FOOS	ZKM	Sette, Gabon
FOOT	TCH	Tchibanga, Gabon
FOOY	MYB	Mayumba, Gabon
FPPR	PCP	Principe, Sao Tome and Principe
FPST	TMS	Sao Tom, Sao Tome and Principe
FQAG	ANO	Angoche, Mozambique
FQBR	BEW	Beira, Mozambique
FQCB	FXO	Cuamba, Mozambique
FQCH	VPY	Chimoio, Mozambique
FQIN	INH	Inhambane, Mozambique
FQLC	VXC	Lichinga, Mozambique
FQMA	MPM	Maputo, Mozambique
FQMP	MZB	Mocimboa Da Praia, Mozambique
FQNC	MNC	Nacala, Mozambique
FQNP	APL	Nampula, Mozambique
FQPB	POL	Pemba, Mozambique
FQQL	UEL	Quelimane, Mozambique
FQTT	TET	Chingozi, Mozambique
FQVL	VNX	Vilankulu, Mozambique
FSDR	DES	Desroches, Seychelles
FSIA	SEZ	Seychelles Intl, Seychelles
FSPP	PRI	Praslin, Seychelles
FSSB	BDI	Bird Island, Seychelles
FSSD	DEI	Denis Island, Seychelles
FSSF	FRK	Fregate, Seychelles
FTTA	SRH	Sarh, Chad
FTTB	OGR	Bongor, Chad
FTTC	AEH	Abeche, Chad
FTTD	MQQ	Moundou, Chad
FTTH	LTC	Lai, Chad

ICAO	IATA	Airport & Country
FTTI	ATV	Ati, Chad
FTTJ	NDJ	N'Djamena, Chad
FTTK	BKR	Bokoro, Chad
FTTL	OTC	Berim, Chad
FTTM	MVO	Mongo, Chad
FTTN	AMC	Am, Chad
FTTP	PLF	Pala, Chad
FTTS	OUT	Bousso, Chad
FTTU	AMO	Mao, Chad
FTTY	FYT	Faya Largeau, Chad
FVBU	BUQ	Bulawayo, Zimbabwe
FVCZ	BFO	Buffalo Range, Zimbabwe
FVFA	VFA	Victoria Falls, Zimbabwe
FVHA	HRE	Harare Intl, Zimbabwe
FVKB	KAB	Kariba, Zimbabwe
FVMU	UTA	Mutare, Zimbabwe
FVMV	MVZ	Masvingo, Zimbabwe
FVTL	GWE	Thornhill, Zimbabwe
FVWN	HWN	Hwange National Park, Zimbabwe
FVWT	WKI	Hwange Town, Zimbabwe
FWCD	CEH	Chelinda, Malawi
FWCL	BLZ	Chileka, Malawi
FWCM	CMK	Club Makokola, Malawi
FWDW	DWA	Dwangwa, Malawi
FWKA	KGJ	Karonga, Malawi
FWKG	KBQ	Kasungu, Malawi
FWLI	LLW	Lilongwe Intl, Malawi
FWLK	LIX	Likoma, Malawi
FWMG	MAI	Mangochi, Malawi
FWMY	MYZ	Monkey Bay, Malawi
FWSM	LMB	Salima, Malawi
FWUU	ZZU	Mzuzu, Malawi
FXLR	LRB	Leribe, Lesotho
FXMF	MFC	Mafeteng, Lesotho
FXMK	MKH	Mokhotlong, Lesotho
FXMM	MSU	Moshoeshoe I Intl, Lesotho
FXQN	UNE	Qacha's Nek, Lesotho
FXSH	SHK	Sehonghong, Lesotho
FXSM	SOK	Semonkong, Lesotho
FYAR	ADI	Arandis, Namibia
FYGF	GFY	Grootfontein, Namibia
FYKM	MPA	Katima Mulilo, Namibia
FYKT	KMP	Keetmanshoop, Namibia
FYLZ	LUD	Luderitz, Namibia
FYNA	NNI	Namutoni, Namibia
FYOA	OND	Ondangwa, Namibia
FYOG	OMD	Oranjemund, Namibia
FYOO	OKF	Okaukuejo, Namibia
FYRU	NDU	Rundu, Namibia
FYSM	SWP	Swakopmund, Namibia
FYTM	TSB	Tsumeb, Namibia
FYWB	WVB	Walvis Bay, Namibia
FYWE	ERS	Eros, Namibia
FYWH	WDH	Hosea Kutako Intl, Namibia
FZAA	FIH	N'djili Intl, Congo
FZAB	NLO	N'dolo, Congo
FZAJ	BOA	Boma, Congo
FZAL	LZI	Luozi, Congo
FZAM	MAT	Matadi, Congo
FZBA	INO	Inongo, Congo

ICAO	IATA	Airport & Country
FZBI	NIO	Nioki, Congo
FZBO	FDU	Bandundu, Congo
FZCA	KKW	Kikwit, Congo
FZCB	IDF	Idiofa, Congo
FZCE	LUS	Lusanga, Congo
FZCV	MSM	Masi, Congo
FZEA	MDK	Mbandaka, Congo
FZEN	BSU	Basankusu, Congo
FZFA	LIE	Libenge, Congo
FZFD	BDT	Gbadolite, Congo
FZFK	GMA	Gemena, Congo
FZFP	KLI	Kotakoli, Congo
FZFU	BMB	Bumba, Congo
FZGA	LIQ	Lisala, Congo
FZGN	BNB	Boende, Congo
FZGV	IKL	Ikela, Congo
FZIC	FKI	Bangoka Intl, Congo
FZJH	IRP	Isiro, Congo
FZKA	BUX	Bunia, Congo
FZKJ	BZU	Buta, Congo
FZMA	BKY	Kavumu, Congo
FZNA	GOM	Goma Intl, Congo
FZNP	BNC	Beni, Congo
FZOA	KND	Kindu, Congo
FZOD	KLY	Kalima, Congo
FZOK	KGN	Kasongo, Congo
FZOP	PUN	Punia, Congo
FZQA	FBM	Lubumbashi Intl, Congo
FZQC	PWO	Pweto, Congo
FZQG	KEC	Kasenga, Congo
FZQM	KWZ	Kolwezi, Congo
FZRA	MNO	Manono, Congo
FZRB	BDV	Moba, Congo
FZRF	FMI	Kalemie, Congo
FZRM	KBO	Kabalo, Congo
FZRQ	KOO	Kongolo, Congo
FZSA	KMN	Kamina Base, Congo
FZSK	KAP	Kapanga, Congo
FZTK	KNM	Kaniama, Congo
FZUA	KGA	Kananga, Congo
FZUG	LZA	Luiza, Congo
FZUK	TSH	Tshikapa, Congo
FZVA	LJA	Lodja, Congo
FZVI	LBO	Lusambo, Congo
FZVM	MEW	Mweka, Congo
FZVR	BAN	Basongo, Congo
FZVS	PFR	Ilebo, Congo
FZWA	MJM	Mbuji, Congo
FZWC	GDJ	Gandajika, Congo
FZWT	KBN	Tunta, Congo
GABS	BKO	Senou, Mali
GAGM	GUD	Goundam, Mali
GAGO	GAQ	Korogoussou, Mali
GAKA	KNZ	Kenieba, Mali
GAKO	KTX	Koutiala, Mali
GAKY	KYS	Kayes, Mali
GAMB	MZI	Barbe, Mali
GANK	NRM	Keibane, Mali
GANR	NIX	Nioro, Mali
GASK	KSS	Sikasso, Mali

ICAO	IATA	Airport & Country
GATB	TOM	Tombouctou, Mali
GAYE	EYL	Yelimane, Mali
GBYD	BJL	Banjul Intl, Gambia
GCFV	FUE	Fuerteventura Airport, Spain
GCGM	GMZ	La Gomera Airport, Spain
GCHI	VDE	El Hierro Airport, Spain
GCLA	SPC	La Palma Airport, Spain
GCLP	LPA	Gran Canaria Intl, Spain
GCRR	ACE	Lanzarote Airport, Spain
GCTS	TFS	Tenerife Reina Sofia Airport, Spain
GCXO	TFN	Tenerife Los Rodeos Airport, Spain
GECT	JCU	Ceuta Heliport, Spain
GEML	MLN	Melilla Airport, Spain
GFBN	BTE	Bonthe, Sierra Leone
GFBO	KBS	Bo, Sierra Leone
GFGK	GBK	Gbangbatoke, Sierra Leone
GFHA	HGS	Hastings, Sierra Leone
GFKB	KBA	Kabala, Sierra Leone
GFKE	KEN	Kenema, Sierra Leone
GFLL	FNA	Lungi, Sierra Leone
GFYE	WYE	Yengema, Sierra Leone
GGOV	OXB	Osvaldo Vieira, Guinea Bissau
GLBU	UCN	Buckanan, Liberia
GLCP	CPA	Cape Palmas, Liberia
GLGE	SNI	Sinoe, Liberia
GLMR	MLW	Spriggs Payne, Liberia
GLNA	NIA	Nimba, Liberia
GLRB	ROB	Roberts Intl, Liberia
GLTN	THC	Tchien, Liberia
GMAT	TTA	Plage Blanche, Morocco
GMFF	FEZ	Saiss, Morocco
GMFK	ERH	Moulay Ali Cherif, Morocco
GMFO	OUD	Angads, Morocco
GMMC	CAS	Anfa, Morocco
GMME	RBA	Sale, Morocco
GMMF	SII	Sidi Ifni, Morocco
GMMN	CMN	Mohamed V, Morocco
GMMS	SFI	Safi, Morocco
GMMX	RAK	Menara, Morocco
GMMZ	OZZ	Ouarzazate, Morocco
GMTA	AHU	Cherif Al Idrissi, Morocco
GMTN	TTU	Sania Ramel, Morocco
GMTT	TNG	Ibn Batouta, Morocco
GOGG	ZIG	Ziguinchor, Senegal
GOGK	KDA	Kolda, Senegal
GOGS	CSK	Cap Skiring, Senegal
GOOK	KLC	Kaolack, Senegal
GOOY	DKR	Leopold Sedar Senghor, Senegal
GOSM	MAX	Ouro Sogui, Senegal
GOSP	POD	Podor, Senegal
GOSR	RDT	Richard Toll, Senegal
GOSS	XLS	St Louis, Senegal
GOTB	BXE	Bakel, Senegal
GOTK	KGG	Kedougou, Senegal
GOTS	SMY	Simenti, Senegal
GOTT	TUD	Tambacounda, Senegal
GQNA	AEO	Aioun, Mauritania
GQNB	OTL	Boutilimit, Mauritania
GQNC	THI	Tichit, Mauritania
GQND	TIY	Tidjikja, Mauritania

ICAO	IATA	Airport & Country
GQNE	BGH	Bogue, Mauritania
GQNF	KFA	Kiffa, Mauritania
GQNH	TMD	Timbedra, Mauritania
GQNI	EMN	Nema, Mauritania
GQNJ	AJJ	Akjoujt, Mauritania
GQNK	KED	Kaedi, Mauritania
GQNL	MOM	Letfotar, Mauritania
GQNN	NKC	Nouakchott, Mauritania
GQNS	SEY	Selibabi, Mauritania
GQNT	THT	Tamchakett, Mauritania
GQPA	ATR	Atar, Mauritania
GQPF	FGD	F'derik, Mauritania
GQPP	NDB	Nouadhibou, Mauritania
GQPZ	OUZ	Tazadit, Mauritania
GUCY	CKY	Gbessia, Guinea
GUFA	FIG	Katourou, Guinea
GUFH	FAA	Badala, Guinea
GUKU	KSI	Kissi, Guinea
GULB	LEK	Tata, Guinea
GUMA	MCA	Macenta, Guinea
GUNZ	NZE	Konia, Guinea
GUOK	BKJ	Baralande, Guinea
GUSB	SBI	Sambailo, Guinea
GUSI	GII	Siguiri, Guinea
GUXD	KNN	Kankan, Guinea
GVAC	SID	Amilcar Cabral, Cape Verde
GVBA	BVC	Rabil, Cape Verde
GVFM	RAI	Francisco Mendes Cape Verde
GVMA	MMO	Maio, Cape Verde
GVSN	SNE	Preguica, Cape Verde
GVSV	VXE	S. Pedro, Cape Verde
HAAB	ADD	Addis Abeba Bole Intl, Ethiopia
HAAM	AMH	Arba Minch, Ethiopia
HAAX	AXU	Axum, Ethiopia
HABC	BCO	Baco, Ethiopia
HABD	BJR	Bahir Dar, Ethiopia
HABE	BEI	Beica, Ethiopia
HADC	DSE	Combolcha, Ethiopia
HADD	DEM	Dembi Dollo, Ethiopia
HADM	DBM	Debre Marcos, Ethiopia
HADR	DIR	A.T.D. Yilma Intl, Ethiopia
HADT	DBT	Debre Tabor, Ethiopia
HAFN	FNH	Fincha, Ethiopia
HAGB	GOB	Robe, Ethiopia
HAGH	GNN	Ghinnir, Ethiopia
HAGM	GMB	Gambella, Ethiopia
HAGN	GDQ	Azezo, Ethiopia
HAGR	GOR	Gore, Ethiopia
HAHU	HUE	Humera, Ethiopia
HAJM	JIM	Aba Segud, Ethiopia
HAKD	ABK	Kebri Dehar, Ethiopia
HALA	AWA	Awasa, Ethiopia
HALL	LLI	Lalibella, Ethiopia
HAMA	MKS	Mekane Salam, Ethiopia
HAMK	MQX	Alula Aba Nega, Ethiopia
HAML	MZX	Masslo, Ethiopia
HAMM	ETE	Metema, Ethiopia
HAMN	NDM	Mendi, Ethiopia
HAMT	MTF	Mizan Teferi, Ethiopia
HANJ	NEJ	Nejjo, Ethiopia

ICAO	IATA	Airport & Country
HANK	NEK	Nekemte, Ethiopia
HASD	SXU	Soddo, Ethiopia
HASK	SKR	Shakiso, Ethiopia
HASO	ASO	Asosa, Ethiopia
HATP	TIE	Tippi, Ethiopia
HAWC	WAC	Wacca, Ethiopia
HBBA	BJM	Bujumbura Intl, Burundi
HBBE	GID	Gitega, Burundi
HBBO	KRE	Kirundo, Burundi
HCMA	ALU	Alula, Somalia
HCMC	CXN	Candala, Somalia
HCME	HCM	Eil, Somalia
HCMF	BSA	Bosaso, Somalia
HCMG	GSR	Gardo, Somalia
HCMI	BBO	Berbera, Somalia
HCMK	KMU	Kisimayu, Somalia
HCMM	MGQ	Mogadishu, Somalia
HCMO	CMO	Obbia, Somalia
HCMR	GLK	Galcaio, Somalia
HCMS	CMS	Scusciuban, Somalia
HCMU	ERA	Erigavo, Somalia
HCMV	BUO	Burao, Somalia
HEAR	AAC	El Arish Intl, Egypt
HEAT	ATZ	Asyut Intl, Egypt
HEAX	ALY	Alexandria Intl, Egypt
HEBA	HBE	Borg El Arab Intl, Egypt
HEBL	ABS	Abu Simbel Airport, Egypt
HECA	CAI	Cairo Intl, Egypt
HEDK	DAK	Dakhla Airport, Egypt
HEGN	HRG	Hurghada Intl, Egypt
HEKG	UVL	El Kharga Airport, Egypt
HELX	LXR	Luxor Intl, Egypt
HEMA	RMF	Marsa Alam Intl, Egypt
HEMM	MUH	Mersa Matruh Airport, Egypt
HEOW	GSQ	Shark El Oweinat Intl, Egypt
HEPS	PSD	Port Said Airport, Egypt
HESC	SKV	St Catherine Intl, Egypt
HESH	SSH	Sharm El Sheikh Intl, Egypt
HESN	ASW	Aswan Intl, Egypt
HETB	TCP	Taba Intl, Egypt
HETR	ELT	El Tor Airport, Egypt
HFFF	JIB	Djibouti Ambouli, Djibouti
HKAM	ASV	Amboseli, Kenya
HKED	EDL	Eldoret, Kenya
HKES	EYS	Eliye Springs, Kenya
HKFG	FER	Ferguson's Gulf, Kenya
HKGA	GAS	Garissa, Kenya
HKHO	HOA	Hola, Kenya
HKJK	NBO	Jomo Kenyatta, Kenya
HKKI	KIS	Kisumu, Kenya
HKKL	ILU	Kilaguni, Kenya
HKKR	KEY	Kericho, Kenya
HKKT	KTL	Kitale, Kenya
HKLO	LOK	Lodwar, Kenya
HKLU	LAU	Lamu/Manda, Kenya
HKLY	LOY	Loyangalani, Kenya
HKMA	NDE	Mandera, Kenya
HKMB	RBT	Marsabit, Kenya
HKML	MYD	Malindi, Kenya
HKMO	MBA	Moi, Kenya

Appendix F

ICAO	IATA	Airport & Country
HKMY	OYL	Oda, Kenya
HKNI	NYE	Nyeri, Kenya
HKNK	NUU	Nakuru, Kenya
HKNW	WIL	Wilson, Kenya
HKNY	NYK	Nanyuki, Kenya
HKSB	UAS	Buffalo Spring, Kenya
HKWJ	WJR	Waghala, Kenya
HLKF	AKF	Kufra, Libya
HLLS	SEB	Sebha, Libya
HLMB	LMQ	Marsa Brega, Libya
HLON	HUQ	Hon, Libya
HRYG	GYI	Gisenyi, Rwanda
HRYI	BTQ	Butare, Rwanda
HRYR	KGL	Gregoire Kayibanda, Rwanda
HRYU	RHG	Ruhengeri, Rwanda
HRZA	KME	Kamembe, Rwanda
HSAT	ATB	Atbara, Sudan
HSDN	DOG	Dongola, Sudan
HSFS	ELF	El Fasher, Sudan
HSGF	GSU	Gedaref, Sudan
HSGG	DNX	Galegu, Sudan
HSGN	EGN	Geneina, Sudan
HSKA	KSL	Kassala, Sudan
HSKI	KST	Kosti, Sudan
HSMR	MWE	Merowe, Sudan
HSNH	NUD	El Nahud, Sudan
HSNL	UYL	Nyala, Sudan
HSNW	NHF	New Halfa, Sudan
HSOB	EBD	El Obeid, Sudan
HSPN	PZU	Port Sudan, Sudan
HSSJ	JUB	Juba, Sudan
HSSM	MAK	Malakal, Sudan
HSSS	KRT	Khartoum, Sudan
HSSW	WHF	Wadi Halfa, Sudan
HSWW	WUU	Wau, Sudan
HTAR	ARK	Arusha, Tanzania
HTBU	BKZ	Bukoba, Tanzania
HTDA	DAR	Dar, Tanzania
HTDO	DOD	Dodoma, Tanzania
HTIR	IRI	Iringa, Tanzania
HTKA	TKQ	Kigoma, Tanzania
HTKI	KIY	Kilwa Masoko, Tanzania
HTKJ	JRO	Kilimanjaro Intl, Tanzania
HTLI	LDI	Lindi, Tanzania
HTLM	LKY	Lake Manyara, Tanzania
HTMA	MFA	Mafia, Tanzania
HTMB	MBI	Mbeya, Tanzania
HTMD	MWN	Mwadui, Tanzania
HTMI	XMI	Masasi, Tanzania
HTMT	MYW	Mtwara, Tanzania
HTMU	MUZ	Musoma, Tanzania
HTMW	MWZ	Mwanza, Tanzania
HTNA	NCH	Nachingwea, Tanzania
HTNJ	JOM	Njombe, Tanzania
HTPE	PMA	Pemba, Tanzania
HTSN	SEU	Seronera, Tanzania
HTSO	SGX	Songea, Tanzania
HTSU	SUT	Sumbawanga, Tanzania
HTSY	SHY	Shinyanga, Tanzania
HTTB	TBO	Tabora, Tanzania

ICAO	IATA	Airport & Country
HTTG	TGT	Tanga, Tanzania
HTZA	ZNZ	Kisauni, Tanzania
HUAR	RUA	Arua, Uganda
HUEN	EBB	Entebbe Intl, Uganda
HUGU	ULU	Gulu, Uganda
HUJI	JIN	Jinja, Uganda
HUKS	KSE	Kasese, Uganda
HUMA	MBQ	Mbarara, Uganda
HUMI	KCU	Masindi, Uganda
HUPA	PAF	Pakuba, Uganda
HUSO	SRT	Soroti, Uganda
HUTO	TRY	Tororo, Uganda
KABE	ABE	Lehigh Valley Intl, USA
KABI	ABI	Abilene Regional Airport, USA
KABQ	ABQ	Albuquerque Intl Sunport, USA
KABR	ABR	Aberdeen Regional Airport, USA
KABY	ABY	Southwest Georgia Regional, USA
KACK	ACK	Nantucket Memorial Airport, USA
KACT	ACT	Waco Regional Airport, USA
KACV	ACV	Arcata Airport, USA
KACY	ACY	Atlantic City Intl, USA
KAEX	AEX	Alexandria Intl, USA
KAGS	AGS	Augusta Regional, USA
KAHN	AHN	Athens, USA
KALB	ALB	Albany Intl, USA
KALO	ALO	Waterloo Regional Airport, USA
KALW	ALW	Walla Walla Regional Airport, USA
KAMA	AMA	Rick Husband Amarillo Intl, USA
KAOO	AOO	Altoona, USA
KAPF	APF	Naples Municipal Airport, USA
KAPN	APN	Alpena County Regional Airport, USA
KASE	ASE	Aspen, USA
KATL	ATL	Hartsfield, USA
KATW	ATW	Outagamie County Regional, USA
KAUS	AUS	Austin, USA
KAVL	AVL	Asheville Regional Airport, USA
KAVP	AVP	Wilkes, USA
KAZO	AZO	Kalamazoo/Battle Creek Intl, USA
KBDL	BDL	Bradley Intl, USA
KBED	BED	Laurence G. Hanscom Field, USA
KBFI	BFI	King County Intl, USA
KBFL	BFL	Meadows Field Airport, USA
KBGM	BGM	Greater Binghamton Airport, USA
KBGR	BGR	Bangor Intl, USA
KBHB	BHB	Hancock County, USA
KBHM	BHM	Birmingham Intl, USA
KBIL	BIL	Billings Logan Intl, USA
KBIS	BIS	Bismarck Municipal Airport, USA
KBJI	BJI	Bemidji Regional Airport, USA
KBLI	BLI	Bellingham Intl, USA
KBMI	BMI	Central Illinois Regional Airport, USA
KBNA	BNA	Nashville Intl, USA
KBOI	BOI	Boise Air Terminal, USA
KBOS	BOS	Gen. Edward Lawrence Logan, USA
KBPT	BPT	Southeast Texas Regional, USA
KBQK	BQK	Brunswick Golden Isles Airport, USA
KBRD	BRD	Brainerd Lakes Regional Airport, USA
KBRO	BRO	Brownsville/South Padre Island Intl, USA
KBTM	BTM	Bert Mooney Airport, USA

Appendix F

ICAO	IATA	Airport & Country
KBTR	BTR	Baton Rouge Metropolitan, USA
KBTV	BTV	Burlington Intl, USA
KBUF	BUF	Buffalo Niagara Intl, USA
KBUR	BUR	Bob Hope Airport, USA
KBWI	BWI	Baltimore, USA
KBZN	BZN	Gallatin Field Airport, USA
KCAE	CAE	Columbia Metropolitan Airport, USA
KCAK	CAK	Akron, USA
KCDC	CDC	Cedar City Regional Airport, USA
KCEC	CEC	Jack McNamara Field Airport, USA
KCHA	CHA	Chattanooga Metropolitan, USA
KCHO	CHO	Charlottesville, USA
KCHS	CHS	Charleston Intl, USA
KCIC	CIC	Chico Municipal Airport, USA
KCID	CID	The Eastern Iowa Airport, USA
KCIU	CIU	Chippewa County Intl, USA
KCKB	CKB	Marion Regional Airport, USA
KCLE	CLE	Cleveland, USA
KCLL	CLL	Easterwood Airport, USA
KCLM	CLM	William R. Fairchild Intl, USA
KCLT	CLT	Charlotte/Douglas Intl, USA
KCMH	CMH	Port Columbus Intl, USA
KCMI	CMI	University of Illinois, USA
KCMX	CMX	Houghton County Memorial, USA
KCOD	COD	Yellowstone Regional Airport, USA
KCOS	COS	Colorado Springs Municipal, USA
KCOU	COU	Columbia Regional Airport, USA
KCPR	CPR	Natrona County Intl, USA
KCRP	CRP	Corpus Christi Intl, USA
KCRQ	CRQ	McClellan, USA
KCRW	CRW	Yeager Airport, USA
KCSG	CSG	Columbus Metropolitan Airport, USA
KCVG	CVG	Northern Kentucky Intl, USA
KCVX	CVX	Charlevoix Municipal Airport, USA
KCWA	CWA	Central Wisconsin Airport, USA
KCYS	CYS	Cheyenne Regional Airport, USA
KDAB	DAB	Daytona Beach Intl, USA
KDAL	DAL	Dallas Love Field, USA
KDAY	DAY	James M. Cox Dayton Intl, USA
KDBQ	DBQ	Dubuque Regional Airport, USA
KDCA	DCA	Washington National Airport, USA
KDEC	DEC	Decatur Airport, USA
KDEN	DEN	Denver Intl, USA
KDFW	DFW	Dallas, USA
KDHN	DHN	Dothan Regional Airport, USA
KDLH	DLH	Duluth Intl, USA
KDRO	DRO	Durango, USA
KDSM	DSM	Des Moines Intl, USA
KDTW	DTW	Detroit Metropolitan, USA
KDUJ	DUJ	DuBois, USA
KEAT	EAT	Pangborn Memorial Airport, USA
KEAU	EAU	Chippewa Valley Regional, USA
KEFD	EFD	Ellington Field, USA
KEGE	EGE	Eagle County Regional Airport, USA
KEKO	EKO	Elko Regional Airport, USA
KELM	ELM	Elmira/Corning Regional Airport, USA
KELP	ELP	El Paso Intl, USA
KERI	ERI	Erie Intl, USA
KEUG	EUG	Eugene Airport, USA
KEVV	EVV	Evansville Regional Airport, USA

ICAO	IATA	Airport & Country
KEWB	EWB	New Bedford Regional Airport, USA
KEWN	EWN	Craven County Regional Airport, USA
KEWR	EWR	Newark Liberty Int , USA
KEYW	EYW	Key West Intl, USA
KFAR	FAR	Hector Intl, USA
KFAT	FAT	Fresno Yosemite Intl, USA
KFAY	FAY	Fayetteville Regional Airport, USA
KFHR	FHR	Friday Harbor Airport, USA
KFLG	FLG	Flagstaff Pulliam Airport, USA
KFLL	FLL	Fort Lauderdale, USA
KFLO	FLO	Florence Regional Airport, USA
KFMN	FMN	Four Corners Regional Airport, USA
KFNT	FNT	Bishop Intl, USA
KFOE	FOE	Forbes Field, USA
KFSD	FSD	Sioux Falls Regional Airport, USA
KFSM	FSM	Fort Smith Regional Airport, USA
KFWA	FWA	Fort Wayne Intl, USA
KGCC	GCC	Gillette, USA
KGCN	GCN	Grand Canyon National Park, USA
KGEG	GEG	Spokane Intl, USA
KGFK	GFK	Grand Forks Intl, USA
KGGG	GGG	East Texas Regional Airport, USA
KGJT	GJT	Walker Field Airport, USA
KGNV	GNV	Gainesville Regional Airport, USA
KGPI	GPI	Glacier Park Intl, USA
KGPT	GPT	Gulfport, USA
KGRB	GRB	Austin Straubel Intl, USA
KGRK	GRK	Killeen, USA
KGRR	GRR	Gerald R. Ford Intl, USA
KGSO	GSO	Piedmont Triad Intl, USA
KGSP	GSP	Greenville, USA
KGTF	GTF	Great Falls Intl, USA
KGTR	GTR	Golden Triangle Regional Airport, USA
KGUC	GUC	Gunnison, USA
KHDN	HDN	Yampa Valley Airport, USA
KHGR	HGR	Hagerstown Regional Airport, USA
KHLN	HLN	Helena Regional Airport, USA
KHOU	HOU	William P. Hobby Airport, USA
KHPN	HPN	Westchester County Airport, USA
KHRL	HRL	Valley Intl, USA
KHSV	HSV	Huntsville Intl, USA
KHTS	HTS	Tri, USA
KHVN	HVN	Tweed, USA
KHXD	HXD	Hilton Head Airport, USA
KHYA	HYA	Barnstable Municipal Airport, USA
KIAD	IAD	Washington Dulles Intl, USA
KIAH	IAH	George Bush Intercontinental, USA
KICT	ICT	Wichita Mid, USA
KIDA	IDA	Idaho Falls Regional Airport, USA
KIFP	IFP	Laughlin/Bullhead Intl, USA
KILM	ILM	Wilmington Intl, USA
KIND	IND	Indianapolis Intl, USA
KINL	INL	Falls Intl, USA
KIPL	IPL	Imperial County Airport, USA
KIPT	IPT	Williamsport Regional Airport, USA
KISP	ISP	Long Island MacArthur Airport, USA
KITH	ITH	Ithaca Tompkins Regional, USA
KIYK	IYK	Inyokern Airport, USA
KJAC	JAC	Jackson Hole Airport, USA
KJAN	JAN	Jackson, USA

ICAO	IATA	Airport & Country
KJAX	JAX	Jacksonville Intl, USA
KJFK	JFK	John F. Kennedy Intl, USA
KJHW	JHW	Chautauqua County Airport, USA
KJLN	JLN	Joplin Regional Airport, USA
KJST	JST	John Murtha Johnstown, USA
KLAF	LAF	Purdue University Airport, USA
KLAN	LAN	Capital City Airport, USA
KLAS	LAS	McCarran Intl, USA
KLAW	LAW	Lawton, USA
KLAX	LAX	Los Angeles Intl, USA
KLBB	LBB	Lubbock Preston Smith Intl, USA
KLBE	LBE	Arnold Palmer Regional Airport, USA
KLCH	LCH	Lake Charles Regional Airport, USA
KLEX	LEX	Blue Grass Airport, USA
KLFT	LFT	Lafayette Regional Airport, USA
KLGA	LGA	LaGuardia Airport, USA
KLGB	LGB	Long Beach Municipal Airport, USA
KLIT	LIT	Little Rock National Airport, USA
KLMT	LMT	Klamath Falls Airport, USA
KLNK	LNK	Lincoln Airport, USA
KLNS	LNS	Lancaster Airport, USA
KLRD	LRD	Laredo Intl, USA
KLSE	LSE	La Crosse Municipal Airport, USA
KLWS	LWS	Lewiston, USA
KLYH	LYH	Lynchburg Regional Airport, USA
KMAF	MAF	Midland Intl, USA
KMBS	MBS	MBS Intl, USA
KMCI	MCI	Kansas City Intl, USA
KMCN	MCN	Middle Georgia Regional Airport, USA
KMCO	MCO	Orlando Intl, USA
KMCW	MCW	Mason City Municipal Airport, USA
KMDT	MDT	Harrisburg Intl, USA
KMDW	MDW	Chicago Midway Intl, USA
KMEI	MEI	Meridian Regional Airport, USA
KMEM	MEM	Memphis Intl, USA
KMFE	MFE	McAllen, USA
KMFR	MFR	Rogue Valley Intl, USA
KMGM	MGM	Montgomery Regional Airport, USA
KMGW	MGW	Morgantown Municipal Airport, USA
KMHK	MHK	Manhattan Regional Airport, USA
KMHT	MHT	Manchester, USA
KMIA	MIA	Miami Intl, USA
KMKE	MKE	General Mitchell Intl, USA
KMKG	MKG	Muskegon County Airport, USA
KMKT	MKT	Mankato Regional Airport, USA
KMLB	MLB	Melbourne Intl, USA
KMLI	MLI	Quad City Intl, USA
KMLU	MLU	Monroe Regional Airport, USA
KMOB	MOB	Mobile Regional Airport, USA
KMOD	MOD	Modesto City, USA
KMOT	MOT	Minot Intl, USA
KMRY	MRY	Monterey Peninsula Airport, USA
KMSN	MSN	Dane County Regional Airport, USA
KMSO	MSO	Missoula Intl, USA
KMSP	MSP	Minneapolis, USA
KMSY	MSY	Louis Armstrong New Orleans, USA
KMTJ	MTJ	Montrose Regional Airport, USA
KMVY	MVY	Martha's Vineyard Airport, USA
KMWA	MWA	Williamson County Regional, USA
KMYR	MYR	Myrtle Beach Intl, USA

ICAO	IATA	Airport & Country
KOAJ	OAJ	Albert J. Ellis Airport, USA
KOAK	OAK	Metropolitan Oakland Intl, USA
KOKC	OKC	Will Rogers World Airport, USA
KOMA	OMA	Eppley Airfield, USA
KONT	ONT	Ontario Intl, USA
KORD	ORD	Chicago O'Hare Intl, USA
KORF	ORF	Norfolk Intl, USA
KORH	ORH	Worcester Regional Airport, USA
KOTH	OTH	Southwest Oregon Regional, USA
KOXR	OXR	Oxnard Airport, USA
KPAH	PAH	Barkley Regional Airport, USA
KPBI	PBI	Palm Beach Intl, USA
KPCW	PCW	Erie, USA
KPDT	PDT	Eastern Oregon Regional Airport, USA
KPDX	PDX	Portland Intl, USA
KPFN	PFN	Panama City, USA
KPGA	PGA	Page Municipal Airport, USA
KPGV	PGV	Pitt, USA
KPHF	PHF	Williamsburg Intl, USA
KPHL	PHL	Philadelphia Intl, USA
KPHX	PHX	Phoenix Sky Harbor Intl, USA
KPIA	PIA	Greater Peoria Regional Airport, USA
KPIB	PIB	Hattiesburg, USA
KPIE	PIE	St. Petersburg, USA
KPIH	PIH	Pocatello Regional Airport, USA
KPIR	PIR	Pierre Regional Airport, USA
KPIT	PIT	Pittsburgh Intl, USA
KPKB	PKB	Mid, USA
KPLN	PLN	Pellston Regional Airport , USA
KPNS	PNS	Pensacola Regional Airport, USA
KPQI	PQI	Northern Maine Regional Airport, USA
KPSC	PSC	Tri, USA
KPSM	PSM	Pease Intl Tradeport Airport, USA
KPSP	PSP	Palm Springs Intl, USA
KPUW	PUW	Pullman, USA
KPVC	PVC	Provincetown Municipal Airport, USA
KPVD	PVD	Theodore Francis Green Statet, USA
KPWM	PWM	Portland Intl Jetport, USA
KRAP	RAP	Rapid City Regional Airport, USA
KRDD	RDD	Redding Municipal Airport, USA
KRDG	RDG	Reading Regional Airport, USA
KRDM	RDM	Redmond Municipal Airport, USA
KRDU	RDU	Raleigh, USA
KRHI	RHI	Rhinelander, USA
KRIC	RIC	Richmond Intl, USA
KRIW	RIW	Riverton Regional Airport, USA
KRKD	RKD	Knox County Regional Airport, USA
KRNO	RNO	Tahoe Intl, USA
KROA	ROA	Roanoke Regional Airport, USA
KROC	ROC	Greater Rochester Intl, USA
KRST	RST	Rochester Intl, USA
KRSW	RSW	Southwest Florida Intl, USA
KSAF	SAF	Santa Fe Municipal Airport, USA
KSAN	SAN	San Diego Intl, USA
KSAT	SAT	San Antonio Intl, USA
KSAV	SAV	Savannah Intl, USA
KSAW	SAW	Sawyer Intl, USA
KSBA	SBA	Santa Barbara Municipal Airport, USA
KSBN	SBN	South Bend Regional Airport, USA
KSBP	SBP	San Luis Obispo County, USA

ICAO	IATA	Airport & Country
KSBY	SBY	Salisbury, USA
KSCK	SCK	Stockton Metropolitan Airport, USA
KSDF	SDF	Louisville Intl, USA
KSDY	SDY	Sidney, USA
KSEA	SEA	Seattle, USA
KSFB	SFB	Orlando Sanford Intl, USA
KSFO	SFO	San Francisco Intl, USA
KSGF	SGF	Springfield, USA
KSGU	SGU	St. George Municipal Airport, USA
KSHR	SHR	Sheridan County Airport, USA
KSHV	SHV	Shreveport Regional Airport, USA
KSJC	SJC	Norman Y. Mineta San Jos, USA
KSJT	SJT	San Angelo Regional Airport, USA
KSLC	SLC	Salt Lake City Intl, USA
KSMF	SMF	Sacramento Intl, USA
KSMX	SMX	Santa Maria Public Airport, USA
KSNA	SNA	John Wayne Airport, USA
KSPI	SPI	Abraham Lincoln Capital Airport, USA
KSPS	SPS	Sheppard Air Force Base, USA
KSRQ	SRQ	Sarasota, USA
KSTC	STC	St. Cloud Regional Airport, USA
KSTL	STL	Lambert, USA
KSUN	SUN	Friedman Memorial Airport, USA
KSUX	SUX	Sioux Gateway Airport, USA
KSWF	SWF	Stewart Intl, USA
KSYR	SYR	Syracuse Hancock Intl, USA
KTEX	TEX	Telluride Regional Airport, USA
KTLH	TLH	Tallahassee Regional Airport USA
KTOL	TOL	Toledo Express Airport, USA
KTPA	TPA	Tampa Intl, USA
KTRI	TRI	Tri, USA
KTTN	TTN	Trenton, USA
KTUL	TUL	Tulsa Intl, USA
KTUP	TUP	Tupelo Regional Airport, USA
KTUS	TUS	Tucson Intl, USA
KTVC	TVC	Cherry Capital Airport, USA
KTWF	TWF	Magic Valley Regional Airport, USA
KTXK	TXK	Texarkana Regional Airport, USA
KTYR	TYR	Tyler Pounds Regional Airport USA
KTYS	TYS	McGhee Tyson Airport, USA
KUIN	UIN	Quincy Regional Airport, USA
KUNV	UNV	University Park Airport, USA
KVCT	VCT	Victoria Regional Airport, USA
KVCV	VCV	Southern California Logistics, USA
KVGT	VGT	North Las Vegas Airport, USA
KVLD	VLD	Valdosta Regional Airport, USA
KVPS	VPS	Okaloosa Regional Airport, USA
KXNA	XNA	Northwest Arkansas Regional, USA
KYKM	YKM	Yakima Air Terminal, USA
KYUM	YUM	Yuma Intl / MCAS Yuma, USA
LATI	TIA	Rinas Mother Teresa Airport, Albania
LBBG	BOJ	Burgas Intl, Bulgaria
LBGO	GOZ	Gorna Oryahovitsa Airport, Bulgaria
LBPD	PDV	Plovdiv Intl, Bulgaria
LBSF	SOF	Sofia Airport, Bulgaria
LBWN	VAR	Varna Intl, Bulgaria
LCEN	ECN	Ercan Intl, Cyprus
LCLK	LCA	Larnaca Intl, Cyprus
LCPH	PFO	Paphos Intl, Cyprus
LDDU	DBV	Dubrovnik Airport, Croatia
LDOS	OSI	Osijek Airport, Croatia
LDPL	PUY	Pula Airport, Croatia
LDRI	RJK	Rijeka Airport, Croatia
LDSB	BWK	Airport Brac, Croatia
LDSP	SPU	Airport Split, Croatia
LDZA	ZAG	Zagreb Airport, Croatia
LDZD	ZAD	Zadar Airport, Croatia
LEAB	ABC	Albacete Airport, Spain
LEAL	ALC	Alicante Airport, Spain
LEAM	LEI	Almeria Intl, Spain
LEAS	OVD	Asturias Airport, Spain
LEBA	ODB	Cordoba Airport, Spain
LEBB	BIO	Bilbao Airport, Spain
LEBL	BCN	Barcelona Intl, Spain
LEBZ	BJZ	Badajoz Airport, Spain
LECO	LCG	A Coruna Airport, Spain
LEGE	GRO	Girona, Spain
LEGR	GRX	Granada, Spain
LEIB	IBZ	Ibiza Airport, Spain
LEJR	XRY	Jerez Airport, Spain
LELC	MJV	Murcia, Spain
LELL	QSA	Sabadell Airport, Spain
LELN	LEN	Leon Airport, Spain
LELO	RJL	Logrono, Spain
LEMD	MAD	Madrid Barajas Intl, Spain
LEMG	AGP	Malaga Airport, Spain
LEMH	MAH	Menorca Airport, Spain
LEPA	PMI	Palma de Mallorca Airport, Spain
LEPP	PNA	Pamplona Airport, Spain
LERS	REU	Reus Airport, Spain
LESA	SLM	Salamanca Airport, Spain
LESO	EAS	San Sebastian Airport, Spain
LEST	SCQ	Santiago Airport, Spain
LETO	TOJ	Madrid Torrejon Airport Spain
LEVC	VLC	Valencia Airport, Spain
LEVD	VLL	Valladolid Airport, Spain
LEVT	VIT	Vitoria Airport, Spain
LEVX	VGO	Vigo Airport, Spain
LEXJ	SDR	Santander Airport, Spain
LEZG	ZAZ	Zaragoza Airport, Spain
LEZL	SVQ	Seville Airport, Spain
LFAB	DPE	Dieppe, France
LFAC	CQF	Calais, France
LFAT	LTQ	Le Touquet, France
LFBA	AGF	Agen, France
LFBD	BOD	Bordeaux Airport Airport, France
LFBE	EGC	Bergerac, France
LFBG	CNG	Cognac, France
LFBH	LRH	La Rochelle, France
LFBI	PIS	Poitiers, France
LFBK	MCU	Montlucon, France
LFBL	LIG	Limoges Airport, France
LFBN	NIT	Souche Airport, France
LFBO	TLS	Toulouse, France
LFBP	PUF	Pau, France
LFBT	LDE	Tarbes, France
LFBU	ANG	Angouleme, France
LFBV	BVE	Brive, France
LFBX	PGX	Perigueux, France
LFBZ	BIQ	Biarritz, France

ICAO	IATA	Airport & Country
LFCC	ZAO	Cahors, France
LFCI	LBI	Albi, France
LFCK	DCM	Castres, France
LFCR	RDZ	Rodez, France
LFCY	RYN	Royan, France
LFDH	AUC	Auch, France
LFDN	RCO	Rochefort, France
LFEY	IDY	d'Yeu, France
LFGA	CMR	Colmar, France
LFGJ	DLE	Dole, France
LFHM	MVV	Megeve Airport, France
LFHO	OBS	Aubenas Ardeche Airport, France
LFHP	LPY	Le Puy, France
LFJL	ETZ	Metz, France
LFJR	ANE	Angers Loire Aeroport Airport, France
LFKB	BIA	Bastia, France
LFKC	CLY	Calvi, France
LFKF	FSC	Figari, France
LFKJ	AJA	Campo Dell Oro Airport, France
LFKO	PRP	Tavaria Airport, France
LFKS	SOZ	Solenzara, France
LFKX	MFX	Meribel Airport, France
LFLA	AUF	Auxerre, France
LFLB	CMF	Chambery, France
LFLC	CFE	Clermont, France
LFLD	BOU	Bourges Airport, France
LFLJ	CVF	Courchevel Airport, France
LFLL	LYS	Lyon Saint Exupery Airport, France
LFLO	RNE	Roanne, France
LFLP	NCY	Annecy, France
LFLS	GNB	Grenoble, France
LFLU	VAF	Valence, France
LFLV	VHY	Vichy, France
LFLW	AUR	Aurillac Airport, France
LFLX	CHR	Chateauroux, France
LFLY	LYN	Lyon, France
LFMD	CEQ	Cannes, France
LFMH	EBU	Saint, France
LFMK	CCF	Carcassonne en Pays, France
LFML	MRS	Marseille, France
LFMN	NCE	Nice, France
LFMP	PGF	Perpignan, France
LFMQ	CTT	Le Castellet Airport, France
LFMT	MPL	Montpellier, France
LFMU	BZR	Beziers, France
LFMV	AVN	Avignon Airport, France
LFNA	GAT	Tallard Airport, France
LFNB	MEN	Mende, France
LFOB	BVA	Beauvais, France
LFOE	EVX	Evreux, France
LFOH	LEH	Le Havre, France
LFOI	XAB	Abbeville, France
LFOJ	ORE	Orleans, France
LFOP	URO	Rouen, France
LFOQ	XBQ	Blois, France
LFOT	TUF	Tours, France
LFOU	CET	Cholet Lepontreau Airport, France
LFOV	LVA	Laval, France
LFPB	LBG	Paris, France
LFPC	CSF	Creil Airport, France

ICAO	IATA	Airport & Country
LFPG	CDG	Paris, France
LFPN	TNF	Toussus – le Noble Airport, France
LFPO	ORY	Paris, France
LFPT	POX	Pontoise, France
LFQD	QRV	Arras, France
LFQF	XXG	Autun, France
LFQG	NVS	Nevers, France
LFQM	QBQ	Besancon, France
LFQQ	LIL	Lille, France
LFQT	HZB	Merville, France
LFRB	BES	Brest Bretagne Airport, France
LFRC	CER	Cherbourg, France
LFRD	DNR	Dinard, France
LFRE	LBY	Labaule, France
LFRF	GFR	Granville, France
LFRG	DOL	Deauville, France
LFRH	LRT	Lorient, France
LFRI	EDM	La Roche sur Yon, France
LFRK	CFR	Caen, France
LFRM	LME	Le Mans, France
LFRN	RNS	Rennes, France
LFRO	LAI	Lannion, France
LFRQ	UIP	Quimper, France
LFRS	NTE	Nantes Atlantique Airport, France
LFRT	SBK	Saint, France
LFRU	MXN	Morlaix, France
LFRV	VNE	Vannes, France
LFRZ	SNR	Saint, France
LFSB	MLH	EuroAirport Basel, France
LFSD	DIJ	Dijon, France
LFSF	MZM	Metz, France
LFSG	EPL	Epinal, France
LFSN	ENC	Nancy, France
LFSR	RHE	Reims, France
LFST	SXB	Strasbourg Airport, France
LFSZ	VTL	Vittel, France
LFVP	FSP	St. Pierre Airport, Saint
LFXC	VTL	Vittel, France
LGAL	AXD	Alexandroupolis Intl, Greece
LGAV	ATH	Athens Intl, Greece
LGBL	VOL	Aghialos National Airport, Greece
LGHI	JKH	Chios Island National Airport, Greece
LGIK	JIK	Ikaria Island National Airport, Greece
LGIO	IOA	Ioannina National Airport, Greece
LGIR	HER	Heraklion Intl, Greece
LGKA	KSO	Kastoria National Airport, Greece
LGKC	KIT	Kithira Island National Airport, Greece
LGKF	EFL	Kefalonia Island Intl, Greece
LGKJ	KZS	Kastelorizo Island Public, Greece
LGKL	KLX	Kalamata Intl, Greece
LGKO	KGS	Kos Island Intl, Greece
LGKP	AOK	Karpathos Island National, Greece
LGKR	CFU	Corfu Intl, Greece
LGKS	KSJ	Kassos Island Public Airport, Greece
LGKV	KVA	Kavala Intl, Greece
LGKZ	KZI	Kozani National Airport, Greece
LGLM	LXS	Lemnos Intl, Greece
LGMK	JMK	Mykonos Island National, Greece
LGML	MLO	Milos Island National Airport, Greece
LGMT	MJT	Mytilene Intl, Greece

Appendix F

ICAO	IATA	Airport & Country
LGNX	JNX	Naxos Island National Airport, Greece
LGPA	PAS	Paros National Airport, Greece
LGPL	JTY	Astypalaia Island National, Greece
LGPZ	PVK	Aktion National Airport, Greece
LGRP	RHO	Rhodes Intl, Greece
LGRX	GPA	Araxos National Airport, Greece
LGSA	CHQ	Chania Intl, Greece
LGSK	JSI	Skiathos Island National, Greece
LGSM	SMI	Samos Intl, Greece
LGSO	JSY	Syros Island National Airport, Greece
LGSR	JTR	Santorini National Airport, Greece
LGST	JSH	Sitia Public Airport, Greece
LGSY	SKU	Skyros Island National Airport, Greece
LGTS	SKG	Thessaloniki Intl, Greece
LGZA	ZTH	Zakynthos Intl, Greece
LHBP	BUD	Budapest Ferihegy Intl, Hungary
LHDC	DEB	Debrecen Intl, Hungary
LHMC	MCQ	Miskolc Airport, Hungary
LHPR	QGY	Gyor, Hungary
LHSM	SOB	S, Hungary
LIBC	CRV	Crotone Airport, Italy
LIBD	BRI	Palese Macchie Airport, Italy
LIBF	FOG	Gino Lisa Airport, Italy
LIBG	TAR	Grottaglie Airport, Italy
LIBN	LCC	Lecce Airport, Italy
LIBP	PSR	Abruzzo Intl, Italy
LIBR	BDS	Casale Airport, Italy
LICA	SUF	Lamezia Terme Intl, Italy
LICC	CTA	Catania, Italy
LICD	LMP	Lampedusa Airport, Italy
LICG	PNL	Pantelleria Airport, Italy
LICJ	PMO	Palermo Intl, Italy
LICR	REG	Reggio Calabria Airport, Italy
LICT	TPS	Vincenzo Florio Airport, Italy
LIDB	BLX	Belluno Airport, Italy
LIDR	RAN	Ravenna Airport, Italy
LIEA	AHO	Alghero Airport, Italy
LIEE	CAG	Cagliari, Italy
LIEO	OLB	Olbia, Italy
LIET	TTB	Tortoli, Italy
LIMC	MXP	Malpensa Intl, Italy
LIME	BGY	Orio al Serio Intl, Italy
LIMF	TRN	Torino Caselle Airport, Italy
LIMG	ALL	Villanova d'Albenga Intl, Italy
LIMJ	GOA	Genoa Cristoforo Colombo, Italy
LIML	LIN	Linate Airport, Italy
LIMP	PMF	Parma Airport, Italy
LIMW	AOT	Aosta Airport, Italy
LIMZ	CUF	Cuneo Levaldigi Airport, Italy
LIPB	BZO	Bolzano Dolomiti Airport, Italy
LIPD	UDN	Campoformido Airport, Italy
LIPE	BLQ	Aeroporto G. Marcon di Bologna, Italy
LIPH	TSF	Treviso Airport, Italy
LIPK	FRL	Forli Airport, Italy
LIPO	VBS	Montichiari Airport, Italy
LIPQ	TRS	Friuli Venezia Giulia Airport, Italy
LIPR	RMI	Federico Fellini Intl, Italy
LIPT	VIC	Vicenza Trissino Airport, Italy
LIPX	VRN	Verona Airport, Italy
LIPY	AOI	Ancona Falconara Airport, Italy

ICAO	IATA	Airport & Country
LIPZ	VCE	Marco Polo Venice Airport, Italy
LIQL	LCV	Tassignano Airport, Italy
LIQS	SAY	Siena Airport, Italy
LIRA	CIA	Ciampino Airport, Italy
LIRF	FCO	Fiumicino, Italy
LIRJ	EBA	Aeroporto Marina di Campo, Italy
LIRL	QLT	Latina Airport, Italy
LIRN	NAP	Naples Intl, Italy
LIRP	PSA	Galileo Galilei Airport, Italy
LIRQ	FLR	A. Vespucci Florence Airport, Italy
LIRS	GRS	Grosseto Airport, Italy
LIRZ	PEG	San Egidio Airport, Italy
LJLJ	LJU	Aerodrom Ljubljana, Slovenia
LJMB	MBX	Maribor Airport, Slovenia
LJPZ	POW	Portoroz Airport, Slovenia
LKKU	UHE	Kunovice Airport, Czech Republic
LKKV	KLV	Karlovy Vary Intl, Czech Republic
LKMT	OSR	Ostrava, Czech Republic
LKPD	PED	Pardubice Airport, Czech Republic
LKPR	PRG	Prague Ruzyne Intl, Czech Republic
LKTB	BRQ	Brno Turany Airport, Czech Republic
LLBG	TLV	Ben Gurion Intl, Israel
LLBS	BEV	Teyman Airport, Israel
LLET	ETH	Eilat Airport, Israel
LLEY	EIY	Ein Yahav Airfield, Israel
LLHA	HFA	Haifa Airport, Israel
LLIB	RPN	Rosh Pina Airport, Israel
LLKS	KSW	Qiryat Shemona Airport, Israel
LLMR	MIP	Mitzpe Ramon Airfield, Israel
LLMZ	MTZ	Masada Airfield, Israel
LLOV	VDA	Ovda Intl, Israel
LLSD	SDV	Sde Dov Airport, Israel
LMML	MLA	Luqa, Malta
LNMC	MCM	Monaco Heliport, Monaco
LOWG	GRZ	Graz, Austria
LOWI	INN	Innsbruck, Austria
LOWK	KLU	Klagenfurt, Austria
LOWL	LNZ	Linz, Austria
LOWS	SZG	Salzburg, Austria
LOWW	VIE	Wien, Austria
LPAZ	SMA	Santa Maria Airport, Portugal
LPBG	BGC	Braganca Airport, Portugal
LPBR	BGZ	Braga Airport, Portugal
LPCH	CHV	Chaves Airport, Portugal
LPCO	CBP	Coimbra Airport, Portugal
LPCR	CVU	Corvo Airport, Portugal
LPCV	COV	Covilha Airport, Portugal
LPFL	FLW	Flores Airport, Portugal
LPFR	FAO	Faro Airport, Portugal
LPGR	GRW	Graciosa Airport, Portugal
LPHR	HOR	Horta Airport, Portugal
LPMA	FNC	Madeira Airport, Portugal
LPPD	PDL	Joao Paulo II Airport, Portugal
LPPI	PIX	Pico Airport, Portugal
LPPM	PRM	Portimao Airport, Portugal
LPPR	OPO	Francisco Sa Carneiro, Portugal
LPPS	PXO	Porto Santo Airport, Portugal
LPPT	LIS	Portela Airport, Portugal
LPSI	SIE	Sines Airport, Portugal
LPSJ	SJZ	Sao Jorge Airport, Portugal

ICAO	IATA	Airport & Country
LPVR	VRL	Vila Real Airport, Portugal
LPVZ	VSE	Viseu Airport, Portugal
LQBK	BNX	Banja Luka Intl, Bosnia
LQMO	OMO	Mostar Intl, Bosnia
LQSA	SJJ	Sarajevo Intl, Bosnia
LQTZ	TZL	Tuzla Intl, Bosnia
LRAR	ARW	Arad Intl, Romania
LRBC	BCM	Bacau Intl, Romania
LRBM	BAY	Baia Mare Airport, Romania
LRBS	BBU	Bucharest Intl, Romania
LRCK	CND	Constanta Intl, Romania
LRCL	CLJ	Cluj, Romania
LRCS	CSB	Caransebes Airport, Romania
LRCV	CRA	Craiova Airport, Romania
LRIA	IAS	Iasi Intl, Romania
LROD	OMR	Oradea Intl, Romania
LROP	OTP	Bucharest Intl, Romania
LRSB	SBZ	Sibiu Intl, Romania
LRSM	SUJ	Satu Mare Intl, Romania
LRSV	SCV	Suceava Airport, Romania
LRTC	TCE	Tulcea Airport, Romania
LRTM	TGM	Targu Mures Intl, Romania
LRTR	TSR	Timisoara Intl, Romania
LSGG	GVA	Geneva, Switzerland
LSGS	SIR	Sion Airport, Switzerland
LSZA	LUG	Lugano Airport, Switzerland
LSZB	BRN	Bern, Switzerland
LSZH	ZRH	Zurich Airport, Switzerland
LSZR	ACH	St Gallen, Switzerland
LSZS	SMV	Samedan Airport, Switzerland
LTAC	ESB	Ankara Esenboga Intl, Turkey
LTAF	ADA	Adana Airport, Turkey
LTAI	AYT	Antalya Airport, Turkey
LTAJ	GZT	Oguzeli Airport, Turkey
LTAN	KYA	Konya Airport, Turkey
LTAR	VAS	Sivas Airport, Turkey
LTAT	MLX	Malatya Erhac Airport, Turkey
LTAU	ASR	Kayseri Erkilet Intl, Turkey
LTAY	DNZ	Denizli Cardak Airport, Turkey
LTAZ	NAV	Nevsehir Kapadokya Airport, Turkey
LTBA	IST	Istanbul Ataturk Intl, Turkey
LTBH	CKZ	Canakkale Airport, Turkey
LTBJ	ADB	Izmir Adnan Menderes Airport, Turkey
LTBR	YEI	Bursa Yenisehir Airport, Turkey
LTBS	DLM	Dalaman Airport, Turkey
LTBU	TEQ	Corlu Airport, Turkey
LTCA	EZS	Elazig Airport, Turkey
LTCC	DIY	Diyarbakir Airport, Turkey
LTCD	ERC	Erzincan Airport, Turkey
LTCE	ERZ	Erzurum Airport, Turkey
LTCF	KSY	Kars Airport, Turkey
LTCG	TZX	Trabzon Airport, Turkey
LTCH	SFQ	Sanliurfa Airport, Turkey
LTCI	VAN	Van Ferit Melen Airport, Turkey
LTCJ	BAL	Batman Airport, Turkey
LTCK	MSR	Mus Airport, Turkey
LTCL	SXZ	Siirt Airport, Turkey
LTCN	KCM	Kahramanmaras Airport, Turkey
LTCO	AJI	Agri Airport, Turkey
LTCP	ADF	Adiyaman Airport, Turkey

ICAO	IATA	Airport & Country
LTCR	MQM	Mardin Airport, Turkey
LTFC	ISE	Suleyman Demirel Airport, Turkey
LTFD	EDO	Edremit Korfez Airport, Turkey
LTFE	BJV	Milas, Turkey
LTFH	SZF	Samsun Carsamba Airport, Turkey
LTFJ	SAW	Istanbul Sabiha Gokcen Intl, Turkey
LUKK	KIV	Chisinau, Moldova
LWOH	OHD	Ohrid, Macedonia
LWOH	OHD	Ohrid Airport, Macedonia
LWSK	SKP	Skopje, Macedonia
LWSK	SKP	Skopje Airport, Macedonia
LXGB	GIB	Gibraltar, Gibraltar
LYBE	BEG	Belgrade Nikola Tesla Airport, Serbia
LYNI	INI	Nis Constantine the Great Intl, Serbia
LYNS	QND	Novi Sad Airport, Serbia
LYPA	QBG	Pancevo Airport, Serbia
LYPG	TGD	Podgorica, Montenegro
LYPR	PRN	Pristina Intl, Serbia
LYTV	TIV	Tivat Airport, Montenegro
LYUZ	ZZE	Uzice Airport, Serbia
LYVA	QWV	Valjevo Airport, Serbia
LZIB	BTS	Bratislava, Slovakia
LZKZ	KSC	Kosice Airport, Slovakia
LZPP	PZY	Piestany Airport, Slovakia
LZSL	SLD	Sliac Airport, Slovakia
LZTT	TAT	Tatry Airport, Slovakia
LZZI	ILZ	Zilina Airport, Slovakia
MBGT	GDT	Grand Turk Intl, Turks & Caicos
MDBH	BRX	Maria Montez Intl, Dominican Repub
MDCR	CBJ	Cabo Rojo Airport, Dominican Repub
MDCZ	COZ	Constanza Airport, Dominican Repub
MDHE	HEX	Herrera Intl, Dominican Republic
MDLI	SLI	La Isabela Intl, Dominican Republic
MDLR	LRM	La Romana Intl, Dominican Republic
MDPC	PUJ	Punta Cana Intl, Dominican Republic
MDPO	EPS	El Portillo Airport, Dominican Republic
MDPP	POP	Gregorio Luperon, Dominican Repub
MDSB	SNX	Sabana de la Mar, Dominican Repub
MDSD	SDQ	Las Americas, Dominican Republic
MDSJ	SJM	San Juan de la Maguana, Dom Repub
MDST	STI	Cibao Intl, Dominican Republic
MGCB	CBV	Coban Airport, Guatemala
MGCR	CMM	Carmelita Airport, Guatemala
MGCT	CTF	Coatepeque Airport, Guatemala
MGGT	GUA	Guatemala La Aurora Intl, Guatemala
MGHT	HUG	Huehuetenango Airport, Guatemala
MGMM	MCR	Melchor de Mencos, Guatemala
MGPB	PBR	Puerto Barrios Airport, Guatemala
MGPP	PON	Poptun Airport, Guatemala
MGQC	AQB	Quiche Airport, Guatemala
MGQZ	AAZ	Quezaltenango Airport, Guatemala
MGRB	RUV	Rubelsanto Airport, Guatemala
MGRT	RER	Retalhuleu Airport, Guatemala
MGTK	FRS	Mundo Maya Intl, Guatemala
MHCA	CAA	Catacamas, Honduras
MHLC	LCE	Goloson Intl, Honduras
MHLE	LEZ	La Esperanza, Honduras
MHLM	SAP	La Mesa Intl, Honduras
MHPL	PEU	Puerto Lempira, Honduras
MHRO	RTB	Roatan Intl, Honduras

ICAO	IATA	Airport & Country	ICAO	IATA	Airport & Country
MHTE	TEA	Tela, Honduras	MMZC	ZCL	La Calera Airport, Mexico
MHTG	TGU	Toncontin Intl, Honduras	MMZH	ZIH	Ixtapa, Mexico
MKJP	KIN	Norman Manley Intl, Jamaica	MMZO	ZLO	Playa de Oro Intl, Mexico
MKJS	MBJ	Sangster Intl, Jamaica	MNBL	BEF	Bluefields, Nicaragua
MMAA	ACA	General Juan N. Alvarez Intl, Mexico	MNMG	MGA	Augusto Cesar Sandino, Nicaragua
MMAS	AGU	Lic. Jesus Teran Peredo Intl, Mexico	MNPC	PUZ	Puerto Cabezas, Nicaragua
MMBT	HUX	Bah, Mexico	MPBO	BOC	Bocas Del Toro Intl, Panama
MMCB	CVJ	General Marianc Matamoros, Mexico	MPCH	CHX	Cap. Manuel Nino Intl, Panama
MMCE	CME	Ciudad del Carmen Intl, Mexico	MPDA	DAV	Enrique Malek Intl, Panama
MMCL	CUL	Federal de Bachigualato Intl, Mexico	MPEJ	ONX	Enrique Adolfo Jimenez, Panama
MMCM	CTM	Chetumal Intl, Mexico	MPJE	JQE	Jaque, Panama
MMCN	CEN	Ciudad Obregon Intl, Mexico	MPTO	PTY	Tocumen Intl, Panama
MMCP	CPE	Ing. Alberto Acuna Ongay Intl, Mexico	MRAN	FON	La Fortuna Airport, Costa Rica
MMCS	CJS	Abraham Gonzalez Intl, Mexico	MRAO	TTQ	Tortuguero Airport, Costa Rica
MMCU	CUU	Gen Roberto Fierro Villalobos, Mexico	MRBA	BAI	Buenos Aires Airport, Costa Rica
MMCV	CVM	General Pedro J. Mendez, Mexico	MRBC	BCL	Barra del Colorado Airport, Costa Rica
MMCZ	CZM	Cozumel Intl, Mexico	MRCC	OTR	Coto 47 Airport, Costa Rica
MMDO	DGO	General Guadalupe Victoria, Mexico	MRCR	RIK	Carrillo Airport, Costa Rica
MMEP	TPQ	Amado Nervo National Airport, Mexico	MRDK	DRK	Drake Bay Airport, Costa Rica
MMGL	GDL	Don Miguel Hidalgo y Costilla, Mexico	MRGF	GLF	Golfito Airport, Costa Rica
MMGM	GYM	Gen Jose Maria Yanez Intl, Mexico	MRGP	GPL	Guapiles Airport, Costa Rica
MMGR	GUB	Guerrero Negro Airport, Mexico	MRIA	PBP	Punta Islita Airport, Costa Rica
MMHO	HMO	Ignacio Pesqueira Garcia, Mexico	MRLB	LIR	Daniel Oduber Intl, Costa Rica
MMIA	CLQ	Lic. Miguel de Madrid Airport, Mexico	MRLC	LSL	Los Chiles Airport, Costa Rica
MMIO	SLW	Plan de Guadalupe Intl, Mexico	MRLM	LIO	Limon Intl, Costa Rica
MMJA	JAL	El Lencero Airport, Mexico	MRNS	NOM	Nosara Airport, Costa Rica
MMLC	LZC	Lazaro Cardenas Airport, Mexico	MROC	SJO	Juan Santamaria Intl, Costa Rica
MMLM	LMM	Federal del Valle del Fuerte, Mexico	MRPJ	PJM	Puerto Jimenez Airport, Costa Rica
MMLO	BJX	Del Bajio Intl, Mexico	MRPM	PMZ	Palmar Sur Airport, Costa Rica
MMLP	LAP	Manuel Marquez de Leon Intl, Mexico	MRPV	SYQ	Tobias Bolanos Intl, Costa Rica
MMLT	LTO	Loreto Intl, Mexico	MRQP	XQP	La Managua Airport, Costa Rica
MMMA	MAM	General Servando Canales, Mexico	MRTM	TNO	Tamarindo Airport, Costa Rica
MMMD	MID	Manuel Crescencio Rej, Mexico	MRTR	TMU	Tambor Airport, Costa Rica
MMML	MXL	General Rodolfo S. Mexico	MRUP	UPL	Upala Airport, Costa Rica
MMMM	MLM	General Francisco J. Mujica, Mexico	MTCH	CAP	Cap Haitien Intl, Haiti
MMMT	MTT	Coatzacoalcos National, Mexico	MTJA	JAK	Jacmel, Haiti
MMMV	LOV	Venustiano Carranza Intl, Mexico	MTJE	JEE	Jeremie, Haiti
MMMX	MEX	Mexico City Intl, Mexico	MTPP	PAP	Port, Haiti
MMMY	MTY	General Mariano Escobedo, Mexico	MTPX	PAX	Port De Paix, Haiti
MMMZ	MZT	General Rafael Buelna Intl, Mexico	MUBA	BCA	Gustavo Rizo Airport, Cuba
MMNL	NLD	Quetzalcoatl Intl, Mexico	MUBY	BYM	Carlos Manuel de Cespedes, Cuba
MMOX	OAX	Xoxocotlan Intl, Mexico	MUCA	AVI	Maximo Gomez Intl, Cuba
MMPA	PAZ	El Tajin National Airport, Mexico	MUCF	CFG	Jaime Gonzalez Airport, Cuba
MMPB	PBC	Hermanos Serdan Intl, Mexico	MUCL	CYO	Vilo Acuna Airport, Cuba
MMPG	PDS	Piedras Negras Intl, Mexico	MUCM	CMW	Ignacio Agramonte Int , Cuba
MMPN	UPN	Gen. Ignacio Lopez Rayon, Mexico	MUCU	SCU	Antonio Maceo Intl, Cuba
MMPR	PVR	Lic. Gustavo Diaz Ordaz Intl, Mexico	MUGT	GAO	Mariana Grajales Airport, Cuba
MMPS	PXM	Puerto Escondido Intl, Mexico	MUHA	HAV	Jose Marti Intl, Cuba
MMRX	REX	General Lucio Blanco Intl, Mexico	MUHG	HOG	Frank Pais Airport, Cuba
MMSD	SJD	Los Cabos Intl, Mexico	MUKW	VRO	Kawama Airport, Cuba
MMSP	SLP	Ponciano Arriaga Intl, Mexico	MULM	LCL	La Coloma Airport, Cuba
MMTC	TRC	Torreon Intl, Mexico	MUMO	MOA	Orestes Acosta Airport, Cuba
MMTG	TGZ	Llano San Juan Airport, Mexico	MUMZ	MZO	Sierra Maestra Airport, Cuba
MMTJ	TIJ	General Abelardo, Mexico	MUNB	QSN	San Nicolas de Bari Airport, Cuba
MMTM	TAM	Gen Francisco Javier Mina, Mexico	MUNC	ICR	Nicaro Airport, Cuba
MMTO	TLC	Lic. Adolfo Lopez Mateos, Mexico	MUNG	GER	Rafael Cabrera Airport, Cuba
MMTP	TAP	Tapachula Intl, Mexico	MUOC	CCC	Cayo Coco Airport, Cuba
MMUN	CUN	Cancun Intl, Mexico	MUPR	QPD	Pinar del R, Cuba
MMVA	VSA	Carlos Rovirosa Perez, Mexico	MUSC	SNU	Abel Santa Maria Airport, Cuba
MMVR	VER	General Heriberto Jara Intl, Mexico	MUSN	SZJ	Siguanea Airport, Cuba

ICAO	IATA	Airport & Country
MUTD	TND	Alberto Delgado Airport, Cuba
MUVR	VRA	Juan Gualberto Gomez, Cuba
MUVT	VTU	Hermanos Ameijeiras Airport, Cuba
MWCB	CYB	Gerrard, Cayman Islands
MWCR	GCM	Roberts Intl, Cayman Islands
MYAB	MAY	Clarence Bain Airport, Bahamas
MYAF	ASD	Andros Town Intl, Bahamas
MYAK	COX	Congo Town Airport, Bahamas
MYAM	MHH	Marsh Harbour Airport, Bahamas
MYAN	SAQ	San Andros Airport, Bahamas
MYAP	AXP	Spring Point Airport, Bahamas
MYAT	TCB	Treasure Cay Airport, Bahamas
MYBC	CCZ	Chub Cay Intl, Bahamas
MYBG	GHC	Great Harbour Cay Airport, Bahamas
MYBS	BIM	South Bimini Airport, Bahamas
MYCA	ATC	Arthurs Town Airport, Bahamas
MYCB	CAT	New Bight Airport, Bahamas
MYCI	CRI	Colonial Hill Airport, Bahamas
MYEF	GGT	Exuma Intl, Bahamas
MYEH	ELH	North Eleuthera Airport, Bahamas
MYEM	GHB	Governor's Harbour Airport, Bahamas
MYEN	NMC	Norman's Cay Airport, Bahamas
MYER	RSD	Rock Sound Intl, Bahamas
MYES	TYM	Staniel Cay Airport, Bahamas
MYGF	FPO	Grand Bahama Intl , Bahamas
MYIG	IGA	Inagua Airport , Bahamas
MYLD	LGI	Deadman's Cay Airport, Bahamas
MYLS	SML	Stella Maris Airport, Bahamas
MYMM	MYG	Mayaguana Airport, Bahamas
MYNN	NAS	Nassau Intl, Bahamas
MYPI	PID	New Providence Airport, Bahamas
MYSM	ZSA	San Salvador Airport , Bahamas
MZBZ	BZE	Philip S W Goldson Intl, Belize
N55	UIT	Jaluit, Marshall Islands
NCAI	AIT	Avarua, Cook Islands
NCMK	MUK	Akatoka Manava, Cook Islands
NCPY	PYE	Tongareva, Cook Islands
NCRG	RAR	Rarotonga Intl, Cook Islands
NFFN	NAN	Nadi Intl, Fiji
NFNA	SUV	Nausori Intl, Fiji
NFNL	LBS	Labasa, Fiji
NFNR	RTA	Rotuma, Fiji
NFTF	TBU	Fua'amotu Intl, Tonga
NFTL	HPA	Ha'apai, Tonga
NFTP	NTT	Niuatoputapu, Tonga
NFTV	VAV	Vava'u, Tonga
NGFU	FUN	Funafuti Intl, Tuvalu
NGTA	TRW	Bonriki Intl, Kiribati
NGTU	BBG	Butaritari, Kiribati
NTTB	BOB	Bora Bora Airport, French Polynesia
NTTG	RGI	Rangiroa Airport, French Polynesia
NTTR	RFP	Raiatea Airport, French Polynesia
NVSS	SON	Santo, Vanuatu
NVVV	VLI	Bauerfield, Vanuatu
NWWD	KNQ	Kone, New Caledonia
NWWE	ILP	Moue, New Caledonia
NWWH	HLU	Nesson, New Caledonia
NWWK	KOC	Koumac, New Caledonia
NWWL	LIF	Ouanaham, New Caledonia
NWWM	GEA	Magenta, New Caledonia
NWWR	MEE	La Roche Aero, New Caledonia
NWWU	TOU	Touho, New Caledonia
NWWV	UVE	Ouloup, New Caledonia
NWWW	NOU	Tontouta, New Caledonia
NZAA	AKL	Auckland Intl, New Zealand
NZAP	TUO	Taupo, New Zealand
NZAS	ASG	Ashburton, New Zealand
NZCH	CHC	Christchurch Intl, New Zealand
NZCI	CHT	Chatham Is/Tuuta, New Zealand
NZDN	DUD	Dunedin, New Zealand
NZGB	GBZ	Great Barrier, New Zealand
NZGM	GMN	Greymouth, New Zealand
NZGS	GIS	Gisborne, New Zealand
NZGT	GTN	Glentanner, New Zealand
NZHK	HKK	Hokitika, New Zealand
NZHN	HLZ	Hamilton Intl, New Zealand
NZKI	KBZ	Kaikoura, New Zealand
NZKK	KKE	Kerikeri, New Zealand
NZKO	KKO	Kaikohe, New Zealand
NZKT	KAT	Kaitaia, New Zealand
NZLX	ALR	Alexandra, New Zealand
NZMA	MTA	Matamata, New Zealand
NZMC	MON	Mount Cook, New Zealand
NZMF	MFN	Milford Sound, New Zealand
NZMS	MRO	Masterton, New Zealand
NZNP	NPL	New Plymouth, New Zealand
NZNR	NPE	Napier, New Zealand
NZNS	NSN	Nelson, New Zealand
NZNV	IVC	Invercargill, New Zealand
NZOH	OHA	Ohakea, New Zealand
NZOU	OAM	Oamaru, New Zealand
NZPM	PMR	Palmerston North, New Zealand
NZPP	PPQ	Paraparaumu, New Zealand
NZQN	ZQN	Queenstown, New Zealand
NZRA	RAG	Raglan, New Zealand
NZRO	ROT	Rotorua, New Zealand
NZTG	TRG	Tauranga, New Zealand
NZTH	TMZ	Thames, New Zealand
NZTU	TIU	Timaru, New Zealand
NZWB	BHE	Woodbourne , New Zealand
NZWF	WKA	Wanaka, New Zealand
NZWK	WHK	Whakatane, New Zealand
NZWN	WLG	Wellington Intl, New Zealand
NZWO	WIR	Wairoa, New Zealand
NZWR	WRE	Whangarei, New Zealand
NZWS	WSZ	Westport, New Zealand
NZWU	WAG	Wanganui, New Zealand
OABN	BIM	Bamyan, Afghanistan
OABT	BST	Bost, Afghanistan
OACC	CCN	Charkhcharan, Afghanistan
OAFR	FAH	Farah, Afghanistan
OAFZ	FBD	Faizabad, Afghanistan
OAGZ	GRG	Gardez, Afghanistan
OAHN	KWH	Khwahan, Afghanistan
OAHR	HEA	Herat, Afghanistan
OAJL	JAA	Jalalabad, Afghanistan
OAKB	KBL	Kabul Intl, Afghanistan
OAKN	KDH	Kandahar, Afghanistan
OAKS	KHT	Khost, Afghanistan
OAMN	MMZ	Maimama, Afghanistan

Appendix F

ICAO	IATA	Airport & Country
OAMS	MZR	Mazar, Afghanistan
OASN	SGA	Sheghnan, Afghanistan
OAUZ	UND	Kunduz, Afghanistan
OAZJ	ZAJ	Zaranj, Afghanistan
OBBI	BAH	Bahrain Intl, Bahrain
OEAB	AHB	Abha Regional Airport, Saudi Arabia
OEBH	BHH	Bisha Domestic Airport, Saudi Arabia
OEDF	DMM	King Fahd Intl, Saudi Arabia
OEDW	DWD	Dawadmi Domestic, Saudi Arabia
OEGN	GIZ	Gizan Regional Airport, Saudi Arabia
OEGS	ELQ	Gassim Regional Airport, Saudi Arabia
OEGT	URY	Gurayat Domestic, Saudi Arabia
OEHL	HAS	Hail Regional Airport, Saudi Arabia
OEJN	JED	King Abdulaziz Intl, Saudi Arabia
OEKK	HBT	Hafr al, Saudi Arabia
OEMA	MED	Moh Bin Abdulaziz, Saudi Arabia
OENG	EAM	Najran Domestic Airport, Saudi Arabia
OEPA	EPA	Qaisumah Domestic, Saudi Arabia
OERF	RAH	Rafha Domestic Airport, Saudi Arabia
OERK	RUH	King Khalid Intl, Saudi Arabia
OERR	RAE	Arar Domestic Airport, Saudi Arabia
OESH	ESH	Sharorah Domestic, Saudi Arabia
OETB	TUU	Tabuk Regional Airport, Saudi Arabia
OETF	TIF	Taif Regional Airport, Saudi Arabia
OETR	TUI	Turaif Domestic Airport, Saudi Arabia
OEWD	EWD	Wadi al, Saudi Arabia
OEWJ	EJH	Wedjh Domestic Airport, Saudi Arabia
OEYN	YNB	Yanbu Domestic Airport, Saudi Arabia
OIAA	ABD	Abadan Airport, Iran
OIAM	MRX	Mahshahr Airport, Iran
OIAW	AWZ	Ahwaz Airport, Iran
OIBB	BUZ	Bushehr Airport, Iran
OIBI	YEH	Asalouyeh Airport, Iran
OIBK	KIH	Kish Airport, Iran
OIBL	BDH	Bandar Lengeh Airport, Iran
OIBQ	KHK	Khark Airport, Iran
OIBS	SXI	Sirri Island Airport, Iran
OIBV	LVP	Lavan Airport, Iran
OICC	KSH	Shahid Ashrafi Esfahani Airport, Iran
OICK	KHD	Khoram Abad Airport, Iran
OICS	SDG	Sanandaj Airport, Iran
OIFM	IFN	Isfahan Intl, Iran
OIGG	RAS	Rasht Airport, Iran
OIHH	HDM	Hamadan Airport, Iran
OIIE	IKA	Imam Khomeini Intl Iran
OIII	THR	Mehrabad Intl, Iran
OIKB	BND	Bandar Abbass Intl, Iran
OIKK	KER	Kerman Airport, Iran
OIKM	BXR	Bam Airport, Iran
OIKR	RJN	Rafsanjan Airport, Iran
OIKY	SYJ	Sirjan Airport, Iran
OIMB	XBJ	Birjand Airport, Iran
OIMC	CKT	Sarakhs Airport, Iran
OIMM	MHD	Mashhad Intl, Iran
OIMN	BJB	Bojnord Airport, Iran
OIMT	TCX	Tabas Airport, Iran
OINR	RZR	Ramsar Airport, Iran
OINZ	SRY	Dasht, Iran
OISS	SYZ	Shiraz Intl, Iran
OITL	ADU	Ardabil Airport, Iran
OITT	TBZ	Tabriz Intl, Iran
OIYY	AZD	Shahid Sadooghi Airport, Iran
OIZB	ACZ	Zabol Airport, Iran
OIZC	ZBR	Konarak Airport, Iran
OIZH	ZAH	Zahedan Intl, Iran
OJAI	AMM	Queen Alia Intl, Jordan
OJAM	ADJ	Marka Intl, Jordan
OJAQ	AQJ	Aqaba Intl, Jordan
OKBK	KWI	Kuwait Intl, Kuwait
OLBA	BEY	Beirut Intl, Lebanon
OLKA	KYE	Rene Mouawad AB, Lebanon
OMAA	AUH	Abu Dhabi Intl, United Arab Emirates
OMAD	AZI	Bateen, United Arab Emirates
OMAL	AAN	Al Ain Intl, United Arab Emirates
OMDB	DXB	Dubai Intl, United Arab Emirates
OMFJ	FJR	Fujairah Intl, United Arab Emirates
OMRK	RKT	Khaimah Intl, United Arab Emirates
OMSJ	SHJ	Sharjah Intl, United Arab Emirates
OOKB	KHS	Khasab AB, Oman
OOMA	MSH	Masirah AB, Oman
OOMS	MCT	Seeb Intl, Oman
OONR	OMM	Marmul, Oman
OOSA	SLL	Salalah, Oman
OOTH	TTH	Thumrait AB, Oman
OPBN	BNP	Bannu Airport, Pakistan
OPBW	BHV	Bahawalpur Airport, Pakistan
OPCH	CJL	Chitral Airport, Pakistan
OPCL	CHB	Chilas Airport, Pakistan
OPDB	DBA	Dalbandin Airport, Pakistan
OPDG	DEA	Dera Ghazi Khan Airport, Pakistan
OPDI	DSK	Dera Ismail Khan Airport, Pakistan
OPFA	LYP	Faisalabad Intl, Pakistan
OPGD	GWD	Gwadar Intl, Pakistan
OPGT	GIL	Gilgit Airport, Pakistan
OPJI	JIW	Jiwani Airport, Pakistan
OPKC	KHI	Jinnah Intl, Pakistan
OPKD	HDD	Hyderabad Airport, Pakistan
OPKH	KDD	Khuzdar Airport, Pakistan
OPLA	LHE	Allama Iqbal Intl, Pakistan
OPMA	XJM	Mangla Airport, Pakistan
OPMF	MFG	Muzaffarabad Airport, Pakistan
OPMJ	MJD	Moenjodaro Airport, Pakistan
OPMP	MPD	Sindhri Airport, Pakistan
OPMT	MUX	Multan Intl, Pakistan
OPNH	WNS	Nawabshah Airport, Pakistan
OPOR	ORW	Ormara Airport, Pakistan
OPPC	PAJ	Parachinar Airport, Pakistan
OPPG	PJG	Panjgur Airport, Pakistan
OPPI	PSI	Pasni Airport, Pakistan
OPPS	PEW	Peshawar Intl, Pakistan
OPQT	UET	Quetta Intl, Pakistan
OPRK	RYK	Shaikh Zayed Intl, Pakistan
OPRN	ISB	Islamabad Intl, Pakistan
OPRT	RAZ	Rawalakot Airport, Pakistan
OPSB	SBQ	Sibi Airport, Pakistan
OPSD	KDU	Skardu Airport, Pakistan
OPSK	SKZ	Sukkur Airport, Pakistan
OPSN	SYW	Sehwan Sharif Airport, Pakistan
OPSS	SDT	Saidu Sharif Airport, Pakistan
OPSU	SUL	Sui Airport, Pakistan

ICAO	IATA	Airport & Country
OPTA	TLB	Tarbela Dam Airport, Pakistan
OPTU	TUK	Turbat Airport, Pakistan
OPZB	PZH	Zhob Airport, Pakistan
OSAP	ALP	Aleppo Intl, Syria
OSDI	DAM	Damascus Intl, Syria
OSDZ	DEZ	Deir Zzor, Syria
OSKL	KAC	Kamishly, Syria
OSLK	LTK	Bassel Al, Syria
OSPR	PMS	Palmyra, Syria
OTBD	DOH	Doha Intl, Qatar
OYAA	ADE	Aden Intl, Yemen
OYAB	EAB	Abbs, Yemen
OYAT	AXK	Ataq, Yemen
OYBN	BHN	Beihan, Yemen
OYBQ	BUK	Al, Yemen
OYGD	AAY	Al, Yemen
OYHD	HOD	Hodeidah Intl, Yemen
OYMB	MYN	Marib, Yemen
OYMK	UKR	Mukeiras, Yemen
OYQN	IHN	Qishn, Yemen
OYRN	RIY	Riyan, Yemen
OYSH	SYE	Saadah, Yemen
OYSN	SAH	Sanaa Intl, Yemen
OYSQ	SCT	Moori, Yemen
OYSY	GXF	Sayun, Yemen
OYTZ	TAI	Ganed, Yemen
PABE	BET	Bethel Airport, USA
PABR	BRW	Wiley Post, USA
PACV	CDV	Merle K. Mudhole Smith Airport, USA
PADL	DLG	Dillingham Airport, USA
PADQ	ADQ	Kodiak Airport, USA
PADU	DUT	Unalaska Airport, USA
PAEN	ENA	Kenai Municipal Airport, USA
PAFA	FAI	Fairbanks Intl, USA
PAGA	GAL	Edward G. Pitka Sr. Airport, USA
PAHO	HOM	Homer Airport, USA
PAJN	JNU	Juneau Intl, USA
PAKN	AKN	King Salmon Airport, USA
PAKT	KTN	Ketchikan Intl, USA
PALH	LHD	Lake Hood Seaplane Base, USA
PAMR	MRI	Merrill Field, USA
PANC	ANC	Ted Stevens Anchorage Intl, USA
PANI	ANI	Aniak Airport, USA
PAOM	OME	Nome Airport, USA
PAOT	OTZ	Ralph Wien Memorial Airport, USA
PAPG	PSG	Petersburg James A. Johnson, USA
PASC	SCC	Deadhorse Airport, USA
PASI	SIT	Sitka Rocky Gutierrez Airport, USA
PAVD	VDZ	Valdez Airport, USA
PAYA	YAK	Yakutat Airport, USA
PCIS	CIS	Canton Afld, Kiribati
PGRO	ROP	Rota Island, Northern Mariana Islands
PGSN	SPN	Obyan Intl, Northern Mariana Islands
PGUM	GUM	Guam Intl, Guam
PHHN	HNM	Hana Airport, USA
PHKO	KOA	Kona Intl at Keahole, USA
PHLI	LIH	Lihue Airport, USA
PHMK	MKK	Molokai Airport, USA
PHNL	HNL	Honolulu Intl, USA
PHNY	LNY	Lanai Airport, USA

ICAO	IATA	Airport & Country
PHOG	OGG	Kahului Airport, USA
PHTO	ITO	Hilo Intl, USA
PKMA	ENT	Enewetak Aux Af, Marshall Islands
PKMJ	MAJ	Marshall Is Intl, Marshall Islands
PKWA	KWA	Bucholz Aaf, Marshall Islands
PLCH	CXI	Cassidy Intl, Kiribati
PTKK	TKK	Chuuk Intl, Micronesia
PTPN	PNI	Pohnpei Intl, Micronesia
PTRO	ROR	Babelthuap/Koror, Micronesia
PTRO	ROR	Koror, Palau
PTSA	KSA	Kosrae, Micronesia
PTYA	YAP	Yap Intl, Micronesia
RCKH	KHH	Kaohsiung Intl, Taiwan
RCSS	TSA	Taipei Songshan Airport, Taiwan
RCTP	TPE	Chiang Kai, Taiwan
RJAA	NRT	Narita Intl, Japan
RJAF	MMJ	Matsumoto Airport, Japan
RJBB	KIX	Kansai Intl, Japan
RJBD	SHM	Nanki, Japan
RJBE	UKB	Kobe Airport, Japan
RJCB	OBO	Obihiro Airport , Japan
RJCC	CTS	New Chitose Airport, Japan
RJCH	HKD	Hakodate Airport, Japan
RJCK	KUH	Kushiro Airport, Japan
RJCM	MMB	Memanbetsu Airport, Japan
RJCN	SHB	Nakashibetsu Airport, Japan
RJCR	RBJ	Rebun Airport, Japan
RJCW	WKJ	Wakkanai Airport, Japan
RJDB	IKI	Iki Airport, Japan
RJDC	UBJ	Yamaguchi Ube Airport, Japan
RJDT	TSJ	Tsushima Airport, Japan
RJEB	MBE	Monbetsu Airport , Japan
RJEC	AKJ	Asahikawa Airport, Japan
RJEO	OIR	Okushiri Airport, Japan
RJER	RIS	Rishiri Airport, Japan
RJFC	KUM	Yakushima Airport, Japan
RJFE	FUJ	Goto, Japan
RJFF	FUK	Fukuoka Airport, Japan
RJFG	TNE	Tanegashima Airport, Japan
RJFK	KOJ	Kagoshima Airport, Japan
RJFM	KMI	Miyazaki Airport, Japan
RJFO	OIT	Oita Airport, Japan
RJFR	KKJ	New Kitakyushu Airport, Japan
RJFS	HSG	Saga Airport, Japan
RJFT	KMJ	Kumamoto Airport, Japan
RJFU	NGS	Nagasaki Airport, Japan
RJGG	NGO	Chubu Intl , Japan
RJKA	ASJ	Amami Airport, Japan
RJKB	OKE	Okinoerabu Airport, Japan
RJKI	KKX	Kikai Airport, Japan
RJKN	TKN	Tokunoshima Airport, Japan
RJNA	NKM	Nagoya Airport , Japan
RJNF	FKJ	Fukui Airport, Japan
RJNO	OKI	Oki Airport, Japan
RJNT	TOY	Toyama Airport, Japan
RJNW	NTQ	Noto Airport, Japan
RJOA	HIJ	Hiroshima Airport, Japan
RJOB	OKJ	Okayama Airport, Japan
RJOC	IZO	Izumo Airport, Japan
RJOK	KCZ	Kochi Airport, Japan

Appendix F

ICAO	IATA	Airport & Country
RJOM	MYJ	Matsuyama Airport, Japan
RJOO	ITM	Osaka Intl , Japan
RJOR	TTJ	Tottori Airport, Japan
RJOT	TAK	Takamatsu Airport, Japan
RJOW	IWJ	Iwami Airport, Japan
RJSA	AOJ	Aomori Airport, Japan
RJSC	GAJ	Yamagata Airport, Japan
RJSD	SDS	Sado Airport, Japan
RJSF	FKS	Fukushima Airport, Japan
RJSI	HNA	Hanamaki Airport, Japan
RJSK	AXT	Akita Airport, Japan
RJSN	KIJ	Niigata Airport, Japan
RJSR	ONJ	Odate, Japan
RJSS	SDJ	Sendai Airport, Japan
RJSY	SYO	Shonai Airport, Japan
RJTH	HAC	Hachijojima Airport, Japan
RJTO	OIM	Oshima Airport, Japan
RJTQ	MYE	Miyakejima Airport, Japan
RJTT	HND	Tokyo Intl , Japan
RKJJ	KWJ	Kwangju Aero, South Korea
RKJK	KUV	Kunsan Ab, South Korea
RKJM	MPK	Mokpo, South Korea
RKJY	RSU	Yeosu, South Korea
RKND	SHO	Sokcho Aero, South Korea
RKNN	KAG	Kangnung Aero, South Korea
RKNW	WJU	Wonju, South Korea
RKPC	CJU	Cheju Intl, South Korea
RKPE	CHF	R, South Korea
RKPK	PUS	Kimhae Intl, South Korea
RKPU	USN	Ulsan, South Korea
RKSM	SSN	Seoul Ab, South Korea
RKSO	OSN	Osan Ab, South Korea
RKSS	SEL	Kimpo Intl, South Korea
RKSW	SWU	Suwon, South Korea
RKTH	KPO	Pohang Aero, South Korea
RKTN	TAE	Taegu Aero, South Korea
RKTU	CJJ	Chongju Intl, South Korea
RKTY	YEC	Yechon Aero, South Korea
ROAH	OKA	Naha Airport, Japan
ROIG	ISG	Ishigaki Airport, Japan
ROKJ	UEO	Kumejima Airport, Japan
ROKR	KJP	Kerama Airport, Japan
ROMD	MMD	Minami, Japan
ROMY	MMY	Miyako Airport, Japan
RORA	AGJ	Aguni Airport, Japan
RORE	IEJ	Iejima Airport, Japan
RORH	HTR	Hateruma Airport, Japan
RORK	KTD	Kita, Japan
RORS	SHI	Shimojishima Airport, Japan
RORT	TRA	Tarama Airport, Japan
RORY	RNJ	Yoron Airport, Japan
ROYN	OGN	Yonaguni Airport, Japan
RPLB	SFS	Subic Bay Intl, Philippines
RPLC	CRK	Diosdado Macapagal Intl, Philippines
RPLI	LAO	Laoag Intl, Philippines
RPLL	MNL	Ninoy Aquino Intl, Philippines
RPLO	CYU	Cuyo Airport, Philippines
RPLP	LGP	Legazpi Airport, Philippines
RPLU	LBX	Lubang Airport, Philippines
RPMA	AAV	Allah Valley Airport, Philippines
RPMC	CBO	Awang Airport, Philippines
RPMD	DVO	Francisco Bangoy Intl, Philippines
RPME	BXU	Bancasi Airport, Philippines
RPMF	BPH	Bislig Airport, Philippines
RPMG	DPL	Dipolog Airport, Philippines
RPMH	CGM	Camiguin Airport, Philippines
RPMI	IGN	Maria Cristina Airport, Philippines
RPMJ	JOL	Jolo Airport, Philippines
RPML	CGY	Lumbia Airport, Philippines
RPMM	MLP	Malabang Airport, Philippines
RPMN	SGS	Sanga, Philippines
RPMO	OZC	Labo Airport, Philippines
RPMP	PAG	Pagadian Airport, Philippines
RPMQ	MXI	Imelda R. Marcos Airport, Philippines
RPMR	GES	General Santos Intl, Philippines
RPMS	SUG	Surigao Airport, Philippines
RPMU	CDY	Cagayan de Sulu Airport, Philippines
RPMV	IPE	Ipil Airport, Philippines
RPMW	TDG	Tandag Airport, Philippines
RPMX	LLY	Liloy Airport, Philippines
RPMZ	ZAM	Zamboanga Intl, Philippines
RPNS	SIA	Siargao Airport, Philippines
RPUB	BAG	Loakan Airport, Philippines
RPUD	DTE	Daet Airport, Philippines
RPUH	SJI	McGuire Field, Philippines
RPUK	CPP	Calapan Airport, Philippines
RPUM	MBO	Mamburao Airport, Philippines
RPUN	WNP	Naga Airport, Philippines
RPUO	BSO	Basco Airport, Philippines
RPUQ	VGN	Mindoro Airport, Philippines
RPUR	BQA	Baler Airport, Philippines
RPUS	SFE	San Fernando Airport, Philippines
RPUT	TUG	Tuguegarao Airport, Philippines
RPUV	VRC	Virac Airport, Philippines
RPUW	MRQ	Marinduque Airport, Philippines
RPUY	CYZ	Cauayan Airport, Philippines
RPUZ	BGN	Bagabag Airport, Philippines
RPVA	TAC	Daniel Z. Romualdez Philippines
RPVB	BCD	Bacolod City Domestic, Philippines
RPVC	CYP	Calbayog Airport, Philippines
RPVD	DGT	Sibulan Airport, Philippines
RPVE	MPH	Godofredo P. Ramos, Philippines
RPVF	CRM	Catarman National Airport, Philippines
RPVG	SAA	Guiuan Airport, Philippines
RPVH	HIL	Hilongos Airport, Philippines
RPVI	ILO	Mandurriao Airport, Philippines
RPVJ	MBT	Masbate Airport, Philippines
RPVK	KLO	Kalibo Airport, Philippines
RPVM	CEB	Mactan, Philippines
RPVO	OMC	Ormoc Airport, Philippines
RPVP	PPS	Puerto Princesa Airport, Philippines
RPVR	RXS	Roxas Airport, Philippines
RPVS	EUQ	Evelio Javier Airport, Philippines
RPVT	TAG	Tagbilaran Airport, Philippines
RPVU	TBH	Tugdan Airport, Philippines
RPVV	USU	Busuanga Airport, Philippines
SAAP	PRA	General Urquiza Airport, Argentina
SAAR	ROS	Rosario Intl, Argentina
SABE	AEP	Aeroparque Jorge Newbery, Argentina
SACO	COR	Ingeniero Ambrosio Intl, Argentina

ICAO	IATA	Airport & Country	ICAO	IATA	Airport & Country
SADF	FDO	San Fernando Airport, Argentina	SBMQ	MCP	Macapa Intl, Brazil
SAEZ	EZE	Ezeiza Intl, Argentina	SBNF	NVT	Ministro Victor Konder Intl, Brazil
SAME	MDZ	El Plumerillo Intl, Argentina	SBNT	NAT	Augusto Severo Intl, Brazil
SAMM	LGS	Comodoro Ricardo, Argentina	SBPA	POA	Salgado Filho Intl, Brazil
SAMR	AFA	Suboficial Aytes Germano, Argentina	SBPJ	PMW	Palmas Airport, Brazil
SANC	CTC	Coronel Felipe Varela, Argentina	SBPP	PMG	Ponta Pora Intl, Brazil
SANE	SDE	Vicecomodoro Aragonez, Argentina	SBPS	BPS	Porto Seguro Airport, Brazil
SANL	IRJ	Capit, Argentina	SBRB	RBR	Presidente Medici Airport, Brazil
SANT	TUC	Benjamin Matienzo Intl, Argentina	SBRF	REC	Guararapes Intl, Brazil
SANU	UAQ	San Juan Airport, Argentina	SBRJ	SDU	Santos Dumont Regional, Brazil
SAOC	RCU	Las Higueras Airport, Argentina	SBRP	RAO	Leite Lopes Airport, Brazil
SAOR	VME	Villa Reynolds Airport, Argentina	SBSL	SLZ	Marechal Cunha Machado Intl, Brazil
SAOU	LUQ	San Luis Airport, Argentina	SBSN	STM	Santarem Airport, Brazil
SARE	RES	Resistencia Intl, Argentina	SBSP	CGH	Congonhas Intl, Brazil
SARF	FMA	Formosa Intl, Argentina	SBSR	SJP	Sao Jose do Rio Preto Airport, Brazil
SARI	IGR	Cataratas del Iguazu Intl, Argentina	SBSV	SSA	Dep Luis Eduardo Magalhaes, Brazil
SARP	PSS	Gen Jose de San Martin, Argentina	SBTE	THE	Senador Petronio Portella, Brazil
SASA	SLA	El Aybal Airport, Argentina	SBUL	UDI	Uberlandia Airport, Brazil
SATR	RCQ	Daniel Jurkic Airport, Argentina	SBVT	VIX	Goiabeiras Airport, Brazil
SAVC	CRD	General Enrique Mosconi, Argentina	SCAC	ZUD	Pupelde, Chile
SAVE	EQS	Esquel Airport, Argentina	SCAN	LOB	San Rafael, Chile
SAVR	ARR	Alto Rio Senguer Airport, Argentina	SCAR	ARI	Chacalluta Intl, Chile
SAVV	VDM	Gobernador Castello, Argentina	SCAS	WPA	Cabo Juan Roman, Chile
SAVY	PMY	El Tehuelche Airport, Argentina	SCBA	BBA	Balmaceda, Chile
SAWE	RGA	Hermes Quijada Airport, Argentina	SCBE	TOQ	Barriles, Chile
SAWG	RGL	Piloto Civil N. Fernandez, Argentina	SCCC	CCH	Chile Chico, Chile
SAWH	USH	Ushuaia Intl, Argentina	SCCF	CJC	El Loa, Chile
SAZB	BHI	Comandante Espora, Argentina	SCCH	YAI	Gen. Bernardo O'higgins, Chile
SAZG	GPO	General Pico Airport, Argentina	SCCI	PUQ	Carlos Ibanez Del Campo Intl, Chile
SAZM	MDQ	Mar Del Plata Intl, Argentina	SCCY	GXQ	Teniente Vidal, Chile
SAZR	RSA	Santa Rosa Airport, Argentina	SCDA	IQQ	Diego Aracena Intl, Chile
SAZS	BRC	San Carlos de Bariloche Intl, Argentina	SCEL	SCL	Arturo Merino Benitez Intl, Chile
			SCES	ESR	El Salvador Bajo, Chile
SBAR	AJU	Santa Maria Airport, Brazil	SCFA	ANF	Cerro Moreno Intl, Chile
SBBE	BEL	Val de C, Brazil	SCFM	WPR	Capitan Fuentes Martinez, Chile
SBBH	PLU	Pampulha Domestic Airport, Brazil	SCFT	FFU	Futaleufu, Chile
SBBR	BSB	Pres Juscelino Kubitschek, Brazil	SCGE	LSQ	Maria Dolores, Chile
SBBV	BVB	Boa Vista Intl, Brazil	SCGZ	WPU	Guardiamarina Zanartu, Chile
SBCF	CNF	Tancredo Neves Intl, Brazil	SCHA	CPO	Chamonate, Chile
SBCG	CGR	Campo Grande Intl, Brazil	SCHR	LGR	Cochrane, Chile
SBCR	CMG	Corumb, Brazil	SCIE	CCP	Carriel Sur Intl, Chile
SBCT	CWB	Afonso Pena Intl, Brazil	SCJO	ZOS	Canal Bajo/Carlos H Siebert, Chile
SBCY	CGB	Marechal Rondon Airport, Brazil	SCLL	VLR	Vallenar, Chile
SBCZ	CZS	Cruzeiro do Sul Intl, Brazil	SCLN	ZLR	Linares, Chile
SBEG	MAO	Eduardo Gomes Intl, Brazil	SCNT	PNT	Teniente Julio Gallardo, Chile
SBFI	IGU	Foz do Iguacu Intl, Brazil	SCPC	ZPC	Pucon, Chile
SBFL	FLN	Herc, Brazil	SCRA	CNR	Chanaral, Chile
SBFZ	FOR	Pinto Martins Intl, Brazil	SCRG	QRC	De La Independencia, Chile
SBGL	GIG	Galeao, Brazil	SCSB	SMB	Franco Bianco, Chile
SBGO	GYN	Santa Genoveva Airport, Brazil	SCSE	LSC	La Florida, Chile
SBGR	GRU	Guarulhos Intl, Brazil	SCSF	SSD	Victor Lafon, Chile
SBIL	IOS	Jorge Amado Airport, Brazil	SCTC	ZCO	Maquehue, Chile
SBIZ	IMP	Prefeito Renato Moreira Airport, Brazil	SCTE	PMC	El Tepual Intl, Chile
SBJP	JPA	Presidente Castro Pinto Intl, Brazil	SCTI	ULC	Los Cerrillos, Chile
SBJV	JOI	Joinville, Brazil	SCTL	TLX	Panguilemo, Chile
SBKP	VCP	Viracopos Intl, Brazil	SCTN	WCH	Chaiten, Chile
SBLO	LDB	Londrina Airport, Brazil	SCTO	ZIC	Victoria, Chile
SBMA	MAB	Maraba Airport, Brazil	SCTT	TTC	Las Breas, Chile
SBMG	MGF	Maringa Domestic Airport, Brazil	SCVD	ZAL	Pichoy, Chile
SBMO	MCZ	Zumbi dos Palmares Airport, Brazil	SCVM	KNA	Vina Del Mar, Chile

ICAO	IATA	Airport & Country
SEAM	ATF	Chachoan, Ecuador
SECO	OCC	Francisco De Orellana, Ecuador
SECU	CUE	Mariscal Lamar, Ecuador
SEGS	GPS	Seymour, Ecuador
SEGS	GPS	Seymour Airport, Ecuador
SEGU	GYE	Simon Bolivar Intl, Ecuador
SELA	LGQ	Lago Agrio, Ecuador
SEMA	MRR	J M Velasco Ibarra, Ecuador
SEMC	XMS	Macas, Ecuador
SEMH	MCH	General Serrano, Ecuador
SEMT	MEC	Eloy Alfaro Intl, Ecuador
SEPV	PVO	Reales Tamarindos, Ecuador
SEQU	UIO	Mariscal Sucre Intl, Ecuador
SESA	SNC	Gen Ulpiano Paez, Ecuador
SESC	SUQ	Sucua, Ecuador
SESM	PTZ	Rio Amazonas, Ecuador
SEST	SCY	San Cristobal, Ecuador
SESV	BHA	Los Perales, Ecuador
SETH	TSC	Taisha, Ecuador
SETI	TPN	Tiputini, Ecuador
SETN	ESM	General Rivadeneira, Ecuador
SETR	TPC	Tarapoa, Ecuador
SETU	TUA	El Rosal, Ecuador
SGAS	ASU	Asuncion Silvio Pettirossi, Paraguay
SGEN	ENO	Quiteria, Paraguay
SKAC	ACR	Araracuara, Colombia
SKAO	MCJ	San Jose De Maicao, Colombia
SKAR	AXM	El Eden, Colombia
SKAS	PUU	Tres De Mayo, Colombia
SKBC	ELB	El Banco Apt., Colombia
SKBG	BGA	Palonegro, Colombia
SKBO	BOG	Eldorado Intl, Colombia
SKBQ	BAQ	Ernesto Cortissoz, Colombia
SKBS	BSC	Jose Celestino Mutis, Colombia
SKBU	BUN	Buenaventura, Colombia
SKCC	CUC	Camilo Daza Intl, Colombia
SKCD	COG	Mandinga, Colombia
SKCG	CTG	Rafael Nunez, Colombia
SKCL	CLO	Alfonso Bonilla Aragon Intl, Colombia
SKCM	CIM	Cimitarra, Colombia
SKCN	RAV	Cravo Norte, Colombia
SKCO	TCO	La Florida, Colombia
SKCR	CUO	Caruru, Colombia
SKCU	CAQ	Caucasia, Colombia
SKCV	CVE	Covenas, Colombia
SKCZ	CZU	Las Brujas, Colombia
SKEB	EBG	El Bagre, Colombia
SKEJ	EJA	Yariguies, Colombia
SKFL	FLA	Gustavo Artunduaga P, Colombia
SKGI	GIR	Santiago Vila, Colombia
SKGO	CRC	Santa Ana, Colombia
SKGP	GPI	Guapi, Colombia
SKHA	CPL	Gen Navas Pardo, Colombia
SKHC	HTZ	Hato Corozal, Colombia
SKIB	IBE	Perales, Colombia
SKIG	IGO	Chigorodo, Colombia
SKIP	IPI	San Luis, Colombia
SKLG	LQM	Caucaya, Colombia
SKLP	LPD	La Pedrera, Colombia
SKLT	LET	Alfredo Vasquez Cobo, Colombia
SKMD	EOH	Olaya Herrera, Colombia
SKMF	MFS	Miraflores, Colombia
SKMG	MGN	Baracoa, Colombia
SKMP	MMP	San Bernardo, Colombia
SKMR	MTR	Los Garzones, Colombia
SKMU	MVP	Fabio A Leon Bentley, Colombia
SKNV	NVA	Benito Salas, Colombia
SKOC	OCV	Aguas Claras, Colombia
SKOT	OTU	Otu, Colombia
SKPC	PCR	Puerto Carreno, Colombia
SKPD	PDA	Obando, Colombia
SKPE	PEI	Matecana, Colombia
SKPI	PTX	Pitalito, Colombia
SKPP	PPN	Guillermo Leon Valencia, Colombia
SKPQ	PAL	German Olano Ab, Colombia
SKPR	PBE	Puerto Berrio, Colombia
SKPS	PSO	Antonio Narino, Colombia
SKPV	PVA	Providencia, Colombia
SKPZ	PZA	Paz De Ariporo, Colombia
SKQU	MQU	Mariquita, Colombia
SKRG	MDE	Jose Maria Cordova, Colombia
SKRH	RCH	Almirante Padilla, Colombia
SKSA	RVE	Los Colonizadores, Colombia
SKSJ	SJE	Jorge E Gonzalez, Colombia
SKSM	SMR	Simon Bolivar, Colombia
SKSO	SOX	Alberto Lieras Camargo, Colombia
SKSV	SVI	San Vicente Del Caguan, Colombia
SKTB	TIB	Tibu, Colombia
SKTD	TDA	Trinidad, Colombia
SKTM	TME	Tame, Colombia
SKTQ	TQS	Tres Esquinas, Colombia
SKTU	TRB	Gonzalo Mejia, Colombia
SKUC	AUC	Santiago Perez, Colombia
SKUI	UIB	El Carano, Colombia
SKUL	ULQ	Farfan, Colombia
SKVG	VGZ	Villagarzon, Colombia
SKVP	VUP	Alfonso Lopez, Colombia
SKVV	VVC	Vanguardia, Colombia
SKYP	EYP	El Yopal, Colombia
SLAG	MHW	Monteagudo, Bolivia
SLAP	APB	Apolo, Bolivia
SLBJ	BJO	Bermejo, Bolivia
SLCA	CAM	Camiri, Bolivia
SLCB	CBB	Jorge Wilsterman, Bolivia
SLCO	CIJ	Cobija, Bolivia
SLCP	CEP	Concepcion, Bolivia
SLET	SRZ	El Trompillo, Bolivia
SLGY	GYA	Cap Av Emilio Beltran, Bolivia
SLJO	SJB	San Joaquin, Bolivia
SLJV	SJV	San Javier, Bolivia
SLLP	LPB	El Alto Intl, Bolivia
SLMG	MGD	Magdalena, Bolivia
SLOR	ORU	Juan Mendoza, Bolivia
SLPS	PSZ	Salvador Ogaya, Bolivia
SLRA	SRD	San Ramon, Bolivia
SLRB	RBO	Robore, Bolivia
SLRI	RIB	Cap De Av Selin Zeitun Lopez, Bolivia
SLRQ	RBQ	Rurrenabaque, Bolivia
SLRY	REY	Reyes, Bolivia
SLSB	SRJ	Capitan German Quiroga, Bolivia

ICAO	IATA	Airport & Country
SLSM	SNM	San Ignacio De Moxos, Bolivia
SLSU	SRE	Juana Azurduy De Padilla, Bolivia
SLTJ	TJA	Capt Oriel Lea Plaza, Bolivia
SLTR	TDD	Jorge Henrich Arauz, Bolivia
SLVG	VAH	Vallegrande, Bolivia
SLVM	VLM	Rafael Pabon, Bolivia
SLVR	VVI	Viru Viru Intl, Bolivia
SLYA	BYC	Yacuiba, Bolivia
SMJP	PBM	J.A. Pengel Intl, Suriname
SMPA	OEM	Vincent Faiks, Suriname
SMZO	ORG	Zorg En Hoop, Suriname
SOCA	CAY	Cayenne, French Guiana
SPAR	ALD	Alerta, Peru
SPBB	MBP	Moyobamba, Peru
SPBL	BLP	Huallaga, Peru
SPBR	IBP	Iberia, Peru
SPCL	PCL	David Abenzur Rengifo, Peru
SPEO	CHM	Teniente Jaime A De Montreuil, Peru
SPGM	TGI	Tingo Maria, Peru
SPHI	CIX	Jose Abelardo, Peru
SPHO	AYP	Col Alfredo Mendivil Duarte, Peru
SPHY	ANS	Andahuaylas, Peru
SPIL	UMI	Quincemil, Peru
SPIM	LIM	Jorge Chavez Intl, Peru
SPJA	RIJ	Rioja, Peru
SPJI	JJI	Juanjui, Peru
SPJJ	JAU	Jauja, Peru
SPJL	JUL	Inca Manco Capac, Peru
SPJN	SJA	San Juan De Marcona, Peru
SPJR	CJA	Armando Revoredo Iglesias, Peru
SPLN	RIM	San Nicolas, Peru
SPME	TBP	Pedro Canga, Peru
SPMS	YMS	Moises Benzaquen Rengifo, Peru
SPNC	HUU	Alferez David Figueroa Fernan, Peru
SPOV	SYC	Shiringayoc O Hda Mejia, Peru
SPPY	CHH	Chachapoyas, Peru
SPQT	IQT	Col Francisco Secada Vignetta, Peru
SPQU	AQP	Rodriguez Ballon, Peru
SPRN	SMG	Santa Maria De Fatima, Peru
SPRU	TRU	Cap Carlos Martinez De Pinill, Peru
SPSO	PIO	Pisco, Peru
SPST	TPP	Cdte.Guillermo D Castillo Par, Peru
SPTN	TCQ	Col Carlos Ciriani Santa Rosa, Peru
SPTU	PEM	Padre Aldamiz, Peru
SPUR	PIU	Capt Guillermo Concha Iberico, Peru
SPYL	TYL	Capitan Montes, Peru
SPZO	CUZ	Velazco Astete, Peru
SUAG	ATI	Artigas Intl, Uruguay
SUCA	CYR	Colonia International, Uruguay
SUDU	DZO	Santa Bernardina Intl, Uruguay
SULS	PDP	Capitan Curbelo Intl, Uruguay
SUMO	MLZ	Cerro Largo Intl, Uruguay
SUMU	MVD	Carrasco Intl, Uruguay
SUPU	PDU	Tydeo Larre Borges Intl, Uruguay
SURV	RVY	Rivera Intl, Uruguay
SUSO	STY	Salto Nueva Hesperides Intl, Uruguay
SUTB	TAW	Tacuarembo, Uruguay
SUTR	TYT	Treinta Y Tres, Uruguay
SUVO	VCH	Vichadero, Uruguay
SVAC	AGV	Oswaldo Guevara Mujica, Venezuela
SVAN	AAO	Anaco, Venezuela
SVBC	BLA	Jose Antonio Anzoategui, Venezuela
SVBI	BNS	Barinas, Venezuela
SVBM	BRM	Barquisimeto, Venezuela
SVCB	CBL	Ciudad Bolivar, Venezuela
SVCL	CLZ	Calabozo, Venezuela
SVCN	CAJ	Canaima, Venezuela
SVCO	VCR	Carora, Venezuela
SVCP	CUP	Jose Francisco Bermudez, Venezuela
SVCR	CZE	Jose L Chirinos Intl, Venezuela
SVCU	CUM	Antonio Jose De Sucre, Venezuela
SVED	EOR	El Dorado, Venezuela
SVEZ	EOZ	Elorza, Venezuela
SVGD	GDO	Guasdualito, Venezuela
SVGI	GUI	Guiria, Venezuela
SVGU	GUQ	Guanare, Venezuela
SVIC	ICA	Icabaru, Venezuela
SVKA	KAV	Bolivar, Venezuela
SVLF	LFR	La Fria, Venezuela
SVMC	MAR	La Chinita Intl, Venezuela
SVMD	MRD	Alberto Carnevalli, Venezuela
SVMG	PMV	Del Caribe Intl, Venezuela
SVMI	CCS	Simon Bolivar Intl, Venezuela
SVMT	MUN	Maturin Intl, Venezuela
SVPA	PYH	Puerto Ayacucho, Venezuela
SVPC	PBL	Gen. Bartolome Salom, Venezuela
SVPM	SCI	Paramillo, Venezuela
SVPR	CGU	Manuel Carlos Piar, Venezuela
SVPT	PTM	Palmarito, Venezuela
SVSE	SNV	Santa Elena De Uairen, Venezuela
SVSO	STD	Mayor Buenaventura Vivas,Venezuela
SVSP	SNF	Sub Teniente Nestor Arias, Venezuela
SVSR	SFD	San Fernando De Apure, Venezuela
SVST	SOM	San Tome, Venezuela
SVTC	TUV	Tucupita, Venezuela
SVTM	TMO	Tumeremo, Venezuela
SVUM	URM	Uriman, Venezuela
SVVA	VLN	Arturo Michelena Intl, Venezuela
SVVG	VIG	Juan Pablo Perez Alfonzo, Venezuela
SVVL	VLV	Dr. Antonio Nicolas Briceno, Venezuela
SVVP	VDP	Valle De La Pascua, Venezuela
SYAH	AHL	Aishalton, Guyana
SYAN	NAI	Annai, Guyana
SYCJ	GEO	Cheddi Jagan Intl, Guyana
SYIB	IMB	Imbaimadai, Guyana
SYKM	KAR	Kamarang, Guyana
SYKR	KRM	Karanambo, Guyana
SYKT	KTO	Kato, Guyana
SYLP	LUB	Lumid Pau, Guyana
SYLT	LTM	Lethem, Guyana
SYMD	MHA	Mahdia, Guyana
SYOR	ORJ	Orinduik, Guyana
TAPA	ANU	VC Bird Intl, Antigua and Barbuda
TAPH	BBQ	Codrington Airport, Antigua & Barbuda
TBPB	BGI	Grantley Adams Intl, Barbados
TDCF	DCF	Canefield Airport, Dominica
TDPD	DOM	Melville Hall Airport, Dominica
TFFA	DSD	Grande Anse Airport, Guadeloupe
TFFB	BBR	Baillif Airport, Guadeloupe
TFFC	SFC	Saint, Guadeloupe

ICAO	IATA	Airport & Country
TFFF	FDF	Le Lamentin, Martinique
TFFG	SFG	Grand Case Airport, Guadeloupe
TFFJ	SBH	Saint, Guadeloupe
TFFM	GBJ	Marie Galante Airport, Guadeloupe
TFFR	PTP	Pointe, Guadeloupe
TFFS	LSS	Les Saintes Airport, Guadeloupe
TGPY	GND	Point Salines Intl, Grenada
TIST	STT	King, US Virgin Islands
TISX	STX	Henry E Rohlsen, US Virgin Islands
TJAB	ABO	Antonio Juarbe Pol, Puerto Rico
TJBQ	BQN	Rafael Hernandez Airport, Puerto Rico
TJCP	CPX	Benjamin Rivera Noriega, Puerto Rico
TJFA	FAJ	Diego Jimenez Torres, Puerto Rico
TJIG	SIG	Isla Grande Airport, Puerto Rico
TJMZ	MAZ	Eugenio Mar, Puerto Rico
TJPS	PSE	Mercedita Airport, Puerto Rico
TJSJ	SJU	Luis Munoz Marin Intl, Puerto Rico
TJVQ	VQS	Vieques Airport, Puerto Rico
TLPC	SLU	George F.L. Charles, Saint Lucia
TLPL	UVF	Hewanorra Intl, Saint Lucia
TNCA	AUA	Queen Beatrix Intl Aruba
TNCB	BON	Flamingo Intl, Netherlands Antilles
TNCC	CUR	Hato Intl, Netherlands Antilles
TNCE	EUX	F.D. Roosevelt, Netherlands Antilles
TNCM	SXM	Princess Juliana, Netherlands Antilles
TNCS	SAB	Juancho, Netherlands Antilles
TQPF	AXA	Anguilla Wallblake, Anguilla
TT02	ULI	Ulithi, Micronesia
TTPP	POS	Piarco Intl, Trinidad & Tobago
TUPJ	EIS	Beef I Intl, British Virgin Islands
TUPW	VIJ	Virgin Gorda, British Virgin Islands
TVSU	UNI	Union I. Intl, St. Vincent & Grenadines
TVSV	SVD	E T Joshua, St. Vincent & Grenadines
TXKF	BDA	Hamilton Bermuda Intl, Bermuda
UAAA	ALA	Almaty, Kazakhstan
UAAH	BXH	Balkhash, Kazakhstan
UACC	TSE	Astana, Kazakhstan
UAFM	FRU	Manas, Kyrgyzstan
UAFO	OSS	Osh, Kyrgyzstan
UAKD	DZN	Zhezkazgan, Kazakhstan
UAKK	KGF	Karaganda, Kazakhstan
UARR	URA	Uralsk, Kazakhstan
UATG	GUW	Atyrau, Kazakhstan
UATT	AKX	Aktyubinsk, Kazakhstan
UAUU	KSN	Narimanovka, Kazakhstan
UBBB	BAK	Bina, Azerbaijan
UBBG	KVD	Gyandzha, Azerbaijan
UEAA	ADH	Aldan Airport, Russia
UEEE	YKS	Yakutsk Airport, Russia
UELL	CNN	Chulman Airport, Russia
UERP	PYJ	Polyarny Airport, Russia
UERR	MJZ	Mirny Airport, Russia
UESO	CKH	Chokurdakh Airport, Russia
UGEE	EVN	Zvartnots, Armenia
UGGG	TBS	Lochini, Georgia
UGGG	TBS	Tbilisi Intl, Georgia
UGSS	SUI	Babushara Airport, Georgia
UHBB	BQS	Ignatyevo Airport, Russia
UHBI	GDG	Magdagachi Airport, Russia
UHHH	KHV	Novy Airport, Russia
UHMA	DYR	Ugolny Airport, Russia
UHMD	PVS	Provideniya Bay Airport, Russia
UHMM	GDX	Sokol Airport, Russia
UHMP	PWE	Pevek Airport, Russia
UHPP	PKC	Yelizovo Airport, Russia
UHSS	UUS	Yuzhno, Russia
UHWW	VVO	Vladivostok Intl, Russia
UIAA	HTA	Kadala Airport, Russia
UIBB	BTK	Bratsk Airport, Russia
UIUU	UUD	Mukhino Airport, Russia
UKBB	KBP	Boryspil Intl, Ukraine
UKCC	DOK	Donetsk Airport, Ukraine
UKDD	DNK	Dnipropetrovsk Airport, Ukraine
UKDE	OZH	Zaporizhzhia Intl, Ukraine
UKDR	KWG	Lozuvatka Intl, Ukraine
UKFF	SIP	Simferopol Airport, Ukraine
UKHH	HRK	Osnova Airport, Ukraine
UKKK	IEV	Zhuliany Intl, Ukraine
UKLI	IFO	Ivano, Ukraine
UKLL	LWO	Lviv Airport, Ukraine
UKLR	RWN	Rivne Airport, Ukraine
UKLU	UDJ	Uzhhorod Airport, Ukraine
UKON	NLV	Mykolaiv Airport, Ukraine
UKOO	ODS	Odessa Airport, Ukraine
UKWW	VIN	Vinnytsia Airport, Ukraine
ULAA	ARH	Talagi Airport, Russia
ULAM	NNM	Naryan, Russia
ULDD	AMV	Amderma Airport, Russia
ULKK	KSZ	Kotlas Airport, Russia
ULLI	LED	Pulkovo Airport, Russia
ULMM	MMK	Murmansk Airport, Russia
ULOO	PKV	Pskov Airport, Russia
ULPB	PES	Besovets Airport, Russia
UMBB	BQT	Brest, Belarus
UMGG	GME	Gomel, Belarus
UMII	VTB	Vitebsk, Belarus
UMKK	KGD	Khrabrovo Airport, Russia
UMMG	GNA	Grodno, Belarus
UMMM	MHP	Minsk, Belarus
UMMS	MSQ	Minsk, Belarus
UNBB	BAX	Barnaul Airport, Russia
UNEE	KEJ	Kemorovo Airport, Russia
UNKL	KJA	Krasnoyarsk Yemelyanovo, Russia
UNKY	KYZ	Kyzyl Airport, Russia
UNNT	OVB	Novosibirsk Tolmachevo, Russia
UNOO	OMS	Tsentralny Airport, Russia
UNWW	NOZ	Novokuznetsk Spichenkovo, Russia
UOOO	NSK	Norilsk Airport, Russia
URKA	AAQ	Vityazevo Airport, Russia
URKK	KRR	Pashkovsky Airport, Russia
URMM	MRV	Mineralnye Vody Airport, Russia
URMN	NAL	Nalchik Airport, Russia
URMO	OGZ	Beslan Airport, Russia
URMT	STW	Shpakovskoye Airport, Russia
URRR	ROV	Rostov, Russia
URWA	ASF	Astrakhan Airport, Russia
URWW	VOG	Gumrak Airport, Russia
USCC	CEK	Balandino Airport, Russia
USCM	MQF	Magnitogorsk Airport, Russia
USKK	KVX	Kirov Airport, Russia

ICAO	IATA	Airport & Country
USNN	NJC	Nizhnevartovsk Airport, Russia
USPP	PEE	Bolshoye Savino Airport, Russia
USRR	SGC	Surgut Airport, Russia
USSS	SVX	Koltsovo Intl, Russia
UTAA	ASB	Ashgabat, Turkmenistan
UTDD	DYU	Dushanbe, Tajikistan
UTDL	LBD	Khudzhand, Tajikistan
UTNU	UGC	Urgench, Uzbekistan
UTSB	BHK	Bukhara, Uzbekistan
UTSS	SKD	Samarkand, Uzbekistan
UTST	TMJ	Termez, Uzbekistan
UTTT	TAS	Tashkent Yuzhny, Uzbekistan
UUDD	DME	Domodedovo Intl, Russia
UUEE	SVO	Sheremetyevo Intl, Russia
UUII	IKT	Irkutsk Intl, Russia
UUOB	EGO	Belgorod Airport, Russia
UUOO	VOZ	Chertovitskoye Airport, Russia
UUWW	VKO	Vnukovo Airport, Russia
UUYH	UCT	Ukhta Airport, Russia
UUYY	SCW	Syktyvkar Airport, Russia
UWGG	GOJ	Strigino Airport, Russia
UWKD	KZN	Kazan Airport, Russia
UWKS	CSY	Cheboksary Airport, Russia
UWOO	REN	Tsentralny Airport, Russia
UWOR	OSW	Orsk Airport, Russia
UWPP	PEZ	Penza Airport, Russia
UWSS	RTW	Tsentralny Airport, Russia
UWUU	UFA	Ufa Airport, Russia
UWWW	KUF	Kurumoch Airport, Russia
VA1A	HBX	Hubli Airport, India
VA1P	DIU	Diu Airport, India
VAAH	AMD	Sardar Vallabhbhai Patel Intl, India
VAAK	AKD	Akola Airport, India
VAAU	IXU	Aurangabad Airport, India
VABB	BOM	Chhatrapati Shivaji Intl, India
VABI	PAB	Bilaspur Airport, India
VABJ	BHJ	Bhuj Rudra Mata Airport, India
VABM	IXG	Belgaum Airport, India
VABO	BDQ	Vadodara Airport, India
VABP	BHO	Bhopal Airport, India
VABV	BHU	Bhavnagar Airport, India
VADN	NMB	Daman Airport, India
VAGO	GOI	Dabolim Airport , India
VAID	IDR	Devi Ahilyabai Holkar Intl, India
VAJB	JLR	Jabalpur Airport, India
VAJM	JGA	Jamnagar Airport, India
VAKE	IXY	Kandla Airport, India
VAKJ	HJR	Khajuraho Airport, India
VAKP	KLH	Kolhapur Airport, India
VAKS	IXK	Junagadh Airport, India
VANP	NAG	Dr. Babasaheb Ambedkar Intl, India
VAPO	PNQ	Pune Airport, India
VAPR	PBD	Porbandar Airport, India
VARG	RTC	Ratnagiri Airport, India
VARK	RAJ	Rajkot Airport, India
VARP	RPR	Raipur Airport, India
VASL	SSE	Sholapur Airport, India
VASU	STV	Surat Airport, India
VAUD	UDR	Udaipur Airport, India
VCBI	CMB	Bandaranaike Intl, Sri Lanka
VCCA	ADP	Anuradhapura, Sri Lanka
VCCB	BTC	Batticaloa AB, Sri Lanka
VCCC	RML	Ratmalana, Sri Lanka
VCCG	GOY	Amparai, Sri Lanka
VCCJ	JAF	Kankesanturai AB, Sri Lanka
VCCT	TRR	China Bay AB, Sri Lanka
VDBG	BBM	Battambang, Cambodia
VDPP	PNH	Pochentong Intl, Cambodia
VDSR	REP	Siem Reap, Cambodia
VE46	JGB	Jagdalpur Airport, India
VEAN	IXV	Along Airport, India
VEAT	IXA	Agartala Airport, India
VEBD	IXB	Bagdogra Airport, India
VEBG	RGH	Balurghat Airport, India
VEBI	SHL	Shillong Airport, India
VEBS	BBI	Biju Patnaik Airport, India
VEC1	DIB	Chabua Airport, India
VECC	CCU	Netaji Subhash Airport Intl, India
VECO	COH	Cooch Behar Airport, India
VEGT	GAU	Guwahati Intl, India
VEGY	GAY	Gaya Airport, India
VEIM	IMF	Imphal Airport, India
VEJS	IXW	Jamshedpur Airport, India
VEJT	JRH	Jorhat Airport, India
VEKM	IXQ	Kamalpur Airport, India
VEKR	IXH	Kailashahar Airport, India
VEKU	IXS	Silchar Airport, India
VEKW	IXN	Khowai Airport, India
VELR	IXI	Lilabari Airport, India
VEMH	LDA	Malda Airport, India
VEMR	DMU	Dimapur Airport, India
VEMZ	MZU	Muzzafarpur Airport, India
VEPG	IXT	Pasighat Airport, India
VEPT	PAT	Patna Airport, India
VEPU	PUI	Purnea Airport, India
VERC	IXR	Birsa Munda Airport, India
VERK	RRK	Rourkela Airport, India
VERU	RUP	Rupsi Airport, India
VETJ	TEI	Tezu Airport, India
VETZ	TEZ	Tezpur Airport, India
VEVZ	VTZ	Visakhapatnam Airport, India
VEZO	ZER	Zero Airport, India
VGBR	BZL	Barisal Airport, Bangladesh
VGCB	CXB	Cox's Bazar Airport, Bangladesh
VGCM	CLA	Comilla Airport, Bangladesh
VGEG	CGP	Shah Amanat Intl, Bangladesh
VGJR	JSR	Jessore Airport, Bangladesh
VGRJ	RJH	Rajshahi Airport, Bangladesh
VGSD	SPD	Saidpur Airport, Bangladesh
VGSG	TKR	Thakuragaon Airport, Bangladesh
VGSY	ZYL	Osmani Intl, Bangladesh
VGZR	DAC	Zia Intl, Bangladesh
VIAG	AGR	Agra Airport, India
VIAR	ATQ	Raja Sansi Intl, India
VIBN	VNS	Varanasi Airport, India
VIBR	KUU	Bhuntar Airport, India
VICG	IXC	Chandigarh Airport, India
VIDN	DED	Jolly Grant Airport, India
VIDP	DEL	Indira Gandhi Intl, India
VIGG	DHM	Gaggal Airport, India

ICAO	IATA	Airport & Country
VIGR	GWL	Gwalior Airport, India
VIJO	JDH	Jodhpur Airport, India
VIJP	JAI	Jaipur Airport, India
VIJR	JSA	Jaisalmer Airport, India
VIJU	IXJ	Jammu Airport, India
VIKA	KNU	Kanpur Airport, India
VIKO	KTU	Kota Airport, India
VILD	LUH	Sahnewal Airport, India
VILK	LKO	Amausi Airport, India
VIPT	PGH	Pantnagar Airport, India
VISM	SLV	Shimla Airport, India
VISR	SXR	Srinagar Airport, India
VIST	TNI	Satna Airport, India
VLAP	AOU	Attopeu, Laos
VLHS	OUI	Ban Houeisay, Laos
VLLB	LPQ	Luang Prabang, Laos
VLLN	LXG	Luang Namtha, Laos
VLOS	ODY	Oudomsay, Laos
VLPS	PKZ	Pakse, Laos
VLSB	ZBY	Sayaboury, Laos
VLSK	ZVK	Savannakhet, Laos
VLSN	NEU	Sam Neua, Laos
VLSV	VNA	Saravane, Laos
VLTK	THK	Thakhek, Laos
VLVT	VTE	Wattay Intl, Laos
VLXK	XKH	Xieng Khouang, Laos
VNBG	BJH	Bajhang, Nepal
VNBJ	BHP	Bhojpur, Nepal
VNBL	BGL	Baglung, Nepal
VNBP	BHR	Bharatpur, Nepal
VNBR	BJU	Bajura, Nepal
VNBT	BIT	Baitadi, Nepal
VNBW	BWA	Bhairahawa, Nepal
VNDG	DNP	Dang, Nepal
VNDH	DHI	Dhangadhi, Nepal
VNDL	DAP	Darchula, Nepal
VNDP	DOP	Dolpa, Nepal
VNGK	GKH	Gorkha, Nepal
VNJL	JUM	Jumla, Nepal
VNJP	JKR	Janakpur, Nepal
VNJS	JMO	Jomsom, Nepal
VNKT	KTM	Tribhuvan Intl, Nepal
VNLD	LDN	Lamidada, Nepal
VNLK	LUA	Lukla, Nepal
VNMA	NGX	Manang, Nepal
VNMG	MEY	Meghauli, Nepal
VNNG	KEP	Nepalgunj, Nepal
VNPK	PKR	Pokhara, Nepal
VNRB	RJB	Rajbiraj, Nepal
VNRC	RHP	Ramechhap, Nepal
VNRK	RUK	Rukumkot, Nepal
VNRT	RUM	Rumjatar, Nepal
VNSI	SIF	Simara, Nepal
VNSK	SKH	Surkhet, Nepal
VNSR	FEB	Sanfebagar, Nepal
VNST	IMK	Simikot, Nepal
VNTR	TMI	Tumlingtar, Nepal
VNVT	BIR	Biratnagar, Nepal
VOAT	AGX	Agatti Aerodrome, India
VOBG	BLR	Bangalore Intl, India

ICAO	IATA	Airport & Country
VOBI	BEP	Bellary Airport, India
VOBZ	VGA	Vijayawada Airport, India
VOCB	CJB	Coimbatore Airport, India
VOCL	CCJ	Calicut Intl, India
VOCP	CDP	Cuddapah Airport, India
VOHY	HYD	Hyderabad Airport, India
VOMD	IXM	Madurai Airport, India
VOML	IXE	Mangalore Airport, India
VOMM	MAA	Chennai Intl, India
VOMY	MYQ	Mysore Airport, India
VOPB	IXZ	Port Blair Airport, India
VOPC	PNY	Pondicherry Airport, India
VOPN	BEK	Sri Sathya Sai Airport, India
VORY	RJA	Rajahmundry Airport, India
VOSM	SXV	Salem Airport, India
VOTP	TIR	Tirupati Airport, India
VOTR	TRZ	Tiruchirapalli Airport, India
VOTV	TRV	Thiruvananthapuram Intl, India
VOWA	WGC	Warangal Airport, India
VQPR	PBH	Paro Airport, Bhutan
VRMG	GAN	Gan, Maldives
VRMH	HAQ	Hanimaadhoo, Maldives
VRMM	MLE	Male Intl, Maldives
VRMT	KDO	Kaadedhdhoo, Maldives
VTBD	BKK	Bangkok Intl, Thailand
VTBS	QHI	Sattahip Airport, Thailand
VTBU	UTP	U, Thailand
VTCC	CNX	Chiang Mai Intl, Thailand
VTCH	HGN	Mae Hong Son Airport, Thailand
VTCL	LPT	Lampang Airport, Thailand
VTCN	NNT	Nan Airport, Thailand
VTCP	PRH	Phrae Airport, Thailand
VTCR	N/A	Chiang Rai Airport, Thailand
VTCT	CEI	Chiang Rai Intl, Thailand
VTPH	HHQ	Hua Hin Airport, Thailand
VTPM	MAQ	Mae Sot Airport, Thailand
VTPO	THS	Sukhothai Airport, Thailand
VTPP	PHS	Phitsanulok Airport, Thailand
VTPT	TKT	Tak Airport, Thailand
VTPU	UTR	Uttaradit Airport, Thailand
VTSB	URT	Surat Thani Airport, Thailand
VTSC	NAW	Narathiwat Airport, Thailand
VTSG	KBV	Krabi Airport, Thailand
VTSH	SGZ	Songkhla Airport, Thailand
VTSK	PAN	Pattani Airport, Thailand
VTSM	USM	Samui Airport, Thailand
VTSN	NST	Cha Ian Airport, Thailand
VTSP	HKT	Phuket Intl, Thailand
VTSR	UNN	Ranong Airport, Thailand
VTSS	HDY	Hat Yai Intl, Thailand
VTST	TST	Trang Airport, Thailand
VTUD	UTH	Udon Thani Airport, Thailand
VTUD	UTP	Udon Thani Intl, Thailand
VTUI	SNO	Sakon Nakhon Airport, Thailand
VTUK	KKC	Khon Kaen Airport, Thailand
VTUL	LOE	Loei Airport, Thailand
VTUQ	NAK	Nakhon Ratchasima Airport, Thailand
VTUU	UBP	Ubon Ratchathani Airport, Thailand
VTUW	KOP	Nakhon Phanom Airport, Thailand
VVBM	BMV	Buon Ma Thuot Airport, Vietnam

ICAO	IATA	Airport & Country
VVCI	HPH	Cat Bi Airport, Vietnam
VVCM	CAH	Ca Mau Airport, Vietnam
VVCR	CXR	Cam Ranh Airport, Vietnam
VVCS	VCS	Co Ong Airport, Vietnam
VVCT	VCA	Tra Noc Airport, Vietnam
VVDB	DIN	Dien Bien Phu Airport, Vietnam
VVDL	DLI	Lien Khuong Airport, Vietnam
VVDN	DAD	Da Nang Intl, Vietnam
VVNB	HAN	Noi Bai Intl, Vietnam
VVNS	SQH	Na San Airport, Vietnam
VVPB	HUI	Phu Bai Airport, Vietnam
VVPC	UIH	Phu Cat Airport, Vietnam
VVPK	PXU	Pleiku Airport, Vietnam
VVPQ	PQC	Duong Dong Airport, Vietnam
VVRG	VKG	Rach Gia Airport, Vietnam
VVTH	TBB	Dong Tac Airport, Vietnam
VVTS	SGN	Tan Son Nhat Intl, Vietnam
VVVH	VII	Vinh Airport, Vietnam
VYBG	NYU	Bagan, Myanmar
VYCZ	MDL	Chanmyathazi, Myanmar
VYDW	TVY	Dawei, Myanmar
VYGG	GAW	Gantgaw, Myanmar
VYGW	GWA	Gwa, Myanmar
VYHH	HEH	Heho, Myanmar
VYHL	HOX	Hommalin, Myanmar
VYKG	KET	Kengtung, Myanmar
VYKI	KHM	Kanti, Myanmar
VYKP	KYP	Kyaukpyu, Myanmar
VYKT	KAW	Kawthoung, Myanmar
VYLK	LIW	Loikaw, Myanmar
VYLS	LSH	Lashio, Myanmar
VYME	MGZ	Myeik, Myanmar
VYMK	MYT	Pamti, Myanmar
VYMM	MNU	Mawlamyine, Myanmar
VYMN	MGU	Manaung, Myanmar
VYMO	MOE	Momeik, Myanmar
VYMS	MOG	Mong, Myanmar
VYMT	MGK	Mong Tong, Myanmar
VYMW	MWQ	Magway, Myanmar
VYNS	NMS	Namsang, Myanmar
VYPA	PAA	Hpa, Myanmar
VYPK	PAU	Pauk, Myanmar
VYPN	BSX	Pathein, Myanmar
VYPP	PPU	Hpapun, Myanmar
VYPT	PBU	Putao, Myanmar
VYPU	PKK	Pakhokku, Myanmar
VYPY	PRU	Pyay, Myanmar
VYSW	AKY	Sittwe, Myanmar
VYTD	SNW	Mazin, Myanmar
VYTL	THL	Tachilek, Myanmar
VYYE	XYE	Ye, Myanmar
VYYY	RGN	Yangon Intl, Myanmar
WAAA	UPG	Hasanuddin Airport, Indonesia
WAAU	KDI	Wolter Monginsidi Airport, Indonesia
WABB	BIK	Frans Kaisiepo Airport, Indonesia
WADD	DPS	Bali Intl, Indonesia
WAJJ	DJJ	Sentani Airport, Indonesia
WALL	BPN	Sepinggan Intl, Indonesia
WAML	PLW	Mutiara Airport, Indonesia
WAMM	MDC	Sam Ratulangi Airport, Indonesia

ICAO	IATA	Airport & Country
WAPP	AMQ	Pattimura Airport, Indonesia
WBGB	BTU	Bintulu, Malaysia
WBGG	KCH	Kuching Intl, Malaysia
WBGK	MKM	Mukah, Malaysia
WBGM	MUR	Marudi, Malaysia
WBGR	MYY	Miri, Malaysia
WBGW	LWY	Lawas, Malaysia
WBGZ	BBN	Bario, Malaysia
WBKD	LDU	Lahad Datu, Malaysia
WBKK	BKI	Kota Kinabalu, Malaysia
WBKL	LBU	Labuan I, Malaysia
WBKS	SDK	Sandakan, Malaysia
WBKW	TWU	Tawau, Malaysia
WBSB	BWN	Brunei Intl, Brunei Darussalam
WIBB	PKU	Sultan Syarif Kasim II, Indonesia
WIIB	BDO	Husein Sastranegara, Indonesia
WIIH	HLP	Halim Perdanakusuma Intl, Indonesia
WIII	CGK	Soekarno, Indonesia
WIIJ	JOG	Adisucipto Intl, Indonesia
WIIS	SRG	Achmad Yani Airport, Indonesia
WIIT	TKG	Radin Inten II Airport, Indonesia
WIKB	BTH	Hang Nadim Airport, Indonesia
WIKN	TNJ	Kijang Airport, Indonesia
WIMM	MES	Polonia Intl, Indonesia
WIOO	PNK	Supadio Airport, Indonesia
WIPP	PLM	Sultan Mahmud Badaruddin Indonesia
WIPT	PDG	Minangkabau Intl, Indonesia
WITT	BTJ	Sultan Iskandarmuda, Indonesia
WMBI	TPG	Taiping, Malaysia
WMKA	AOR	Sultan Abdul Halim, Malaysia
WMKB	BWH	Butterworth, Malaysia
WMKC	KBR	Sultan Ismail Petra, Malaysia
WMKD	KUA	Kuantan, Malaysia
WMKE	KTE	Kerteh, Malaysia
WMKI	IPH	Sultan Azlan Shah, Malaysia
WMKJ	JHB	Sultan Ismail, Malaysia
WMKK	KUL	Kuala Lumpur Intl, Malaysia
WMKL	LGK	Langkawi Intl, Malaysia
WMKM	MKZ	Malacca, Malaysia
WMKN	TGG	Sultan Mahmud, Malaysia
WMKP	PEN	Penang Intl, Malaysia
WMSA	SZB	Sultan Abdul Aziz Shah, Malaysia
WPDL	DIL	Comoro Airport, East Timor
WPMN	MPT	Maliana Airport, East Timor
WRBB	BDJ	Syamsudin Noor Airport, Indonesia
WRBP	PKY	Tjilik Riwut Airport, Indonesia
WRKK	KOE	El Tari Airport, Indonesia
WRLR	TRK	Juwata Airport, Indonesia
WRLS	SRI	Temindung Airport, Indonesia
WRRA	AMI	Selaparang Airport, Indonesia
WRSJ	SUB	Juanda Airport, Indonesia
WRSQ	SOC	Adisumarmo Intl, Indonesia
WSSS	SIN	Singapore Changi Intl, Singapore
YABA	ALH	Albany Airport, Australia
YAPH	ABH	Alpha Airport, Australia
YARA	ARY	Ararat Airport, Australia
YARM	ARM	Armidale Airport, Australia
YAVV	AVV	Avalon Airport, Australia
YAYE	AYQ	Ayers Rock Airport, Australia
YBAS	ASP	Alice Springs Airport, Australia

ICAO	IATA	Airport & Country
YBBN	BNE	Brisbane Airport, Australia
YBCG	OOL	Gold Coast Airport, Australia
YBCK	BKQ	Blackall Airport, Australia
YBCS	CNS	Cairns Intl, Australia
YBCV	CTL	Charleville Airport, Australia
YBHI	BHQ	Broken Hill Airport, Australia
YBHM	HTI	Hamilton Island Airport, Australia
YBIE	BEU	Bedourie Airport, Australia
YBKE	BRK	Bourke Airport, Australia
YBLA	BLN	Benalla Airport, Australia
YBLN	BQB	Busselton Regional Airport, Australia
YBMA	ISA	Mount Isa Airport, Australia
YBMC	MCY	Sunshine Coast Airport, Australia
YBMK	MKY	Mackay Airport, Australia
YBNA	BNK	Ballina, Australia
YBNS	BSJ	Bairnsdale Airport, Australia
YBOU	BQL	Boulia Airport, Australia
YBPN	PPP	Proserpine, Australia
YBRK	ROK	Rockhampton Airport, Australia
YBRM	BME	Broome Intl, Australia
YBRN	BZD	Balranald Airport, Australia
YBRW	BWQ	Brewarrina Airport, Australia
YBTH	BHS	Bathurst Airport, Australia
YBTI	BRT	Bathurst Island Airport, Australia
YBTL	TSV	Townsville Intl, Australia
YBTR	BLT	Blackwater Airport, Australia
YBUD	BDB	Bundaberg Airport, Australia
YBWP	WEI	Weipa Airport, Australia
YCAR	CVQ	Carnarvon Airport, Australia
YCBA	CAZ	Cobar Airport, Australia
YCBB	COJ	Coonabarabran Airport, Australia
YCBP	CPD	Coober Pedy Airport, Australia
YCBR	CRB	Collarenebri Airport, Australia
YCCA	CCL	Chinchilla Airport, Australia
YCCY	CNJ	Cloncurry Airport, Australia
YCDU	CED	Ceduna Airport, Australia
YCEE	CVC	Cleve Airport, Australia
YCKI	CKI	Croker Island Airport, Australia
YCMT	CMQ	Clermont Airport, Australia
YCNM	CNB	Coonamble Airport, Australia
YCOE	CUQ	Coen Airport, Australia
YCOM	OOM	Cooma, Australia
YCOR	CWW	Corowa Airport, Australia
YCRG	CYG	Corryong Airport, Australia
YCTM	CMD	Cootamundra Airport, Australia
YCUE	CUY	Cue Airport, Australia
YCWR	CWT	Cowra Airport, Australia
YDBI	DRN	Dirranbandi Airport, Australia
YDBY	DRB	Derby Airport, Australia
YDLQ	DNO	Deniliquin Airport, Australia
YDPO	DPO	Devonport Airport, Australia
YDYS	DYA	Dysart Airport, Australia
YECH	ECH	Echuca Airport, Australia
YELD	ELC	Elcho Island Airport, Australia
YEML	EMD	Emerald Airport, Australia
YESP	EPR	Esperance Airport, Australia
YFBS	FRB	Forbes Airport, Australia
YFLI	FLS	Flinders Island Airport Australia
YFRT	FOS	Forrest Airport, Australia
YFTZ	FIZ	Fitzroy Crossing Airport, Australia
YFTZ	FIZ	Fitzroy Crossing Airport, Australia
YGDH	GUH	Gunnedah Airport, Australia
YGEL	GET	Geraldton Airport, Australia
YGFN	GFN	Grafton Airport, Australia
YGLA	GLT	Gladstone Airport, Australia
YGLB	GUL	Goulburn Airport, Australia
YGLI	GLI	Glen Innes Airport, Australia
YGPT	GPN	Garden Point Airport, Australia
YGTE	GTE	Groote Eylandt Airport, Australia
YGTH	GFF	Griffith Airport, Australia
YHAY	HXX	Hay Airport, Australia
YHBA	HVB	Hervey Bay Airport, Australia
YHID	HID	Horn Island Airport, Australia
YHLC	HCQ	Halls Creek Airport, Australia
YHML	HLT	Hamilton Airport, Australia
YHOT	MHU	Mount Hotham Airport, Australia
YHPN	HTU	Hopetoun Airport, Australia
YHSM	HSM	Horsham Airport, Australia
YIVL	IVR	Inverell Airport, Australia
YKER	KRA	Kerang Airport, Australia
YKII	KNS	King Island Airport, Australia
YKMB	KRB	Karumba Airport, Australia
YKMP	KPS	Kempsey Airport, Australia
YKOW	KWM	Kowanyama Airport, Australia
YKRY	KGY	Kingaroy Airport, Australia
YKSC	KGC	Kingscote Airport, Australia
YLEC	LGH	Leigh Creek Airport, Australia
YLEO	LNO	Leonora Airport, Australia
YLHI	LDH	Lord Howe Island Airport, Australia
YLHR	IRG	Lockhart River Airport, Australia
YLIS	LSY	Lismore Airport, Australia
YLRD	LHG	Lightning Ridge Airport, Australia
YLRE	LRE	Longreach Airport, Australia
YLST	LER	Leinster Airport, Australia
YLTV	LTB	Latrobe Valley Airport, Australia
YMAY	ABX	Albury Airport, Australia
YMBA	MRG	Mareeba Airport, Australia
YMCO	XMC	Mallacoota Airport, Australia
YMDG	DGE	Mudgee Airport, Australia
YMEK	MKR	Meekatharra Airport, Australia
YMEN	MEB	Essendon Airport, Australia
YMER	MIM	Merimbula Airport, Australia
YMGD	MNG	Maningrida Airport, Australia
YMHB	HBA	Hobart Intl, Australia
YMIA	MQL	Mildura Airport, Australia
YMLT	LST	Launceston Airport, Australia
YMMB	MBW	Moorabbin Airport, Australia
YMML	MEL	Melbourne Intl, Australia
YMNE	WME	Mount Keith Airport, Australia
YMOG	MMG	Mount Magnet Airport, Australia
YMOR	MRZ	Moree Airport, Australia
YMRB	MOV	Moranbah Airport, Australia
YMRY	MYA	Moruya Airport, Australia
YMTG	MGB	Mount Gambier Airport, Australia
YNAR	NRA	Narrandera Airport, Australia
YNBR	NAA	Narrabri Airport, Australia
YNGU	RPM	Ngukurr Airport, Australia
YNRM	QRM	Narromine Airport, Australia
YNTN	NTN	Normanton Airport, Australia
YNWN	ZNE	Newman Airport, Australia

ICAO	IATA	Airport & Country
YORB	RBS	Orbost Airport, Australia
YORG	OAG	Orange Airport, Australia
YPAD	ADL	Adelaide Intl, Australia
YPAG	PUG	Port Augusta Airport, Australia
YPBO	PBO	Paraburdoo Airport, Australia
YPCC	CCK	Cocos Island Intl, Australia
YPDN	DRW	Darwin Intl, Australia
YPGV	GOV	Gove Airport, Australia
YPIR	PPI	Port Pirie Airport, Australia
YPJT	JAD	Jandakot Airport, Australia
YPKA	KTA	Karratha Airport, Australia
YPKG	KGI	Kalgoorlie, Australia
YPKS	PKE	Parkes Airport, Australia
YPKT	PKT	Port Keats Airport, Australia
YPKU	KNX	Kununurra Airport, Australia
YPLC	PLO	Port Lincoln Airport, Australia
YPLM	LEA	Learmonth Airport, Australia
YPMQ	PQQ	Port Macquarie Airport, Australia
YPOD	PTJ	Portland Airport, Australia
YPPD	PHE	Port Hedland Intl, Australia
YPPH	PER	Perth Intl, Australia
YPXM	XCH	Christmas Island Airport, Australia
YQLP	ULP	Quilpie Airport, Australia
YRED	RCL	Redcliffe Airport, Australia
YREN	RMK	Renmark Airport, Australia
YROI	RBC	Robinvale Airport, Australia
YROM	RMA	Roma Airport, Australia
YRTI	RTS	Rottnest Island Airport, Australia
YSBK	BWU	Bankstown Airport, Australia
YSCB	CBR	Canberra Intl, Australia
YSCH	CFS	Coffs Harbour Airport, Australia
YSCN	CDU	Camden Airport, Australia
YSDU	DBO	Dubbo Airport, Australia
YSGE	SGO	Saint George Airport, Australia
YSHT	SHT	Shepparton Airport, Australia
YSMI	SIO	Smithton Airport, Australia
YSNB	SNB	Snake Bay Airport, Australia
YSNF	NLK	Norfolk Island Airport, Australia
YSPT	SHQ	Southport Airport, Australia
YSRN	SRN	Strahan Airport, Australia
YSSY	SYD	Sydney Intl, Australia
YSTH	HLS	St Helens Airport, Australia
YSTW	TMW	Tamworth Airport, Australia
YSWG	WGA	Wagga Wagga Airport, Australia
YSWH	SWH	Swan Hill Airport, Australia
YSWL	SWC	Stawell Airport, Australia
YTAM	XTO	Taroom Airport, Australia
YTEM	TEM	Temora Airport, Australia
YTGM	XTG	Thargomindah Airport, Australia
YTIB	TYB	Tibooburra Airport, Australia
YTMU	TUM	Tumut Airport, Australia
YTNG	THG	Thangool Airport, Australia
YTNK	TCA	Tennant Creek Airport, Australia
YTRE	TRO	Taree Airport, Australia
YTWB	TWB	Toowoomba Airport, Australia
YWDH	WNR	Windorah Airport, Australia
YWGT	WGT	Wangaratta Airport, Australia
YWHA	WYA	Whyalla Airport, Australia
YWKB	WKB	Warracknabeal Airport, Australia
YWLG	WGE	Walgett Airport, Australia

ICAO	IATA	Airport & Country
YWLM	NTL	Newcastle, Australia
YWLU	WUN	Wiluna Airport, Australia
YWOL	WOL	Wollongong Airport, Australia
YWRN	QRR	Warren Airport, Australia
YWSL	SXE	West Sale Airport, Australia
YWTN	WIN	Winton Airport, Australia
YWWL	WWA	West Wyalong Airport, Australia
YWYY	BWT	Burnie Airport, Australia
YYNG	NGA	Young Airport, Australia
ZBAA	PEK	Beijing Capital Intl, China
ZBBB	NAY	Beijing Nanyuan Airport, China
ZBCF	CIF	Chifeng Airport, China
ZBCZ	CIH	Changzhi Airport, China
ZBDT	DAT	Datong Airport, China
ZBHH	HET	Hohhot Baita Intl, China
ZBLA	HLD	Hailar Dongshan Airport, China
ZBOW	BAV	Baotou Airport, China
ZBSH	SHP	Qinhuangdao Shanhaiguan, China
ZBSJ	SJW	Shijiazhuang Daguocun Intl, China
ZBTJ	TSN	Tianjin Binhai Intl, China
ZBTL	TGO	Tongliao Airport, China
ZBUL	HLH	Ulanhot Airport, China
ZBXT	XNT	Xingtai Airport, China
ZBYN	TYN	Taiyuan Wusu Airport, China
ZGBH	BHY	Beihai Airport, China
ZGGG	CAN	Guangzhou Baiyun Intl, China
ZGHA	CSX	Changsha Huanghua Intl, China
ZGHY	HNY	Hengyang Airport, China
ZGKL	KWL	Guilin Liangjiang Intl, China
ZGNN	NNG	Nanning Wuxu Intl, China
ZGOW	SWA	Shantou Airport, China
ZGSD	ZUH	Zhuhai Intl, China
ZGSY	SYX	Sanya Fenghuang Intl, China
ZGSZ	SZX	Shenzhen Bao'an Intl, China
ZGWZ	WUZ	Wuzhou Changzhoudao Airport, China
ZGZH	LZH	Liuzhou Airport, China
ZGZJ	ZHA	Zhanjiang Airport, China
ZHAY	AYN	Anyang Airport, China
ZHCC	CGO	Zhengzhou Xinzheng Intl, China
ZHHH	WUH	Wuhan Tianhe Airport, China
ZHLY	LYA	Luoyang Airport, China
ZHNY	NNY	Nanyang Airport, China
ZHSS	SHS	Shashi Airport, China
ZHXF	XFN	Xiangfan Airport, China
ZHYC	YIH	Yichang Airport, China
ZJHK	HAK	Haikou Meilan Intl, China
ZKPY	FNJ	Sunan, North Korea
ZKPY	FNJ	Sunan, South Korea
ZLAN	LHW	Lanzhou Airport, China
ZLDH	DNH	Dunhuang Airport, China
ZLGM	GOQ	Golmud Airport, China
ZLHZ	HZG	Hanzhong Airport, China
ZLIC	INC	Yinchuan Helanshan Airport, China
ZLJN	JNG	Jining Airport, China
ZLJQ	CHW	Jiuquan Airport, China
ZLLL	ZGC	Lanzhou Zhongchuan Airport, China
ZLQY	IQN	Qingyang Airport, China
ZLXN	XNN	Xining Airport, China
ZLXY	XIY	Xi'an Xianyang Intl, China
ZLYA	ENY	Yan'an Airport, China

ICAO	IATA	Airport & Country
ZLYL	UYN	Yulin Airport, China
ZMAH	AVK	Arvaikheer, Mongolia
ZMAT	LTI	Altai, Mongolia
ZMBH	BYN	Bayankhongor, Mongolia
ZMBN	UGA	Bulgan, Mongolia
ZMBU	UUN	Baruun, Mongolia
ZMCD	COQ	Choibalsan, Mongolia
ZMUB	ULN	Buyant, Mongolia
ZPBS	BSD	Baoshan Airport, China
ZPJH	JHG	Jinghong Gasa Airport, China
ZPLJ	LJG	Lijiang Airport, China
ZPLX	YUM	Luxi Mangshi Airport, China
ZPPP	KMG	Kunming Wujiaba Intl, China
ZPSM	SYM	Simao Airport, China
ZPZT	ZAT	Zhaotong Airport, China
ZSAM	XMN	Xiamen Gaoqi Intl, China
ZSAQ	AQG	Anqing Airport, China
ZSBB	BFU	Bengbu Airport, China
ZSCG	CZX	Changzhou Airport, China
ZSCN	KHN	Nanchang Intl, China
ZSFY	FUG	Fuyang Airport, China
ZSFZ	FOC	Fuzhou Chengle Intl, China
ZSGZ	KOW	Ganzhou Airport, China
ZSHC	HGH	Hangzhou Xiaoshan Intl, China
ZSJD	JDZ	Jingdezhen Airport, China
ZSJJ	JIU	Jiujiang Lushan Airport, China
ZSJN	TNA	Jinan Yaoqiang Airport, China
ZSLG	LYG	Lianyungang Airport, China
ZSLQ	HYN	Huangyan Luqiao Airport, China
ZSNB	NGB	Ningbo Lishe Intl, China
ZSNJ	NKG	Nanjing Lukou Intl, China
ZSOF	HFE	Hefei Luogang Intl, China
ZSPD	PVG	Shanghai Pudong Intl, China
ZSQD	TAO	Qingdao Liuting Intl, China
ZSQZ	JJN	Quanzhou Jinjiang Airport, China
ZSSS	SHA	Shanghai Hongqiao Airport, China
ZSSZ	SZV	Suzhou Guangfu Airport, China
ZSTX	TXN	Huangshan Tunxi Intl, China
ZSWF	WEF	Weifang Airport, China
ZSWX	WUX	Wuxi Airport, China
ZSWY	WUS	Nanping Wuyishan Airport, China
ZSWZ	WNZ	Wenzhou Intl, China
ZSXZ	XUZ	Xuzhou Airport, China
ZSYT	YNT	Yantai Laishan Airport, China
ZSYW	YIW	Yiwu Airport, China
ZSZS	HSN	Zhoushan Airport, China
ZUCK	CKG	Chongqing Jiangbei Intl, China
ZUGY	KWE	Guiyang Longdongbao Airport, China
ZULS	LXA	Lhasa Gonggar Airport, China
ZUNC	NAO	Nanchong Airport, China
ZUUU	CTU	Chengdu Shuangliu Intl, China
ZUXC	XIC	Xichang Qingshan Airport, China
ZUYB	YBP	Yibin Airport, China
ZUZY	ZYI	Zunyi Airport, China
ZWAK	AKU	Aksu Airport, China
ZWAT	AAT	Altay Airport, China
ZWFY	FYN	Fuyun Airport, China
ZWHM	HMI	Hami Airport, China
ZWKC	KCA	Kuqa Airport, China
ZWKL	KRL	Korla Airport, China
ZWKM	KRY	Karamay Airport, China
ZWSH	KHG	Kashgar Airport, China
ZWTN	HTN	Hotan Airport, China
ZWWW	URC	Diwopu Airport, China
ZWYN	YIN	Yining Airport, China
ZYAS	AOG	Anshan Airport, China
ZYCC	CGQ	Changchun Longjia Intl, China
ZYDD	DDG	Dandong Airport, China
ZYHB	HRB	Harbin Taiping Intl, China
ZYHE	HEK	Heihe Airport, China
ZYJL	JIL	Jilin Airport, China
ZYJM	JMU	Jiamusi Airport, China
ZYJZ	JNZ	Jinzhou Airport, China
ZYMD	MDG	Mudanjiang Airport, China
ZYQQ	NDG	Qiqihar Airport, China
ZYTL	DLC	Dalian Zhoushuizi Intl, China
ZYTN	TNH	Tonghua Liuhe Airport, China
ZYTX	SHE	Shenyang Taoxian Intl, China
ZYYJ	YNJ	Yanji Airport, China

ICAO / IATA Airline Codes & Callsigns

ICAO	IATA	Airline	Callsign	Country
AAB	W9	Abelag Aviation	Abg	Belgium
AAF	ZI	Aigle Azur	Aigle Azur	France
AAG	KI	Air Atlantique	Atlantic	United Kingdom
AAH	KH	Aloha Air Cargo	Aloha	USA
AAL	AA	American Airlines	American	USA
AAN	WD	Amsterdam Airlines	Amstel	Netherlands
AAR	OZ	Asiana Airlines	Asiana	South Korea
AAS	4K	Askari Aviation	Al-Aas	Pakistan
AAW	8U	Afriqiyah Airways	Afriqiyah	Libya
AAY	G4	Allegiant Air	Allegiant	USA
ABB	4P	Business Aviation	African Business	Congo
ABD	CC	Air Atlanta Icelandic	Atlanta	Iceland
ABE	K5	Aban Air	Aban	Iran
ABR	AG	Air Contractors	Contract	Ireland
ABS	9T	Transwest Air	Athabaska	Canada
ABW	RU	AirBridgeCargo Airlines	Airbridge Cargo	Russia
ABX	GB	ABX Air	Abex	USA
ABY	G9	Air Arabia	Arabia	United Arab Emirates
ACA	AC	Air Canada	Air Canada	Canada
ACI	SB	Aircalin (Air Caledonie International)	Aircalin	New Caledonia
ACK	DV	Nantucket Airlines	Ack Air	USA
ACL	9X	ItAli Airlines	Itali	Italy
ACP	8V	Astral Aviation	Astral Cargo	Kenya
ADE	ZY	Ada Air	Ada Air	Albania
ADH	AP	Air One	Heron	Italy
ADO	HD	Hokkaido International Airlines	Air Do	Japan
ADR	JP	Adria Airways	Adria	Slovenia
AEA	UX	Air Europa	Europa	Spain
AEB	EM	Aero Benin	Aeroben	Benin
AEE	A3	Aegean Airlines	Aegean	Greece
AEI	4Q	Air Italy Polska	Polish Bird	Poland
AER	KO	Alaska Central Express	Ace Air	USA
AEU	5W	Astraeus	Flystar	United Kingdom
AEW	VV	Aerosvit Airlines	Aerosvit	Ukraine
AEY	I9	Air Italy	Air Italy	Italy
AFG	FG	Ariana Afghan Airlines	Ariana	Afghanistan
AFL	SU	Aeroflot Russian Airlines	Aeroflot	Russia
AFN	AF	Air Freight NZ	Air Freight	New Zealand
AFR	AF	Air France	Airfrans	France
AGV	7T	Air Glaciers	Air Glaciers	Switzerland
AGX	JJ	Aviogenex	Genex	Serbia
AHA	GD	Air Alpha Greenland	Air Alpha	Denmark
AHK	LD	Air Hong Kong	Air Hong Kong	China
AHW	HT	Aeromist-Kharkiv	Aeromist	Ukraine
AHY	J2	Azerbaijan Airlines	Azal	Azerbaijan
AIA	U3	Avies	Avies	Estonia
AIB	AP	Airbus Industrie	Airbus Industrie	France
AIC	AI	Air India	Airindia	India
AIE	3H	Air Inuit	Air Inuit	Canada
AIJ	4O	Interjet	Interjet	Mexico
AIP	5A	Alpine Air Express	Alpine Air	USA
AIQ	FD	Thai AirAsia	Thai Asia	Thailand
AIZ	IZ	Arkia Israel Airlines	Arkia	Israel
AJM	JM	Air Jamaica	Jamaica	Jamaica
AJT	M6	Amerijet International	Amerijet	USA
AJV	9N	ANA & JP Express	Ayjay Cargo	Japan

ICAO	IATA	Airline	Callsign	Country
AJX	NQ	Air Japan	Air Japan	Japan
AKK	6L	Aklak Air	Aklak	Canada
AKX	EH	Air Nippon Network Co. Ltd.	Alfa Wing	Japan
ALK	UL	SriLankan Airlines	Srilankan	Sri Lanka
ALX	EO	Hewa Bora Airways	Allcongo	Congo
AMB	1I	DRF Luftrettung	Civil Air Ambulance	Germany
AMC	KM	Air Malta	Air Malta	Malta
AMF	A8	Ameriflight	Amflight	USA
AML	QM	Air Malawi	Malawi	Malawi
AMU	NX	Air Macao	Air Macao	China
AMX	AM	AeroMéxico	Aeromexico	Mexico
ANA	NH	All Nippon Airways	All Nippon	Japan
ANE	YW	Air Nostrum	Air Nostrum	Spain
ANG	PX	Air Niugini	Nuigini	Papua New Guinea
ANK	EL	Air Nippon	Ank Air	Japan
ANO	TL	Airnorth	Topend	Australia
ANS	OY	Andes Líneas Aéreas	Aeroandes	Argentina
ANT	4N	Air North	Air North	Canada
ANZ	NZ	Air New Zealand	New Zealand	New Zealand
APG	3D	Air People International	Air People	Thailand
APP	WL	Aeroperlas	Aeroperlas	Panama
APW	JW	Arrow Air	Big A	USA
ARA	W3	Arik Air	Arik Air	Nigeria
ARD	2B	Aerocondor	Aerocondor	Portugal
ARE	4C	Aires, Aerovias de Integracion Regional, S.A.	Aires	Colombia
ARG	AR	Aerolineas Argentinas	Argentina	Argentina
ARR	QN	Air Armenia	Air Armenia	Armenia
ASA	AS	Alaska Airlines	Alaska	USA
ASD	4D	Air Sinai	Air Sinai	Egypt
ASE	PL	Airstars	Morozov	Russia
ASH	YV	Mesa Airlines	Air Shuttle	USA
ASJ	6O	Air Satellite	Satellite	Canada
ASQ	EV	Atlantic Southeast Airlines	Acey	USA
ASZ	OB	Astrakhan Airlines	Air Astrakhan	Russia
ATI	HC	Aero-Tropics Air Services	Aerotropics	Australia
ATM	FO	Airlines Of Tasmania	Airtas	Australia
ATN	8C	Air Transport International LLC	Air Transport	USA
AUA	OS	Austrian Airlines	Austrian	Austria
AUB	IQ	Augsburg Airways GmbH	Augsburg-Air	Germany
AUH	MO	Abu Dhabi Amiri Flight	Sultan	United Arab Emirates
AUI	PS	Ukraine International Airlines	Ukraine International	Ukraine
AUL	5N	Aeroflot-Nord	Dvina	Russia
AUR	GR	Aurigny Air Services	Ayline	United Kingdom
AUT	AU	Austral Lineas Aereas	Austral	Argentina
AVA	AV	Avianca - Aerovias Nacionales de Colombia, S.A.	Avianca	Colombia
AVI	A0	L'Avion	Elysair	France
AVJ	TF	Avia Traffic Company	Atomic	Kyrgyzstan
AVN	NF	Air Vanuatu	Air Van	Vanuatu
AWC	ZT	Titan Airways	Zap	United Kingdom
AWE	US	US Airways	Cactus	USA
AWI	ZW	Air Wisconsin	Air Wisconsin	USA
AWQ	QZ	Indonesia AirAsia	Wagon Air	Indonesia
AWU	7E	Sylt Air	Sylt-Air	Germany
AXB	IX	Air India Express	Express India	India
AXF	HJ	Asian Express Airlines	Freightexpress	Australia
AXK	XU	African Express Airways	Express Jet	Kenya
AXM	AK	AirAsia	Asian Express	Malaysia
AXY	6V	Axis Airways	Axis	France
AYZ	3G	Atlant-Soyuz Airlines	Atlant-Soyuz	Russia
AZA	AZ	Alitalia	Alitalia	Italy

ICAO	IATA	Airline	Callsign	Country
AZE	ZE	Arcus-Air Logistic	Arcus Air	Germany
AZN	Z8	Amaszonas	Amaszonas	Bolivia
AZQ	ZP	Silk Way Airlines	Silk Line	Azerbaijan
AZS	ZR	Aviacon Zitotrans	Zitotrans	Russia
AZU	AD	Azul Brazilian Airlines	Azul	Brazil
AZW	UM	Air Zimbabwe	Air Zimbabwe	Zimbabwe
BAB	2B	Bahrain Air	Bahrain Air	Bahrain
BAW	BA	British Airways	Speedbird	United Kingdom
BBC	BG	Biman Bangladesh Airlines	Bangladesh	Bangladesh
BBD	BF	Bluebird Cargo	Blue Cargo	Iceland
BBO	F7	Flybaboo	Baboo	Switzerland
BBR	S3	Santa Barbara Airlines	Santa Barbara	Venezuela
BCF	B4	BACH Flugbetriebsgesellschaft mbH	Bach	Austria
BCI	SI	Blue Islands	Blue Island	United Kingdom
BCS	QY	European Air Transport	Eurotrans	Belgium
BCY	WX	CityJet	City-Ireland	Ireland
BDA	BZ	Blue Dart Aviation	Blue Dart	India
BEA	5Q	Best Air	Best Air	Bangladesh
BEE	BE	Flybe	Jersey	United Kingdom
BEL	SN	Brussels Airlines	Bee-Line	Belgium
BER	AB	Air Berlin	Air Berlin	Germany
BES	W4	Aero Services Executive	Bird Express	France
BFL	J4	Buffalo Airways	Buffalo	Canada
BGH	1B	BH Air (Balkan Holidays)	Balkan Holidays	Bulgaria
BGL	A8	Benin Golf Air	Benin Golf	Benin
BHP	4T	Belair Airlines	Belair	Switzerland
BHS	UP	Bahamasair	Bahamas	Bahamas
BIE	DR	Air Mediterranee	Mediterranee	France
BIH	BS	British International Helicopters	Brintel	United Kingdom
BKA	B4	Bankair	Bankair	USA
BKP	PG	Bangkok Airways	Bangkok Air	Thailand
BLE	4Y	Blue Line	Blue Berry	France
BLF	KF	Blue1	Bluefin	Finland
BLS	JV	Bearskin Lake Air Service	Bearskin	Canada
BLV	B3	Bellview Airlines	Bellview Airlines	Nigeria
BLX	6B	TUIfly Nordic	Bluescan	Sweden
BMJ	CH	Bemidji Airlines	Bemidji	USA
BML	5Z	Bismillah Airlines	Bismillah	Bangladesh
BMM	8A	Atlas Blue	Atlas Blue	Morocco
BMR	BD	BMI Regional		United Kingdom
BNX	KG	LAI - Linea Aerea IAACA	Air Barinas	Venezuela
BON	JA	B&H Airlines	Air Bosna	Bosnia-Hercegovina
BOS	EC	OpenSkies	Mistral	United Kingdom
BOT	BP	Air Botswana	Botswana	Botsuana
BPA	BV	Blue Panorama Airlines	Blue Panoroma	Italy
BRG	8E	Bering Air	Bering Air	USA
BRI	FQ	Brindabella Airlines	Brindabella	Australia
BRQ	UZ	Buraq Air	Buraqair	Libya
BRU	B2	Belavia Belarusian Airlines	Belarus Avia	Belarus
BRV	K6	Bravo Air Congo	Bravo	Congo
BSK	GL	Miami Air International	Biscayne	USA
BSR	G6	Guine Bissaur Airlines	Bissau Airlines	Guinea Bissau
BST	T1	Bestair	Barbie	Turkey
BTA	XE	ExpressJet Airlines	Jet Link	USA
BTI	BT	Air Baltic	Airbaltic	Latvia
BTR	B8	Botir-Avia	Botir-Avia	Kyrgyzstan
BTV	7P	Batavia Air	Batavia	Indonesia
BUC	1T	Bulgarian Air Charter	Bulgarian Charter	Nigeria
BUG	MW	Mokulele Airlines	Speedbuggy	USA
BVT	J8	Berjaya Air	Berjaya	Malaysia

ICAO	IATA	Airline	Callsign	Country
BWA	BW	Caribbean Airlines	Caribbean Airlines	Trinidad & Tobago
BWG	QW	Blue Wings	Blue Wings	Germany
BZH	DB	Brit Air	Britair	France
CAL	CI	China Airlines	Dynasty	Taiwan
CAO	CA	Air China Cargo	Airchina Freight	China
CAV	MO	Calm Air	Calm Air	Canada
CAW	MN	Comair	Commercial	South Africa
CAY	KX	Cayman Airways	Cayman	Cayman Islands
CBB	BB	Cargo B Airlines	Cargo-Bee	Belgium
CBC	B9	Caribair	Caribair	Dominican Republic
CBE	QA	MexicanaClick	Click	Mexico
CCA	CA	Air China	Air China	China
CCI	PT	Capital Cargo International Airlines	Cappy	USA
CCM	XK	CCM Airlines	Corsica	France
CDG	SC	Shandong Airlines	Shandong	China
CDP	Q6	Aero Condor Peru	Condor-Peru	Peru
CEB	5J	Cebu Pacific	Cebu Air	Philippines
CES	MU	China Eastern Airlines	China Eastern	China
CFE	CJ	BA CityFlyer	Flyer	United Kingdom
CFG	DE	Condor Flugdienst	Condor	Germany
CFS	EM	Empire Airlines	Empire	USA
CGK	4C	Click Airways	Click Air	United Arab Emirates
CGL	SJ	Seagle Air	Seagle	Slovakia
CGN	2Z	Chang'an Airlines	Changan	China
CGP	8L	Cargo Plus Aviation	Cargo Plus	United Arab Emirates
CHB	PN	China West Air	West China	China
CHH	HU	Hainan Airlines	Hainan	China
CHP	6A	Aviacsa	Aviacsa	Mexico
CHQ	RP	Chautauqua Airlines	Chautauqua	USA
CIM	QI	Cimber Air	Cimber	Denmark
CIR	5F	Arctic Circle Air Service	Air Arctic	USA
CIU	A2	Cielos Airlines	Cielos	Peru
CIX	G3	City Connexion Airlines	Connexion	Burundi
CJA	C6	CanJet	Canjet	Canada
CJC	9L	Colgan Air	Colgan	USA
CJT	W8	Cargojet Airways	Cargojet	Canada
CKK	CK	China Cargo Airlines	Cargo King	China
CKS	K4	Kalitta Air	Connie	USA
CLH	CL	Lufthansa CityLine	Hansaline	Germany
CLI	XG	Clickair	Clickjet	Spain
CLU	3A	Triple Alpha Luftfahrtgesellschaft	Carolus	Germany
CLW	C0	Centralwings	Centralwings	Poland
CLX	CV	Cargolux	Cargolux	Luxembourg
CMI	CS	Continental Micronesia	Air Mike	Guam (USA)
CMM	I5	Compagnie Aérienne du Mali	Camali	Mali
CMP	CM	Copa Airlines	Copa	Panama
COA	CO	Continental Airlines	Continental	USA
COM	OH	Comair	Comair	USA
COY	7C	Coyne Aviation	Coyne Air	United Kingdom
COZ	F5	Cosmic Air	Cosmic Air	Nepal
CPA	CX	Cathay Pacific	Cathay	China
CPN	RV	Caspian Airlines	Caspian	Iran
CPZ	CP	Compass Airlines	Compass Rose	USA
CQH	9S	Spring Airlines	Air Spring	China
CQN	OQ	Chongqing Airlines	Chong Qing	China
CRD	QC	Air Corridor	Air Corridor	Mozambique
CRF	NV	Air Central	Air Central	Japan
CRG	2G	Cargoitalia	White Pelican	Italy
CRK	N8	Hong Kong Airlines	Bauhinia	China
CRL	SS	Corsairfly	Corsair	France

ICAO	IATA	Airline	Callsign	Country
CRN	7L	Aero Caribbean	Aerocaribbean	Cuba
CRQ	YN	Air Creebec	Cree	Canada
CSA	OK	Czech Airlines	Csa-Lines	Czech Republic
CSC	3U	Sichuan Airlines	Si Chuan	China
CSH	FM	Shanghai Airlines	Shanghai Air	China
CSN	CZ	China Southern Airlines	China Southern	China
CSQ	II	IBC Airways	Chasqui	USA
CSZ	ZH	Shenzhen Airlines	Shenzhen Air	China
CTN	OU	Croatia Airlines	Croatia	Croatia
CTT	5R	Custom Air Transport	Catt	USA
CUA	HR	China United Airlines	Lianhang	China
CUB	CU	Cubana de Aviacion	Cubana	Cuba
CVA	CV	Air Chathams	Chatham	New Zealand
CVC	J7	Centre-Avia	Aviacentre	Russia
CVU	YR	Grand Canyon Airlines	Canyon View	USA
CWC	WE	Centurion Air Cargo	Challenge Cargo	USA
CWM	CW	Air Marshall Islands	Air Marshalls	Marshall Islands
CXA	MF	Xiamen Airlines	Xiamen Air	China
CXH	XO	China Xinhua Airlines	Xinhua	China
CXI	8C	Shanxi Airlines	Shanxi	China
CXP	XP	Xtra Airways	Ruby Mountain	USA
CYP	CY	Cyprus Airways	Cyprus	Cyprus
CYZ	8Y	China Postal Airlines	China Post	China
DAE	D5	DHL Aero Expreso	Yellow	Panama
DAG	N2	Dagestan Airlines	Dagal	Russia
DAH	AH	Air Algerie	Air Algerie	Algeria
DAL	DL	Delta Air Lines	Delta	USA
DAO	D3	Daallo Airlines	Daallo Airlines	United Arab Emirates
DER	JD	Deer Jet	Deer Jet	China
DHK	D0	DHL Air UK	Eurotrans	United Kingdom
DHL	ER	Astar Air Cargo	Dhl	USA
DHX	ES	DHL International Aviation ME	Dilmun	Bahrain
DIR	AW	Dirgantara Air Service	Dirgantara	Indonesia
DJB	D8	Djibouti Airlines	Djibouti Air	Djibouti
DKH	HO	Juneyao Airlines	Air Juneyao	China
DKN	DN	Kingfisher Red	Deccan	India
DLA	EN	Air Dolomiti	Dolomoti	Italy
DLH	LH	Lufthansa	Lufthansa	Germany
DNL	9H	Dutch Antilles Express	Dutch Antilles	Netherlands Antilles
DNM	3D	Denim Air	Denim	Netherlands
DNU	R6	DOT LT	Danu	Lithuania
DNV	D9	Aeroflot-Don	Donavia	Russia
DQA	Q2	Maldivian	Island Aviation	Maldives
DRK	KB	Druk Air	Royal Bhutan	Bhutan
DRU	6R	Alrosa Mirny Air Enterprise	Mirny	Russia
DSM	4M	LAN Argentina	Lan Air	Argentina
DTA	DT	TAAG Angola Airlines (Linhas Aéreas de Angola)	Dta	Angola
DTH	SF	Tassili Airlines	Tassili Air	Algeria
DTR	DX	DAT Danish Air Transport	Danish	Denmark
DWT	0D	Darwin Airline	Darwin	Switzerland
DXH	8C	East Star Air	East Star	China
EAG	NZ	Eagle Airways	Eagle	New Zealand
EAK	5B	Euro-Asia Air	Eakaz	Kazakhstan
EAQ	QF	Eastern Australia Airlines	Eastern	Australia
ECA	UI	Eurocypria Airlines	Eurocypria	Cyprus
ECV	8Y	Ecuato Guineana	Ecuatoguinea	Equatorial Guinea
EDW	WK	Edelweiss Air	Edelweiss	Switzerland
EEA	EU	Empresa Ecuatoriana De Aviacion	Ecuatoriana	Ecuador
EEU	GJ	Eurofly	Eurofly	Italy
EGF	MQ	American Eagle Airlines	Eagle Flight	USA

ICAO	IATA	Airline	Callsign	Country
EGJ	YR	Scenic Airlines	Scenic	USA
EGU	H7	Eagle Air	African Eagle	Uganda
EIA	EZ	Evergreen International Airlines	Evergreen	USA
EIN	EI	Aer Lingus	Shamrock	Ireland
EJA	1I	NetJets	Execjet	USA
ELL	OV	Estonian Air	Estonian	Estonia
ELO	K2	Eurolot	Eurolot	Poland
ELY	LY	El Al Israel Airlines	Elal	Israel
ENK	G8	Enkor	Enkor	Russia
EPA	J5	Shenzhen Donghai Airlines	Donghai Air	China
ERG	7U	Aviaenergo	Aviaenergo	Russia
ERH	7H	Era Aviation	Erah	USA
ERO	7L	Sun d'Or Internationa Airlines	Echo Romeo	Israel
ERT	B8	Eritrean Airlines	Eritrean	Eritrea
ESF	E7	Estafeta Carga Aerea	Estafeta	Mexico
ESK	NE	SkyEurope	Relax	Slovakia
ESL	P7	Russian Sky Airlines	Raduga	Russia
ESY	EF	EasyFly	Easyfly	Colombia
ETD	EY	Etihad Airways	Etihad	United Arab Emirates
ETH	ET	Ethiopian Airlines	Ethiopian	Ethiopia
ETS	2Q	Avitrans	Extrans	Sweden
EUP	6M	EuroAir	Eurostar	Greece
EVA	BR	EVA Air	Eva	Taiwan
EWG	EW	Eurowings	Eurowings	Germany
EXK	OW	Executive Airlines	Executive Eagle	Puerto Rico
EXL	CQ	Sunshine Express Airlines	Sea	Australia
EXS	LS	Jet2.com	Channex	United Kingdom
EXV	8D	Expo Aviation	Expoavia	Sri Lanka
EXY	YB	South African Express	Expressways	South Africa
EYE	4A	FS Air Service	Sockeye	USA
EZA	ZY	Eznis Airways	Eznis	Mongolia
EZE	T3	Eastern Airways	Eastflight	United Kingdom
FAB	7F	First Air	First Air	Canada
FAJ	PC	Air Fiji	Fijiair	Fiji
FCR	7Y	Flying Carpet	Flying Carpet	Lebanon
FDN	ZD	Dolphin Air	Flying Dolphin	United Arab Emirates
FDX	FX	FedEx Express	Fedex	USA
FFM	FY	Firefly	Firefly	Malaysia
FFT	F9	Frontier Airlines	Frontier Flight	USA
FFV	5H	Fly540	Swift Tango	Kenya
FFX	JH	Flex Linhas Aéreas	Flex	Brazil
FHE	HW	Hello	Flyhello	Switzerland
FHY	XD	Freebird Airlines	Free Bird	Turkey
FIF	OF	Air Finland	Air Finland	Finland
FIN	AY	Finnair	Finnair	Finland
FJI	FJ	Air Pacific	Pacific	Fiji
FLG	9E	Pinnacle Airlines	Flagship	USA
FLI	RC	Atlantic Airways	Faroeline	Faroe Islands (Denmark)
FPO	5O	Europe Airpost	French Post	France
FPY	E9	Compagnie Africaine d'Aviation	Africompany	Congo
FRE	FP	Freedom Air	Freedom	Guam (USA)
FRJ	6F	Afrijet Airlines	Afrijet	Nigeria
FRL	F8	Freedom Airlines	Freedom Air	USA
FSC	HK	Four Star Aviation / Four Star Cargo	Four Star	Puerto Rico
FSW	F3	Faso Airways	Faso	Burkina Faso
FTA	2F	Frontier Flying Service	Frontier-Air	USA
FWA	I4	Interstate Airline	Freewayair	Netherlands
FWI	TX	Air Caraibes	French West	Guadeloupe,French Antilles
FWL	RF	Florida West International Airways	Flo West	USA
FXI	NY	Air Iceland (Flugfélag Íslands)	Faxi	Iceland

ICAO	IATA	Airline	Callsign	Country
GAI	3R	Moskovia Airlines	Gromov Airline	Russia
GAL	7O	Galaxy Air	Galaxy	Kyrgyzstan
GAO	DC	Golden Air	Golden	Sweden
GAP	2P	Air Philippines	Orient Pacific	Philippines
GBA	GF	Gulf Air Bahrain	Gulf Bahrain	Bahrain
GBK	GY	Gabon Airlines	Gabon Airlines	Gabon
GCR	GS	Grand China Express Air	China Dragon	China
GDR	GP	Gadair European Airlines	Gadair	Spain
GEC	LH	Lufthansa Cargo	Lufthansa Cargo	Germany
GES	GP	Gestair	Gestair	Spain
GFG	QB	Georgian National Airlines	National	Georgia
GFT	3M	Gulfstream International Airlines	Gulf Flight	USA
GGN	ZX	Air Georgian	Georgian	Canada
GHB	G0	Ghana International Airlines	Ghana Airlines	Ghana
GIA	GA	Garuda Indonesia	Indonesia	Indonesia
GIF	J9	Guinee Airlines	Guinee Airlines	Guinea
GJS	G7	GoJet Airlines	Lindbergh	USA
GLA	ZK	Great Lakes Airlines	Lakes Air	USA
GLG	2K	Aerolineas Galapagos (Aerogal)	Aerogal	Ecuador
GLO	G3	Gol Transportes Aéreos	Gol Transporte	Brazil
GLR	9M	Central Mountain Air	Glacier	Canada
GMI	ST	Germania	Germania	Germany
GMT	UJ	Magnicharters	Grupomonterrey	Mexico
GNC	LQ	Air Guinea Cargo	Guinea Cargo	Equatorial Guinea
GOM	YD	Gomelavia	Gomel	Belarus
GOT	XW	WaltAir	Gothic	Sweden
GOW	G8	GoAir	Goair	India
GRL	GL	Air Greenland	Greenland	Denmark
GRO	LL	Allegro	Allegro	Mexico
GSM	B4	Flyglobespan	Globespan	United Kingdom
GSS	XH	Global Supply Systems	Jet Lift	United Kingdom
GTI	5Y	Atlas Air	Giant	USA
GTV	KG	Aerogaviota	Gaviota	Cuba
GUN	GS	Grant Aviation	Hoot	USA
GUY	GG	Air Guyane Express	Green Bird	French Guiana
GWI	4U	Germanwings	German Wings	Germany
GWL	IJ	Great Wall Airlines	Great Wall	China
GWY	U5	USA 3000 Airlines	Getaway	USA
GXL	9E	XL Airways Germany	Star Dust	Germany
GZP	4G	Gazpromavia	Gazpromavia	Russia
HAG	H6	Hageland Aviation Services	Hageland	USA
HAL	HA	Hawaiian Airlines	Hawaiian	USA
HDA	KA	Dragonair, Hong Kong Dragon Airlines	Dragon	China
HEJ	T4	Hellas Jet	Hellas Jet	Greece
HER	UD	Hex'Air	Hex Airline	France
HFY	5K	Hi Fly	Sky Flyer	Portugal
HHA	ZF	Atlantic Airlines de Honduras	Atlantic Honduras	Honduras
HHI	4R	Hamburg International	Hamburg Jet	Germany
HHN	HR	Hahn Air	Rooster	Germany
HKA	SO	Superior Aviation	Spend Air	USA
HKE	UO	Hong Kong Express Airways	Hongkong Shuttle	China
HKS	L5	CHC Helikopter Service	Helibus	Norway
HLX	X3	TUIfly	Yellow Cab	Germany
HMS	DU	Hemus Air	Hemus Air	Bulgaria
HOA	H5	Hola Airlines	Hola	Spain
HPA	HP	Pearl Airways	Pearl Airways	Haiti
HSA	S9	East African Safari Air Express	Duma	Kenya
HSV	HS	Direktflyg	Highswede	Sweden
HVN	VN	Vietnam Airlines	Viet Nam Airlines	Vietnam
HVY	HN	Heavylift Cargo Airlines	Heavy Cargo	Australia

ICAO	IATA	Airline	Callsign	Country
HWY	8H	Highland Airways	Hiway	United Kingdom
HZT	8C	Air Horizon	Horizon Togo	Togo
IAD	6P	Fly Wex	Flywex	Italy
IAW	IA	Iraqi Airways	Iraqi	Iraq
IBB	NT	Binter Canarias	Binter	Spain
IBE	IB	Iberia Airlines	Iberia	Spain
IBX	FW	Ibex Airlines	Ibex	Japan
IBZ	6I	International Business Air	Interbiz	Sweden
ICD	X8	Icaro Air	Icaro	Ecuador
ICE	FI	Icelandair	Iceair	Iceland
ICL	5C	CAL Cargo Air Lines	Cal	Israel
IDA	I8	Indonesia Air Transport	Intra	Indonesia
IGO	6E	IndiGo Airlines	Ifly	India
IKA	G1	Gorkha Airlines	Gorkha Airlines	Nepal
IKA	GI	Itek Air	Itek-Air	Kyrgyzstan
ILN	D6	Interair South Africa	Inline	South Africa
IMP	HT	Hellenic Imperial Airways	Imperial	Greece
IMX	C4	Zimex Aviation	Zimex	Switzerland
INC	7I	Insel Air	Inselair	Netherlands Antilles
IOS	5Y	Isles of Scilly Skybus	Scillonia	United Kingdom
IRA	IR	Iran Air	Iranair	Iran
IRC	EP	Iran Aseman Airlines	Iaa	Iran
IRK	Y9	Kish Air	Kishair	Iran
IRM	W5	Mahan Air	Mahan Air	Iran
IRP	2F	Payam Air	Payamair	Iran
ISK	3L	InterSky	Intersky	Austria
ISR	6H	Israir Airlines	Israir	Israel
ISS	IG	Meridiana	Merair	Italy
ISW	IF	Islas Airways	Pintadera	Spain
ITK	ID	Interlink Airlines	Interlink	South Africa
ITX	IK	Imair Airlines	Improtex	Azerbaijan
IWD	TY	Iberworld	Iberworld	Spain
IYE	IY	Yemenia - Yemen Airways	Yemeni	Yemen
IZM	H9	Izair	Izmir	Turkey
JAB	W9	Air Bagan	Air Bagan	Myanmar (Burma)
JAC	3X	Japan Air Commuter	Commuter	Japan
JAE	JI	Jade Cargo International	Jade Cargo	China
JAF	JF	Jetairfly	Beauty	Belgium
JAI	9W	Jet Airways	Jet Airways	India
JAL	JL	Japan Airlines	Japanair	Japan
JAT	JU	Jat Airways	Jat	Serbia
JAV	R5	Jordan Aviation	Jordan Aviation	Jordan
JAZ	JO	JALways	Jalways	Japan
JBA	JB	Helijet	Helijet	Canada
JBU	B6	JetBlue Airways	Jetblue	USA
JCS	0J	Jetclub	Jetclub	Switzerland
JEA	O2	Jet Air	Jeta	Poland
JEC	JX	Jett8 Airlines Cargo	Taipan	Singapore
JET	IV	Wind Jet	Ghibli	Italy
JEX	JC	JAL Express	Janex	Japan
JFU	8J	Jet4you	Argan	Morocco
JIA	US	PSA Airlines	Blue Streak	USA
JJA	7C	Jeju Air	Jeju Air	South Korea
JKK	JK	Spanair	Spanair	Spain
JLJ	XM	J-Air	J-Air	Japan
JLL	S2	JetLite	Lite Jet	India
JNA	LJ	Jin Air	Jin Air	South Korea
JOL	IP	Atyrau Air Ways	Edil	Kazakhstan
JOR	0B	Blue Air	Blue Transport	Romania
JSA	3K	Jetstar Asia Airways	Jetstar Asia	Singapore

ICAO	IATA	Airline	Callsign	Country
JST	JQ	Jetstar Airways	Jetstar	Australia
JTA	NU	Japan Transocean Air	Jai Ocean	Japan
JUB	6J	Jubba Airways	Jubba	Somalia
JUS	UJ	USA Jet Airlines	Jet Usa	USA
JXX	GX	Primera Air	Jetbird	Iceland
JZA	QK	Air Canada Jazz	Jazz	Canada
JZR	J9	Jazeera Airways	Jazeera	Kuwait
KAC	KU	Kuwait Airways	Kuwaiti	Kuwait
KAE	3Y	Kartika Airlines	Kartika	Indonesia
KAJ	5R	Karthago Airlines	Karthago	Tunesia
KAL	KE	Korean Air	Koreanair	South Korea
KAP	9K	Cape Air	Cair	USA
KBA	4K	Kenn Borek Air	Borek Air	Canada
KBR	K7	KoralBlue Airlines	Koral Blue	Egypt
KDC	XC	KD Air	Kay Dee	Canada
KDR	6D	Royal Daisy Airlines	Darlines	Uganda
KEE	BZ	Keystone Air Services	Keystone	Canada
KEN	M5	Kenmore Air	Kenmore	USA
KFA	KW	Kelowna Flightcraft Air Charter	Flightcraft	Canada
KFR	IT	Kingfisher Airlines	Kingfisher	India
KFS	K9	Kalitta Charters	Kalitta	USA
KGA	R8	Kyrgyzstan Airlines	Kyrgyz	Kyrgyzstan
KGL	7K	Kogalymavia	Kogalym	Russia
KHO	X9	Khors Aircompany	Aircompany Khors	Ukraine
KIL	GW	Kuban Airlines	Air Kuban	Russia
KIS	C3	Contact Air	Contactair	Germany
KKK	KK	Atlasjet	Atlasjet	Turkey
KLB	XG	Air Mali International	Trans Mali	Mali
KLC	WA	KLM Cityhopper	City	Netherlands
KLM	KL	KLM Royal Dutch Airlines	Klm	Netherlands
KMF	RQ	Kam Air	Kamgar	Afghanistan
KMP	E2	Kampuchea Airlines	Kampuchea	Cambodia
KNE	XY	Nas Air	Nas Express	Saudi Arabia
KNI	KD	KD Avia	Kaliningrad Air	Russia
KOR	JS	Air Koryo	Air Koryo	North Korea
KPA	VD	Kunpeng Airlines	Kun Peng	China
KQA	KQ	Kenya Airways	Kenya	Kenya
KRE	6N	AeroSucre	Aerosucre	Colombia
KRP	V3	Carpatair	Carpatair	Romania
KRT	0K	Air Kokshetau	Kokta	Kazakhstan
KYV	KY	Cyprus Turkish Airlines Kibris Turk Hava Yollari)	Airkibris	Turkey
KZR	KC	Air Astana	Astanaline	Kazakhstan
KZU	GO	Kuzu Airlines Cargo	Kuzu Cargo	Turkey
LAA	LN	Libyan Airlines	Libair	Libya
LAB	JF	L.A.B. Flying Service	Lab	USA
LAL	WJ	Air Labrador	Lab Air	Canada
LAM	LM	LAM Mozambique Airlines	Mozambique	Mozambique
LAN	LA	LAN Airlines	Lan	Chile
LAO	QV	Lao Airlines	Lao	Laos
LAP	PZ	TAM Airlines	Paraguaya	Paraguay
LAV	VH	Aeropostal Alas de Venezuela	Aeropostal	Venezuela
LBC	LV	Albanian Airlines	Albanian	Albania
LBT	BJ	Nouvelair	Nouvelair	Tunesia
LBY	LZ	Belle Air	Alban-Belle	Albania
LCG	6V	Lignes Aériennes Congolaises	Congolaise	Congo
LCO	UC	LAN Cargo	Lan Cargo	Chile
LDA	NG	Lauda Air	Lauda Air	Austria
LDE	5U	LADE - Líneas Aéreas del Estado	Lade	Argentina
LER	8z	LASER Airlines	Laser	Venezuela
LGL	LG	Luxair	Luxair	Luxembourg

ICAO	IATA	Airline	Callsign	Country
LGW	HE	Luftfahrtgesellschaft Walter	Walter	Germany
LHN	EO	Express One International	Longhorn	USA
LIA	LI	Leeward Islands Air Transport	Liat	Antigua and Barbuda
LID	D4	Alidaunia	Alida	Italy
LIL	TE	FlyLal (Lithuanian Airlines)	Lithuania Air	Lithuania
LKE	8L	Lucky Air	Lucky Air	China
LKN	IK	Lankair	Lankair	Sri Lanka
LLM	YL	Yamal Airlines	Yamal	Russia
LLR	CD	Air India Regional	Allied	India
LMT	6T	Almaty Aviation	Almaty	Kazakhstan
LMZ	DZ	Starline.kz	Alunk	Kazakhstan
LNE	XL	LAN Ecuador	Lan Ecuador	Ecuador
LNI	JT	Lion Air (Lion Mentari Airlines)	Lion Inter	Indonesia
LNK	4Z	Airlink	Link	South Africa
LOF	AX	Trans States Airlines	Waterski	USA
LOG	LC	Loganair	Logan	United Kingdom
LOT	LO	LOT Polish Airlines	Pollot	Poland
LPE	LP	LAN Peru	Lanperu	Peru
LPV	A6	Air Alps Aviation	Air Alps	Austria
LRC	LR	LACSA	Lacsa	Costa Rica
LTC	6Y	SmartLynx Airlines	Latcharter	Latvia
LTF	DV	Lufttaxi Fluggesellschaft	Garfield	Germany
LTR	L5	Lufttransport	Luft Transport	Norway
LTU	LT	LTU International	Ltu	Germany
LUR	TD	Atlantis European Airways	Atlantis Liner	Armenia
LVG	LM	Livingston Energy Flight	Livingston	Italy
LXP	LU	LAN Express	Lanex	Chile
LYC	L2	Lynden Air Cargo	Lynden	USA
LYN	QH	Kyrgyzstan	Altyn Avia	Kyrgyzstan
LZB	FB	Bulgaria Air	Flying Bulgaria	Bulgaria
MAA	M7	MasAir	Mas Carga	Mexico
MAH	MA	Malev Hungarian Airlines	Malev	Hungary
MAK	IN	MAT Macedonian Airlines	Makavio	Macedonia
MAS	MH	MASkargo (Malaysia Airlines Kargo)	Malaysian Cargo	Malaysia
MAS	MH	Malaysia Airlines	Malaysian	Malaysia
MAT	MV	Maldivian Air Taxi	Maldivian	Maldives
MAU	MK	Air Mauritius	Airmauritius	Mauritius
MBN	Q3	Zambian Airways	Zambiana	Zambia
MCK	CC	Macair Airlines	Macair	Australia
MCM	YO	Heli Air Monaco	Heli Air	Monaco
MDA	AE	Mandarin Airlines	Mandarin	Taiwan
MDG	MD	Air Madagascar	Air Madagascar	Madagascar
MDL	RI	Mandala Airlines	Mandala	Indonesia
MDM	N5	Medavia	Medavia	Malta
MDV	2M	Moldavian Airlines	Moldavian	Moldova
MDW	JI	Midway Airlines	Midway	USA
MEA	ME	Middle East Airlines	Cedar Jet	Lebanon
MEP	MY	Midwest Airlines	Midex	Egypt
MES	XJ	Mesaba Airlines	Mesaba	USA
MGL	OM	MIAT Mongolian Airlines	Mongol Air	Mongolia
MGX	YM	Montenegro Airlines	Montair	Montenegro
MJN	RS	Royal Air Force of Oman	Majan	Oman
MKA	7G	MK Airlines	Kruger Air	United Kingdom
MKU	WP	Island Air	Moku	USA
MLD	9U	Air Moldova	Air Moldova	Moldova
MLR	MJ	Mihin Lanka	Mihin Lanka	Sri Lanka
MNA	MZ	Merpati Nusantara Airlines	Merpati	Indonesia
MNB	MB	MNG Airlines	Black Sea	Turkey
MNG	M0	Aero Mongolia	Aero Mongolia	Mongolia
MNJ	IM	Menajet	Menajet	Lebanon

ICAO	IATA	Airline	Callsign	Country
MNO	JE	Mango	Tulca	South Africa
MON	ZB	Monarch Airlines	Monarch	United Kingdom
MOV	NN	VIM Airlines	Mov Air	Russia
MPD	A7	Air Comet	Red Comet	Spain
MPE	5T	Canadian North	Empress	Canada
MPH	MP	Martinair	Martinair	Netherlands
MPX	QO	Aeromexpress	Aeromexpress	Mexico
MRW	6V	Mars RK	Aviamars	Ukraine
MSE	MS	EgyptAir Express	Egyptair Express	Egypt
MSI	M9	Motor Sich	Motor Sich	Ukraine
MSL	M7	Marsland Aviation	Marslandair	Sudan
MSR	MS	Egyptair	Egyptair	Egypt
MSX	MS	EgyptAir Cargo	Egyptair Cargo	Egypt
MTW	YD	Mauritania Airways	Mauritania Airways	Mauritania
MTZ	Z8	Mali Airways	Mali Airways	Mali
MUA	5M	National Airlines	Murray Air	USA
MVD	KV	Kavminvodyavia	Air Minvody	Russia
MWG	MH	MASwings	Maswings	Malaysia
MXA	MX	Mexicana	Mexicana	Mexico
MXL	8M	Maxair	Maxair	Sweden
MYD	MW	Maya Island Air	Myland	Belize
MYW	8I	MyAir	Franky	Italy
NAC	NC	Northern Air Cargo	Yukon	USA
NAO	NA	North American Airlines	North American	USA
NAS	UE	Nasair	Nasairways	Eritrea
NAX	DY	Norwegian Air Shuttle	Nor Shuttle	Norway
NAY	ZN	Navegacion y Servicios Aéreos Canarios (NAYSA)	Naysa	Spain
NCA	KZ	Nippon Cargo Airlines	Nippon Cargo	Japan
NCH	3U	Chanchangi Airlines	Chanchangi	Nigeria
NEA	EJ	New England Airlines	New England	USA
NFA	M3	Air Norway	North Flying	Norway
NFA	M3	North Flying	North Flying	Denmark
NGE	8G	Angel Airlines	Angel Air	Thailand
NIG	AJ	Aero Contractors	Aeroline	Nigeria
NJE	1I	NetJets Europe	Fraction	Portugal
NJS	NC	National Jet Systems	National Jet	Australia
NKF	8N	Barents AirLink	Nordflight	Sweden
NKS	NK	Spirit Airlines	Spirit Wings	USA
NLY	HG	Niki	Flyniki	Austria
NMB	SW	Air Namibia	Namibia	Namibia
NMI	LW	Pacific Wings	Tsunami	USA
NOK	DD	Nok Air	Nok Air	Thailand
NOS	NO	Neos	Moonflower	Italy
NOV	M4	Nova Airline	Novanile	Sudan
NRD	6N	Nordic Airways	North Rider	Sweden
NRD	6N	Nordic Regional	North Rider	Sweden
NRR	5C	Nature Air	Natureair	Costa Rica
NSE	9N	SATENA	Satena	Colombia
NSO	P4	Aerolineas Sosa	Sosa	Honduras
NTJ	2N	Nextjet	Nextjet	Sweden
NTN	YJ	National Airways	Natchair	South Africa
NVR	1I	Novair	Navigator	Sweden
NWA	NW	Northwest Airlines	Northwest	USA
NWL	HW	North-Wright Airways	Northwright	Canada
NXA	7A	Air Next	Blue-Dolphin	Japan
NYL	7Y	Mid Airlines	Nile	Sudan
NZM	NM	Mount Cook Airlines	Mountcook	New Zealand
OAE	OY	Omni Air International	Omni-Express	USA
OAL	OA	Olympic Airlines	Olympic	Greece
OAW	2L	Helvetic Airways	Helvetic	Switzerland

ICAO	IATA	Airline	Callsign	Country
OCA	R7	Aserca Airlines	Arosca	Venezuela
ODS	5K	Odessa Airlines	Odessa Air	Ukraine
OEA	OX	Orient Thai Airlines	Orient Thai	Thailand
OHY	8Q	Onur Air	Onur Air	Turkey
OKA	BK	Okay Airways	Okayjet	China
OLA	OJ	Overland Airways	Overland	Nigeria
OLT	OL	OLT - Ostfriesische Lufttransport	Oltra	Germany
OMA	WY	Oman Air	Oman Air	Oman
ONA	OE	Yeongnam Air	Yeongnam Air	South Korea
ONE	O6	Oceanair	Oceanair	Brazil
ORB	R2	Orenair (Orenburg Airlines)	Orenburg	Russia
OST	2D	Alania Airlines	Alania	Russia
OTG	OX	One-Two-GO Airlines	Thai Express	Thailand
OTL	YG	South Airlines	Southline	Ukraine
OZJ	O7	Ozjet Airlines	Ausjet	Australia
OZW	XR	Skywest Airlines	Ozwest	Australia
PAC	PO	Polar Air Cargo	Polar	USA
PAG	4B	Perimeter Aviation (Perimeter Airlines)	Perimeter	Canada
PAL	PR	Philippine Airlines	Philippine	Philippines
PAO	PH	Polynesian Airlines	Polynesian	Samoa
PAS	6D	Pelita Air Service	Pelita	Indonesia
PBA	9Q	PB Air	Peebee Air	Thailand
PBN	DJ	Pacific Blue Airlines	Bluebird	New Zealand
PCE	Y5	Pace Airlines	Pace	USA
PCO	8P	Pacific Coastal Airline	Pasco	Canada
PDF	7V	Pelican Air Services	Pelican Airways	South Africa
PDT	PI	Piedmont Airlines	Piedmont	USA
PEC	Q8	Pacific East Asia Cargo Airlines	Pac-East Cargo	Philippines
PEL	OT	Aeropelican Air Services	Pelican	Australia
PEN	KS	PenAir (Peninsula Airways)	Peninsula	USA
PGA	NI	Portugalia	Portugalia	Portugal
PGP	P9	Perm Airlines	Perm Air	Russia
PGT	H9	Pegasus Airlines	Sunturk	Turkey
PHW	2E	AVE.com	Phoenix Sharjah	United Arab Emirates
PIA	PK	Pakistan International Airlines	Pakistan	Pakistan
PIC	BL	Jetstar Pacific	Pacific Airlines	Vietnam
PIR	NR	Pamir Airways	Pamir	Afghanistan
PJS	PP	Jet Aviation	Jet Aviation	Switzerland
PLM	EB	Air Pullmantur	Pullmantur	Spain
PLR	J3	Northwestern Air	Polaris	Canada
PMT	U4	PMTair	Multitrade	Cambodia
PMW	I7	Paramount Airways	Paraway	India
PNF	PQ	Panafrican Airways	Panways	Ivory Coast
PNR	PV	PAN Air	Skyjet	Spain
PNW	PF	Palestinian Airlines	Palestinian	Egypt
POE	PD	Porter Airlines	Porter Air	Canada
POT	YQ	Polet Airlines	Polet	Russia
PPW	RL	Royal Phnom Penh Airways	Phnom-Penh Air	Cambodia
PRF	PW	Precision Air	Precision Air	Tanzania
PSD	TO	President Airlines		Cambodia
PSV	5S	Servicios Aereos Profesionales	Proservicios	Dominican Republic
PTN	P8	Pantanal Linhas Aereas Sul-Matogrossenses	Pantanal	Brazil
PUA	PU	PLUNA	Pluna	Uruguay
PVV	PC	Continental Airways	Contair	Russia
PWF	8W	Private Wings Flugcharter	Private Wings	Germany
QCL	QD	Air Class Lineas Aereas	Acla	Uruguay
QFA	QF	Qantas	Qantas	Australia
QNK	N2	Kabo Air	Kabo	Nigeria
QNZ	QF	JetConnect	Qantas	New Zealand
QTR	QR	Qatar Airways	Qatari	Qatar

ICAO	IATA	Airline	Callsign	Country
QXE	QX	Horizon Air	Horizon Air	USA
RAE	YS	Regional Compagnie Aerienne Europeenne	Regional Europe	France
RAM	AT	Royal Air Maroc	Royalair Maroc	Morocco
RBA	BI	Royal Brunei Airlines	Brunei	Brunei Darussalam
RCF	SU	Aeroflot-Cargo	Aeroflot Cargo	Russia
RCH	MC	Air Mobility Command	Reach	USA
REA	RE	Aer Arann	Aer Arann	Ireland
REU	UU	Air Austral	Reunion	Reunion
RFR	RR	Royal Air Force	Rafair	United Kingdom
RGL	FN	Regional Air Lines	Maroc Regional	Morocco
RHC	8L	Redhill Aviation	Redair	United Kingdom
RIT	6K	Zest Airways	Asian Spirit	Philippines
RIU	PK	Riau Airlines	Riau Air	Indonesia
RJA	RJ	Royal Jordanian	Jordanian	Jordan
RKH	RK	Royal Khmer Airlines	Khmer Air	Cambodia
RKM	RT	RAK Airways	Rakair	United Arab Emirates
RLA	A5	Airlinair	Airlinair	France
RLE	C7	Rico Linhas Aereas	Rico	Brazil
RLK	NZ	Air Nelson	Link	New Zealand
RLN	QL	Aero Lanka	Aero Lanka	Sri Lanka
RMV	WQ	Romavia	Aeromavia	Romania
RNA	RA	Nepal Airlines	Royal Nepal	Nepal
RNV	U8	Armavia	Armavia	Armenia
ROI	9V	Avior Airlines	Avior	Venezuela
RON	ON	Nauru Air Corporation	Air Nauru	Nauru
ROT	RO	Tarom	Tarom	Romania
RPA	RW	Republic Airlines	Brickyard	USA
RPB	P5	AeroRepublica	Aerorepublica	Colombia
RPH	RH	Republic Express Airlines	Public Express	Indonesia
RPK	R0	Royal Airlines	Royal Pakistan	Pakistan
RSI	YI	Air Sunshine	Air Sunshine	USA
RSO	E4	Aero Asia International	Aero Asia	Pakistan
RSR	BF	Aero-Service	Congoserv	Congo
RSU	5L	Aerosur	Aerosur	Bolivia
RUN	9T	ACT Airlines	Cargo Turk	Turkey
RUS	C9	Cirrus Airlines	Cirrus Air	Germany
RVL	DO	Air Vallée	Air Vallee	Italy
RWD	WB	Rwandair Express	Rwandair	Rwanda
RXA	ZL	Regional Express Airlines	Rex	Australia
RYN	RD	Ryan International Airlines	Ryan International	USA
RYR	FR	Ryanair	Ryanair	Ireland
RZO	S4	SATA International	Air Azores	Portugal
SAA	SA	South African Airways	Springbok	South Africa
SAH	W7	Sayakhat Airlines	Sayakhat	Kazakhstan
SAI	NL	Shaheen Air International	Shaheen Air	Pakistan
SAM	MM	SAM Colombia	Sam	Colombia
SAS	SK	Scandinavian Airlines System (SAS)	Scandinavian	Sweden
SAT	SP	SATA Air Acores	Sata	Portugal
SAX	SA	Sabah Air	Sabah Air	Malaysia
SAY	CB	ScotAirways	Suckling	United Kingdom
SBI	S7	S7 Airlines (Siberia Airlines)	Siberian Airlines	Russia
SBS	BB	Seaborne Airlines	Seaborne	US Virgin Islands
SBU	PV	Saint Barth Commuter	Black Fin	France
SCH	AW	CHC Airways	Schreiner	Netherlands
SCW	TF	Malmö Aviation	Scanwings	Sweden
SCX	SY	Sun Country Airlines	Sun Country	USA
SDA	DA	Sol Dominicana Airlines	Sol Airlines	Dominican Republic
SDM	FV	Rossiya - Russian Airlines	Russia	Russia
SDR	CF	City Airline	Swedestar	Sweden
SDY	2S	Island Express	Sandy Isle	USA

ICAO	IATA	Airline	Callsign	Country
SEH	G3	Sky Express	Air Crete	Greece
SEJ	SG	Spicejet	Spicejet	India
SEQ	I6	Sky Eyes	Sky Eyes	Thailand
SEU	SE	XL Airways France	Starway	France
SEY	HM	Air Seychelles	Seychelles	Seychelles
SFJ	7G	Star Flyer	Starflyer	Japan
SFR	FA	Safair	Cargo	South Africa
SGN	5E	SGA Airlines	Siam	Thailand
SHQ	F4	Shanghai Airlines Cargo	Shanghai Cargo	China
SHU	HZ	SAT Airlines	Satair	Russia
SHY	SY	Sky Airlines	Antalya Bird	Turkey
SIA	SQ	Singapore Airlines	Singapore	Singapore
SJY	SJ	Sriwijaya Air	Sriwijaya	Indonesia
SKP	NP	Skytrans Airlines	Skytrans	Australia
SKU	H2	Sky Airline	Aerosky	Chile
SKW	OO	SkyWest Airlines	Skywest	USA
SKX	JZ	Skyways Express	Sky Express	Sweden
SKY	BC	Skymark Airlines	Skymark	Japan
SKZ	KI	Skyway Enterprises	Skyway-Inc	USA
SLA	LJ	Sierra National Airlines	Selair	Sierra Leone
SLI	5D	Aeroméxico Connect	Costera	Mexico
SLK	MI	SilkAir	Silkair	Singapore
SLM	PY	Surinam Airways	Surinam	Suriname
SMJ	Z3	Avient Aviation	Avavia	Zimbabwe
SMX	XM	Alitalia Express	Aliexpress	Italy
SMY	ZS	Sama Airlines	Najim	Saudi Arabia
SNC	2Q	Air Cargo Carriers	Night Cargo	USA
SNG	V7	Air Senegal International	Air Senegal	Senegal
SNJ	6J	Skynet Asia Airways	Newsky	Japan
SOA	PL	Southern Air Charter	South Aircharter	Bahamas
SOL	IE	Solomon Airlines	Solomon	Solomon Islands
SOO	9S	Southern Air	Southern Air	USA
SOV	6W	Saravia	Saratov Air	Russia
SOZ	HZ	Sat Airlines	Satco	Kazakhstan
SPA	SI	Sierra Pacific Airlines	Sierra Pacific	USA
SPM	PJ	Air Saint Pierre	Saint Pierre	Saint-Pierre and Miquelon
SPR	PB	Provincial Airlines	Speedair	Canada
SQC	SQ	Singapore Airlines Cargo	Singcargo	Singapore
SRQ	DG	South East Asian Airlines	Seair	Philippines
SRR	S6	Star Air	Whitestar	Denmark
SRU	2I	Star Perú	Star Up	Peru
SSQ	QF	Sunstate Airlines	Sunstate	Australia
SSV	5G	Skyservice Airlines	Skytour	Canada
SSX	L4	Lynx Aviation	Shasta	USA
STU	FS	Servicios de Transportes Aereos Fueguinos	Fueguino	Argentina
SUD	SD	Sudan Airways	Sudanair	Sudan
SUS	EZ	Sun Air of Scandinavia	Sunscan	Denmark
SVA	SV	Saudi Arabian Airlines	Saudia	Saudi Arabia
SVK	GM	Air Slovakia	Slovakia	Slovakia
SVR	U6	Ural Airlines	Sverdlovsk Air	Russia
SWA	WN	Southwest Airlines	Southwest	USA
SWG	WG	Sunwing Airlines	Sunwing	Canada
SWN	PT	West Air Sweden	Air Sweden	Sweden
SWQ	Q7	Swift Air	Swiftflight	USA
SWR	LX	Swiss International Air Lines	Swiss	Switzerland
SWT	W3	Swiftair	Swift	Spain
SWU	LX	Swiss European Air Lines	Euroswiss	Switzerland
SXR	XW	Sky Express	Skystorm	Russia
SXS	XQ	SunExpress	Sunexpress	Turkey
SYL	R3	Yakutia Airlines	Air Yakutia	Russia

ICAO	IATA	Airline	Callsign	Country
SYR	RB	Syrian Arab Airlines (Syrianair)	Syrianair	Syria
SZL	SA	Swaziland Airlink	Swazilink	Swaziland
TAE	EQ	TAME	Tame	Ecuador
TAK	U9	Tatarstan Airlines	Tatarstan	Russia
TAM	JJ	TAM Airlines (TAM Linhas Aereas)	Tam	Brazil
TAO	VW	Aeromar	Trans-Aeromar	Mexico
TAP	TP	TAP Portugal	Air Portugal	Portugal
TAR	TU	Tunisair	Tunair	Tunesia
TAS	T2	Lotus Air	Lotus Flower	Egypt
TAY	3V	TNT Airways	Quality	Belgium
TCF	S5	Shuttle America	Mercury	USA
TCI	JY	Air Turks and Caicos	Kerrmont	Turks & Caicos
TCV	VR	TACV	Caboverde	Cape Verde
TCV	VR	TACV Cabo Verde Airlines	Caboverde	Cape Verde
TCW	FQ	Thomas Cook Airlines	Thomas Cook	Belgium
TCX	MT	Thomas Cook Airlines	Kestrel	United Kingdom
TDM	TQ	Tandem Aero	Tandem	Moldova
TDX	WI	Tradewinds Airlines	Tradewinds Express	USA
TFL	OR	Arkefly	Arkefly	Netherlands
TGN	TN	Trigana Air Service	Trigana	Indonesia
TGW	TR	Tiger Airways	Go Cat	Singapore
TGW	TT	Tiger Airways Australia	Go Cat	Australia
TGZ	A9	Georgian Airways	Tamazi	Georgia
THA	TG	Thai Airways International	Thai	Thailand
THE	9D	Toumaï Air Tchad	Toumai Air	Chad
THT	TN	Air Tahiti Nui	Tahiti Airlines	French Polynesia
THY	TK	Turkish Airlines	Turkair	Turkey
TIB	8R	TRIP Linhas Aereas	Trip	Brazil
TIW	T9	Transcarga	Tiaca	Venezuela
TJT	T7	Twin Jet	Twinjet	France
TLR	7Q	Air Libya	Air Libya	Libya
TMA	TL	Trans Mediterranean Airlines	Tango Lima	Lebanon
TMG	GY	Tri-MG Intra Asia Airlines	Trilines	Indonesia
TMW	M8	Trans Maldivian Airways	Trans Maldivian	Maldives
TNA	GE	TransAsia Airways	Transasia	Taiwan
TNB	N4	Trans Air Benin	Trans-Benin	Benin
TNM	3P	Tiara Air	Tiara	Aruba
TOB	7T	Tobruk Air	Tobruk Air	Libya
TOK	CG	Airlines PNG	Balus	Papua New Guinea
TOM	BY	Thomson Airways	Tomson	United Kingdom
TOS	PM	Tropic Air	Tropiser	Belize
TPA	QT	Tampa Cargo	Tampa	Colombia
TPC	TY	Air Caledonie	Aircal	New Caledonia
TPU	T0	TACA Peru	Trans Peru	Peru
TRS	FL	AirTran Airways	Citrus	USA
TSC	TS	Air Transat	Transat	Canada
TSD	R9	TAF Linhas Aéreas	Tafi	Brazil
TSE	TH	Transmile Air Services	Transmile	Malaysia
TSG	Q8	Trans Air Congo	Trans-Congo	Congo
TSO	UN	Transaero Airlines	Transoviet	Russia
TUA	T5	Turkmenistan Airlines	Turkmenistan	Turkmenistan
TUD	4Y	Flight Alaska	Tundra	USA
TUI	UG	Sevenair	Sevenair	Tunesia
TUP	4B	Aviastar-TU	Tupolevair	Russia
TUS	M3	ABSA Cargo Airline	Absa Cargo	Brazil
TUX	2T	Tulpar Air Service	Tulpa	Kazakhstan
TUY	LD	Linea Turistica Aerotuy	Aereotuy	Venezuela
TVR	T6	Tavrey Airlines	Tavrey	Ukraine
TVS	QS	Smart Wings	Skytravel	Czech Republic
TWE	5T	Transwede Airways	Transwede	Sweden

ICAO	IATA	Airline	Callsign	Country
TWN	EC	Avialeasing Aviation Company	Twinarrow	Uzbekistan
TXC	AL	TransAVIAexport Airlines	Transexport	Belarus
TYR	VO	Austrian Arrows (Tyrolean Airways)	Tyrolean	Austria
TZK	7J	Tajik Air	Tajikistan	Tajikistan
TZT	ZT	Air Zambezi	Zambesi	Zimbabwe
UAE	EK	Emirates Airline	Emirates	United Arab Emirates
UAL	UA	United Airlines	United	USA
UBA	UB	Myanma Airways	Unionair	Myanmar
UBA	8M	Myanmar Airways International	Unionair	Myanmar
UBD	4H	United Airways (Bangladesh)	United Bangladesh	Bangladesh
UCA	C5	CommutAir	Commutair	USA
UCR	DW	Aero-Charter Ukraine	Charter Ukraine	Ukraine
UDC	5D	DonbassAero	Donbass Aero	Ukraine
UDN	Z6	Dniproavia	Dniepro	Ukraine
UEA	EU	United Eagle Airlines	United Eagle	China
UGA	U7	Air Uganda	Uganda	Uganda
UGX	QU	East African	Crane	Uganda
UIA	B7	Uni Air	Glory	Taiwan
UKM	UF	UM Airlines	Ukraine Mediterranee	Ukraine
UKS	6Z	Ukrainian Cargo Airways	Cargotrans	Ukraine
UKW	5V	Lviv Airlines	Ukraine West	Ukraine
UMK	2N	Yuzmashavia	Yuzmash	Ukraine
UPS	5X	United Parcel Service	Ups	USA
URG	3N	Air Urga	Urga	Ukraine
URJ	6S	Star Air Aviation	Starav	Pakistan
URN	3T	Turan Air	Turan	Azerbaijan
USH	UH	US Helicopter	Us Heli	USA
UTA	UT	UTair Aviation	Utair	Russia
UTY	QQ	Alliance Airlines	Unity	Australia
UZB	HY	Uzbekistan Airways	Uzbek	Uzbekistan
VAL	VC	Voyageur Airways	Voyageur	Canada
VAP	9R	Phuket Air	Phuket Air	Thailand
VAS	V8	ATRAN Cargo Airlines	Atran	Russia
VAZ	WZ	Red Wings Airlines	Remont Air	Russia
VBW	2J	Air Burkina	Burkina	Burkina Faso
VCV	V0	Conviasa	Conviasa	Venezuela
VDA	VI	Volga-Dnepr Airlines	Volga-Dnepr	Russia
VEC	RV	Venezolana	Vecar	Venezuela
VES	VI	Vieques Air Link	Viques	Puerto Rico
VGN	VK	Virgin Nigeria Airways	Virgin Nigeria	Nigeria
VIK	4P	Viking Airlines	Swedjet	Sweden
VIM	VL	Air VIA	Via Airways	Bulgaria
VIR	VS	Virgin Atlantic Airways	Virgin	United Kingdom
VIV	VB	VivaAerobus	Aeroenlaces	Mexico
VKG	DK	Thomas Cook Airlines Scandinavia	Viking	Denmark
VLE	VA	Volare Airlines	Vola	Italy
VLG	VY	Vueling Airlines	Vueling	Spain
VLK	XF	Vladivostok Air	Vladair	Russia
VLM	VG	VLM Airlines	Rubens	Belgium
VLO	LC	Varig Logistica (VarigLog)	Velog	Brazil
VNR	3W	Wan Air	Wan Air	French Polynesia
VNZ	L6	Tbilaviamsheni	Tbilavia	Georgia
VOA	VM	Viaggio Air	Viaggio	Bulgaria
VOZ	DJ	Virgin Blue	Virgin	Australia
VPP	VQ	Vintage Props and Jets	Vintage	USA
VRD	VX	Virgin America	Redwood	USA
VRN	RG	VRG Linhas Aereas (VARIG)	Varig	Brazil
VSV	DV	Scat Aircompany	Vlasta	Kazakhstan
VTA	VT	Air Tahiti	Air Tahiti	French Polynesia
VTS	3Z	Everts Air Cargo	Everts	USA

ICAO	IATA	Airline	Callsign	Country
VUN	VU	Air Ivoire	Airivoire	Ivory Coast
VUR	V6	VIP Ecuador	Vip	Ecuador
VVM	ZG	Viva Macau	Jackpot	China
VXG	G2	Avirex	Avirex-Gabon	Gabon
WAK	K5	Wings of Alaska	Wings Alaska	USA
WBA	FC	Finncomm Airlines	Westbird	Finland
WDA	9C	Wimbi Dira Airways	Wimbi Dira	Congo
WDL	W1	WDL Aviation	Wdl	Germany
WEB	WJ	WebJet Linhas Aéreas	Webjet	Brazil
WIA	WM	Windward Islands Airways	Winair	Netherlands Antilles
WIF	WF	Wideroe	Wideroe	Norway
WIG	WG	Wiggins Airways	Wiggins Airways	USA
WJA	WS	WestJet	Westjet	Canada
WLC	2W	Welcome Air	Welcomeair	Austria
WOA	WO	World Airways	World	USA
WON	1W	Wings Air	Wings Abadi	Indonesia
WOW	WO	Air Southwest	Swallow	United Kingdom
WRC	7W	Wind Rose Aviation	Wind Rose	Ukraine
WRF	8V	Wright Air Service	Wright Flyer	USA
WSG	WT	Wasaya Airways	Wasaya	Canada
WTA	FK	Africa West	West Togo	Togo
WVL	W6	Wizz Air	Wizzbul	Bulgaria
WZZ	W6	Wizz Air	Wizz Air	Hungary
XAK	P2	Airkenya Express	Airkenya	Kenya
XAX	D7	AirAsia X	Xanadu	Malaysia
XME	XM	Australian air Express	Jetex	Australia
YZR	Y8	Yangtze River Express	Yangtze River	China
ZAK	K8	Zambia Skyways	Zambia Skies	Zambia

ICAO Aircraft Codes

ICAO	Manufacturer	Type/Model
A1	Douglas	AD-1 / A-1 / EA-1 Skyraider
A10	Fairchild	A-10 Thunderbolt 2
A109	Agusta	A-109
A119	Agusta	A-119 Koala
A124	Antonow	An-124 Ruslan
A129	Agusta	A-129 Mangusta
A139	Agusta	AB139 / AW139
A140	Antonow	An-140
A140	Hesa	IRAN-140 Faraz
A148	Antonow	An-148
A20	Douglas	A-20 Havoc
A225	Antonow	An-225 Mriya
A270	Ibis	Ae-270 Ibis
A270	Aero	Ae-270 Ibis
A2RT	Kazan	Ansat 2RT
A3	Douglas	A-3 Skywarrior
A306	Airbus	A300B4-600 /C4-600 / F4-600
A30B	Airbus	A300B2 / B4 / C4 / F4
A310	Airbus	A310 / CC-150 Polaris
A318	Airbus	A318
A319	Airbus	A319
A320	Airbus	A320
A321	Airbus	A321
A332	Airbus	A330-200
A333	Airbus	A330-300
A342	Airbus	A340-200
A343	Airbus	A340-300
A345	Airbus	A340-500
A346	Airbus	A340-600
A37	Cessna	318 / A-37 Dragonfly
A388	Airbus	A380-800
A3ST	Airbus	A300-600ST Beluga
A4	Douglas	A-4 Skyhawk
A50	Beriev	A-50
A500	Adam	A-500
A504	Avro	504
A6	Grumman	A-6 Intruder
A6	Grumman	EA-6 Prowler
A660	Ayres	S-2R-T660 Turbo Thrush
A660	Thrush	S-2R-T660 Turbo Thrush
A7	Chance-Vought	A-7 Corsair 2
A7	Ltv	A-7 Corsair 2
A700	Adam	A-700 AdamJet
A743	Antonow	An-74-300
A748	AVRO	748
A748	Hawker-Siddeley	HS-748 Andover
A748	BAe	BAe-748
A9	Aero Commander	A-9 Ag Commander
A9	N. Amer Rockwell	A-9 Quail Commander
AA1	American	AA-1
AA1	American	AA-1
AA5	American	AA-5
AA5	AGAC	AG-5 Tiger
AA5	American	AA-5
AB11	Aero Boero	AB-115
AB15	Aero Boero	AB-150
AB18	Aero Boero	AB-180
AB95	Aero Boero	AB-95
AC11	Rockwell	112 Commander 112
AC11	Commander	Commander 114
AC11	Commander	Commander 115
AC11	N. Amer Rockwell	112 Commander 112
AC11	Rockwell	114 Commander 114
AC50	N. Amer Rockwell	500 Commander 500
AC50	N. Amer Rockwell	500 Shrike Commander
AC50	Rockwell	500 Shrike Commander
AC50	Aero Commander	500 Commander 500
AC56	Aero Commander	560 Commander 560
AC68	Aero Commander	680F Commander 680F
AC6L	Rockwell	685 Commander 685
AC6L	N. Amer Rockwell	685 Commander 685
AC6L	N. Amer Rockwell	680FL Courser Commander
AC6L	Aero Commander	680FL Grand Commander
AC6L	N. Amer Rockwell	Grand Commander
AC72	Aero Commander	Alti Cruiser
AC72	Aero Commander	720 Alti Cruiser
AC80	Aero Commander	680T Turbo Commander
AC80	N. Amer Rockwell	680V Turbo Commander
AC90	N. Amer Rockwell	690 Turbo Commander 690
AC90	Rockwell	690 Jetprop Commander 840
AC90	American	690 Jetprop Commander 900
AC90	Rockwell	690 Turbo Commander 690
AC95	American	695 Jetprop Commander 1000
AC95	Rockwell	695 Jetprop Commander 980
AC95	American	Jetprop Commander 980 / 1000
ACAR	Auster	J-5 Autocar
ACSR	Victa	Aircruiser
ADVE	Auster	J-5 Adventurer
AE45	LET	Super Aero 145
AE45	LET	Aero 45
AE45	AERO	Ae-45 / Ae-145
AEST	Ted Smith	Aerostar
AEST	Piper	PA-60 Aerostar
AIGT	Auster	J-5 Aiglet Trainer
AIRD	Beagle	A-109 Airedale
AJET	Dornier	Alpha Jet
AJET	Dassault-Breguet	Alpha Jet
ALH	HAL	Dhruv
ALIZ	Breguet	1050 Aliz
ALO2	Aerospatiale	SA-318 Alouette 2
ALO2	Sud-Est	SE-3130 Alouette 2
ALO2	Sud	SA-318 / SA-3180 / SE-313
ALO3	Sud	SA-316 / Alouette 3
ALO3	HAL	SE-3160 Chetak / Chetan
ALO3	Sud	SA-319 Alouette 3
ALO3	Aerospatiale	SA-316 / SA-319 Alouette 3
ALPI	Auster	J-5 Alpine
AM3	Atlas	AM-3 Bosbok
AM3	Aermacchi	AM-3
AMX	Aermacchi	AMX
AMX	Aeritalia	AMX
AMX	Embraer	A-1
AMX	Amx	AMX

ICAO	Manufacturer	Type/Model
AN12	Antonow	An-12
AN2	Antonow	An-2
AN2	Nanchang	Y-5
AN2	PZL Mielec	An-2 Antek
AN22	Antonow	An-22 Antheus
AN24	Antonow	An-24
AN26	Antonow	An-26
AN28	PZL Mielec	M-28 Bryza
AN28	Antonow	An-28
AN28	PZL Mielec	An-28 Bryza
AN3	Antonow	An-3
AN30	Antonow	An-30
AN32	Antonow	An-32
AN38	Antonow	An-38
AN70	Antonow	An-70
AN72	Antonow	An-72
AN72	Antonow	An-74
AN8	Antonow	An-8
ANSN	AVRO	652 Anson
ANST	Kazan	Ansat
AR11	Aeronca	11 Chief
AR11	HAL	HUL-26 Pushpak
AR15	Aeronca	15 Sedan
AR79	Arado	Ar-79
ARON	General Avia	F-220 Airone
ARVA	IAI	Arava
AS02	FFA	AS-202 Bravo
AS2T	FFA	AS-202-32TP Turbine Bravo
AS32	Aerospatiale	AS-532 Mk1 Cougar
AS32	Eurocopter	AS-332 Super Puma
AS32	Aerospatiale	AS-332 Mk1 Super Puma
AS32	Atlas	SA-330 Oryx
AS3B	Eurocopter	AS-532 Mk2 Cougar
AS3B	Eurocopter	AS-332 Mk2 Super Puma
AS3B	Aerospatiale	AS-332 Mk2 Super Puma
AS3B	Aerospatiale	AS-532 Mk2 Cougar
AS50	Eurocopter	AS-350 AStar
AS50	Aerospatiale	AS-350 SuperStar
AS50	Aerospatiale	AS-350 Ecureuil
AS50	Eurocopter	AS-550 Fennec
AS50	Aerospatiale	AS-550 Fennec
AS50	Eurocopter	AS-350 Ecureuil
AS50	Eurocopter	AS-350 SuperStar
AS50	Aerospatiale	AS-350 AStar
AS55	Aerospatiale	AS-555 Fennec
AS55	Eurocopter	AS-355 TwinStar
AS55	Aerospatiale	AS-355 TwinStar
AS55	Eurocopter	AS-355 Ecureuil 2
AS55	Aerospatiale	AS-355 Ecureuil 2
AS55	Eurocopter	AS-555 Fennec
AS65	Aerospatiale	AS-365 Dauphin 2
AS65	Chance-Vought	SA-366 Panther 800
AS65	HAMC / Harbin	Z-9 Haitun
AS65	Eurocopter	AS-565 Panther
AS65	Eurocopter	AS-365 Dauphin 2
AS65	Aerospatiale	AS-565 Panther
ASTR	IAI	1125 Astra
ASTR	IAI	Gulfstream G100
AT3	AIDC	AT-3 Tzu-Chung
AT3P	Air Tractor	AT-300 / AT-301 / AT-401

ICAO	Manufacturer	Type/Model
AT3T	Air Tractor	AT-302 / AT-400 / AT-402
AT43	ATR	ATR 42-200 / 42-300
AT44	ATR	ATR-42-400
AT45	ATR	ATR-42-500
AT5P	Air Tractor	AT-501
AT5T	Air Tractor	AT-502 / AT-503
AT6T	Air Tractor	AT-602
AT72	ATR	ATR 72
AT8T	Air Tractor	AT-802
ATLA	Dassault-Breguet	1150 Atlantic / Atlantique 2
ATP	BAe	ATP
AU11	Beagle	E-3 Auster AOP11
AUJ2	Auster	J-2 Arrow
AUJ4	Auster	J-4 Archer
AUS3	Taylorcraft	Auster 3
AUS4	Taylorcraft	Auster 4
AUS5	Auster	Auster 5 Alpha
AUS5	Taylorcraft	Auster 5 Alpha
AUS6	Beagle	A-61 Terrier / Tugmaster
AUS6	Auster	Auster AOP6
AUS6	Taylorcraft	Auster AOP6
AUS7	Auster	Auster T7
AUS9	Auster	Auster AOP9
AVIN	AVRO	594 / 616 Avian
B06	Agusta	AB-206 JetRanger
B06	Bell Helicopter	JetRanger / OH-58 Kiowa
B06T	Bell Helicopter	206LT TwinRanger
B06T	Tridair	206L-ST Gemini ST
B1	Rockwell	B-1 Lancer
B103	Beriev	Be-103 Bekas
B105	MBB	BO-105
B14A	Bellanca	14 Cruisair / Cruisemaster
B17	Boeing	B-17 Flying Fortress
B18T	Beech	18 (turbine)
B190	Beech	1900
B2	Northrop	B-2 Spirit
B209	Bölkow	BO-209 Monsun
B212	Agusta	AB-212
B212	Bell Helicopter	UH-1N
B212	Bell Helicopter	212 Twin Two-Twelve
B214	Bell Helicopter	214C BigLifter
B222	Bell Helicopter	222
B23	Douglas	B-23 / UC-67 Dragon
B230	Bell Helicopter	230
B24	Consolidated	B-24 Liberator
B25	North American	B-25 Mitchell
B26	Douglas	A-26 Invader
B26M	Martin	B-26 Marauder
B29	Boeing	B-29 Superfortress
B350	Beech	300 (B300) Super King Air 350
B36T	Beech	36 Bonanza (turbine)
B407	Bell Helicopter	407
B412	Bell Helicopter	412
B412	Bell Helicopter	CH-146 Griffon
B412	Agusta	AB-412 Griffon
B427	Bell Helicopter	427
B427	KAI	SB-427
B429	Bell Helicopter	429 GlobalRanger
B430	Bell Helicopter	430
B461	BAe	BAe-146-100

ICAO	Manufacturer	Type/Model
B462	BAe	BAe-146-200
B463	BAe	BAe-146-300
B47G	Kawasaki	47G
B47G	Agusta	AB-47G
B47G	Bell Helicopter	47
B47G	Westland	Sioux
B47J	Agusta	AB-47J
B47J	Bell Helicopter	47J Ranger
B52	Boeing	B-52 Stratofortress
B609	Bell-Agusta	BA-609
B701	Boeing	707-100
B703	Boeing	707-300
B703	Boeing	C-137 / KC-137
B712	Boeing	717-200
B720	Boeing	720
B721	Boeing	727-100
B721	Boeing	C-22
B722	Boeing	727-200
B731	Boeing	737-100
B732	Boeing	737-200
B733	Boeing	737-300
B734	Boeing	737-400
B735	Boeing	737-500
B736	Boeing	737-600
B737	Boeing	737-700
B737	Boeing	C-40 Clipper
B738	Boeing	737-800
B739	Boeing	737-900
B741	Boeing	747-100
B742	Boeing	E-4 / VC-25
B742	Boeing	747-200
B743	Boeing	747-300
B744	Boeing	747-400
B74R	Boeing	747SR
B74S	Boeing	747SP
B752	Boeing	C-32
B752	Boeing	757-200
B753	Boeing	757-300
B762	Boeing	767-200
B763	Boeing	767-300
B764	Boeing	767-400
B772	Boeing	777-200
B773	Boeing	777-300
B77L	Boeing	777-200LR
B77W	Boeing	777-300ER
B783	Boeing	787-3 Dreamliner
B788	Boeing	787-8 Dreamliner
B789	Boeing	787-9 Dreamliner
BA11	ROMBAC	Rombac 1-11 One-Eleven
BA11	BAC	111 One-Eleven
BASS	Beagle	B-206
BCAT	Grumman	F8F Bearcat
BDOG	Beagle	B-125 Bulldog
BDOG	Scottish Aviation	Bulldog
BDOG	BAe	Bulldog
BE10	Beech	100 King Air
BE12	Beriev	Be-12 Tchaika
BE17	Beech	17 Staggerwing
BE18	Beech	18
BE20	Beech	1300 Commuter
BE20	Beech	200 Super King Air
BE23	Beech	23 Musketeer
BE23	Beech	23 Sundowner
BE24	Beech	24 Sierra
BE24	Beech	24 Musketeer Super
BE30	Beech	300 Super King Air
BE32	Beriev	Be-30
BE32	Beriev	Be-32
BE33	Beech	33 Debonair
BE33	Beech	33 Bonanza
BE33	HESA	Parastu
BE35	Beech	35 Bonanza
BE36	Beech	36 Bonanza
BE40	Hawker-Beechcraft	400 Beechjet
BE40	Beech	400 Beechjet
BE50	Beech	Seminole (U-8D/E/G)
BE50	Beech	50 Twin Bonanza
BE55	Beech	55 Baron
BE58	Beech	58 Baron
BE60	Beech	60 Duke
BE65	Beech	65 Queen Air
BE70	Beech	70 Queen Air
BE76	Beech	76 Duchess
BE77	Beech	77 Skipper
BE80	Beech	80 Queen Air
BE88	Beech	88 Queen Air
BE95	Beech	95 Travel Air
BE99	Beech	99 Airliner
BE9L	Beech	90 King Air
BE9T	Beech	90 (F90) King Air
BELF	Shorts	SC-5 Belfast
BER2	Beriev	Be-200 Altair
BER4	Beriev	A-40 Albatross
BFIT	Bristol	F-2B Fighter
BFIT	Bristol	Fighter
BK17	MBB-Kawasaki	BK-117
BK17	Eurocopter	BK-117
BK17	Kawasaki	BK-117
BK17	Eurocopter-Kawasaki	BK-117
BK17	MBB	BK-117
BL11	Bleriot	11
BL17	Bellanca	17 Super Viking
BL19	Bellanca	19 Skyrocket
BL8	Bellanca	8 Scout
BL8	American Champion	8 Scout
BL8	Campion	8 Decathlon
BL8	Bellanca	8 Decathlon
BL8	American Champion	8 Super Decathlon
BLCF	Boeing	747-400LCF Dreamlifter
BLEN	Bristol	149 Blenheim
BLEN	Bristol	149 Bolingbroke
BN2P	Britten Norman	BN-2 Islander
BN2T	Britten Norman	BN-2T Defender 4000
BR14	Breguet	14 Replica
BRB2	Brantly	B-2
BROU	Max Holste	MH-1521 Broussard
BSCA	Boeing	747SCA Shuttle Carrier
BSTP	Bell Helicopter	214ST SuperTransport
BU31	Bücker	B?-131 Jungmann
BU31	CASA	1-131

ICAO	Manufacturer	Type/Model
BU33	Bücker	B?-133 Jungmeister
BU33	CASA	1-133
BU81	Zlin	Z-183
BU81	Heliopolis	Gomhouria
BU81	Bücker	B?-181 Bestmann
BU81	Zlin	Z-181
BU81	Zlin	Z-182
BUC	Hawker-Siddeley	Buccaneer
C02T	Cessna	402 (turbine)
C04T	Cessna	404 (turbine)
C06T	Cessna	206 (turbine)
C07T	Cessna	207 (turbine)
C1	Kawasaki	C-1
C101	CASA	C-101 Aviojet
C10T	Cessna	P210 (turbine)
C119	Fairchild	C-119 Flying Boxcar
C120	Cessna	120
C123	Fairchild	C-123 Provider
C125	Northrop	C-125 Raider
C130	Lockheed	C-130 Hercules
C133	Douglas	C-133 Cargomaster
C135	Boeing	C-135 Stratolifter
C140	Cessna	140
C141	Lockheed	C-141 Starlifter
C14T	Cessna	414 (turbine)
C150	Cessna	150
C150	Cessna	A150 Aerobat
C152	Cessna	A152 Aerobat
C152	Cessna	152
C160	Transport Allianz	C-160
C162	Cessna	162 SkyCatcher
C17	Boeing	C-17 Globemaster 3
C17	McDonnell Douglas	C-17 Globemaster 3
C170	Cessna	170
C172	FMA	P-172
C172	Cessna	172
C175	Cessna	175
C177	Cessna	177
C180	Cessna	180
C182	Cessna	182
C182	FMA	A-182
C182	Cessna	T182 Turbo Skylane
C182	FMA	A-182
C185	Cessna	A185 AgCarryall
C185	Cessna	185 Skywagon
C188	FMA	A-A188 AgTruck
C188	Cessna	188 AgPickup / AgWagon
C190	Cessna	190
C195	Cessna	195
C2	Grumman	C-2 Greyhound
C205	Cessna	205
C206	Cessna	206 Stationair
C206	Cessna	T206 Turbo Stationair
C207	Cessna	207 Stationair 7 / 8
C207	Cessna	T207 Turbo Skywagon 207
C207	Cessna	207 Skywagon 207
C207	Cessna	T207 Turbo Stationair 7 / 8
C208	Cessna	208 Caravan 1
C210	Cessna	210 Centurion
C212	CASA	C-212 Aviocar
C21T	Cessna	421 (turbine)
C25A	Cessna	525A Citation CJ2
C25B	Cessna	525B Citation CJ3
C270	Caudron	C-275 Luciole
C270	Caudron	C-272 / C-275 Luciole
C27J	Aeritalia / Alenia	C-27J Spartan
C295	CASA	C-295
C303	Cessna	T303 Crusader
C30J	Lockheed	C-130J Hercules
C310	Cessna	310
C320	Cessna	320 Executive Skyknight
C335	Cessna	335
C336	Cessna	336 Skymaster
C337	Cessna	337 Super Skymaster
C340	Cessna	340
C365	EKW / K+W	C-3605
C402	Cessna	401
C402	Cessna	402
C404	Cessna	404 Titan
C411	Cessna	411
C414	Cessna	414
C421	Cessna	421 Golden Eagle
C425	Cessna	425 Corsair
C425	Cessna	425 Conquest 1
C441	Cessna	Conquest
C441	Cessna	441 Conquest 2
C46	Curtiss	C-46 Commando
C5	Lockheed	C-5 Galaxy
C500	Cessna	500 Citation 1
C501	Cessna	501 Citation 1SP
C510	Cessna	510 Citation Mustang
C525	Cessna	525 Citation CJ1
C526	Cessna	526 CitationJet
C550	Cessna	550 Citation Bravo
C550	Cessna	S550 Citation S2
C550	Cessna	550 Citation 2
C551	Cessna	551 Citation 2SP
C560	Cessna	560 Citation 5 Ultra
C560	Cessna	560 Citation 5 Ultra Encore
C560	Cessna	560 Citation 5
C56X	Cessna	560XL Citation XLS
C56X	Cessna	560XL Citation Excel
C650	Cessna	650 Citation 6
C650	Cessna	650 Citation 7
C650	Cessna	650 Citation 3
C680	Cessna	680 Citation Sovereign
C72R	Cessna	172RG Cutlass RG
C750	Cessna	750 Citation X
C77R	Cessna	177RG Cardinal RG
C82	Fairchild	C-82 Packet
C82R	Cessna	TR182 Turbo Skylane RG
C82R	Cessna	R182 Skylane RG
C97	Boeing	C-97 Stratofreighter
CA19	CAC	Boomerang
CA25	CAC	CA-25 Winjeel
CAML	Sopwith	Camel
CARV	Aviation Traders	ATL-98 Carvair
CAT	Consolidated	Catalina / Canso
CE43	Cerva	CE-43 Guepard
CG3	Caudron	G-3

ICAO	Manufacturer	Type/Model
CH1	AIDC	A-CH-1 Chung-Tsing
CH2T	JAI	CH-2000 Sama
CH40	Campion	402 Lancer
CH7A	Bellanca	Citabria (7ECA)
CH7A	American Champion	7ACA Champ
CH7A	Aeronca	7 Champion
CH7A	Campion	Traveler
CH7A	Bellanca	Champ
CH7A	American Champion	7ECA Citabria Aurora
CH7A	Campion	Citabria (7ECA)
CH7B	Bellanca	Citabria (7GCBC/7KCAB)
CH7B	American Champion	Citabria Adventure
CH7B	American Champion	Citabria Explorer
CH80	JAI	CH-8000 Hawk 1
CJ6	Nanchang	CJ-6
CKUO	AIDC	F-CK-1 Ching-Kuo
CL2P	Canadair	CL-215
CL2T	Canadair	CL-415
CL2T	Canadair	CL-215T
CL30	Bombardier	BD-100 Challenger 300
CL41	Canadair	CL-41 Tutor
CL41	Canadair	CT-114 Tutor
CL44	Canadair	CL-44 Forty Four
CL4G	Canadair	CL-44-O Guppy
CL60	Canadair	CL-600 Challenger 600
CL60	Canadair	CL-600 Challenger 604
CL60	Canadair	CL-600 Challenger 601
CL60	Canadair	CL-600 Challenger 605
CLB1	Aero Commander	Ag Commander (B-1)
CLB1	N. Amer Rockwell	B-1 Snipe Commander
CMAS	Cessna	Airmaster
CN35	Airtech	CN-235
CN35	CASA	CN-235
CNBR	BAC	Canberra
CONI	Lockheed	Super Constellation
CORS	Vought-Sikorsky	F4U Corsair
CORS	Chance-Vought	F4U Corsair
COUR	Helio	Courier
CP10	CAP	CAP-10
CP10	Mudry	CAP-10
CP13	Piel	Super Emeraude (CP-1310/ 1315/1330)
CP20	Mudry	CAP-20
CP21	Mudry	CAP-21
CP22	CAP	CAP-222
CP23	Mudry	CAP-230
CP30	Piel	Emeraude
CP32	Piel	Super Emeraude
CP60	Piel	Diamant
CP75	Piel	B?ryl
CP80	Piel	Z?phir
CP90	Piel	Pinocchio
CRES	PAC	Cresco
CRJ1	Canadair	CL-600 Regional Jet CRJ-100
CRJ2	Canadair	CL-600 Regional Jet CRJ-200
CRJ7	Canadair	CL-600 Regional Jet CRJ-700
CRJ9	Canadair	CL-600 Regional Jet CRJ-900
CT4	PAC	CT-4 Airtrainer
CT4	AESL	CT-4 Airtrainer
CVLP	Convair	C-131
CVLP	Convair	CV-340 Convairliner
CVLP	Convair	CV-440 Metropolitan
CVLP	Convair	CV-240 Convairliner
CVLT	Convair	CV-640
CVLT	Canadair	Cosmopolitan
CVLT	Convair	CV-580
CVLT	Convair	CV-600
CVLT	Canadair	CV-580
CYGT	Hawker	Cygnet
D11	Jodel	D-120
D11	Wassmer	D-120 Paris-Nice
D11	Wassmer	D-112
D11	Jodel	D-11
D140	Mudry	D-140 Mousquetaire
D140	Jodel	D-140 Abeille
D140	Jodel	D-140 Mousquetaire
D150	Jodel	D-150 Mascaret
D18	Jodel	D-18
D228	HAL	228
D228	Dornier	228
D250	Robin / Apex	DR-200
D253	Robin / Apex	DR-253 Regent
D28D	Dornier	Do-28D Skyservant
D28T	Dornier	128-6 Turbo Skyservant
D328	Dornier	328
D328	Fairchild-Dornier	328
D4	Auster	D-4
D4	Beagle	D-4
D5	Beagle	D-5
D5	Auster	D-5
D5	Beagle	D-5 Husky
D5	Beagle	D-5
D6	Auster	D-6
D6	Beagle	D-6
D7	Fokker	D-7 Replica
D8	Fokker	D-8 Replica
DA40	Diamond	DA-40
DA42	Diamond	DA-42
DA50	Diamond	DA-50
DC10	McDonnell Douglas	DC-10
DC10	McDonnell Douglas	KC-10 Extender
DC2	Douglas	DC-2
DC3	Douglas	DC-3
DC3S	Douglas	Super DC-3
DC3T	Basler	BT-67 Turbo 67
DC4	Douglas	DC-4
DC6	Douglas	DC-6
DC7	Douglas	DC-7
DC85	Douglas	DC-8-50
DC86	Douglas	DC-8-60
DC87	Douglas	DC-8-70
DC91	Douglas	DC-9-10
DC91	McDonnell Douglas	DC-9-10
DC92	McDonnell Douglas	DC-9-20
DC92	Douglas	DC-9-20
DC93	Douglas	DC-9-30
DC93	McDonnell Douglas	DC-9-30
DC94	Douglas	DC-9-40
DC94	McDonnell Douglas	DC-9-40
DC95	McDonnell Douglas	DC-9-50

ICAO	Manufacturer	Type/Model
DC95	Douglas	DC-9-50
DH2T	De Havilland Can	DHC-2 Mk3 Turbo Beaver
DH3T	De Havilland Can	DHC-3 Turbo Otter
DH60	De Havilland	DH-60 Moth
DH80	De Havilland	DH-80 Puss Moth
DH82	De Havilland	DH-82 Tiger Moth
DH83	De Havilland	DH-83 Fox Moth
DH85	De Havilland	DH-85 Leopard Moth
DH87	De Havilland	DH-87 Hornet Moth
DH88	De Havilland	DH-88 Comet Replica
DH89	De Havilland	DH-89 Dragon Rapide
DH8A	De Havilland Can	DHC-8-100 Dash 8
DH8B	De Havilland Can	DHC-8-200 Dash 8
DH8C	De Havilland Can	DHC-8-300 Dash 8
DH8D	De Havilland Can	DHC-8-400 Dash 8
DH90	De Havilland	DH-90 Dragonfly
DH94	De Havilland	DH-94 Moth Minor
DHA3	De Havilland Aust	DHA-3 Drover
DHC1	De Havilland	DHC-1 Chipmunk
DHC2	De Havilland Can	DHC-2 Mk1 Beaver
DHC3	De Havilland Can	DHC-3 Otter
DHC4	De Havilland Can	DHC-4 Caribou
DHC5	De Havilland Can	DHC-5 Buffalo
DHC6	De Havilland Can	DHC-6 Twin Otter
DHC7	De Havilland Can	DHC-7 Dash 7
DJET	Diamond	D-Jet
DJIN	Sud	SO-1221 Djinn
DJIN	Sud-Ouest	SO-1221 Djinn
DO27	Dornier	Do-27
DO28	Dornier	Do-28A / Do-28B
DOVE	De Havilland	DH-104 Dove
DOVE	Hawker-Siddeley	DH-104 Dove
DR1	Fokker	Dr-1 Replica
DR10	Robin / Apex	Ambassadeur
DV20	Diamond	Katana (DA-20/DV-20)
DWD2	EKW / K+W	D-27
DWD2	Dewoitine	D-26
DWD2	EKW / K+W	D-26
DWD2	Dewoitine	D-27
E110	Embraer	EMB-111 Bandeirulha
E110	Embraer	EMB-110 Bandeirante
E120	Embraer	EMB-120 Brasilia
E121	Embraer	EMB-121 Xingu
E135	Embraer	EMB-135 / ERJ-135
E135	Embraer	EMB-140 / ERJ-140
E145	Embraer	EMB-145 / ERJ-145
E170	Embraer	EMB-170 / EMB-175
E190	Embraer	EMB-190 / EMB-195
E2	Grumman	E-2 Hawkeye
E2	Northrop	E-2 Hawkeye
E200	Extra	EA-200
E230	Extra	EA-230
E300	Extra	EA-300
E314	Embraer	EMB-314 Super Tucano
E3CF	Boeing	E-3 (CFM56) Sentry
E3TF	Boeing	E-3 (TF33) Sentry
E400	Extra	EA-400
E45X	Embraer	EMB-145XR / ERJ-145XR
E500	Extra	EA-500
E50P	Embraer	EMB-500 Phenom 100
E55P	Embraer	EMB-505 Phenom 300
E6	Boeing	E-6 Mercury
EA50	Eclipse	Eclipse 500
EAGL	Christen	Eagle
EC20	HAMC / Harbin	HC-120
EC20	Eurocopter	EC-120 Colibri
EC25	Eurocopter	EC-225 Super Puma Mk2+
EC25	Eurocopter	EC-725 Cougar Mk2+
EC30	Eurocopter	EC-130
EC35	Eurocopter	EC-635
EC35	Eurocopter	EC-135
EC45	Eurocopter-Kawasaki	BK-117C-2
EC45	Eurocopter	BK-117C-2
EC45	Eurocopter-Kawasaki	EC-145
EC45	Kawasaki	BK-117C-2
EC45	Eurocopter	EC-145
EC55	Eurocopter	EC-155
EDGE	Zivko	Edge 540
EH10	Kawasaki	KHI-01
EH10	Agusta	EH-101
EH10	EH Industries	CH-149 Cormorant
EH10	EH Industries	EH-101
ELST	Pützer	Elster
EN28	Enstrom	F-28
EN28	Enstrom	280 Shark
EN48	Enstrom	480
ERCO	ERCO	Ercoupe
ERCO	Air Products	Aircoupe
ERCO	Forney / Fornaire	Aircoupe
ERCO	Mooney	Aircoupe
ETAR	Dassault	Etendard 4
ETAR	Dassault	Super Etendard
EUFI	Eurofighter	C-16 Typhoon
EUFI	Eurofighter	Typhoon
EUFI	Eurofighter	CE-16 Typhoon
EUFI	Eurofighter	Eurofighter 2000
EXPL	MD Helicopters	MD-902 Explorer
F1	Mitsubishi	F-1
F100	Fokker	100
F104	Lockheed	F-104 Starfighter
F106	Convair	QF-106 Delta Dart
F111	General Dynamics	F-111
F117	Lockheed	F-117 Nighthawk
F14	Grumman	F-14 Tomcat
F15	Boeing	F-15 Eagle
F156	Morane-Saulnier	Criquet
F156	Fieseler	Fi-156 Storch
F156	Benes-Mraz	K-65 Cap
F16	Lockheed	F-16 Fighting Falcon
F16	General Dynamics	F-16 Fighting Falcon
F18	McDonnell Douglas	FA-18 Hornet
F18	Boeing	FA-18 Hornet
F18	Boeing	FA-18 Super Hornet
F18	McDonnell Douglas	FA-18 Super Hornet
F2	Mitsubishi	F-2
F22	Lockheed	F-22 Raptor
F260	Aermacchi	SF-260
F260	SIAI-Marchetti	SF-260
F26T	SIAI-Marchetti	SF-260TP
F27	Fairchild-Hiller	FH-227

ICAO	Manufacturer	Type/Model
F27	Fokker	F-27 Friendship
F28	Fokker	F-28 Fellowship
F2TH	Dassault	Falcon 2000
F35	Lockheed	F-35 Lightning II
F3F	Grumman	F3F Replica
F3F	Grumman	G-32 Replica
F3F	Grumman	G-11 Replica
F4	McDonnell	F-4 Phantom 2
F406	Reims	F406 Vigilant
F406	Cessna	F406 Caravan 2
F406	Reims	F406 Caravan 2
F5	AIDC	F-5 Chung-Cheng
F5	Northrop	F-5 Chung-Cheng
F5	Canadair	CF-5
F50	Fokker	50
F60	Fokker	60
F600	SIAI-Marchetti	SF-600 Canguro
F70	Fokker	70
F8	LTV	F-8 Crusader
F8	Chance-Vought	F8 Crusader
F86	Canadair	CL-13 Sabre
F86	North American	F-86 Sabre
F8L	Aviamilano	F-8L Falco
F900	Dassault	Falcon 900
F900	Dassault	Myst?re 900
F9F	Grumman	F9F Panther
FA10	Dassault	Myst?re 10
FA10	Dassault	Myst?re 10
FA10	Dassault	Myst?re 100
FA10	Dassault	Falcon 10
FA11	Fairchild	F-11 Husky
FA20	Dassault	Myst?re 200
FA20	Dassault	Falcon 20
FA20	Dassault	Myst?re 20
FA24	Fairchild	UC-61 Argus
FA24	Fairchild	UC-61 Forwarder
FA50	Dassault	Falcon 50
FA50	Dassault	Myst?re 50
FA62	Fairchild	Cornell
FA7X	Dassault	Falcon 7X
FALM	Miles	M-3 Falcon Major
FANT	RFB	Fantrainer
FC1	Chengdu	FC-1 Super 7
FFLY	Fairey	Firefly
FH11	Fairchild-Hiller	FH-1100
FLAM	Dassault	Flamant
FN33	SIAI-Marchetti	FN-333 Riviera
FOUG	Aerospatiale	CM-170R Magister
FOUG	Potez	CM-175 Z?phyr
FOUG	Fouga	CM-170R Magister
FOUG	Sud	CM-170R Magister
FOUG	Potez	CM-170R Magister
FREL	Sud	SA-321 Super Frelon
FREL	Aerospatiale	SA-321 Super Frelon
FU24	Fletcher	FU-24
FURY	Hawker	Sea Fury
FURY	Hawker	Fury
FW44	Focke-Wulf	Fw-44 Stieglitz
FW90	Focke-Wulf	Fw-190 Replica
G109	Grob	G-109

ICAO	Manufacturer	Type/Model
G115	Grob	G-115
G120	Grob	G-120
G140	Grob	G-140TP
G150	IAI	Gulfstream G150
G159	Grumman	G-159 Gulfstream 1
G15T	Grob	G-115T Acro
G160	Grob	G-160 Ranger
G164	American	G-164 Ag-Cat
G164	Grumman	G-164 Ag-Cat
G164	Schweizer	G-164 Ag-Cat
G21	Grumman	G-21A Goose
G222	Aeritalia / Alenia	C-27A Spartan
G222	Aeritalia / Alenia	G-222
G2GL	SOKO	G-2 Galeb
G44	Grumman	G-44 Widgeon
G46	Fiat	G-46
G4SG	SOKO	G-4 Super Galeb
G59	Fiat	G-59
G64T	Schweizer	G-164 Turbo Ag-Cat
G64T	Ag-Cat	G-164 Super Turbine
G64T	Schweizer	G-164 Ag-Cat Turbine
G64T	Grumman	G-164 Turbo Ag-Cat
G64T	American	G-164 Turbo Ag-Cat
G73	Grumman	G-73 Mallard
G73T	Grumman	G-73T Turbo Mallard
G96	Grumman	G-96 Trader
GA20	Gippsland	Fatman
GA20	Gippsland	GA-200 Fatman
GA7	SOCATA	TB-360 Tangara
GA7	American	GA-7 Cougar
GA8	Gippsland	GA-8 Airvan
GALX	IAI	Gulfstream G200
GALX	IAI	1126 Galaxy
GANT	Fairey	Gannet
GAUN	Gloster	Gauntlet
GAZL	SOKO	H-45 Partizan
GAZL	Sud	SA-341 / SA-342 Gazelle
GAZL	Aerospatiale	SA-341 / SA-342 Gazelle
GC1	Globe	GC-1 Swift
GEMI	Miles	M-65 Gemini
GF20	Grob	GF-200
GL5T	Bombardier	BD-700 Global 5000
GLAD	Gloster	Gladiator
GLEX	Bombardier	BD-700 Global Express
GLF2	Gulfstream	G-1159 Gulfstream 2
GLF2	Grumman	G-1159 Gulfstream 2
GLF3	Gulfstream	G-1159A Gulfstream 3
GLF4	Gulfstream	G-4X Gulfstream G450
GLF4	Gulfstream	G-4 Gulfstream G350
GLF4	Gulfstream	G-4 Gulfstream 4
GLF4	Gulfstream	G-4 Gulfstream G400
GLF4	Gulfstream	G-4 Gulfstream G300
GLF5	Gulfstream	G-5SP Gulfstream G550
GLF5	Gulfstream	G-5 Gulfstream 5
GLF5	Gulfstream	G-5SP Gulfstream G500
GNAT	Hawker-Siddeley	Gnat
GNAT	Folland	Fo-144 Gnat
GSPN	Grob	G-180 SPn Utility Jet
GY80	SOCATA	GY-80 Horizon
H111	CASA	2-111

ICAO	Manufacturer	Type/Model
H111	Heinkel	He-111
H12T	Hiller	UH-12ET
H2	Kaman	SH-2 Seasprite
H25A	De Havilland	DH-125
H25A	Hawker-Siddeley	HS-125-1
H25B	Hawker-Beechcraft	Hawker 850
H25B	Hawker-Siddeley	HS-125-700
H25B	BAe	BAe-125-700
H25B	Hawker-Beechcraft	Hawker 800
H25C	BAe	BAe-125-1000
H25C	Hawker-Beechcraft	Hawker 1000
H269	Hughes	269
H269	Hughes	300
H269	Schweizer	269
H269	Hughes	TH-55 Osage
H43A	Kaman	HH-43A
H43B	Kaman	HH-43B Huskie
H46	Kawasaki	KV-107
H46	Boeing Vertol	HH-46 Sea Knight
H46	Boeing Vertol	CH-113 Labrador
H46	Boeing Vertol	107
H46	Boeing Vertol	UH-46 Sea Knight
H46	Boeing Vertol	CH-46 Sea Knight
H47	Boeing Vertol	MH-47 Chinook
H47	Boeing Vertol	CH-47 Chinook
H500	Hughes	500
H500	Hughes	369
H500	MD Helicopters	MD-500
H500	Hughes	OH-6 Cayuse
H500	MD Helicopters	MD-530
H53	Sikorsky	S-65
H53	Sikorsky	CH-53
H53S	Sikorsky	CH-53E Super Stallion
H53S	Sikorsky	MH-53E Sea Dragon
H60	Sikorsky	S-70 Black Hawk
H60	Mitsubishi	S-70 Seahawk
H60	Sikorsky	MH-60 Black Hawk
H60	Sikorsky	AH-60 Black Hawk
H64	Hughes	77 Apache
H64	Fuji	AH-64 Longbow Apache
H64	McDonnell Douglas	AH-64 Apache
H64	Boeing Vertol	AH-64 Longbow Apache
H64	Hughes	AH-64 Apache
H64	McDonnell Douglas	AH-64 Longbow Apache
H66	Boeing-Sikorsky	RAH-66 Comanche
HA31	HAL	HA-31 Basant
HA4T	Hawker-Beechcraft	Hawker 4000
HA4T	Hawker-Beechcraft	4000 Hawker Horizon
HAR	McDonnell Douglas	AV-8 Harrier
HAR	BAe	Harrier
HAR	BAe	Sea Harrier
HAR	Hawker-Siddeley	Harrier
HAR	Boeing	AV-8 Harrier
HAWK	BAe	Hawk
HAWK	BAe	Hawk
HAWK	Hawker-Siddeley	Hawk
HCAT	Grumman	F6F Hellcat
HDJT	Honda	HA-420 HondaJet
HERN	De Havilland	DH-114 Heron
HERN	Hawker-Siddeley	DH-114 Heron

ICAO	Manufacturer	Type/Model
HF20	HFB	HFB-320 Hansa
HF20	MBB	HFB-320 Hansa
HI27	Hirth	Hi-27 Acrostar
HIND	Hawker	Hind
HR10	Robin / Apex	HR-100
HR20	Robin / Apex	HR-200
HT16	HAL	HJT-16 Kiran
HT2	HAL	HT-2
HT32	HAL	HPT-32 Deepak
HT36	HAL	HJT-36 Sitara
HUCO	Bell Helicopter	209 HueyCobra
HUNT	Hawker	Hunter
HURI	Hawker	Hurricane
HURI	Hawker	Sea Hurricane
HUSK	Aviat	A-1 Husky
I103	Ilyuschin	Il-103
I114	Ilyuschin	Il-114
I153	Polikarpov	I-153
I15B	Polikarpov	I-15bis
I16	Polikarpov	I-16
I23	PZL Swidnik	I-23 Manager
I3	Technoavia	I-3
IA46	FMA	IA-46 Ranquel
IA46	FMA	IA-46 Super Ranquel
IA50	FMA	IA-50 Guarani 2
IA50	FMA	IA-50 Guarani 2
IA51	FMA	IA-51 Tehuelche
IA51	FMA	IA-51 Tehuelche
IA58	FMA	IA-58 Pucar
IA63	FMA	IA-63 Pampa
IL14	Ilyuschin	Il-14
IL18	Ilyuschin	Il-18
IL18	Ilyuschin	Il-20
IL18	Ilyuschin	Il-24
IL18	Ilyuschin	Il-22 Zebra
IL28	Ilyuschin	Il-28
IL28	HAMC / Harbin	H-5
IL38	Ilyuschin	Il-38
IL62	Ilyuschin	Il-62
IL76	Ilyuschin	Il-78
IL76	Ilyuschin	Il-76
IL76	Ilyuschin	Il-82
IL86	Ilyuschin	Il-87
IL86	Ilyuschin	Il-86
IL96	Ilyuschin	Il-96
IPAN	Embraer	EMB-200 Ipanema
IR27	ROMBAC	IAR-827 Dacic
IR46	IAR	IAR-46
IS28	IAR	IS-28M2
J1	Taylorcraft	J-1 Autocrat
J1	Auster	J-1 Aiglet
J10	Chengdu	F-10
J10	Chengdu	J-10
J2	Piper	Cub (J-2)
J2	Piper	J-2 Cub
J3	Piper	Cub (J-3/L-4/NE)
J328	Fairchild-Dornier	Envoy 3
J328	Fairchild-Dornier	328JET
J4	Piper	J-4 Cub Coupe
J5	Piper	J-5 Cub Cruiser

ICAO	Manufacturer	Type/Model
J5	Piper	L-14 Cub Cruiser
J8A	Shenyang	F-8-1
J8A	Shenyang	J-8-1
J8B	Shenyang	F-8-2 /-3 /-4
J8B	Shenyang	J-8-2 /-3 /-4
JAGR	SEPECAT	Jaguar
JAGR	Breguet	Jaguar
JAGR	HAL	Shamsher
JAGR	BAC	Jaguar
JAGR	BAe	Jaguar
JAGR	SEPECAT	Jaguar
JAST	SOKO	Jastreb
JCOM	Aero Commander	1121 Jet Commander
JCOM	IAI	1121 Commodore Jet
JN76	Caudron	CR-760 Cyclone Replica
JN76	Caudron	JN-760 Cyclone Replica
JP10	GAP	JP100 Kestrel
JPRO	Hunting	P-84 Jet Provost
JPRO	BAC	167 Strikemaster
JPRO	BAe	BAC-167 Strikemaster
JPRO	Hunting Percival	P-84 Jet Provost
JPRO	BAC	145 Jet Provost
JS1	Handley Page	HP-137 Jetstream 1
JS20	Scottish Aviation	Jetstream T.Mk.1
JS20	Handley Page	Jetstream 200
JS20	Handley Page	HP-137 Jetstream 200
JS20	Scottish Aviation	Jetstream T.Mk.2
JS31	BAe	Jetstream T.Mk.3
JS31	BAe	BAe-3100 Jetstream 31
JS31	BAe	Jetstream 31
JS32	BAe	BAe-3200 Jetstream Super 31
JS41	BAe	BAe-4100 Jetstream 41
JU52	CASA	352L
JU52	Junkers	Ju-52/3m
JUNR	Bölkow	BO-208 Junior
JUNR	MFI	MFI-9 Junior
K126	Kamov	Ka-126
K226	Kamov	Ka-226
K35A	Boeing	KC-135A Stratotanker
K35E	Boeing	KC-135D/E Stratotanker
K35R	Boeing	KC-135R/T Stratotanker
K50	KAI	A-50 Golden Eagle
K50	KAI	T-50 Golden Eagle
K8	Nanchang	JL-8 Karakorum
K8	Nanchang	K-8 Karakorum
KA25	Kamov	Ka-25
KA26	Kamov	Ka-26
KA27	Kamov	Ka-31
KA27	Kamov	Ka-27
KA27	Kamov	Ka-32
KA27	Kamov	Ka-29
KA27	Kamov	Ka-28
KA50	Kamov	Ka-50
KA52	Kamov	Ka-52
KA62	Kamov	Ka-62
KA62	Kamov	Ka-60
KE3	Boeing	KE-3
KFIR	IAI	Kfir
KH4	Kawasaki	KH-4
KL07	Klemm	Kl-107
KL07	Bölkow	Kl-107
KL25	Klemm	L-25
KL35	Klemm	Kl-35
KM2	Fuji	KM-2
KM2	Fuji	TL-1
KMAX	Kaman	K-1200 K-Max
KR34	Fairchild	KR-34 Challenger
KR34	Fairchild	Challenger
KRAG	SOKO	P-2 Kraguj
KRAG	SOKO	J-20 Kraguj
KT1	KAI	KT-1 Woong-Bee
KT1	KAI	KO-1 Woong-Bee
L10	Lockheed	L-10 Electra
L101	Lockheed	L-1011 TriStar
L11	Luscombe	11A Sedan
L12	Lockheed	L-12 Electra Junior
L13	Convair	L-13
L14	Lockheed	L-14 Hudson
L14	Lockheed	L-14 Super Electra
L159	AERO	L-159 Albatross 2
L18	Lockheed	L-18 Lodestar
L18	Learjet	Learstar
L188	Lockheed	L-188 Electra
L200	LET	L-200 Morava
L29	AERO	L-29 Delfin
L29A	Lockheed	L-1329 Jetstar 6 / 8
L29B	Lockheed	L-1329 Jetstar 2
L37	Lockheed	B-34 Lexington
L37	Lockheed	PV-2 Harpoon
L37	Lockheed	PV-1 Ventura
L39	AERO	L-39 Albatross
L39	AERO	L-139 Albatross
L40	Orlican	L-40 Meta Sokol
L410	LET	L-410 Turbolet
L410	LET	L-420 Turbolet
L5	Stinson	L-5 Sentinel
L59	AERO	L-59
L60	AERO	L-60 Brigadyr
L610	LET	L-610
L8	Luscombe	8
L8	Luscombe	50
L90	Aermacchi	M-290TP Redigo
LA25	Lake Aircraft	LA-250 / LA-270
LA4	Lake Aircraft	LA-4 / LA-200 Buccaneer
LA60	Lockheed-Azcarate	LASA-60 Santa Maria
LA60	Aermacchi	AL-60
LA60	Atlas	AL-60 Kudu
LA60	Lockheed	LASA-60
LAMA	Aerospatiale	SA-315 Lama
LAMA	HAL	SA-315 Cheetah / Cheetal / Lancer
LAMA	Sud	SA-315 Lama
LANC	AVRO	683 Lancaster
LARK	N. Amer Rockwell	100 Lark Commander
LJ23	Learjet	23
LJ24	Learjet	24
LJ25	Learjet	25
LJ31	Learjet	31
LJ35	Shin Meiwa	U-36
LJ35	Learjet	35

ICAO	Manufacturer	Type/Model
LJ40	Learjet	40
LJ45	Learjet	45
LJ55	Learjet	55
LJ60	Learjet	60
LTNG	BAC	Lightning
LYNX	Westland	Lynx
LYNX	Westland	Super Lynx
LYSA	Westland	Lysander
M10	Mooney	M-10 Cadet
M101	Myasishchev	M-101
M110	Aviat	110 Specal
M15	PZL Mielec	M-15 Belphegor
M17	Myasishchev	M-17 Stratosfera
M18	PZL Mielec	M-18 Dromader
M18T	PZL Mielec	M-18 Turbine Dromader
M200	Aero Commander	Commander 200
M200	N. Amer Rockwell	200 Commander 200
M203	Myasishchev	M-203 Barsuk
M20P	Mooney	M-20
M20T	Mooney	M-20K 252TSE / M-20M
M22	Mooney	M-22 Mustang
M28	PZL Mielec	M-28 Skytruck
M2HK	Miles	M-2 Hawk Speed Six
M2HK	Miles	M-2 Hawk Major
M308	Aermacchi	MB-308
M326	Aermacchi	MB-326
M326	CAC	MB-326
M326	Embraer	EMB-326 Xavante
M326	Atlas	MB-326 Impala
M326	CAC	CA-30
M326	Embraer	AT-26 Xavante
M326	Aermacchi	MB-326
M339	Aermacchi	MB-339
M404	Martin	404
M55	Myasishchev	M-55 Geophysica
MAGI	Miles	M-14 Magister
MARS	Martin	JRM Mars
MD11	McDonnell Douglas	MD-11
MD52	McDonnell Douglas	AH-6J
MD52	McDonnell Douglas	MD-520N
MD52	MD Helicopters	MD-520N
MD52	McDonnell Douglas	MH-6J
MD52	McDonnell Douglas	MD-530N
MD60	McDonnell Douglas	MD-600N
MD60	MD Helicopters	MD-600N
MD81	McDonnell Douglas	MD-81
MD82	McDonnell Douglas	MD-82
MD83	McDonnell Douglas	MD-83
MD87	McDonnell Douglas	MD-87
MD88	McDonnell Douglas	MD-88
MD90	McDonnell Douglas	MD-90
ME08	Messerschmitt	Bf-108 Taifun
ME08	Nord	1001 Pingouin 1
ME08	Nord	1002 Pingouin 2
ME09	Hispano	HA-1112 Buchon
ME09	Messerschmitt	Bf-109
ME62	Messerschmitt	Me-262 Replica
MESS	Miles	M-38 Messenger
METR	Gloster	Meteor
METR	Armstrong Withworth	Meteor

ICAO	Manufacturer	Type/Model
MF17	Saab	MFI-15 Safari
MF17	Saab	MFI-17 Supporter
MG15	PZL Mielec	LiM-1
MG15	AERO	S-103
MG15	Mikoyan	MiG-15
MG15	PZL Mielec	LiM-2
MG15	AERO	S-102
MG17	PZL Mielec	LiM-6
MG17	Chengdu	JJ-5
MG17	Shenyang	J-5
MG17	Chengdu	FT-5
MG17	Mikoyan	MiG-17
MG17	PZL Mielec	LiM-5
MG17	Shenyang	F-5
MG19	Mikoyan	MiG-19
MG19	Shenyang	F-6
MG19	Nanchang	J-6
MG19	Shenyang	J-6
MG19	Nanchang	F-6
MG21	Chengdu	J-7
MG21	Mikoyan	MiG-21
MG21	Chengdu	F-7
MG23	Mikoyan	MiG-27
MG23	HAL	MiG-27 Bahadur
MG23	Mikoyan	MiG-23
MG25	Mikoyan	MiG-25
MG29	Mikoyan	MiG-29
MG29	Mikoyan	MiG-33
MG31	Mikoyan	MiG-31
MG44	Mikoyan	MiG 1-44
MGAT	Mikoyan	MiG-AT
MH20	Mitsubishi	MH-2000
MI10	Mil	Mi-10
MI14	Mil	Mi-14
MI2	Mil	Mi-2
MI2	PZL Swidnik	Mi-2
MI24	Mil	Mi-25
MI24	Mil	Mi-24
MI24	Mil	Mi-35
MI26	Mil	Mi-26
MI28	Mil	Mi-28
MI34	Mil	Mi-34
MI38	Mil	Mi-38
MI4	HAMC / Harbin	Z-5
MI4	Mil	Mi-4
MI6	Mil	Mi-22
MI6	Mil	Mi-6
MI8	Mil	Mi-8
MI8	Mil	Mi-17
MI8	Mil	Mi-9
MI8	Mil	Mi-19
MIR2	Dassault	Mirage 2000
MIR4	Dassault	Mirage 4
MIRA	Dassault	Mirage 50
MIRA	Dassault	Mirage 3
MIRA	IAI	Dagger
MIRA	Dassault	Mirage 5
MIRA	Atlas	Cheetah
MIRA	CAC	CA-29 Mirage 3
MITE	Mooney	M-18

ICAO	Manufacturer	Type/Model
MONA	Miles	M-17 Monarch
MOSQ	De Havilland	DH-98 Mosquito
MRF1	Dassault	Mirage F1
MS18	SOCATA	MS-200FG Morane
MS23	Morane-Saulnier	MS-230
MS25	SOCATA	MS-200RG Morane
MS30	SOCATA	MS-300 Epsilon 2
MS31	Morane-Saulnier	MS-315
MS31	Morane-Saulnier	MS-317
MS73	Morane-Saulnier	MS-733 Alcyon
MS76	Morane-Saulnier	MS-760 Paris
MSAI	Morane-Saulnier	MoS-29
MSAI	Morane-Saulnier	AI
MSAI	Morane-Saulnier	MoS-27
MSAI	Morane-Saulnier	MoS-30
MT2	Mitsubishi	T-2
MU2	Mitsubishi	MU-2
MU30	Mitsubishi	MU-300 Diamond
MYA4	Myasishchev	M-4
MYS4	Dassault	MD-454A Myst?re 4A
N110	Nord	1100 Noralpha
N120	Nord	1200 Norecrin
N260	Max Holste	MH-260 Super Broussard
N260	Nord	260 Super Broussard
N262	Aerospatiale	N-262 Fr?gate
N262	Nord	262
N262	Aerospatiale	Fr?gate
N320	Nord	3202
N340	Nord	3400
N5	Nanchang	N-5
NAVI	Ryan	Navion
NAVI	North American	Navion
NC85	Nord	NC-858
NC85	Nord	NC-854
NI28	Nieuport	28 Replica
NIBB	Aviamilano	F-14 Nibbio
NIM	BAe	Nimrod
NIM	BAe	Nimrod
NIM	Hawker-Siddeley	Nimrod
NIPR	Slingsby	T-66 Nipper
NIPR	Avions Fairey	T-66 Nipper
NOMA	GAF	Nomad
NORA	Nord	2501 Noratlas
NORS	Noorduyn	Norseman
O1	Fuji	Bird Dog
O1	Cessna	Bird Dog
OH1	Kawasaki	OH-1
OPCA	Edgley / Optica	EA-7 Optica
OSCR	Partenavia	P-66 Charlie
OSCR	Partenavia	P-64 Oscar
P136	Piaggio	P-136
P148	Piaggio	P-148
P149	Piaggio	P-149
P149	Focke-Wulf	FWP-149
P180	Piaggio	P-180 Avanti
P19	Aviamilano	P-19 Scricciolo
P2	Lockheed	P-2 Neptune
P210	Cessna	P210 Pressurized Centurion
P28A	Embraer	Tupi
P28A	Embraer	Carioquinha
P28A	Embraer	EMB-712 Tupi
P28A	Embraer	EMB-712
P28A	Piper	Cherokee PA-28
P28B	Piper	Cherokee (PA-28-235)
P28B	Embraer	EMB-710 Carioca
P28R	Piper	PA-28R-180 Cherokee Arrow
P28R	Embraer	EMB-711B Corisco
P28R	Piper	PA-28R-201T Turbo Cherokee
P28R	Piper	PA-28R-200 Cherokee Arrow
P28R	Piper	PA-28R-201 Cherokee Arrow
P28T	Piper	PA-28RT-201T Turbo Arrow 4
P28T	Piper	PA-28RT-201 Arrow 4
P28T	Embraer	EMB-711ST Corisco 2 Turbo
P3	Kawasaki	P-3 Orion
P3	Lockheed	P-3 Orion
P3	Lockheed	P-3 Orion
P3	Lockheed	CP-140 Aurora
P32R	Piper	PA-32R-300 Lance
P32R	Piper	PA-32R-301 Saratoga 2 HP
P32R	Piper	PA-32R-300 Cherokee Lance
P32R	Embraer	EMB-721 Sertanejo
P32T	Piper	PA-32RT-300T Turbo Lance 2
P337	Cessna	P337 Pressurized Skymaster
P337	Reims	FT337G Pressz'd Skymaster
P38	Lockheed	F-5 Lightning
P38	Lockheed	P-38 Lightning
P39	Bell Aircraft	P-39 Airacobra
P40	Curtiss	P-40 Warhawk
P40	Curtiss	Kittyhawk
P46T	Piper	PA-46-500TP Malibu Meridian
P47	Republic	F-47 Thunderbolt
P4Y	Convair	PB4Y Privateer
P51	CAC	CA-18 Mustang
P51	North American	P-51 Mustang
P57	Partenavia	P-57 Fachiro 2
P61	Northrop	P-61 Black Widow
P63	Bell Aircraft	P-63 Kingcobra
P66P	Piaggio	P-166
P66T	Piaggio	P-166DL3
P66T	Piaggio	P-166DP1
P68	Partenavia	P-68 Victor
P68	Partenavia	P-68 Observer
P68T	Partenavia	AP-68TP-300 Spartacus
P750	PAC	750XL
P808	Piaggio	PD-808
P82	North American	P-82 Twin Mustang
P82	North American	F-82 Twin Mustang
PA11	Piper	PA-11 Cub Special
PA12	Piper	PA-12 Super Cruiser
PA14	Piper	PA-14 Family Cruiser
PA15	Piper	PA-15 Vagabond
PA16	Piper	PA-16 Clipper
PA17	Piper	PA-17 Vagabond
PA18	Piper	PA-18 Super Cub
PA20	Piper	PA-20 Pacer
PA22	Piper	PA-22 Caribbean
PA22	Piper	PA-22 Colt
PA22	Piper	PA-22 Tri-Pacer
PA23	Piper	PA-23 Apache
PA24	Piper	PA-24 Comanche

ICAO	Manufacturer	Type/Model
PA25	Embraer	PA-25 Pawnee
PA25	Piper	PA-25 Pawnee
PA27	Piper	PA-23-250 Turbo Aztec
PA27	Piper	PA-23 Aztec
PA30	Piper	PA-30 Twin Comanche
PA31	Piper	PA-31
PA31	Embraer	EMB-820 Navajo
PA32	Piper	PA-32
PA32	Embraer	EMB-720 Minuano
PA34	Embraer	EMB-810 Seneca
PA34	PZL Mielec	M-20
PA34	Piper	PA-34 Seneca
PA36	Piper	PA-36 Pawnee Brave
PA38	Piper	PA-38 Tomahawk
PA44	Piper	PA-44 Seminole
PA46	Piper	PA-46-350P Malibu Mirage
PA46	Piper	PA-46-310P Malibu
PAT4	Piper	PA-31T3-500 T-1040
PAY1	Piper	PA-31T1-500 Cheyenne 1
PAY2	Piper	PA-31T-620 Cheyenne 2
PAY4	Piper	PA-42-1000 Cheyenne 400
PC12	Pilatus	PC-12
PC21	Pilatus	PC-21
PC6P	Pilatus	PC-6 Porter
PC6T	Pilatus	PC-6A/B/C Turbo-Porter
PC7	Denel	PC-7 Astra
PC7	Atlas	PC-7 Astra
PC7	HESA	S-68
PC7	Pilatus	PC-7 Turbo Trainer
PC9	Pilatus	PC-9
PEGA	General Avia	F-20 Pegaso
PEMB	Hunting Percival	P-66 Pembroke
PEMB	Percival	P-66 Pembroke
PEMB	Hunting	P-66 Pembroke
PICO	General Avia	F-15 Delfino
PICO	General Avia	F-15 Picchio
PILL	Piper	PA-28R-300 Pill?n
PILL	CASA	T-35 Pill?n
PILL	CASA	E-26 Tamiz
PINO	General Avia	F-22 Pinguino
PLUS	Taylorcraft	Auster 1 / Plus C / Plus D
PO2	PZL Mielec	CSS-13
PO2	Polikarpov	Po-2
PO2	PZL Okecie	CSS-13
PO60	Potez	600 Sauterelle
PO60	Potez	60 Sauterelle
PP2	Pilatus	P-2
PP3	Pilatus	P-3
PPRO	Percival	P-56 Provost
PPRO	Hunting	P-56 Provost
PPRO	Hunting Percival	P-56 Provost
PRCE	Percival	P-57 Sea Prince
PREN	Percival	P-40 Prentice
PRM1	Hawker-Beechcraft	390 Premier 1
PROC	Percival	Proctor
PSW4	PZL Swidnik	SW-4
PT22	Ryan	PT-22 Recruit
PT22	Ryan	ST-3KR Recruit
PTMS	Pitts / Aviat	S-12 Macho Stinker
PTMS	Pitts / Aviat	S-12 Super Stinker
PTS1	Christen	Pitts S-1 Special
PTS1	Pitts / Aviat	S-1 Special
PTS1	Aviat	Pitts S-1 Special
PTS1	Aerotek	Pitts S-1 Special
PTS2	Aviat	Pitts S-2 Special
PTS2	Aerotek	Pitts S-2 Special
PTS2	Christen	Pitts S-2 Special
PTS2	Pitts / Aviat	S-2 Special
PTSS	Pitts / Aviat	S-1-11 Super Stinker
PTSS	Aviat	S-1-11 Super Stinker
PUMA	Westland	Puma
PUMA	Aerospatiale	SA-330 Puma
PUMA	Sud	SA-330 Puma
PUMA	IAR	IAR-330 Puma
PUP	Beagle	B-121 Pup
PZ01	PZL Okecie	PZL-101 Gawron
PZ02	PZL Okecie	PZL-102 Kos
PZ04	PZL Okecie	PZL-104 Wilga
PZ05	PZL Okecie	PZL-105 Flaming
PZ06	PZL Okecie	PZL-106 Kruk
PZ12	PZL Okecie	PZL-112 Koliber Junior
PZ26	PZL Okecie	PZL-126 Mr?wka
PZ3T	PZL Okecie	PZL-130 Orlik
PZ4M	PZL Okecie	PZL-104M Wilga 2000
PZ6T	PZL Okecie	PZL-106AT Turbo Kruk
Q5	Nanchang	Q-5
Q5	Nanchang	A-5
R100	Robin / Apex	R-1180 Aiglon
R135	Boeing	RC-135
R200	Alpha	R-2160 Alpha 160
R200	Robin / Apex	Alpha
R300	Robin / Apex	R-3140
R300	Robin / Apex	R-3000
R300	Robin / Apex	R-3100
R300	Robin / Apex	R-3120
R300	Robin / Apex	R-300
R721	Boeing	727-100RE Super 27
R722	Boeing	727-200RE Super 27
R90F	Ruschmeyer	R-90-230FG
R90R	Ruschmeyer	R-90-230RG
R90T	Ruschmeyer	R-90-420AT
RALL	Morane-Saulnier	Super Rallye
RALL	Morane-Saulnier	Rallye 105
RALL	Morane-Saulnier	Rallye Commodore
RALL	PZL Okecie	PZL-110 Koliber
RALL	Morane-Saulnier	Rallye Club
RC3	Republic	RC-3 Seabee
RC70	Rockwell	700 Commander 700
RC70	Fuji	FA-300
RELI	Stinson	Reliant
RF10	Fournier	RF-10
RF4	Sportavia-Pützer	RF-4
RF47	Fournier	RF-47
RF5	Sportavia-Pützer	RF-5
RF6	Slingsby	Firefly
RF6	Fournier	RF-6
RF9	Fournier	RF-9
RFAL	Dassault	Rafale
RJ1H	BAe	Avro RJ-100
RJ1H	BAe	RJ-100

ICAO	Manufacturer	Type/Model
RJ70	BAe	Avro RJ-70
RJ70	BAe	RJ-70
RJ85	BAe	RJ-85
RJ85	BAe	Avro RJ-85
ROND	Ambrosini	F-4 Rondone
ROND	Ambrosini	Rondone
RP1	Mitsubishi	RP-1
RS18	Sportavia-Pützer	RS-180 Sportsman
RV10	Vans	RV-10
RV3	Vans	RV-3
RV4	Vans	RV-4
RV4T	Vans	RV-4T
RV6	Vans	RV-6
RV7	Vans	RV-7
RV8	Vans	RV-8
RV9	Vans	RV-9
RVAL	Denel	CSH-2 Rooivalk
RVAL	Atlas	CSH-2 Rooivalk
RVAL	Denel	AH-2 Rooivalk
RYST	Ryan	PT-20
RYST	Ryan	ST-A / ST-M / ST-R
S05F	SIAI-Marchetti	S-205-18F / S-205-20F
S05R	SIAI-Marchetti	S-205-18R / S-205-20R S10
S108	Stinson	108 Voyager
S108	Piper	108 Voyager
S108	Stinson	108 Station Wagon
S108	Piper	108 Station Wagon
S11	Fokker	S-11 Instructor
S208	SIAI-Marchetti	S-208
S210	Sud-Est	SE-210 Caravelle
S210	Aerospatiale	SE-210 Caravelle
S210	Sud	SE-210 Caravelle
S211	SIAI-Marchetti	S-211
S211	SIAI-Marchetti	M-311
S223	MBB	223 Flamingo
S223	MBB	223 Flamingo
S223	Hispano	223 Flamingo
S223	CASA	223 Flamingo
S223	SIAT	223 Flamingo
S278	HESA	Shahed 278
S2P	De Havilland Can	S-2 Tracker
S2P	Grumman	S-2 Tracker
S2T	IAI	S-2UP Turbo Tracker
S2T	Grumman	S-2 Turbo Tracker
S3	Lockheed	S-3 Viking
S330	Schweizer	269D 330
S330	Schweizer	269D 333
S360	Aerospatiale	SA-360 Dauphin
S37	Sukhoi	S-37 Berkut
S37	Sukhoi	Su-47 Berkut
S38	Sikorsky	S-38 Replica
S39	Sikorsky	S-39
S51	Sikorsky	S-51
S51	Sikorsky	HO3S
S52	Sikorsky	HO5S
S52	Sikorsky	S-52
S55P	Sikorsky	CH-19
S55P	Sikorsky	H-19 Chickasaw
S55P	Sikorsky	S-55
S55P	Sikorsky	HH-19

ICAO	Manufacturer	Type/Model
S55T	Sikorsky	S-55T
S55T	Westland	WS-55 Whirlwind 3
S58P	Sikorsky	CH-34 Chocktaw
S58P	Sikorsky	SH-34 Seabat
S58P	Sikorsky	S-58
S58P	Sikorsky	HH-34 Seahorse
S58T	Sikorsky	S-58T
S601	Aerospatiale	SN-601 Corvette
S61	Sikorsky	S-61N
S61	Sikorsky	S-61A
S61	Sikorsky	S-61L
S61	Sikorsky	SH-3 Sea King
S61	Westland	Commando
S61	Mitsubishi	HSS-2
S61	Agusta	SH-3
S61	Sikorsky	Sea King
S61	Westland	Sea King
S61R	Agusta	HH-3
S61R	Sikorsky	CH-3
S61R	Sikorsky	S-61R
S62	Sikorsky	HH-52 Seaguard
S62	Sikorsky	S-62
S64	Sikorsky	CH-54 Tarhe
S64	Sikorsky	S-64 Skycrane
S65C	Aerospatiale	SA-365C Dauphin 2
S76	Sikorsky	S-76
S92	Sikorsky	S-92 Helibus
SA20	Beriev	SA-20
SA37	Schweizer	SA-2-37A Condor
SAND	Shorts	S-25 Sandringham
SAPH	Piel	CP-1320 Saphir
SASP	Supermarine	Spitfire Mk25
SATA	CASA	HA-220 Super Saeta
SATA	Hispano	HA-220 Super Saeta
SATA	Hispano	HA-200 Saeta
SAVG	Zlin	Savage
SB05	Saab	105
SB20	Saab	2000
SB29	Saab	29 / J29
SB32	Saab	32 / J32 Lansen
SB35	Saab	35 / J35 Draken
SB37	Saab	37 / JA37 Viggen
SB39	Saab	JAS39 Gripen
SB39	Saab	39 Gripen
SB91	Saab	91 Safir
SBD	Douglas	SBD Dauntless
SBR1	N. Amer Rockwell	Sabreliner
SBR1	North American	Sabreliner
SBR2	N. Amer Rockwell	NA-265 Sabre 75
SBR2	Rockwell	NA-265 Sabre 80
SBR2	Rockwell	NA-265 Sabre 75
SC7	Shorts	SC-7 Skyvan
SCOU	Westland	Scout
SE5R	Royal Aircraft Factory	SE-5A Replica
SF34	Saab	340
SG92	Technoavia	SM-92T Turbo Finist
SH33	Shorts	330
SH36	Shorts	360
SH5	HAMC / Harbin	SH-5
SHAC	AVRO	696 Shackleton

ICAO	Manufacturer	Type/Model
SHAW	Armstrong Withworth	Sea Hawk
SHAW	Hawker	Sea Hawk
SJ30	Sino Swearingen	SJ-30
SL90	Technoavia	I-1
SM19	SIAI-Marchetti	SM-1019
SM20	Technoavia	SM-2000
SM60	Stinson	SM-6000 Tri-Motor
SM92	Technoavia	SM-92 Finist
SMB2	Dassault	Super Myst?re B2
SOKL	Benes-Mraz	M-1 Sokol
SP18	Luscombe	11E Spartan 185
SP55	Technoavia	SP-55
SP91	Technoavia	SP-91 Slava
SP95	Technoavia	SP-95
SPIT	Supermarine	Spitfire
SPIT	Supermarine	Seafire
SR20	Cirrus	SR-20
SR22	Cirrus	SR-22
SR71	Lockheed	SR-71 Blackbird
SS2P	N. Amer Rockwell	Thrush Commander
SS2P	Rockwell	Thrush Commander
SS2P	Ayres	Thrush
SS2P	Aero Commander	S-2 Ag Commander
SS2P	Ayres	Bull Thrush
SS2P	N. Amer Rockwell	Ag Commander
SS2T	Ayres	Turbo Thrush (except T660)
SS2T	Thrush	Turbo Thrush (S-2RHG-T34)
SSAB	North American	F-100 Super Sabre
ST10	SOCATA	ST-10
ST75	Stearman	PT-17 Kaydet
ST75	Boeing	PT-13 Kaydet
ST75	Boeing	PT-27 Kaydet
ST75	Stearman	PT-13 Kaydet
ST75	Stearman	75 Kaydet
ST75	Boeing	PT-17 Kaydet
ST75	Stearman	Kaydet
ST75	Boeing	PT-18 Kaydet
ST75	Boeing	75 Kaydet
STAR	Beech	2000 Starship
STLN	Helio	Stallion
STRI	Sopwith	Triplane Replica
SU15	Sukhoi	Su-15
SU17	Sukhoi	Su-22
SU17	Sukhoi	Su-20
SU17	Sukhoi	Su-17
SU24	Sukhoi	Su-24
SU25	Sukhoi	Su-28
SU25	Sukhoi	Su-39
SU25	Sukhoi	Su-25
SU26	Sukhoi	Su-26
SU27	Shenyang	J-11
SU27	Sukhoi	Su-37
SU27	Sukhoi	Su-27
SU27	Sukhoi	Su-34
SU27	Sukhoi	Su-30
SU27	Sukhoi	Su-32
SU27	Sukhoi	Su-35
SU27	Sukhoi	Su-33
SU29	Sukhoi	Su-29
SU31	Sukhoi	Su-31

ICAO	Manufacturer	Type/Model
SU38	Sukhoi	Su-38
SU7	Sukhoi	Su-7
SU80	Sukhoi	Su-80
SUBA	Fuji	FA-200 Aero Subaru
SUCO	Bell Helicopter	SuperCobra
SV4	Nord	SV-4
SW2	Swearingen	SA-26 Merlin 2
SW3	Fairchild	Merlin 3
SW3	Fairchild-Swearingen	Merlin 3
SW3	Swearingen	Merlin 3
SW4	Fairchild	Metro
SW4	Fairchild-Swearingen	Metro
SW4	Swearingen	Merlin 4
SW4	Fairchild	Merlin 23
SW4	Fairchild	Merlin 4
SW4	Fairchild-Swearingen	Merlin 4
SW4	Swearingen	Metro
SWIF	Supermarine	Swift
SWOR	Fairey	Swordfish
SWOR	Blackburn	Swordfish
SYCA	Bristol	Sycamore
SYCA	Bristol	171 Sycamore
T1	Fuji	T-1
T134	Tupolev	Tu-134
T144	Tupolev	Tu-144
T154	Tupolev	Tu-154
T160	Tupolev	Tu-160
T2	North American	T-2 Buckeye
T2	N. Amer Rockwell	T-2 Buckeye
T204	Tupolev	Tu-214
T204	Tupolev	Tu-224
T204	Tupolev	Tu-204
T204	Tupolev	Tu-234
T22M	Tupolev	Tu-22M
T250	Bellanca	T-250 Aries
T28	North American	T-28 Trojan
T33	Lockheed	T-33 Shooting Star
T33	Canadair	CT-133 Silver Star
T33	Lockheed	T-33 T-Bird
T33	Canadair	CL-30 Silver Star
T334	Tupolev	Tu-334
T34P	Beech	45 Mentor
T34P	Beech	T-34 Mentor
T34P	Fuji	T-3 Mentor
T34T	Fuji	T-3Kai
T34T	Beech	T-34C Turbo Mentor
T37	Cessna	318 / T-37
T38	Northrop	T-38 Talon
T4	Kawasaki	T-4
T5	Fuji	KM-2Kai
T5	Fuji	T-5
T6	North American	SNJ Texan
T6	North American	AT-6 Texan
T6	Noorduyn	AT-16 Harvard
T6	North American	T-6 Texan
T6	CCF	T-6 Harvard
T7	Fuji	T-7
TA15	Taylorcraft	15 Foursome
TA15	Taylorcraft	15 Tourist
TA20	Taylorcraft	20 Seabird

ICAO	Manufacturer	Type/Model
TA20	Taylorcraft	20 Ranchwagon
TA20	Taylorcraft	20 Zephyr 400
TA20	Taylorcraft	20 Topper
TAMP	SOCATA	TB-9 Tampico
TAMP	SOCATA	Tampico
TAYA	Taylorcraft	A
TAYB	Taylorcraft	BC
TAYD	Taylorcraft	DC
TB30	SOCATA	TB-30 Epsilon
TB30	Aerospatiale	TB-30 Epsilon
TB31	SOCATA	TB-31 Omega
TBM	Grumman	TBF Avenger
TBM7	SOCATA	TBM-700
TBM8	SOCATA	TBM-850
TCAT	Grumman	F7F Tigercat
TCOU	Helio	Twin Courier
TEX2	Hawker-Beechcraft	CT-156 Harvard 2
TEX2	Hawker-Beechcraft	T-6 Texan 2
TF19	Taylorcraft	Sportsman (F-19)
TF21	Taylorcraft	F-21
TF22	Taylorcraft	F-22
TIGR	Eurocopter	EC-665 Tiger / Tigre
TIJU	Avions Fairey	Tipsy Junior
TIPB	Avions Fairey	Tipsy BC
TIPB	Avions Fairey	Tipsy B
TIPB	Avions Fairey	Tipsy Belfair
TIPB	Avions Fairey	Tipsy Trainer
TOBA	SOCATA	TB-10 Tobago
TOR	Aeritalia / Alenia	Tornado
TOR	BAC	Tornado
TOR	MBB	Tornado
TOR	BAe	Tornado
TOUR	AESL	Airtourer
TOUR	Victa / AESL	Airtourer
TPIN	Scottish Aviation	Twin Pioneer
TRID	De Havilland	DH-121 Trident
TRID	Hawker-Siddeley	HS-121 Trident
TRIM	Ford	4-AT Tri-Motor
TRIM	Ford	5-AT Tri-Motor
TRIN	SOCATA	TB-20 Trinidad
TRIS	Britten Norman	BN-2A Mk3 Trislander
TRMA	Stinson	Tri-Motor (A)
TS11	PZL Mielec	TS-11 Iskra
TS8	PZL Mielec	TS-8 Bies
TU16	Tupolev	Tu-16
TU22	Tupolev	Tu-22
TU4	Tupolev	Tu-4
TU95	Tupolev	Tu-20
TU95	Tupolev	Tu-95
TU95	Tupolev	Tu-142
TUCA	Embraer	EMB-312 Tucano
TUCA	Embraer	T-27 Tucano
TUCA	Shorts	Tucano
TUTR	Avro	621 Tutor
U16	Grumman	Albatross
U2	Lockheed	U-2
U21	Beech	U-21A Ute
UH1	Bell Helicopter	205
UH1	Bell Helicopter	210
UH1	Bell Helicopter	UH-1 Iroquois
UH12	Fairchild-Hiller	OH-23 Raven
UH12	Hiller	OH-23 Raven
UH1Y	Bell Helicopter	UH-1Y
US1	Shin Meiwa	US-1
US1	Shin Meiwa	US-1
UT60	Utva	60
UT65	Utva	65 Privrednik
UT66	Utva	66
UT75	Utva	75
UU12	Udet	U-12 Flamingo Replica
V1	Grumman	OV-1 Mohawk
V10	N. Amer Rockwell	OV-10 Bronco
V10	Rockwell	OV-10 Bronco
V10	North American	OV-10 Bronco
V22	Bell Helicopter	V-22 Osprey
V22	Boeing Vertol	V-22 Osprey
V22	Bell-Boeing	V-22 Osprey
VALI	Vultee	BT-13 Valiant
VALI	Convair	BT-13 Valiant
VALI	Vultee	BT-15 Valiant
VAMP	De Havilland	DH-115 Vampire
VAMP	De Havilland	DH-100 Vampire
VAUT	Sud	SO-4050 Vautour
VC10	Vickers	VC-10
VC10	Bac	VC-10
VF14	Vfw	VFW-614
VF35	Lockheed	F-35B Lightning II
VGUL	Percival	Vega Gull
VIMY	Vickers	FB-27 Vimy Replica
VISC	Vickers	Viscount
VMT	Myasishchev	VM-T Atlant
VNOM	De Havilland	DH-112 Venom
VO10	Aero Commander	100 Commander 100
VO10	N. Amer Rockwell	Darter Commander
VO10	Volaircraft	Volaire 10
VP2	Evans	VP-2 Volksplane
VTOR	Partenavia	AP-68TP-600 Viator
W3	PZL Swidnik	W-3 Sok?l
WA40	Wassmer	WA-40 Super 4
WA41	Wassmer	WA-41 Baladou
WA42	Wassmer	WA-421 Prestige
WA50	Wassmer	WA-51 Pacific
WA50	Wassmer	WA-54 Atlantic
WA50	Wassmer	WA-52 Europa
WA80	Wassmer	WA-80 Piranha
WAC9	Waco	9
WACA	Waco	IBA, PBA, PLA, RBA, UBA,
WACC	Waco	YKC, YKS, YOC, YQC, ZGC
WACC	Waco	AGC, AQC
WACC	Waco	CJC, CUC, DJC, DQC, EGC
WACC	Waco	UEC, UIC, UKC, UKS, VKS
WACD	Waco	S3HD
WACE	Waco	E (ARE/HRE/SRE) Aristocrat
WACF	Waco	CPF, ENF, INF, KNF, PBF
WACF	Waco	RNF
WACF	Waco	UBF, UMF, UPF
WACF	Waco Classic	YMF
WACF	Waco	YMF, YPF, ZPF
WACG	Waco	CRG
WACM	Waco	JWM, JYM

ICAO	Manufacturer	Type/Model
WACN	Waco	ZVN
WACN	Waco	AVN
Waco	Waco	QSO
Waco	Waco	ASO, ATO
Waco	Waco	10
Waco	Waco	GXE
Waco	Waco	125
Waco	Waco	BSO, CSO, CTO, DSO
Waco	Waco	PSO
WACT	Waco	RPT
WASP	Westland	Wasp
WCAT	Grumman	F4F Wildcat
WESX	Westland	Wessex
WG30	Westland	30
WHIT	Miles	M-11 Whitney Straight
WIRR	CAC	CA-16 Wirraway
WW23	IAI	1123 Westwind
WW24	IAI	1124 Westwind
Y11	HAMC / Harbin	Y-11
Y112	Yakovlev	Yak-112
Y12	HAMC / Harbin	Y-12
Y130	Aermacchi	M-346
Y130	Yakovlev	Yak-130
Y141	Yakovlev	Yak-141
Y18T	Technoavia	SM-94
Y18T	Technoavia	SM-2000P
Y18T	Yakovlev	Yak-18T
YAK3	Yakovlev	Yak-3
YAK9	Yakovlev	Yak-9
YALE	North American	Yale
YK11	LET	C-11
YK11	Yakovlev	Yak-11
YK12	PZL Okecie	Yak-12
YK12	Yakovlev	Yak-12
YK18	Yakovlev	Yak-18
YK18	Nanchang	CJ-5
YK18	Yakovlev	Yak-18U
YK28	Yakovlev	Yak-28
YK38	Yakovlev	Yak-38
YK40	Yakovlev	Yak-40
YK42	Yakovlev	Yak-42
YK42	Yakovlev	Yak-142
YK50	Yakovlev	Yak-50
YK52	Yakovlev	Yak-52
YK52	Aerostar	Yak-52
YK53	Yakovlev	Yak-53
YK54	Yakovlev	Yak-54
YK55	Yakovlev	Yak-55
YK58	Yakovlev	Yak-58
YS11	NAMC	YS-11
YURO	IAR	IAR-93 / J-22 Orao
YURO	SOKO	J-22 Orao
Z22	Zlin	Z-22 Junak
Z22	Zlin	Zlin Z-22 Junak
Z26	Zlin	Zlin Z-326 Trener Master
Z26	Zlin	Zlin Z-626
Z26	Zlin	Zlin Z-726 Universal
Z26	Zlin	Z-326 Trener Master
Z26	Zlin	Zlin Z-126 Trener 2
Z26	Zlin	Z-226 Trener 6

ICAO	Manufacturer	Type/Model
Z26	Zlin	Zlin Z-226 Akrobat
Z26	Zlin	Zlin Z-26 Trener
Z26	Zlin	Zlin Z-526 Trener Master
Z26	Zlin	Z-226 Akrobat
Z26	Zlin	Z-626
Z26	Zlin	Z-526 Akrobat
Z26	Zlin	Z-726 Universal
Z26	Zlin	Zlin Z-526 Akrobat
Z26	Zlin	Zlin Z-326 Akrobat
Z26	Zlin	Z-26 Trener
Z26	Zlin	Z-126 Trener 2
Z26	Zlin	Zlin Z-226 Trener 6
Z26	Zlin	Z-326 Akrobat
Z26	Zlin	Z-526 Trener Master
Z37P	LET	Z-37 Cmel?k
Z37P	Zlin	Z-37 Cmel?k
Z37P	Zlin	Z-237 Cmel?k
Z37P	LET	Z-237 Cmel?k
Z37T	Zlin	Z-37T Agro Turbo
Z37T	Zlin	Z-137 Agro Turbo
Z42	Zlin	Z-142
Z42	Zlin	Z-242
Z42	Zlin	Z-42
Z42	Zlin	Zlin Z-242
Z42	Zlin	Zlin Z-142
Z42	Zlin	Zlin Z-42
Z43	Zlin	Z-43
Z43	Zlin	Z-143
Z43	Zlin	Zlin Z-143
Z43	Zlin	Zlin Z-43
Z50	Zlin	Z-50
Z50	Zlin	Zlin Z-50
ZERO	Mitsubishi	A6M Zero

ARINC Documents and Specifications

ARINC 607	Design Guidance for Avionics Equipment. Includes definition of Aircraft Personality Module (APM), required for ARINC 758 CMU installation.
ARINC 429	Specification for receiving and broadcasting ARINC 429 broadcast data (data transfer between avionics LRUs). ARINC 429 is the one way communication data bus (one pair of data bus use for transmit data and another pair of data bus use for receive data)
ARINC 618	Defines the air / ground protocols for communicating between the ACARS / CMU and VHF ground systems. Also defines the format of the ACARS messages sent by the ACARS / CMU as well as received by the ACARS CMU. The format of this message is called a Type A message. This characteristic has been updated to define the future VDL Mode 2 AOA operation.
ARINC 619	Defines the protocols for the ACARS / CMU to use to transfer file data between other avionics in the aircraft. ARINC 619 covers file protocols that are used to interface with FMS, FDAMS, Cabin Terminal, Maintenance Computers, SATCOM systems and HF Voice Data Radios.
ARINC 620	Defines ground-to-ground communication protocols. This includes the message format of messages routed between a service provider and an airline or other ground system. This is referred to as a Type B message (the air/ground Type A message is reformatted to a Type B message for ground transmissions).
ARINC 622	Describes the processing associated with sending ATC application messages over today's ACARS links (including ARINC 623 ATC messages).
ARINC 623	This characteristic identifies ATC related messages that can be generated or received by an ACARS MU / CMU system (does not include FANS-1 or FANS-A messages that are processed by the FMS)
ARINC 629	Specification for receiving and broadcasting ARINC 629 broadcast data (data transfer between avionics LRUs). ARINC 629 was introduce to use on B777 commercial airplane. ARINC 629 is the two ways communication data bus (one pair of data bus is use for transmit and receive data).
ARINC 631	Specification for VHF DIGITAL LINK (VDL) MODE 2. This specification provides general and specific design guidance for the development and installation of the protocols needed to exchange bit-oriented data across an air-ground VHF Digital Link (VDL) in an Open System Interconnection (OSI) environment.
ARINC 724B	Specification for an ACARS MU for ARINC 724B wiring.
ARINC 739	Specification for interfacing with Multi-purpose Cockpit Display Units
ARINC 740	Specification for interfacing to cockpit Printers.
ARINC 758	Specification for a CMU relative to ARINC 758 wiring. This specification actually identifies various levels of functionality, these defining future growth phases for the CMU. Initial CMU systems which perform today's ACARS functions are classified as Level OA.
ARINC 823	Two-part specification that defines a security framework for protecting ACARS datalink messages exchanged between aircraft and ground systems. Security services include confidentiality, data integrity, and message authentication. Part 1, ACARS Message Security (AMS), specifies the security protocol, and Part 2, Key Management, specifies life-cycle management of the cryptographic keys necessary for secure and proper operation of AMS.

Other Books by The Author

The author has published a number of other books most of which are available from Amazon.

ShipPlotter - An Illustrated User Guide

ISBN 978-1445215310

ShipPlotter is a unique piece of software that enables a user to have a live radar type display of shipping in their local coastal region or other regions and waterways around the world. The software decodes radio signals, received using a VHF radio receiver or scanner, from ships transmitting digital data using the marine Automatic Identification System (AIS). The book provides an excellent description of the AIS system and messaging.

ShipPlotter visually displays the position and identification of each ship either as radar view or on a chart created from a graphic image file, a satellite image download or a downloaded Open Street Map.

The Early Days of Digital Computing in the British Army

ISBN 978-0955675362

The story of the first British Army battlefield digital computer then called FADAC and later to become known as FACE. A fascinating insight into the development of digital computers in the 1960's.

PlanePlotter - An Illustrated User Guide

ISBN 978-446130636

PlanePlotter is a unique piece of software receives and decodes live digital position reports from aircraft and plots them on a chart. With PlanePlotter users see a radar-like display of all the aircraft in range of the users radio receiver that are transmitting digital messages in a number of formats such as ACARS, ADS-B and HFDL